D0897356

DATE DUE

DEC 2 3 1989			

DEMCO 38-297

Collective Wisdom

A Sourcebook of Lessons
for Writing Teachers

Collective Wisdom

A Sourcebook of Lessons for Writing Teachers

SONDRA J. STANG
ROBERT WILTENBURG

Washington University

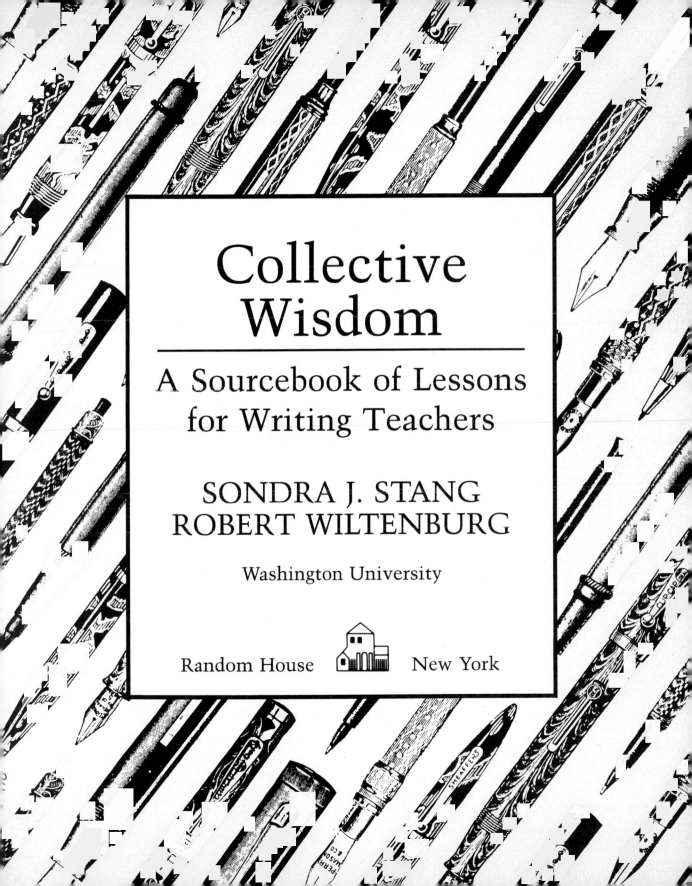

Random House   New York

First Edition

9 8 7 6 5 4 3 2 1

Library of Congress Cataloging-in-Publication Data

Collective wisdom.

  Includes index.
    1. English language—Rhetoric—Study and teaching.
2. English language—Rhetoric—Outlines, syllabi, etc.
I. Stang, Sondra J.   II. Wiltenburg, Robert Edward,
1947–

PE1404.C614   1987   808'.042'07   87-20764
ISBN 0-394-35451-6

Cover Design—Eric Baker
Text Design—Glen M. Edelstein

Manufactured in the United States of America

PREFACE

This collection of lessons and assignments reflects our conviction that good teaching should make the composition classroom a place of initiation as well as instruction, in which the teacher becomes the catalyst for a growing engagement with reading and writing, showing students not only how to read and write but also why they should care about the whole enterprise.

In fulfilling this purpose, most teachers act as practitioners, not theorists or researchers, and are habitually, incorrigibly, and (in our view) appropriately, eclectic in their methods. No theory can be adequate to all situations; what most teachers want to know is, "What works?" The enthusiasm and generosity with which teachers all over the country have responded to our invitation to submit their best lessons and assignments indicates that this need is widely felt, and we hope the collection will be of service not only to new teachers but also to experienced teachers who wish to keep their teaching fresh and effective.

In choosing the lessons we have welcomed widely different styles and strategies in teaching, since we feel that good teaching in composition is necessarily more diverse (and probably more difficult) than in almost any other subject, and that it grows out of a teacher's own instincts and experience. Thus we endorse no single method or vocabulary but have tried to represent a range of temperaments, approaches, teaching levels, student bodies, and institutions. We think that teachers of many kinds will find here material for inspiration, instruction, or emulation.

The table of contents reflects our sense that a composition course should be dynamic, evolving steadily from the apparently simple to the apparently complex, an evolution that is, however, accomplished by continually returning to a few fundamental principles and concerns, consolidating and extending what has been done before. It seems particularly important that the first part of the semester should be rich and suggestive, setting a high standard, and when students are most amenable, changing their awareness of language, their ways of seeing, thinking, reading, and writing.

There are more lessons and assignments here than any one could use in a semester, or even in an entire year. Our aim has been to provide enough material so that teachers can choose and adapt, fashioning a term's or a year's work that fits their style and sense of adventure, as well as their students' needs.

Although the lessons vary in format, contributors have been careful to provide a complete and lucid account of what they do in class and why they do it, showing both the logic of the lesson and the way in which it gives students the intellectual support they need to do the writing assignment. We have indicated in the margin whenever a lesson requires more than one class session, and we have used the following marginalia to make the shape of each more readily discernible:

In-Class Exercise—writing of a paragraph or more done in class.

Writing Assignment—writing done outside class and submitted in standard format (typed, double-spaced, etc.).

Specific readings are either included or indicated when they are necessary or appropriate to the lesson.

It is impossible to edit such a collection without being struck by the amount and diversity of fine teaching these lessons represent. They should give heart to anyone dismayed by the supposed decline of education in America, and particularly to composition teachers, prone as we are to proclaim the importance of our work even as we lament its difficulty. Here we see teachers awakening their students to the power of language, helping them to discover what they think, to narrow the gap between what they mean to say and do say, teaching them, like Prospero, Shakespeare's best teacher, to "endow their purposes with words." These lessons testify that such work is not only essential to education but also richly possible.

We are grateful to Steven Pensinger, our imaginative editor at Random House, who first saw the possibilities of this undertaking and supported it in every way. Cynthia Ward, Tina Barland, and Ron Harris, editors to whom the manuscript was entrusted, brought it to final form with patience and acuity. Kaye Norton and Camelia Hoerner, faithful secretaries of the Washington University Department of English, helped with typing and other essential matters. Candace O'Connor and Richard Stang followed this project from its inception, always encouraging and always critical.

We are much obliged to Scott Elledge for his useful questions and suggestions. For cheering us on, or for helping in one way or another, we thank Victoria Aarons, Thomas Bailey, Kent Bales, Joan Barickman, John Bernard, Ann E. Berthoff, Elizabeth T. Black, Alice Bloom, Leanna Boysko, Robert H. Brinkmeyer, Jr., Ken Bruffee, John F. Callahan, C. Barry Chabot, Maurice Charney, Howell Chickering, DeWitt Clinton, William Coles, John W. Conlee, Jim Corder, George Core, Frederick Crews, Donald A. Daiker, Margaret Dickie, John Dings, Ann Dobyns, Audrey T. Edwards, Norrie Epstein, Wayne Fields, Stephen Fix, Ron Fortune, John Gage, A. Bartlett Giamatti, Thora C. Girke, Bertrand A. Goldgar, Susan Gurewitsch, Tom Hahn, Maxine Hairston, John M. Hanchin, Shirley Brice Heath, William W. Heath, Neil Hertz, Eugene D. Hill, E. D. Hirsch, Jr., Bates L. Hoffer, Martin J. Jacobi, Lee Jacobus, David R. Johnson, Mark Karlins, Ruth M. Kivette, Catherine Lamb, Dagmar Logie, Andrea A. Lunsford, Edward A. Martin, Joanna S. Mink, Donald M. Murray, Charles Muscatine, Elizabeth Neeld,

Virginia Nees-Hatlen, Mary Nyquist, Barbara D. Palmer, Andrew Parker, JoAnne M. Podis, Hephzibah Roskelly, Donald Ross, John J. Ruszkiewicz, Anne Salvatore, Delores K. Schriner, Ronald A. Sharp, Robert E. Streeter, W. O. S. Sutherland, Sally T. Taylor, Douglas H. Thayer, John Trimble, Edward F. J. Tucker, Thomas Van Laan, Joseph Wiesenfarth, and Karl Zender.

Finally, we wish to acknowledge longstanding debts to our own teachers—Leah Brown, Katharine A. Gatch, Robert Knapp, and Joseph Summers—who, early and late, taught us how to listen, to read, and to teach.

S.J.S.
R.W.

CONTENTS

TRANSFORMATIONS

Observation to Essay

Critical Reading

Argument

OPENING OUT

Collective
Wisdom

A Sourcebook of Lessons
for Writing Teachers

First Principles

Of all the lessons in this book, those in this section are among the simplest to teach, introduce the most important concepts on which to build, and raise the most fundamental questions.

What does language do for us? How do reading and writing change our lives (MacKethan)? Why write (Wiltenburg)? Why bother to write well, and what does good writing have in common with the most life-enhancing work (Goleman)?

How do we find something to say that's worth saying (Baker)? How does critical thinking depend on—and in turn support—precise statement (Stang)? How do sentence sound and form reflect relationships between ideas (Flowers, Strout, Doyle)? What is grammar and why should we study it (Berke)? Why do we write in paragraphs (Doyle)? What happens when we fail to communicate—two lessons on clarity and revision (Carlisle, Madsen)?

How can writing be helped or hindered by clearly defined rules and expectations, whether deriving from what the teacher expects (Sonstroem) or from what students agree is necessary (Beidler)? How can attitudes toward authority be used as catalysts for critical thinking (Haddad, Podis)?

What are the intellectual operations that generate and focus writing? They include finding things to say by sharpening one's questions (Justice), adequately defining objects and categories (Lawrence), choosing categories and organizing (Pedersen), grasping the concept of evidence (Flood), anticipating the requirements of an audience (Gopen), and creating one's personality as a writer (Filloy).

And finally, we have an extended sequence formulating step-by-step ways in which the act of writing can create bridges between the self and the world (Lang).

The Power of Language: Liberation Through Literacy

Lucinda H. MacKethan,
North Carolina State University

This assignment uses American fugitive-slave narratives to accomplish several purposes:

- to generate thinking about the functions of literacy: Why do people need to know how to read and write?
- to introduce the concept of language as power: How can people use language to accomplish political and social goals?
- to illustrate the function of style: How does a writer manipulate language to communicate what he or she has to say in a striking, effective way, and what difference does style make?

I use this assignment fairly early in the semester in the basic freshman composition course. It works well to stimulate students to think about their own writing in a way that has usually not occurred to them: as a right, as a privilege, and even as a weapon that they need to possess and to exercise if they are to live productively as free citizens.

Before I introduce the reading, I ask the students to bring in a list of situations occurring in the previous week in which they used their writing skills—*any* situation, from making grocery lists to writing checks, taking phone messages or notes in class, writing papers, or writing letters. I also ask for a list of how other people's writing impinged on them in the course of a day: letters received, directions on labels or in manuals or cookbooks, books read for classes, announcements or bulletins or newspapers, and so on.

CLASS 1   We discuss the lists; then I give them the passage from Douglass's 1845 *Narrative of the Life of Frederick Douglass, an American Slave* in which

3

he tells how he learned the importance of written language. I give some additional background on Douglass's eventual role in American abolitionism, and I mention additional scenes from his and other slave narratives (e.g., James Pennington's account of slavery's worst crime, robbing him of an education, so that he remained a child well into adulthood; William Wells Brown's tale of tricking an illiterate free black man into getting a whipping meant for Brown himself; Harriet Jacob's story of duping her master into thinking that she had escaped to New York by writing letters to him and having a friend take them north and mail them to the master in North Carolina, where she was hiding out very near his home; Douglass's recollection of writing "passes" for himself and several slave friends in an abortive escape attempt—when caught, they had to "eat their own words" literally.)

WRITING
ASSIGNMENT 1
I ask the students to study the passage from Douglass I have distributed as a handout and to select any *three* sentences that seem to them to be particularly interesting because of their style, diction, or syntax. I ask them to explain their choices in one well-developed paragraph to be turned in at the next class meeting.

CLASS 2
We discuss the sentences the students have chosen. They easily catch the use of parallelism and the balancing of antithetical ideas in Douglass's sentences: "What he most dreaded, that I most desired." "What he most loved, that I most hated." We talk about the motive and effect of such sentences, how they distance or separate the slave from the master in order to give the slave equal importance. I read to them the sentence with which Douglass introduces his climactic fight with the overseer Covey: "You have seen how a man was made a slave; you shall see how a slave was made a man."

When I ask the students to pick out one sentence that sums up best for them the process that Douglass is describing, they tend to agree on one of three: "It would forever unfit him to be a slave"; "I now understood what had been to me a most perplexing difficulty—to wit, the white man's power to enslave the black man"; "From that moment, I understood the pathway from slavery to freedom." When we discuss Douglass's overall strategy, students come up with the sense of opposition and contrast that Douglass uses to achieve power, and they appreciate the balancing: *inch* with *ell*, *saddened* with *gladdened*, *revelation* with *dark* and *mysterious things*, *white man* with *black man*, and most important, *slavery* with *freedom*.

WRITING
ASSIGNMENT 2
At this point I allude to Bergen Evans's idea that "the more words one has at his command, the greater the possibility that he may be his own master. It takes words to free us from words." Sometimes I conclude this sequence of discussions and assignments by asking the students to write an out-of-class essay: Speculate on how your life would be if you could not read or write competently. What difficulties would you encounter in your

daily living? What economic, political, aesthetic limitations would you experience? You might begin organizing your thoughts by imagining one day in which you could not use written language in any way. What would you miss? Use the passage from Douglass's essay as a reference point wherever his perceptions help to illustrate your points.

(If I use the following segment, I give this assignment later as a choice with the ones that follow the third class meeting.)

CLASS 3
(OPTIONAL)

If we have time and the students have shown interest, at the end of the second class period I hand out the passage from Douglass's second auto-biography, the 1855 *My Bondage and My Freedom*, which revises the scene covered in the earlier passage we have studied. I ask the students to discuss the differences between the two passages and notice at least four significant changes that Douglass made in his new version. Students usually prefer the 1845 version. I explain some of the differences in Douglass's situation in 1855: He was by then very well known, a prominent man who had been given a hero's welcome in England; he had begun his own newspaper; he had "purchased" his freedom from his former "master"; he was no longer being supported financially by the American abolitionists; the Fugitive Slave Act (1850) had made escaped slaves' situations much more perilous than before. Douglass had undoubtedly read a great deal more, and *Uncle Tom's Cabin* (1851) had achieved enormous popularity around the world for its fictional rendering of slavery. (The character of Uncle Tom can be compared with the personality Douglass projects.)

We talk about specific changes in the later version, changes in wording, sentence structure, characterization, and approach: students see the differences between the early rhetoric, derived from preaching, and the later, largely influenced by contemporary journalism, wider reading, and a larger experience of men and women. Toward the end of the period I give several options for an out-of-class essay of three or four pages.

WRITING
ASSIGNMENT 3

Options include (1) write the essay described at the end of Class 2; (2) compare the two passages that Douglass wrote, in 1845 and then in 1855, evaluating what he gained or lost by the changes he made; (3) read another chapter of Douglass's narrative (available on reserve if the book is not a class text) and discuss how he dramatizes the idea that literacy provides the "pathway from slavery to freedom." Students are free to devise their own topics as well. When they write longer research papers later in the semester, one of their options is to read another slave narrative, noticing how the narrator's experiences shaped his attitudes toward reading and writing.

These anthologies of slave narratives are available in most libraries:

Puttin' On Ole Massa, ed. Gilbert Osofsky

Great Slave Narratives, ed. Arna Bontemps

Five Slave Narratives: A Compendium, ed. William L. Katz

Four Fugitive Slave Narratives, ed. Robin Winks

LESSON READINGS

Frederick Douglass, from *Narrative of the Life of Frederick Douglass, an American Slave, Written by Himself*, ed. Benjamin Quarles (Cambridge, MA: Harvard UP, 1960), pp. 58–59.
———, from *My Bondage and My Freedom* (New York: Miller, Orton & Mulligan, 1855).

READING

Frederick Douglass

NARRATIVE OF THE LIFE OF FREDERICK DOUGLASS, AN AMERICAN SLAVE, WRITTEN BY HIMSELF (1845)

Very soon after I went to live with Mr. and Mrs. Auld, she very kindly commenced to teach me the A, B, C. After I had learned this, she assisted me in learning to spell words of three or four letters. Just at this point of my progress, Mr. Auld found out what was going on, and at once forbade Mrs. Auld to instruct me further, telling her, among other things, that it was unlawful, as well as unsafe, to teach a slave to read. To use his own words, further, he said, "If you give a nigger an inch, he will take an ell. A nigger should know nothing but to obey his master—to do as he is told to do. Learning would spoil the best nigger in the world. Now," said he, "if you teach that nigger (speaking of myself) how to read, there would be no keeping him. It would forever unfit him to be a slave. He would at once become unmanageable, and of no value to his master. As to himself, it could do him no good, but a great deal of harm. It would make him discontented and unhappy." These words sank deep into my heart, stirred up sentiments within that lay slumbering, and called into existence an entirely new train of thought. It was a new and special revelation, explaining dark and mysterious things, with which my youthful understanding had struggled, but struggled in vain. I now understood what had been to me a most perplexing difficulty—to wit, the white man's power to enslave the black man. It was a grand achievement, and I prized it highly. From that moment, I understood the pathway from slavery to freedom. It was just what I wanted, and I got it at a time when I

From *Narrative of the Life of Frederick Douglass, an American Slave, Written by Himself* by Frederick Douglass, ed. Benjamin Quarles (Cambridge, MA: Harvard UP, 1960), pp. 58–59.

least expected it. Whilst I was saddened by the thought of losing the aid of my kind mistress, I was gladdened by the invaluable instruction which, by the merest accident, I had gained from my master. Though conscious of the difficulty of learning without a teacher, I set out with high hope, and a fixed purpose, at whatever cost of trouble, to learn how to read. The very decided manner with which he spoke, and strove to impress his wife with the evil consequences of giving me instruction, served to convince me that he was deeply sensible of the truths he was uttering. It gave me the best assurance that I might rely with the utmost confidence on the results which, he said, would flow from teaching me to read. What he most dreaded, that I most desired. What he most loved, that I most hated. That which to him was a great evil, to be carefully shunned, was to me a great good, to be diligently sought; and the argument which he so warmly urged, against my learning to read, only served to inspire me with a desire and determination to learn. In learning to read, I owe almost as much to the bitter opposition of my master, as to the kindly aid of my mistress. I acknowledge the benefit of both.

Frederick Douglass

MY BONDAGE AND MY FREEDOM (1855)

The frequent hearing of my mistress reading the bible—for she often read aloud when her husband was absent—soon awakened my curiosity in respect to this *mystery* of reading, and roused in me the desire to learn. Having no fear of my kind mistress before my eyes, (she had then given me no reason to fear), I frankly asked her to teach me to read; and, without hesitation, the dear woman began the task, and very soon, by her assistance, I was master of the alphabet, and could spell words of three or four letters. My mistress seemed almost as proud of my progress, as if I had been her own child; and, supposing that her husband would be as well pleased, she made no secret of what she was doing for me. Indeed, she exultingly told him of the aptness of her pupil, of her intention to persevere in teaching me, and of the duty which she felt it to teach me, at least to read *the bible*. Here arose the first cloud over my Baltimore prospects, the precursor of drenching rains and chilling blasts.

Master Hugh was amazed at the simplicity of his spouse, and, probably for the first time, he unfolded to her the true philosophy of slavery, and the peculiar rules necessary to be observed by masters and mistresses, in the management of their human chattels. Mr. Auld promptly forbade continuance of her instruction; telling her, in the first place, that the thing itself was unlawful; that it was also unsafe, and could only lead to mischief. To use his own words, further, he said, "if you give a nigger an inch, he will take an ell;" "he should know nothing but the will of his master, and learn to obey it;" "if you teach that nigger—speaking of myself—how to read the bible, there will be no keeping him;" "it would forever unfit him for the duties of a slave;"

From *My Bondage and My Freedom* by Frederick Douglass (New York: Miller, Orton & Mulligan, 1855).

and "as to himself, learning would do him no good, but probably, a great deal of harm—making him disconsolate and unhappy." "If you learn him how to read, he'll want to know how to write; and, this accomplished, he'll be running away with himself." Such was the tenor of Master Hugh's oracular exposition of the true philosophy of training a human chattel; and it must be confessed that he very clearly comprehended the nature and the requirements of the relation of master and slave. His discourse was the first decidedly anti-slavery lecture to which it has been my lot to listen. Mrs. Auld evidently felt the force of his remarks; and, like an obedient wife, began to shape her course in the direction indicated by her husband. The effect of his words, *on me*, was neither slight nor transitory. His iron sentences—cold and harsh—sunk deep into my heart, and stirred up not only my feelings into a sort of rebellion, but awakened within me a slumbering train of vital thought. It was a new and special revelation, dispelling a painful mystery, against which my youthful understanding had struggled, and struggled in vain, to wit: the *white* man's power to perpetuate the enslavement of the *black* man. "Very well," thought I; "knowledge unfits a child to be a slave." I instinctively assented to the proposition; and from that moment I understood the direct pathway from slavery to freedom. This was just what I needed; and I got it at a time, and from a source, whence I least expected it. I was saddened at the thought of losing the assistance of my kind mistress; but the information, so instantly derived, to some extent compensated me for the loss I had sustained in this direction. Wise as Mr. Auld was, he evidently underrated my comprehension, and had little idea of the use to which I was capable of putting the impressive lesson he was giving to his wife. *He* wanted me to be *a slave*; I had already voted against that on the home plantation of Col. Lloyd. That which he most loved I most hated; and the very determination which he expressed to keep me in ignorance, only rendered me the more resolute in seeking intelligence. In learning to read, therefore, I am not sure that I do not owe quite as much to the opposition of my master, as to the kindly assistance of my amiable mistress. I acknowledge the benefit rendered me by the one, and by the other; believing, that but for my mistress, I might have grown up in ignorance.

Why Write

Robert Wiltenburg,
Washington University

I often use this as a first assignment (beyond the merely diagnostic) in a freshman composition class and have found that it works well even with quite unsophisticated students. Its main purpose is to provide a practical, personal demonstration of why writing matters, what makes it worth the effort. The examined life *is* more worth living, and writing is our chief means of examining it. In coming to terms with a significant experience of their own, students discover the primary possibilities and challenges that writing presents: first, the chance to lift something out of the vague formlessness of unconsidered impressions, opinions, and memories, to work it through, and to learn from it; and second, to share that experience with others.

To prepare for the assignment, I have the class read and discuss two standard anthology pieces, E. B. White's "Once More to the Lake" and George Orwell's "Shooting an Elephant." Many essays would serve the purpose, but I find these sturdy perennials particularly useful both for their qualities in common—blending particular experiences and larger significance in ways that students find clear and engaging—and for the range of contrasts they suggest: White more personal, familiar, evocative, deliberately artful; Orwell more public, exotic, polemical, "artless." And together they exemplify the complementary kinds of experiences students have had: things that happen within the family; things that happen at the boundary between the self and the larger world.

I base the discussions on questions of form, both because these essays lend themselves to such treatment and because students need to start thinking as writers facing technical choices. Everyone is struck by White's ending. The obvious questions are: Has the ending been earned? If so, how? How does the ending fulfill the patterns (constancy and change, father and son, the "religious" quality of the whole experience) upon which the story is built? Are these patterns natural to the subject, or are they artificial impositions? The mode of attack is not quite so obvious with the Orwell, which, though less finely polished, is more ambitious and suggestive than White's piece. I begin by summarizing Orwell's discussion in "Why I Write" of the four motives for writing: egotistical, aesthetic (the pleasure of finding words to fit experience), scientific or historical (getting things straight in one's mind), and political (trying to push the world in a certain direction). We discuss the mixture of motives in this piece—whether it is essentially a story with political reflections or a polemical essay with personal illustrations; how these elements are balanced, interact, and support each other; and how the elephant in its death throes serves not only as the climax of the story but also as a unifying image that suggests the "suffering" of the British Empire in history and the suffering of the young Orwell as he comes to realize his place within it.

WRITING ASSIGNMENT   The assignment must be defined widely enough so that all the students feel that they can do it, yet in a way that guards against the tendency to trivialize. I discourage the easiest options ("My First Day at College") and encourage students to write about such things as falling in or out of love, making and losing friends, death, moving, first experiences in public roles and situations, moments when something building for a long time comes to a crisis. Those who protest that nothing has ever happened to them can write instead about a moment when they first understood something; those who do not admit to understanding anything can describe an experience that typifies their life or personality. Once the assignment is made, we discuss briefly what is essential in fulfilling it: a vivid, appropriately detailed sense of "before" and "after"; a turning point that can bear the causal weight assigned to it ("Did eating that hot dog really change your whole outlook?"); a continuity of description and reflection that enables the reader both to share the essential experience and to evaluate the conclusions drawn from it.

This may sound like a rather sophisticated set of expectations for a first assignment—as indeed it is. But I find that students are better served by an initial assignment that admits, even insists, that good writing is always complex, even when its materials are found right at home. We should not pretend that writing can be divided into simple bits that can be mastered one at a time. It is always difficult to think things through, find the right words, and adequately imagine the reader and his needs. By simplifying the materials rather than the activity of writing, this assignment gives beginning students an accurate picture of what good writing involves and how they should go about it. By encouraging them to learn something about themselves, it also shows them what, at the beginning, they most need to know: why they should write.

LESSON READINGS

George Orwell, "Shooting an Elephant," in *Shooting an Elephant and Other Essays* (Orlando, FL: Harcourt Brace Jovanovich, 1950).

George Orwell, "Why I Write," in *Such, Such Were the Joys* (Orlando, FL: Harcourt Brace Jovanovich, 1953).

E. B. White, "Once More to the Lake," in *Essays of E. B. White* (New York: Harper & Row, 1977).

Writing and Working: The Common Denominator

Judith Goleman,
University of Massachusetts–Boston

In the following introductory sequence of writing assignments for freshman English, I am interested in eliciting thought about what the composing process is and why anyone should want to compose. I am especially interested that the students for whom this sequence is designed (frequently older, working, urban students) will be able to draw on what they already know about composing from their home and work lives to begin their study of college writing as a composing activity. In this way, the following sequence constitutes a lesson in the original sense of the word as the "practice of reading" (*O.E.D.*). Through this incremental sequence, students read from the texts of their own and others' work lives and write about these texts. It is their own sustained action of reading and writing that actually constructs "the lesson," for it is finally a lesson about nothing else but writing as the action of reading, as the construction *of* a reading.

At the same time the sequence addresses the question of why students should want to do the work of construction that writing requires in the following way: Writing about their own work lives and about the work lives of two people in Studs Terkel's book *Working*, the class begins to develop a definition of what they dislike or do not value in their jobs and what they like or value in their jobs. As this definition develops through reading, writing, and class discussion, so too does an analogy develop between working and writing: those aspects of work that are valued (e.g., responsibility for a whole process, creative decision making, a sense of belonging to a community) and those that are not valued (e.g., mechanical participation in a fragmented act of linear production) *also* come to define what the writing process is and is not. Thus through the following sequence of introductory assignments, my students' concept of writing evolves as a mode of *valued* work, consistent with the values expressed in their own descriptions of work they have enjoyed and consistent with the values they have derived from Terkel's book about work in America.

CLASS 1   I begin the course by writing the words *compose, composer,* and *composition* on the board and then inviting quick, associational thinking about these words. I promote associations by asking a lot of who, what, when, where, and how questions. When I am satisfied that all the students have found a context for these words in their lives, I give them an in-class exercise to help us begin generating a lexicon about composing:

IN-CLASS   Write for 15 minutes describing something you have composed. What did you
EXERCISE 1   do? How did you do it? What came of what you did?

Fifteen minutes later each student reads his or her writing aloud while others listen and make lists of all the phrases they hear that describe the action of composing. Then, I ask the students to volunteer items from their lists and I write them on the board. Using this master list, we return to a discussion of the concept *composing*—using the phrases on the board as a new, class-generated lexicon for the process.

For example, when one student described "Creating a Floral Arrangement from Scratch," she wrote that after getting all the "ingredients" together from several stores, "It was a place and look method of creating. After placing and moving, moving and placing, I finally had what I thought was a centerpiece." This phrase, "placing and moving, moving and placing," when transferred to the board and discussed in terms of composing in general, helped to lay the groundwork for the whole course in the way its language rendered the more abstract process of writing and rewriting concrete and self-evident.

With this exercise completed, it is now possible to move into a more sustained, incremental investigation of the relation between composing at work and composing in the writing class. This investigation begins with Assignment 1:

WRITING   Write about a job you've had or work you've done which you did not like,
ASSIGNMENT 1   which you might even call the worst job you've ever done. What did you do?
How did you do it? Why didn't you like it?

CLASS 2   When the students bring Assignment 1 to the next class, they read their papers aloud and follow a procedure similar to that of the previous class: They listen to each other's papers and make lists of examples and characteristics of bad work that they hear. (I make no attempt to distinguish between examples and general characteristics here; we sort this out on the board as part of the classwork.) The following paper is representative of the sort of examples and characterizations the students hear:

The worst job that I've ever had would have to be the job I had last summer at Stryco Electronics in Malden. This was my first factory job and boy was I in for a surprise. Upon entering the buildings we punched our card into a time clock. Just as soon as the entire crew gathered, the doors to the outside world were slammed shut and locked. Only the manager carried the key to the outside world. Every evening I would sit in front of an oven and test electronic parts. We had to wear a band around our wrists which was attached to our work table. They told me it was to prevent any electrical shocks from happening. In reality, I felt like a slave chained to the table. All I did was test electrical parts every minute hour after hour for eight hours with only a half-hour break in between. By the end of the first week there I thought that I was going crazy from the tedious boredom. That was my first factory job and definitely my last.

Papers such as this one lead to an active class: The students generate a master list of items from their notes; then we work at gathering into groups similar examples of bad work and naming them—sometimes with the names or characterizations already on the board (e.g., "tedious boredom") and other times with new-found characterizations.

The students then compose a sentence that defines bad work, using the concepts we have developed. Once these sentences are read aloud, I ask the students, usually as class is ending, how they would characterize the work *we* have done that day. Whatever the students say at this point (there's usually a lot of play on the words from the master list), they usually recognize the difference between work that discourages thought and work that promotes it.

The following three assignments build on the previous one. In Assignment 2 the students are asked to read their first narrative from *Working*, a narrative by the disaffected steel worker, Mike Lefevre. As the following assignment suggests, they are asked to write about Mike Lefevre using, in part, the concepts they have evolved from writing about their own work lives:

WRITING
ASSIGNMENT 2

In Assignment 1, you wrote about a job you had or work you did which you disliked. We have listened to those papers, taken notes, and made observations about what we have heard. From our observations of each other's papers, we have begun to characterize a bad job. For next class, consider the narrative of Mike Lefevre in *Working* as another story by someone who dislikes his job. As you explained specifically in your own stories what you did and how you did it, so too, explain specifically in this paper what Mike Lefevre does and how he does it.

- From what he says, why does Mike dislike his work?

- Do his criticisms resemble any that have shown up in your story or in any of the papers read in class?

- Can you name these resemblances?

CLASS 3   In the next class each student reads his or her paper on Mike Lefevre aloud while the rest make lists of all the concepts the writers have used to discuss Mike's work. Afterward I draw from them the elements of a master list, which I write on the board. This master list may include such concepts as the anonymity of the worker in mass production, Mike's lack of pride in his work, his lack of recognition in a job where there is no chance to see end results, his frustrations about work that is seen by others as "dummy" work, his boredom with a repetitive job, and his fear of automation.

We distinguish between the concepts taken from the prior discussion and the *new* concepts found in the *new* reading. For instance, the concept of boredom as it relates to repetitive work was first formed in relation to the Stryco Electronics paper. However, the concept of recognition comes up for the first time in relation to Mike Lefevre, as does the concept of responsibility for a whole process. The purpose of making this distinction between prior concepts and new concepts is to suggest how the composing–recomposing process is both dialogical and dialectical, that is, how the reading of *new* material can set up a dialogue with *prior* material in a way that makes it possible to expand and to revise the prior material on the basis of new understanding.

In the name of this purpose the students are then asked to revise their sentence defining bad work (from Class 2), and we read a few of these aloud. Finally, I ask the students to try to recall everything we have had to *do* to arrive at this latest definition—writing, listening, listing, sorting, naming, rewriting, reading, further writing, listening, listing, naming, renaming, and so on. As the students recall this process, I try to use phrases from our composing lexicon (Exercise 1) to punctuate their discourse about composing. Because Mike Lefevre's narrative is so explicitly and dramatically about merely rote work that leads to nothing but its own repetition, the work of constructing in which these writers have been engaged reveals itself as different in a telling way, a way that decidedly opposes it to work such as Mike's, where "you never see the end result."

The sequence now turns to defining what constitutes enjoyable and valuable work in Assignment 3:

WRITING ASSIGNMENT 3   For your next assignment, think about a job you have had or work you have done which you have enjoyed. Describe as precisely as you can what you did, how you did it, and why you liked this work. Tell your story in any way that makes it possible for us to appreciate the pleasure you took in your work or your job, whether this involved paid employment, unpaid activity, or hobby.

CLASS 4   With Assignment 3 the students consciously organize their essays to oppose the characteristics of bad work they have been defining. Although the procedure for reading aloud and making lists is identical to that for Assignment 1, the classroom experience is not, for the students now listen to each other as writers with works in progress. They listen actively for the way other writers are rewriting shared concepts about work.

The challenge of this class is to move from lists composed of negatively formed concepts about valued work ("not like a robot"; "not boring") to positively expressed concepts ("discovery of new talents"; "increased self-confidence"; "opportunity for getting it right"). Helping the process along will be a number of students who have chosen to rewrite their papers from Exercise 1 for this assignment on valued work. As a result, many papers will explicitly recall our original composing lexicon in order to describe enjoyable work. *Methods* of composing ("placing and moving, moving and placing") are now rewritten as working *values*—the language of construction offering itself as the positively expressed concepts for valued work that we are looking for.

WRITING ASSIGNMENT 4

This process of defining working values prepares the students for Assignment 4, a reading and writing assignment based on the narrative of the stonemason Carl Murray Bates in *Working:*

> In Assignment 3, you wrote a story about a job you had or work you did which you liked. We have listened to those papers, taken notes, and made observations about what we have heard. From our observations of each other's papers, we can infer what we, as a class, think a good job is. For next class, consider the narrative of Carl Murray Bates in *Working* as another story by someone who likes his job. As you explained in your own stories what you did and how you did it, so too, explain specifically in this paper what Bates does and how he does it.
>
> From what he says, why does Bates like his work? Do his reasons (stated or implied) resemble any that have shown up in your story or in any of the papers read in class? Name these resemblances, and draw any conclusions that you feel are appropriate based on what you have written.

CLASS 5

Students arrive at their reading of Carl Murray Bates's narrative as specialists on the subject of work. Their reflexive awareness of the relationship between working and writing can be seen in the way students read Bates's narrative both as a source of new meaning about work and as a source of metaphor for their own process of constructing meaning. Thus this five-part sequence ends with students consciously constructing a reading about the value of construction itself and about themselves as constructors. Their papers will teach "the lesson" of these assignments and will uniquely position the students to receive and respond to the writing course ahead of them. On this day the students give the lesson to each other as they read and attend to the stage of insight their work has brought them to, a stage of insight powerfully exemplified in the following essay from Assignment 4 by Kathy Evans:

> Carl Murray Bates is an artist, a stonemason who has worked at his job for forty years. His art tools are his hands; they have molded, created and designed stone structures with skill. Carl works on stone projects for his friends, stone projects involving fireplaces and brick walls in his job and daydreams about various stone projects for his home. Laying brick and working with trowel, hammer and mortar has been Carl's life since he was 17 years old. Originally

he did his work by patterning himself after the men who were stonemasons he admired. This admiration became transferred slowly over the years into a self-admiration through learning, correcting, modifying, making mistakes and loving the work. Carl had self-respect, which generated admiration from friends and family. This complete circle not only produced works of stone worthy of Carl's respect but produced Carl's hands.

Forty years of chiseling with a hammer, I imagine, have transferred the grooves of the stone onto Carl's hands. Furrows and channels are indented into his hands like a trench in the ground made by a plow, and rising up from these grooves are aged and hard calluses. Carl's hands are as much his identity as the work he so proudly displays. They are the initials after his name, his M.D., Ph.D., his shingle.

Carl does his job with confidence; he takes the time to work out problems and is proud of his ability to carry on and do the work after the architects and draftsmen draw up the plans. Taking on jobs his boss doesn't think can be done and staying up at night solving problems make Carl's work an adventure.

The pride Carl takes in his work and the knowledge he has about the history of stone I would think might parallel the tradition and background of his name, Carl Murray Bates. Carl Murray Bates, Stonemason, a strong statement like Henry Cabot Lodge, Statesman, and Margaret Chase Smith, Politician; the words have a strength of their own.

The absence of any mention of Mrs. Bates is to me evidence of her existence. Carl's world of men and his world of stone do not encourage conversations about women, but I imagine that his manageable, hard-working life was shared by an equally strong woman. As proudly as Carl refers to his tools and "my hammer" and "my trowel," I imagine that Mrs. Bates, packing his lunch, might just as respectfully mention "my dishes" and "my ironing." Their combined sense of order surely contributed to three sons becoming mathematicians. Sharing his delight while driving to view prior works of Carl's surely is a fond event to Mrs. Bates, but possibly her encouragement of him reached its limit when he began daydreaming about plans to build stone cabinets.

Carl reminds me a little of myself during one incident that I shared concerning my efforts to write a story about an old house. I didn't realize at the time that this writing situation would resemble someone who loved his job. His mortar reminded me of my words, and our efforts to mix them, change them and allow them to fit just right seemed identical to me. As he sketched out the curves in the fireplace, I searched for words to make sentences. Carl's efforts to find just the right mixture of mortar to match the wall he was fixing matched my intensity in trying to find the right phrases and tenses to blend in smoothly. Our results were also similar as we were both pleased with our efforts. Recognizing their similarities, I feel a change of name is in order. Carl Murray Bates, Stonemason, has inspired me. If I am known as Kathleen Curran Evans, possibly an appropriate noun might follow.

LESSON READING

Studs Terkel, "Mike Lefevre," "Carl Murray Bates" in *Working* (New York: Pantheon, 1972).

Themes Off the Top of Your Head

Sheridan Baker,
University of Michigan

I like to start the second meeting of the class by hitting head on the problem of finding something to write about and shaping it into an essay. My first meeting is just getting acquainted, usually asking the class about what kind of writing they did in high school. I usually end with ten or fifteen minutes of writing about what they hope to get out of this course, what they think their problems are, anything, as I tell them, to help me get acquainted with them and how they write.

Now comes the fun. This hour will be a "brainstormer" to illustrate that everyone really does have something to write about, if we just give the old mind a chance. We will also discover what a subject, or topic, is and how to turn it into a thesis and roll it out into an essay.

Teacher: All right. I'm going to proceed around the room, asking each of you to give me the first word, by way of a subject, that pops into your head. I'll put them all on the board, but you have a sheet of paper to write it down for yourself too. All right, here we go.

Students: Canoes. Knitting. Nail polish. Tomatoes. Fishing. . . .

Teacher: Now what we have here is a list of subjects about which you must have some interest and knowledge or some healthy and humorous antipathy, as with "Teachers" here or "Assignments." Now, to turn these subjects into theses, all we have to do is to say something about them, to assert something about them. I'll go around the room again asking each one to assert something about his or her top-of-the-head subject. Canoes?

Students: "Canoes are exciting."

"Knitting is both relaxing and creative."

"I hate nail polish."

Teacher: Nope. You're asserting something about yourself, not about your subject. Start with *nail polish.*

Student: "Nail polish is unnecessary, fussy, and snobbish."

Teacher: Good. Now you really have something to write about, something to prove, an argument to make. Why do you suppose I shifted the focus from I to *nail polish?*

Here we have a discussion of the first person pronoun and the autobiographical in expository writing. The trouble with the wholly personal focus, I say, is that it puts you back in the kindergarten of show and tell in which everyone assumes that he or she is unique.

Student: "But everyone *is* unique."

We toss this around for a few minutes, talking about fingerprints, ear-whorls, intonations of voice recognizable over the phone. I say,

Teacher: But actually, handy and attractive as our uniquenesses are—it would be terrible if we were all identical—they are the least significant things about us. Neither you nor I can be perceived by others as worth anything at all except insofar as we represent some category of value larger than ourselves—a good tennis player, a good student, an independent thinker, a cheerful friend. All of our experiences are different in detail, but they are valuable and significant and interesting to others only insofar as they illustrate something typical about being human—growing up, for instance. When you assert a personal opinion as something generally true, you have objectified it. You have shifted your focus from the personal *I* to the question of validity, which you will now set about proving and demonstrating to your readers. Now here's the point about the personal *I*. Once you have asserted your thesis, you can well bring instances from your own experience to illustrate it. Our canoeist will certainly tell of an exciting white-water experience or two, and our knitter of relaxing and creating. Sure, use the *I* to illustrate, along with other kinds of evidence to. We'll have more to say about this as we go on.

Student: But isn't your assertion, your thesis, still only a personal opinion?

Student: How can you tell what makes a good objectified assertion, something more than just personal opinion? Aren't some assertions more objective than others? How *can* you tell?

Teacher: Good questions. This is right at the heart of the matter, the whole business of what is true and what isn't. In the area of values (judgments about what is good, beautiful, true, immoral, ugly, and so forth, the questions that interest and concern us most, in fact—just think about what you say when you talk about your friends, films, classes, political action, whatever), all we actually have to go on is assertions, strange as that may seem. We cannot check their validity in any physical way. In mathematics we can check the written assertion that 2 times 2 equals 4 by putting down a couple of toothpicks then another couple—that is, putting down 2's two times—and counting them with our fingers and eyes. But in the theses we make we have very few quantifiable objective facts. We have only our assertion that such and such is so, backed by examples and stated reasons that will persuade others, our readers, that what we assert as true is in fact true, reasonably valid. We cannot prove it with mathematical objectivity. We can only persuade our readers that it is probably true. That's the way we humans are. Complete objectivity in this area is simply beyond our reach. But we can be reasonably sure, and that's all we need.

Now let's take the nail-polish thesis, because it has a good argumentative edge to it. What do you think the writer ought to take into account as she goes along thinking up reasons to support her assertion?

Student: Well, some people like nail polish. An awful lot of people use it anyway.

Teacher: Right. This is what I hoped you'd see. To make that thesis stand up well, the writer will have to make some concession to the opposite point of view. Our canoeist should probably admit that his sport is dangerous, even sometimes fatal, and not for the weak of arm and heart, and our knitter that many entrants quit the game before giving it a real chance. What kind of reasons might support the nail-polish thesis?

Students: That fingernails are perfectly OK as they are? After all, about half the people, men, don't use nail polish. That beauty should be natural? That people should be simple and natural? That people should stop fussing with themselves and help others?

Teacher: OK. Now how about opposing points?

Students: That nail polish shows a person who takes care of herself? A person who cares? Not a nail biter, not a neurotic? That beauty consists of enhancing the natural, grooming it? Like a lawn or a garden! Or Japanese flower arrangement?

Teacher: OK. Our writer will have to work it out. Now, just off the top of your heads, which of the two theses, the nail-polish one or the knitting one, seems the more valid, the more provable, the more nearly objective in this area where we can never reach anything like mathematical objectivity?

Discussion seems to back the knitter on the grounds that relaxation and creativity are more generally persuasive than having natural nails but that the nail polisher might have the livelier essay from her minority position, a good chance for something light and humorous.

Teacher: Well, we've certainly covered the ground. If you haven't yet made a sentence asserting something about your top-of-the-head subject, do it now, and go on for the rest of the hour seeing how well you can make it stick, make it persuasive and interesting to someone else; then bring it in next time rounded out to 500 words or so to hand in.

FOR FURTHER READING

Karl R. Popper, *Conjectures and Refutations*, 3rd ed. (New York: Basic Books, 1969).

Sheridan Baker, *The Practical Stylist*, 6th ed. (New York: Harper & Row, 1985).

Thinking Critically: Finding the Right Word, Defining the Right Subject

Sondra J. Stang,
Washington University

This is the last sequence in a unit focusing on accuracy of expression—the idea of choosing the word to fit the meaning and not the other way around. Orwell's "Politics and the English Language" is of course the centerpiece of the whole sequence of lessons, and a good deal of work on euphemism, jargon, cliché, and padding has followed the reading of the essay: For students today it is such a powerful statement that it seems easily to sustain a good many ensuing lessons. Students come away from their reading imbued with Orwell's spirit and willing to do the work of relearning how to write and read. The lesson I am about to describe illustrates his thesis about the need to think about the language we use, to attend to the meaning of individual words, to care about how we use words—and to resist the ready-made phrase. For this lesson I use an old adage—"Honesty is the best policy"—as it appears in the opening of a student paper from a previous year.

CLASS 1   I distribute copies of the paper below, and ask the students to read it to themselves:

> Honesty is the best policy. These days a majority of people do not hold this concept true. They have no faith in the idea of honesty. Honesty is, was, and always will be the best course of action a person can take. This maxim has a concrete and practical basis in human nature, everyday experience, and moral ethics. To assert that it is untrue or to ignore its meaning is a crime against nature and a violation of moral standards. It is to cheat.
>
> Cheating appears in many forms. From the young to the old, the poor to the rich, dishonest inclinations are always winning battles. It almost becomes

an obsession to see who can cheat their company out of the most goods or who can dupe the government for the most on their taxes. It is constantly spreading from the elders to the youngsters. How many times have we seen a father or a mother lie about their thirteen-year-old child's age to save some money on a movie ticket. Or how many times will a student peek at another student's exam to find out what he wrote down for question seven, the only answer stopping him from a perfect paper. How little he realizes that the act of cheating forever bars him from attaining perfection, just as the parent barely realizes what a tainted influence he is setting for his child. Why don't they care?

One of the best reasons that a cheater will give as justification for his dishonesty is the so-called reward he is earning: a higher grade, a few extra dollars, material things which are almost always incorrectly valued. If only the emphasis in life were placed upon the proper things—truth, justice, honesty, love. Then all would realize the actual seriousness of their petty crimes.

Everybody's doing it. This excuse has been heard often enough, and holds a double meaning. The first interpretation is that if a person deludes himself into believing that everyone else is cheating to get ahead of the pack, more than likely he will do the same, so as not to fall behind. He is cheating to uphold his image of fairness. Why should he be the only one to remain honest and be deprived? The other important side is that honesty in a person's actions no longer matters if everyone is cheating. Somehow, in the violator's mind, the numbers decrease the seriousness of the crime. If everyone else is being dishonest then dishonesty must not be bad. The error in the above reasonings lies in the original statement. Everybody is not doing it. If only one solitary person were to uphold the idea of honesty, everyone else's justification of cheating would be worthless. Merely to say to yourself "if I am honest, then honesty must necessarily be the best policy for all." Cheating cannot be justified and therefore cannot be tolerated.

My questions about the paper run something like this: What does the opening sentence mean? What does *policy* mean? What does it suggest? What is the difference between saying "It is best to be honest" or "Honesty is the best of all principles" and saying "Honesty is the best policy"?

Once the difference is established, I ask the class if they know who wrote the apothegm (I define the word for those who don't know it). Invariably someone suggests Benjamin Franklin, and I ask why he or she thinks so. Some discussion follows about Franklin's general point of view, and I enlarge on the distinction between pragmatism, expediency, and immediate usefulness, on the one hand, and the idea of principle or ethical ideal, on the other. Then I tell the class that it wasn't Benjamin Franklin who wrote "Honesty is the best policy." The statement was probably made two centuries earlier—if not before—and was much quoted. "Would you like to hear the most striking use of it I have found?" They would; and I tell them it was by Richard Whately, Archbishop of Dublin (1787–1863). "Honesty is the best policy; but he who is governed by that maxim is not an honest man."

The class *is* surprised. We talk a little more about Whately's point of view and how it is opposed to Franklin's.

I go back to the student paper, and I harp on the opening a little longer: "If you put yourself in this student's frame of mind, can you see why he or she reached for this old maxim?" A student will say, "Yes, this student wanted to write about honesty, but he couldn't think of a real opening, so he pressed a button and out came 'Honesty is the best policy.' " I ask what's to be learned from examining this first sentence and clarifying the word *policy.* What sort of paragraph *could* have followed if the writer had understood the quotation? In answer, a student suggests a paragraph about using honesty as an instrument rather than as an end in itself.

I ask the class to think again about Orwell's point—and he was referring to readers as well as writers—about being indifferent to what words really mean, and I quote the bit about phrases and words "tacked together like a prefabricated hen house"—something that seems to happen automatically when a writer fails to "stop and think about what he is saying." I tell the class about the French ideal, *le mot juste,* the need to care about the detail of what we write. We begin to analyze the paper, starting with the first paragraph as an example not just of faulty construction but of words used irresponsibly.

CLASS 2   I give the students a few minutes in which to reread the paper to themselves. Then we go to work, collectively, taking it apart in the spirit of critical analysis. "What does it mean to analyze a work?" I ask. We talk about their negative feelings—and Wordsworth's—and I quote the line "We murder to dissect." But we conclude, and I think it's important to steer the discussion to this point, that the true purpose of analysis is to take the work—a piece of music, a painting, a story, a poem, or an essay—apart, to examine the parts and see the relationship of each part to the whole.

In trying to see the relationship between the individual sentences and the meaning of the paragraph as a whole, I have found that it helps students to number the sentences in any given paragraph under scrutiny. Sentence by sentence and paragraph by paragraph in this very confused paper on honesty, we consider the sequence of illogical, unrelated, and undeveloped statements. We identify them and discuss possible solutions to the many problems the paper presents. But in addition to the important and pervasive issues of paragraph construction, faulty logic, and general incoherence is another issue. I ask, "What are this writer's real feelings—his personal feelings—about the subject of honesty? Where do you spot them? In other words, where do you really hear this writer speaking?" Everyone identifies the sentence "How many times have we seen a father or a mother lie about their thirteen-year-old child's age to save money on a movie ticket." This is the only fresh observation in the paper, and we know at once that the writer actually saw an incident that left its impression on him. I go on: "Why has this writer failed—except for the one particular moment we've identified—to convince us that a living human being has written this paper?"

This is a difficult question, and there are several answers. "Maybe the subject was so big he felt he had to make general statements about honesty in order to cover the whole subject and so he didn't have time to give his own individual feelings." "Maybe he thought he should sound objective and not put himself into the paper." The discussion goes on for a while, and I ask: "Do you think this writer *intentionally* refrained from developing the observation we all like so much? It's so obviously the real spark behind the paper—but it never catches. It gets smothered. He could have made better use of that moment—developed it, given more specific detail, drawn out its implications."

> *Student:* Maybe he wanted to but didn't know how.
> *Another:* Maybe that's why he fell back on all those clichés.

I ask the students if they have ever faced the same problem. Yes, they tell me: It's their chief problem in transferring their thoughts to paper. Even though they start with an outline—and some do—they can't get in what they most want to write about. Somehow it gets left out because it's too hard—too complicated—to write about. We conclude that often what they leave out is their best material in their attempt to get it into words. It's their best material because it's their own. It's something they themselves have noticed and thought about; it's not in the common domain, yet they find they can't write about it because they don't have the words for it, the sort of prepackaged words that fill up the paper we've been considering. I try to reassure them that the real work of writing—and its greatest value— is to do justice to their own perceptions, that it is very hard to find the right words. The material that might have brought the paper to life re- mained submerged because the writer either panicked or gave up. I read some statements by great writers about how hard they too find writing to be.

WRITING ASSIGNMENT   It is time for the writing assignment—to rewrite the paper on honesty, making it as logical and coherent as possible, paragraph by paragraph, and at the same time to allow the students' own voices to be heard. (Length: two pages maximum.) The assignment becomes clearer as a result of the following discussion.

CLASS 3   I raise a number of questions. *Is* honesty best? Best for what? Should we be honest because it is useful to *seem* honest, because it keeps us out of trouble—or is honesty a good in itself? If it is, is it related to other virtues? Which? What kind of society would we be likely to have if the ideal of honesty—now seriously eroded, if we believe the writer of the paper—were totally discarded? What have you noticed about dishonesty in personal relationships—in the family, among friends? How serious are the conse- quences? And yet, should we always be absolutely honest? How did you as a child feel about witnessing dishonest behavior in adults or in other chil- dren? These are preliminary questions to be thought about before the stu- dents even plan their papers. The questions are meant to stimulate their thinking, encourage them to trust their own perceptions, and value them enough to do the work of trying to express them in their papers—that is, wherever they are relevant. The point is to get the students to begin to think their own thoughts and to try to write about them. Of course, the students will have to take the large, sprawling subject of the paper we have been considering and somehow narrow it. I try to develop a more restricted subject with the class, and we arrive at something like this: Children notice a lot more about adult behavior than adults realize. They are disturbed when adults tell children to do one thing and then proceed to do the opposite themselves. *What is the effect on children of small or not-so-small examples of dishonesty?* What happens to children when they decide to give up trying to make sense of adult behavior and instead join them by imitation? Obviously, this writing assignment is going to produce an altogether different paper from the one we have been analyzing, and I point out that breathing life into lifeless prose and revising something that has not yet been thought through means pretty much making a fresh start and writing an altogether new paper. I promise to bring to class photocopies of manuscripts showing revisions by an eminent writer who almost completely reconceived his essay after several false starts.

LESSON READING

George Orwell, "Politics and the English Language," in *Shooting an Elephant and Other Essays* (Orlando, FL: Harcourt Brace Jovanovich, 1950).

"Real" Sentences and Then the Other Kind

Linda Flowers,
North Carolina Wesleyan College

Students are encouraged enormously by seeing concrete evidence that their teachers are also writers, that they read and write more or less all the time, often simply for their own pleasure, as well as in an effort to come to grips with the world. Every semester, therefore, I try to find a way to use in class something I am currently writing. It need not be a finished essay. Successive drafts of a paragraph or two can be profitably analyzed, especially where I have changed my direction or abandoned a hopeless beginning. An essay on Reagan's visit to Bitburg, for example, which I wrote for myself, proved wonderfully effective for driving home the point that writing can matter to us personally and profoundly. Teachers of composition do well, I am convinced, to put themselves on the line. The best instruction still is by example.

At the start of class, I hand out the following passage that I've written, along with a set of questions, in order to stimulate a discussion of style and meaning.

A sentence, as much as a man, has integrity when it proves as good as its word, when it promises no more than it delivers and yet delivers all that it promises. By itself a sentence, a good, clean sentence, is a glory to behold. Not everybody can write one. Others can, though usually without knowing it. A few people, especially if they have been formally educated, assume that of course they can, and that they habitually do, when, in fact, only by chance is a "real" sentence ever caught in the nets they cast. As scarce almost as hen's teeth are the lone souls for whom constructing a sentence is a deliberate act: as premeditated as murder in the first-degree, and infinitely—or so I suspect—more difficult.

Not every complete thought that begins with a capital and ends with a period needs to be a "real" sentence. A basic clarity is about all even purists ask of most prose, and ordinarily we accept a good deal less. For his own self-respect, however, anybody inflicting his opinion on somebody else ought to be as clear and precise as possible. A farmer plows as straight a furrow as he can; a carpenter takes care to use only seasoned lumber, and he measures before he saws. A writer can have worse models. Why? What is the harm if a field has no rows that are parallel? if a house or barn is not well made, so long as it doesn't actually tumble down? if an article in the newspaper—an office memorandum, a set of instructions, a critical essay—is so clumsily written as to be (more or less) incomprehensible? None, of course. Sloppiness isn't yet a crime, any more than a customary and vague ineptness is. Why, then, do even farmers and carpenters just starting out, but not the majority of students as they plan their papers, tend to be so painstaking?

Simple. Farmers and carpenters are proud people, and their work is not usually just something they have been told to do: it is themselves. Having taken up trades that society values, they have no need to justify themselves to the rest of us. Writers, whose work is so much less self-evident than theirs, do—and to themselves, also. Listen. Crops and construction are what farmers and carpenters talk about most passionately, and they are as competitive among themselves as graduate students or business majors.

In this class, within the society of this college, our work consists in writing as deliberately as we can: you in your papers—and I in mine. Our goal is sentences as clean and clear and sharply defined as the rows in a field or the boards in a house. A "real" sentence says what it means, and only what it means, and exactly what it means—and then it shuts up. We will try to do no less.

QUESTIONS

1. Circle the subjects of the sentences in the first paragraph. What is the effect of the one sentence where the subject is delayed?
2. Consider the effect of the short sentences. Are they used mostly for economy, emphasis, or rhythm?
3. Box in all the words I repeat (except *a*, *an*, and *the*). Why the repetition? What kind of words—what parts of speech—tend to be repeated?
4. Consider the effect of the sentence fragments. Underline two or three, and decide if they should be rewritten as complete sentences. Why or why not?
5. List three or four phrases where you think particular words were used—as opposed to other words meaning about the same thing—because of their sound.
6. Define the tone. Quarrelsome? Preacherlike? What? Is the tone largely a result of emphasis? of rhythm? of what?

Time permitting, these questions also need asking:

1. Define *man* (and the pronouns referring to *man*) in the sense intended here. How would saying "man or woman," "he or she," and the like affect the style of the passage? Would it alter the rhythm? the emphasis?
2. In what sense do the following adjectives describe good sentences? *chiseled, shaped, crafted, honed.* (We consult the dictionary.)
3. Does the passage establish a dialogue with the reader? If so, how? Does this matter?

4. Is the analogy between writing and farming (and carpentering) appropriate? Can it be sustained?

5. In saying that farmers and carpenters are proud people, do I imply that students are not? Evaluate for logic.

6. Should I have said, in the first paragraph, "Not everybody can write one"? Why or why not?

In the discussion that follows, I push for precise and concrete responses. Students should have specific phrases, words, and sentences in mind for every generalization they make. The point is that by first concentrating on the passage, the class will be ready to evaluate it for economy, emphasis, and rhythm. Sentence (and paragraph) effectiveness is inseparable from content: the writer's depth of feeling determines his style. The point needs establishing. As the discussion winds down, I ask something like the following: "If I didn't truly care about writing, would my sentences sound differently . . . even if I lied and said anyway that writing is important?"

WRITING   Read the following essay carefully. (I provide students with a handout of
ASSIGNMENT   a piece I have recently written.) Bear in mind the discussion we have just had as you think about the question of style. Mentally evaluate for economy, emphasis, and rhythm. Consider the tone.

Having read my essay, take something—an event, a college policy, a law, a condition—about which you care passionately, and, in part by imitating my essay here, write a two- to three-page essay (typed) making your opinion—and your feeling—clear. Use what you now know to achieve economy, emphasis, and rhythm. Try to follow my sentence structure closely, at least in your early drafts. See if by following my essay as a model, you will not be led into a similar tone. Is this tone appropriate for *your* topic? If not, what should you do? Bring to class next time your best draft of your first two pages (handwritten). The typed essay is due a week from today.

Sentence-Level Assignments in an Essay Context: A Lesson in Subordinate Clauses

Nathaniel Strout,
Hamilton College

The goal, I suppose, of every composition teacher is to help students understand how language can enable and limit thought, a goal general enough to be met by their writing almost any kind of essay often enough. I have found, however, that students can learn to write wonderfully engaging accounts of personal experiences without learning how to sustain the analytic arguments expected in most college classrooms. To my mind, the proper challenge—for both students and teachers—in a first composition course is the essay that analyzes and argues about ideas in books.

Because effective subordination is crucial in this sort of writing, I try to introduce students to its value as early as the second essay of the term (saving the first to diagnose individual problems). Many students have learned to avoid subordinating altogether, some out of fear of writing fragments, more out of intellectual laziness. Simple subject/verb sentences, after all, look safer and easier to write and are surely easier to think in than more complex forms. At best, students will subordinate temporally with *after* or *when*, or they will use *as* everywhere. The result we know too well: the typically dull, impersonal theme. Encouraging a class to write and think in nontemporal subordinate clauses leads to papers that are more interesting to read and, more important, to write, as students discover that their thoughts are not as shallow or conventional as their flat prose styles have forced them to be.

It helps, though, to do more than exhort a class to subordinate intelligently. Good advice needs to be put into specific practice, especially since the fear of errors often keeps students from changing their prose. To forestall, as much as I can, the notion that errors count for more than anything else, I treat early essays in part as exercises in writing certain kinds of sentences. When assigning the second of ten essays (a one-page affair), for instance, I insist that at least one sentence begin with *because*, one with *although*, one with *even though*. The first invites thinking in terms of a basic conceptual relationship. The second two invite those qualifications of an argument that show a mind at work—the source of lively prose. The assignment also helps students discover ways to write sentences that do not start with the subject, and it immediately reveals whether students understand the difference between a subordinate clause and a fragment.

All this will seem an arid drill, however, unless the essay topic is linked to the thematic focus of the course. Students learn to write better when they are acquiring knowledge and ideas as well as skills. Like many instructors, I start the term with Orwell's "Politics and the English Language," drawing attention away from the list of "rules" near the end and toward the claim early on that language controls us if we are intellectually passive. At first I went to recent political prose for passages students could write about with the help of Orwell's ideas, but using such prose proved too thematically limiting and, more important, too distant from the immediate concerns of the class. A more fruitful topic turned out to be this one: "With the help of Orwell's essay, argue that a new statement of educational purpose is needed in the College Catalog." Like all such statements, the ringing declarations in ours about the value of learning for its own sake do not exactly describe either what happens in classrooms or what students have come to college for. Further, the institution usually appears as the subject of the sentences, the students—grammatically at least—as the acted on rather than the active participants. If this alone does not upset someone's idealism, I will prompt the initial discussion by asking a student what he or she hopes to gain from a college education, or I will ask whether grades further the purpose put forth in the catalog. I also tell the class that one way to show what is wrong with something is to suggest an alternative, and I suggest that the goal of education should be teaching "respect for liberty" and "hatred of war" (taken from Virginia Woolf's *Three Guineas*, Chapter One, though I do not distract the class with the information). In essence, of course, I want students to examine their assumptions about the nature and value of education, to consider what their education has to do, if anything, with preparing them to change or to succeed in existing social and economic systems, a question I hope they will return to throughout their lives. (Thus I think it important that the catalog be that of the institution the students are attending.) Early in the semester, though, the big issues sometimes have to go by the wayside. Having introduced the theme of education, I am content that the topic gives a context in which students can practice subordinating ideas.

How much I say about subordination beforehand depends on the class. I have spent as little as ten minutes or so discussing the general advantages of placing ideas into a hierarchy of importance. I have spent twice that long going over with the class a sample essay, in which even the best students do not subordinate much, talking about ways to clarify the interrelations of the writer's thoughts. It is what happens after the assignment that really matters. When returning the essays they have just written, I give the class unmarked copies of two of them—copies kept anonymous to reduce the tension of criticism—so that we can compare the handling of subordinate clauses. (Somewhere along the way, I will have to show how to join the inevitable sentence beginning *because of this* with the one that precedes it.) The essays will undoubtedly suffer from unsupported generalizations, poor logic, and all the other commonplace faults of writers not practiced in composing arguments or summaries of arguments, so I will also be able to raise key questions about organization and method, especially since students routinely try to fit their ideas into the following pattern: a first paragraph that begins with a general truth about human nature and ends with an overly specific statement of what the author plans to do, a second paragraph that presents a collection of examples in no particular order, a third paragraph that slightly rewords the original thesis. Because the essays are short, the class soon sees how dull and unnecessary are words spent on large generalizations no one would disagree with, on laying out everything about the essay in advance, on restating what a reader readily recalls. Once students begin to give up their allegiance to the outward trappings of organization, they begin to notice the actual lack of it. I am careful, however, not to overload the circuits with too much advice too soon.

To encourage conscious writing further, and to indicate further that the point is not to follow rules mechanically but to practice kinds of sentences, I base other assignments on the principle of this one. To stress the importance of choosing verbs, for instance, I have asked that one page of another early essay not include any form of *to be*, an instruction that immediately yields awkward circumlocutions and ungainly constructions, but like the exercise in subordination, has the advantage of giving students something specific to think about when cobbling sentences together. The differences between good writing and their prose can otherwise look impossibly, self-defeatingly large.

Indeed, early in the term, students often adopt a grumbling defensiveness about their prose. They have, after all, spent twelve years in school memorizing formulas for essays that please the teacher, only to find the formulas not worth very much anymore. Students accept assignments more cheerfully when I stress that they are not requirements for all future writing but chances to experiment without significant penalties for getting things wrong. (I never count early essays as much as later ones.) Obviously, a single, simple assignment cannot possibly counteract the many bad writing habits developed over years of schooling. I merely hope to get students to begin to think regularly about their sentences.

<u>*LESSON READING*</u>

George Orwell, "Politics and the English Language," in *Shooting an Elephant and Other Essays* (Orlando, FL: Harcourt Brace Jovanovich, 1950).

Everything You Always Wanted to Know About Grammar— Including What You Already Know (but Don't Know You Know)

Jacqueline Berke,
Drew University

This lesson requires that you prepare in advance a handout entitled "Everything You Always Wanted to Know About Grammar" (or whatever), consisting of the six (I–VI) passages that follow; each provides a point of departure for what I have come to regard as a *first* lesson in grammar—a first *real* lesson. Like Molière's famous character who is surprised to discover that he has been speaking prose all his life, students should discover through *this* lesson that they have been using grammar all their lives. They have been using it with all the grace and deftness of a natural grammarian. In fact, each of us *is!* and with a firm command achieved long before entering a classroom or beginning to write—indeed, long before learning that there was anything special to learn about the formalities of grammar and its insidious array of dos and don'ts.

I ask the class to read the following passage, a short essay earnestly titled "Gramar (sic) and Why We Study It." Then I read it aloud, since there are a few tricky sentences that are hard to decipher. (For example, after the

fourth sentence—actually, the fourth period—imagine the following punctuation: "the 'and' here, the 'buts' there; *this* is a direct object; *this* is a
preposition and *that* the subject.") The essay was written (presumably in
all seriousness) by a tenth-grade boy in Illinois and was later reprinted in
an educational journal. I have kept it these many years as a treasure in my
file:

Gramar and Why We Study It

I.   I don't know why we study gramar, sometimes it seems like a wastc of time.
      I would rather we us the liture books any day than the gramar books. They
      put the good subjects in nice big books so that you need a truck to pull them
      around with. We study gramar because everybody thinks we need it, there
      usually right, all the professors and doctors and teachers. They say that we
      are not putting the correct words in the right place. the and here the buts
      there, this is a direct object this is a preposition and that the subject all the
      time they are confusing us more and more but we need it. It would be bad if
      someone wasn't there to pound it in because wel'd sound like a pack of
      fourners in our own country and thats not good not good at all we need gramar
      all we can get and not to soon.

                                                      —*tenth-grade boy in Illinois*

What a remarkably revealing and poignant statement this is, reflecting
as it does all the wild confusion and terror that issue from this most
confusing and terrifying of subjects in the school curriculum.

I read it and we laugh (the students in my writing classes laugh—and
identify). If you are an English teacher, of course, you will also weep. For
this tenth-grade Huck Finn is not atypical. Right down to his fanciful
spelling, his run-on sentences, his pervasive anxiety and amusing self-
righteousness ("It would be bad if someone wasn't there to pound it in
because wel'd sound like a pack of fourners in our own country . . .") this
student is everyone who is mystified by grammar—and that is everyone,
from the marginal C student to the Merit Scholar.

To reassure students and to demystify the "problem" of grammar once
and for all, I read aloud the following passage, taken from a slim but inspired
volume by a structural grammarian:

II.   All of us have a grammar. The fact that we use and understand English in
      daily affairs means that we use and understand, for the most part uncon-
      sciously, the major grammatical patterns of our language.
      —*Harold Whitehall*, Structural Essentials of English *(Harcourt Brace Jov-
      anovich, 1954)*

The students hear the good news: *They have already mastered grammar.*
Note that Whitehall tells us that our mastery is *unconscious.* Precisely so:
This is a fact both little known and widely known. Certainly Lewis Carroll
provided an amusing demonstration of the fact in the wonderful "Jabberwocky" poem from *Through the Looking Glass:*

III.   'Twas brillig and the slithy toves
         Did gyre and gimble in the wabe:
         All mimsy were the borogroves,
         And the mome raths outgrabe.

When Alice hears these lines she says: "Somehow it seems to fill my head with ideas—only I don't know exactly what they are!" As I have pointed out elsewhere,[1] "These ideas are actually *patterns*—the structural or grammatical meanings that stand out unmistakably because the lexical meanings have been obliterated. That is, the words themselves do not mean anything, but the *forms* of the words and their arrangement within the line stir the mind to vague recognition."

By reviewing these "vague recognitions" through the lines of the poem you are preparing students to confront specific recognitions about language, additional facts they already know but don't know they know because they have never consciously dealt with them. Only then do they become aware that they *know*—with a deep, gut feeling that makes all explanation or explication unnecessary and irrelevant—that certain things can be done with language (they are grammatically acceptable) and certain things cannot be done (they are grammatically unacceptable). So it is that we all *know* that the first line of "Jabberwocky" cannot be filled in as follows:

'Twas *walked* and the *their slowly*
       (verb)   *(pronoun)(adverb)*

This is an impossible nonsense (no-sense) sequence. The first line *must* read something like this:

'Twas beautiful   and the happy girls
     (adjective)   *(adjective)(noun)*

Whatever specific words a native speaker of English might select, then, to fill in the first line of the poem would necessarily fall into a given pattern: They would never be verb, pronoun, adverb; they appear to be adjective, adjective, noun.

Once these limitations are established, students are ready to move on to the heart of the matter, as embodied in the following passage:

IV.   LANGUAGE: The most important single fact about language is that it has two kinds of symbols, both of which work together to express the total meaning of any statement: these are the VOCABULARY elements and the GRAMMATICAL elements.[2]

---

[1] *Twenty Questions for the Writer*, 4th ed. (Orlando, FL: Harcourt Brace Jovanovich, 1985), pp. 536–538.

[2] This statement, and much of what follows, is drawn from Dona Worrall Brown, Wallace C. Brown, and Dudley Bailey, "Grammar in a New Key," as it appears in Leonard F. Dean and Kenneth G. Wilson, *Essays on Language and Usage* (New York: Oxford University Press, 1959), pp. 198–205.

A. VOCABULARY: The many thousands of single words we use daily. There are more than half a million (approximately 650,000) in an unabridged dictionary.

Children begin to learn language by learning individual words: *mama, baby, bottle* (or "bott-ey"). As children grow, they begin to put words together to form simple sentences. At this point they absorb the second element of language: GRAMMAR.

B. GRAMMAR: A system of signs or devices whereby we put single words together in order to convey meaning:

I want milk. / Bobby is bad. / The girls sing loudly.

There are three major grammatical devices: word order, inflection, and function words.

1. *Word order* refers to how we position words in a sentence.

The dog bit the man.
The old lady wears a purple hat.

Note that in using the same words in different order we can reverse the meaning of a sentence:

Dog bites man. / Man bites dog.

Note also that in the sentences "The old lady wears a purple hat" word order alone conveys unmistakably that it is an *old* lady wearing a *purple* hat and not a *purple* lady wearing an *old* hat (modifiers precede the noun modified).

2. *Inflection* refers to how we change the form of words (i.e., their spelling and pronunciation) in order to indicate changes in meaning.

The dogs bit the men.
The old ladies wear purple hats.
I walk to town. / I walked to town.

Now how we pluralize through inflection (dog/dogs) and how we change tense (I walk today / I walk*ed* yesterday). A dull subject inflection, yet I find that students are comforted by background information that humanizes the process. Thus I generally try to give a little "presentation" here, something like the following:

Although the formal description of an inflectional system is invariably complex, children begin to learn the system on their own at the incredibly early age of two or three, or even earlier. It is an astonishing feat (still mysterious to psychologists), yet it is demonstrably the case that the linguistic process is absorbed through the ear and learned without benefit of formal training. On their own, children pick up the sounds of language and begin to make sense of them.

Take the sound *man*, for example, quickly recognized by the child as indicating *one* such person. (This then becomes a vocabulary element.) On seeing more than one—a whole group, let's say—the child may well exclaim, "Look at the mans over there." Parental correction is sure to follow. "No dear, you mean *men*." To be sure, the child has made a mistake but what a brilliant mistake!—indicating as it does that the child has mastered the intricate linguistic system of pluralization: a specific sound represents a specific object; to demonstrate more than one of that object, you add a final *s* sound (girl/girls, boy/boys, ball/balls).

However, an exception to the rule is at work here. The word *man* is pluralized differently—not by adding a final *s* but by changing the medial vowel from an *a* sound to an *e*. Ah, note how cumbersome it is to try to *explain* the process; indeed, it would be impossible to describe to the child, for even an adult's head begins to spin when confronted with detailed linguistic and historical description. What is useful to keep in mind, then, is that the intellectual leap into language—words (vocabulary elements) and the combining of words (grammar)—comes to us all as a kind of gift.

3. *Function words* refer to how we use little words (like *the* and *and*), which have no meaning in and of themselves, to connect words and to designate different meanings within the sentence.

The dog bit *a* man. / John *and* Mary *will* walk. / John *and* Mary *would not* walk.

Although function words have little or no referential meaning, they often clarify the meaning of an otherwise ambiguous sentence such as the following:

He gave her dog biscuits.

This sentence presents no problems when it is spoken because the things we do with our voice (pitch and pause and stress) would make the point clearly. In writing, however, the sentence has two possible meanings: (1) he gave biscuits to her dog, and (2) he gave dog biscuits to her. Note how function words indicate which of the meanings was intended:

He gave her dog *the* (or *some*) biscuits.

or

He gave her *the* (or *some*) dog biscuits.

Similarly, the following sentence needs clarifying function words:

He loved racing horses.

Does this mean he loved to race horses? Or does it mean he loved horses that race, that is, he loved *the* racing horses?

V.   Grammar *EXERCISE:*[3] Following is a list of vocabulary elements which might appear in a simple sentence: 1. *Henry* 2. *house* 3. *build* 4. *old*
Now let us suppose that we want to express these additional ideas:

5. that *old* qualifies our idea of the man, Henry

6. that *build* expresses an assertion [rather than a question or command]

7. that the building is continuing at the present time

8. that Henry is the builder

9. that the result of the building is the house

10. that there is only one house

11. and that a completed statement is intended

The resulting sentence would be:

Old Henry is building a house.

What makes it possible to condense all of these complex ideas into six words? The answer is, of course, *grammar*. In the preceding sentences the ideas numbered 5–11 have been translated into a code of grammatical "signs"—the devices we use to signal different meanings. By using different signs with the four words that convey the vocabulary meaning—*Henry, house, build*, and *old*—it is possible to express a very different idea:

An old building housed Henry.

IN-CLASS
EXERCISE   I have students improvise additional exercises with groups of words of their own choice.
I have found that through this lesson students are able to understand—for the first time—the grammar they are "reviewing," to see a little more clearly the relation of language to their lives, and of grammar to their language. Students may now be asked to write their own version of "Grammar, and Why We Study It."

WRITING
ASSIGNMENT
I like to conclude—or continue—the lesson by discussing and demonstrating further the differences between writing and speech (see Whitehall article). I also read to them E. B. White's marvelous description of language as a cowpath (cited in Brown et al. from *The New Yorker*):

VI.   The living language is like a cowpath: it is the creation of the cows themselves, who, having created it, follow it or depart from it according to their whims or their needs. From daily use, the path undergoes change. A cow is under no obligation to stay in the narrow path she helped make, following the contour

---

[3] From Brown et al., "Grammar in a New Key."

of the land, but she often profits by staying with it and she would be handi-capped if she didn't know where it was and where it led to. Children obviously do not depend for communication on a knowledge of grammar; they rely on their ear, mostly, which is sharp and quick. But we have yet to see the child who hasn't profited from coming face to face with a relative pronoun at an early age, and from reading books, which follow the paths of centuries.

LESSON READING

Harold Whitehall, ''Writing and Speech,'' in *Structural Essentials of English* (San Diego: Harcourt Brace Jovanovich, 1954, 1956), pp. 1–7.

What Students Can Learn from a Single Paragraph

Dorothy M. Doyle,
Parkway School District,
St. Louis County

What are paragraphs? Why do we, or should we, write in paragraphs? How did they come to be? What use do they have, and how are they different from just any collection of sentences?

These fundamental questions need to be raised early in the term, particularly in courses teaching the fundamentals of writing, though they are useful in advanced courses as well. In a sequence of lessons intended to answer these questions, I concentrate on a single paragraph to demonstrate to students how much information about the craft of writing it can yield.

I build the lessons on the premise that the paragraph is the basic unit for written discourse, and through it I demonstrate the connection between organization and function as well as direct the students' attention to particular details of structure, sentence form, grammatical rule, and style; I end with exercises that give the students enough practice in these matters to achieve some confidence in their ability to write.

The paragraph then becomes the model for study, and I offer it repeatedly until the students learn to put sentences together with grace, variety, and a sense of sequence—and to hold to one topic effectively through the paragraph. In addition, the questions I ask are intended to stimulate students to think about style in a larger way than they are perhaps accustomed to. I try to convey to them that even elementary points of usage involve esthetic judgments, and once students are alerted to the process of making choices—between one word and another, one phrase and another, one mark of punctuation and another—they will more readily accept "rules" for writing, since writing becomes clearer and more communicable with them than it is likely to be without them. Most important, I try to interest students who have never thought very much about the assumptions and reasons that lie behind the rules of writing they are expected to learn.

I give students the following paragraph to read in class:

> 1. Moiseika likes to make himself useful. 2. He gives his companions water and covers them up when they are asleep; he promises each of them to bring him back a kopeck and to make him a new cap; he feeds with a spoon his neighbor on the left, who is paralyzed. 3. He acts in this way, not from compassion nor from any considerations of a humane kind, but through imitation, unconsciously dominated by Gromov, his neighbor on the right hand.
> —*from "Ward Number Six," Anton Chekhov*[1]

How does this paragraph work? Before the students can answer this question I ask the other questions with which I opened this account: What are paragraphs? Why are we expected to write in paragraphs? What use do they have? How did they come to be? How are they different from just any collection of sentences?

I explain to the class: Suppose you and Anton Chekhov were talking to each other, and suppose he made this statement to you: "Moiseika likes to make himself useful." If you knew Moiseika, you might agree or disagree with Chekhov—on the basis of your own observations and knowledge of Moiseika. If you did not know Moiseika, you might ask, "Why do you say that?" In other words, you would call for specific examples of Moiseika's actions to help you agree or disagree with Chekhov's idea.

The particular sentence with which our paragraph opens—"Moiseika likes to make himself useful."—is a generalization, an idea of the author's. In a written context, as opposed to an oral or spoken context (a conversation with Anton Chekhov), this one sentence, standing alone without any further sentences to tell us about Moiseika, would have little power to convince the reader, to persuade him to agree with the author's generalization about Moiseika.

One of the reasons writing is so completely different from informal speaking is that the writer must write to convince a listener who will never ask questions (or whose questions the writer will never hear), to convince a listener whom he can see only in his mind. This silent, invisible listener for whom you write is, in fact, the reader. Just as the incomplete sentence "likes to make himself useful" means nothing to a reader, so the incomplete paragraph "Moiseika likes to make himself useful" means little in a written context and fails utterly to persuade the reader to believe the generalization. Thus the paragraph is an important unit of composition because it allows space and context to develop an idea and to move the reader's mind in the direction of the writer's mind.

Besides providing a larger context for an idea than a single sentence, the paragraph focuses attention on one idea at a time. As a reader, what is your reaction to the following group of sentences?

---

[1] Translated by Constance Garnett. Her translation of this passage is very close to the original. (I am obliged to Professor Milicia Banjanin, Department of Slavic Studies, Washington University, for this observation.)

Moiseika likes to make himself useful. He had a very painful experience in early adolescence. It is surprising to find a man so totally lacking in ambition. In these days almost everyone has done some travelling, but Moiseika has spent his entire fifty years in the village in which he was born.

Though the preceding sentences may look like a paragraph, they are not a paragraph. Each sentence presents a different idea. The writer has provided no connecting link between the ideas, and no one idea controls the entire paragraph. As you read those sentences, your mind, searching for the writer's idea, tries to provide connections to tie the sentences together. But it is not possible to derive the writer's idea from this group of unrelated and unsupported sentences.

The Moiseika paragraph satisfies the reader's expectation of a single idea accompanied by appropriate and sufficient detail; it is full and clear enough to provide the context in which one idea moves from writer's mind to reader's mind. It is as if Chekhov were saying, "The character whom I am calling Moiseika likes to make himself useful. I will tell you why I think so. I have seen him helping his companions by giving them water and by covering them up. I have heard him promise to bring them kopecks and to make them new caps. I have watched him feeding his paralyzed neighbor with a spoon." In his second sentence notice that Chekhov gives all these details to tell *how* Moiseika is useful. That is his method of satisfying the expectation that he set up in the attentive reader's mind with the topic sentence.

But Chekhov does not want the reader to stop attending to his idea; he has more to say. The writer's mind moves from *how* Moiseika acts useful to *why* he acts useful (Sentence 3). The consideration of *why* leads to Gromov, a major influence on Moiseika, and then of course both Chekhov's and the reader's minds move to the next paragraph—about Gromov. I read to the class the next paragraph from Chekhov's "Ward Number 6."

Ivan Dimitritch Gromov, a man of thirty-three, who is a gentleman by birth, and has been a court usher and provincial secretary, suffers from the mania of persecution. He either lies curled up in bed or walks from corner to corner as though for exercise; he very rarely sits down. He is always excited, agitated, and overwrought by a sort of vague, undefined expectation. The faintest rustle in the entry or shout in the yard is enough to make him raise his head and begin listening: whether they are coming for him, whether they are looking for him. And at such times his face expresses the utmost uneasiness and repulsion.

At this point I break down our paragraph to a series of simple sentences that carry the kernels of meaning that Chekhov conveys.

Moiseika likes to make himself useful. (*How?*)
Moiseika gives water to his companions.
Moiseika covers up his companions.

Moiseika's companions are asleep.
Moiseika promises each companion something.
Moiseika will bring back a kopeck to each companion.
Moiseika will make each companion a new cap.
Moiseika feeds with a spoon his neighbor on the left.
Moiseika's neighbor on the left is paralyzed.
Moiseika acts in this way. (*Why?*)
Moiseika does not act from compassion.
Moiseika does not act from considerations of a humane kind.
Moiseika acts through imitation.
Moiseika is unconsciously dominated by Gromov. (*Who?*)
Gromov is Moiseika's neighbor on the right hand.

But compare this series of sentences with the actual sentences that make up Chekhov's paragraph. You will see how much more connected and interesting and varied sentences must be to make a good paragraph. If the subject (Moiseika) were repeated in every sentence, and if every sentence were constructed with the same simple pattern, the content of the paragraph, which is certainly very interesting, would lose a good deal of its interest. It would seem excruciatingly boring, and the reader might very well give up before he reaches the end. Here we would have a good example of style—the way in which something is written—weakening, rather than strengthening, meaning. The discussion that follows turns on the following questions:

1. Why does Chekhov use the name Moiseika only once? Suppose he had repeated it in the course of the paragraph. Where would the repetition be most effective? least effective? most awkward?
2. Why does Chekhov use sentences that seem so simple? What connection can you see between the sort of person Chekhov is writing about and the style in which he writes?
3. Which of the three sentences is most complicated in structure? What connection might there be between this complication in sentence structure and the idea expressed in the sentence? Why do some sentences need to have a more complex structure than others?

Chekhov's opening sentence is, as we have noticed, a generalization. It is a statement that draws a conclusion from a number of separate observations and arrives at an idea that is large enough to fit or include all those separate observations. In the sentences that follow the opening sentence, Chekhov demonstrates all the ways in which the opening statement is true.

WRITING
ASSIGNMENT

You have often, no doubt, made a generalization about another person's character or his intentions. Try now to write a paragraph in which you begin with a general statement about someone you've observed. Then give some specific examples that will help the reader to see why your general statement is true. What Chekhov does before the paragraph is over is to try to interpret Moiseika's behavior—why "he acts in this way." If you can open with a generalization, go on to your evidence for it, and then conclude with a statement explaining or interpreting what you have just observed, you will have communicated something to your reader that is worth communicating.

CLASSES 3
AND 4

Throughout these lessons I show how the basic rules of good writing can be derived from the reading at hand: even a paragraph as short as the one I have chosen has material enough for generating a set of rules. It seems to me important that students see for themselves the value of a set of imperatives that grow out of their reading of writing that engages them, and I begin with fundamental observations. I ask students to keep a notebook in which they write the rules.

RULE 1. *Subject and verb form the base of every sentence and every clause.*

In this paragraph Moiseika (or the pronoun *he,* substituting for *Moiseika*) is the subject of most of the verbs.

Sentence 1: Moiseika likes. . . .

Sentence 2: He gives . . . and covers . . . ; he promises . . . ; he feeds. . . .

Sentence 3: He acts. . . .

RULE 2. *Avoid sentence fragments.*

The distinction between a sentence and a clause is important for you to know. All sentences are clauses, in the sense that they contain a subject and a verb, but a sentence is a self-contained unit, a group of words that "makes sense" and satisfies the reader's expectations about sentence sense. Some clauses—those we label "independent" clauses—also "make sense" when removed from their context. Other clauses, however, we call "dependent," because, even though they contain the required subject and verb, they cannot be taken out of the sentence context in which they appear without violating the reader's expectations and leaving him with a feeling of incompleteness. For example, consider your reaction to the following group of words:

Not because he is compassionate nor because he is humane.

The word *because* is a clue to the reader that these words are linked in a special way to some other group of words, and an attentive reader cannot make sense of these words taken out of context. On the other hand, if we remove the two *because*'s and rearrange the word order slightly, we have a perfectly acceptable sentence:

He is neither compassionate nor humane.

The main reason for understanding the difference between sentences and clauses is that when dependent clauses are punctuated as if they were full sentences, the writer is mistakenly offering a part of the sentence for the whole. A reader needs complete sentences and correct punctuation to help him follow the writer's thought.

RULE 3. *Avoid running sentences together.*

Like sentence fragments, "run-on" sentences distract the reader. Some writers make the mistake of running sentences together because they do not understand how to punctuate sentences.

It is important to keep your sentences clearly defined by correct punctuation. In the following example two complete and separate sentences are run together as one.

Moiseika likes to make himself useful, he gives his companions water.

Use a period or semicolon to separate the sentences. A comma does not do the job of separating them.

Moiseika likes to make himself useful. He gives his companions water.
Moiseika likes to make himself useful; he gives his companions water.

Or join two sentences by *and* (preceded by a comma):

He gives his companions water, and he covers them up when they are asleep.

RULE 4. *To avoid unnecessary repetition, compound sentence elements.*

Consider the sentence

Moiseika gave each of his friends a kopek, a cap, and some food.

Even a young child knows that in effect this sentence means:

Moiseika gave each of his friends a kopek.
Moiseika gave each of his friends a cap.
Moiseika gave each of his friends some food.

Because of our understanding of the deep structure underlying the series of items, we are able to omit tiresome repetition in the "surface" structure of the sentence that we actually speak or write. Most native speakers learn this process of compounding before they enter school.

The words that we use for compounding are the coordinating conjunctions: *and, or, but, either . . . or, neither . . . nor, both . . . and, not only . . . but also.* (In the second paragraph of the Chekhov selection, there are several instances of compounding:

```
                        court usher
   Gromov had been    AND
                        a provincial secretary
      lies curled up in bed.
   He            OR
      walks from corner to corner
                        NEITHER a kopek.
   Gromov gave his enemy
                        NOR a cap.
                   EITHER that they would not listen.
   Gromov thinks
                   OR that they would not understand.
                        NEITHER listen
   Gromov thinks that they would
                        NOR understand.)
```

RULE 5. *Express parallel ideas in parallel structure.*

Parallel structure is merely good compounding. As a rhetorical device, it promotes conciseness and elegance. For your reader, parallel structure makes difficult thoughts much easier to understand.

Chekhov's third sentence, the most complicated of the paragraph we are examining, uses parallel structure to organize comments about *why* Moiseika acts in a useful way. Contrast Chekhov's sentence with the following:

> He doesn't act this way because he is compassionate.
> He has no conscious understanding of humane rather than inhumane behavior.
> He imitates Gromov, his neighbor.
> He is unconsciously dominated by Gromov, his neighbor. . . .

How much more appealing is Chekhov's controlled structure! How much easier Chekhov's sentence is to understand and remember!

> He acts in this way, not from _____ nor from _____, but through _____.

Use parallel grammatical elements to express ideas of equal value.

> I like the man himself, courteous, anxious to be of use, and extraordinarily gentle to everyone except Nikita.

In this sentence the three qualities describing the man are in parallel grammatical order, the information given in the sentence is pulled together neatly, and the shape of the sentence is clear and striking. But look at the following sentence:

> I like the man himself, with his courteous manner, anxious to be of use, and having an extraordinary gentleness to everyone except Nikita.

In this sentence, a deliberately deformed version of the translator's original sentence, the three attributes are not in parallel grammatical order, and the sentence is faulty.

Now take this sentence:

EITHER Gromov thinks that they would not listen
OR that they would not understand.

The words *Gromov thinks* follow EITHER, and the words *that they would not understand* follow OR. In this faulty sentence these two groups of words are not parallel grammatical elements. In the original sentence

EITHER that they would not listen

Gromov thinks

OR that they would not understand

the words that follow EITHER and the words that follow OR are indeed parallel grammatical elements.

CLASS 5   I distribute handouts with exercises that require rewriting with the help of the rules covered in the previous classes. We rewrite the sentences together, and for every change made, I ask students to give their reasons. *Rewrite the following into well-formed sentences.*

EXERCISES FOR
RULE 2:

Avoid sentence fragments.

1. Going home again makes me feel sad. Especially when I see my old room.
2. I refuse to go. Even if I'm paid.
3. I sometimes push myself to finish what I start. Although I have had to stay up all night to finish a paper.
4. She is a woman I admire. A woman who relies on herself.
5. I cannot run fast. Not the way I used to.
6. The first night of our camping trip we all caught colds. Because the rain soaked through the tent.
7. He talked about the chief faults of writing today. Two of these being lack of precision and staleness of imagery.
8. That was the day the fragile tie between us broke. A tie that had been created many years before.

EXERCISES FOR
RULE 3:

Avoid running sentences together.

9. Try to be aware of the possible dangers, do not assume that things will go well.

10. Angrily, she yanked him by the arm off the floor, his small body, so compact and spare, flashed across the room.
11. She forgot all she'd learned, all she could think of was how she'd disgraced herself.
12. Without a doubt, it's the biggest house in the neighborhood, just take a look.
13. The journal from which these excerpts came was written just before his final illness and death, consequently what he writes has a particular authority.

EXERCISES FOR
RULE 4:

To avoid unnecessary repetition, compound sentence elements.

14. François Truffaut directed *Jules and Jim*. He also directed *The Wild Child*.
15. Alfred Hitchcock directed *The Lady Vanishes*. Hitchcock played a minor part in the film.

EXERCISES FOR
RULE 5:

Express parallel ideas in parallel structure.

16. The suspect was thin, with gray hair, and had a hesitant manner.
17. I cannot afford the cost of skis, to fly to Aspen, or paying for a week's stay at a ski lodge there.
18. He disliked his job not just for its long hours but because the work was monotonous.
19. You are either pretending not to understand me or my point is not clear.
20. You are either wrong or I am.
21. He was both an excellent guitarist and knew how to sing besides.
22. He not only has no money but he has no plans to find a job.
23. Pete will either go by bicycle or his father will pay for a bus ticket.
24. I could not decide whether the writer could be taken seriously or to disregard everything he wrote.
25. I felt puzzled, knowing neither how to start nor anyone who might help me.

I have found that my students, rather than suffering from restlessness when they work intensively on a single paragraph, have enjoyed the experience of concentrating on a brief example that opens to them so many possibilities they can adopt for their own use.

When Clear Is Not Clear

Janice Carlisle,
Washington University

Students frequently need to learn that what's clear to the writer is not always clear to the reader and that clarity is measured by an audience's response to a piece of writing, not by an author's unexamined assumptions about its effectiveness. The most forceful way that I have found of conveying this lesson is to let my students know that they, not I, constitute the ideal audience for each writing assignment in the course. By virtue of my position, I assign grades, but I do not ultimately decide whether a sentence or essay conveys the meaning that a student hopes to communicate. That question I leave to the class as a whole. By demonstrating that I trust their collective judgment on the clarity of a particular piece of prose, I hope to teach them that they as individuals can make reliable judgments on their essays as they are composing them. Fairly early in every course, I plan a discussion that puts this principle into practice.

Typically the students have written a set of papers on each of which I have had to write "unclear" at least once. I type up a representative sampling, trying to choose one example from each paper because misery demands company. I also make sure that the examples demonstrate the full range of problems that can impede understanding: errors in grammar or mechanics, faulty word choice, a lack of continuity or coherence, unsatisfactory definitions, fuzzy thinking, or faulty logic. In class we go over each sentence slowly and carefully. Every student is encouraged to say what he or she thinks it means. The multiplicity of the interpretations that emerge is often comic, sometimes dismaying, and always instructive. The perpetrator usually confesses at last, letting us know what the sentence "really says," and the other students offer suggestions to clarify and emphasize its point. At least one student will object that this discussion places an artificial burden on the communicative power of one isolated sentence: Because it has been taken out of context, its clarity cannot be judged fairly. In most cases the students, not the teacher, point out the folly of hoping that a weak sentence can be saved by the strength of its neighbors.

Letting the students do the talking is, indeed, the key to the success of this exercise. Such meticulous critical scrutiny can quickly become defeating, not only to the writer of the example under discussion, but to the class as a whole, particularly if the teacher is offering most of the negative comments. During such a discussion I remain as discreetly silent as possible, serving as a resource on technical matters while the students try to figure out what a particular sentence or phrase means. It is better to let an error go unmentioned than to divert attention from the students' role as a responsive and articulate audience. For all parties involved such restraint is often difficult to practice—teachers, after all, have been taught to lead and students to follow—but it is worth the effort. One liberty, however, that I allow myself is the right to praise whenever a positive response is not forthcoming from the class. Treating even the weakest and most confused sentence as one that has potential for strength and clarity ensures that the students are motivated, not discouraged, by this examination of their work: It should show them what they can do, not what they are always fated to do.

IN-CLASS
EXERCISE

One such discussion recently issued from a previous in-class writing exercise on Joseph Wood Krutch's treatment of the word *normal*, which the students had read for the occasion. Rather than ask them for Krutch's definition, I had invited them to speculate on the intellectual or social assumptions behind his commentary. Since the answer to such a question is not immediately obvious to most students, asking them to formulate it on paper teaches them two apparently contradictory principles: One must know what one wants to say before it can be said, and the process of writing is itself a way of clarifying what one wants to say. Discussing typically unclear responses during the next class meeting emphasized the reciprocity between thought and expression. Since the essays had been written quickly in class, under constraints of time and place, the students felt less responsible for and therefore more objective about their weaknesses than they would have about the shortcomings of more formal essays.

Frequently a sentence yields telling examples of the relation between correctness and clarity. One response to Krutch's comments is typical:

> Writing in mid-century, the cultural "mediocrity" of the common man is seen as contemptuous and dangerously self-complacent rather than a virtue for which to strive.

Here a dangling modifier and faulty parallelism help to obfuscate the meaning of the sentence. This example also provides a good instance of the obscurity attendant on the dragon that every composition teacher was born to slay, the passive voice. Who, after all, is doing the "seeing" here? Is the common man "contemptuous"—or contemptible? Krutch himself is nowhere in sight. After the students had criticized this particularly weak sentence, I tried to point out that it does have the merit of designating the historical moment at which Krutch put forth his analysis. After some effort the class came up with a revision that clarified the implications of this observation:

> Writing at mid-century, Krutch was aware of the dangers of conformity and was contemptuous of the complacency of the common man.

The idea that a norm is a "virtue for which to strive" clearly belongs in a separate sentence.

An example from another student's essay reveals what can be done with even a short paragraph:

> 1. Krutch defines the word normal in a very attitude conscious manner. 2. It lacks the scientific assumptions of a statistician. 3. To this person normal is a norm or average, but does not necessarily denote mediocrity. 4. This definition would use the term normal as designating a "mean" or category in which most people would be grouped. 5. Krutch does not assume that normal might be defined or used in this manner, he assumes that this word is a goal for which most people should strive.

Here is a study in confusion. The first sentence reveals the functionality of the hyphen: "attitude-conscious manner" is easier to read than "attitude conscious manner." For that matter, this example demonstrates the need to avoid phrases that require such hyphenation or that use nouns as modifiers. The most substantial problem here, however, is faulty reference: The *it* in the second sentence or the demonstrative adjective *this* in the third and fourth could refer to at least two elements in the preceding sentences. Does *this person* in the third sentence stand for Krutch or the statistician, or is it perhaps a modest reference to the writer of the essay itself? Such criticism could go to some lengths. *Mediocracy* deserves comment, as does the implication in the final sentence that a word can be a goal. At the end of this discussion, the student who had thought that this paragraph makes sense was unable to sustain that illusion. Having kept myself from mentioning the comma splice in the last sentence because the students had not noticed it, I tried to point out that even in this case there is some thinking going on: If Krutch set up his argument in opposition to the definitions of the statistician and the social scientist, could we discover which discipline informed his thinking? At this point the hour was almost over, but I asked the students to think about how they would go about revising this paragraph. They all agreed that it should begin in a more straightforward manner, and several students worked together to produce the opening of this topic sentence: "Krutch refuses to define the word *normal* as a statistician would; rather, he. . . ." By ending the discussion here I was able to suggest how the students might want to examine Krutch's assumptions, but not what they might decide to say about them.

WRITING ASSIGNMENT   The assignment that naturally follows from such a discussion is obvious: to define the social and intellectual assumptions behind Krutch's analysis of the term *normal*. If the students have responded at all to this conscious-ness-raising in matters of clarity, they should be ready to use the in-class exercises that they have previously written as rough drafts for more care-fully considered formal essays. In the case of Krutch's definition of *normal*, the result might be only a paragraph or a page in length; in either case clarity is the main goal of the assignment. When explaining the purpose of these revisions, I ask the students specifically to look for unclear statements that I may not have pointed out in their first efforts. They are, of course, welcome to throw away what they have done and start over again.

If I feel that the students need more than a day or two to work on this project, I assign for discussion in the next class three essays that deal with the relation between clarity and a sense of one's audience: "Simplicity" and "Clutter" from William Zinsser's *On Writing Well* (third edition) and F. L. Lucas's "On the Fascination of Style." Though these essays do not announce clarity as their subject, it is central to their admonitions to the would-be writer. Furthermore, they work well as companion pieces because their authors' styles differ so greatly: Zinsser's pared-down simplicity makes Lucas's fondness for metaphor seem almost baroque, but both write clearly, forcefully, and engagingly on a topic that would not strike most students as inherently enthralling. Students who need an example of Yeats's contention that the "correction of prose . . . is endless" may find useful an opportunity to see examples of manuscript revisions of any good profes-sional writer.

No matter how much time is spent in discussing the examples provided by these professional writers, no matter how pressing the need to get on to other issues may be, devoting another class or part of a class to the problem of clarity is, I think, necessary if the point of the initial discussion is to be enforced. The students should have a chance to share with each other the rewritten essays on which they have been expected to expend a good deal of time and effort. Whether they read them all aloud or examine a partic-ularly successful attempt to answer the question set in the in-class exercise, the students need—and will need repeatedly throughout the semester—the opportunity to function as their peers' audience. By confronting the quiz-zical looks and persistent questions of their classmates, they will ratify their sense of an audience as a test of clarity.

LESSON READINGS

William Zinsser, "Simplicity" and "Clutter," in *Writing Well*, 3rd ed. (New York: Harper & Row, 1976).

F. L. Lucas, "On the Fascination of Style," in William Smart, *Eight Mod-ern Essayists*, 3rd ed. (New York: St. Martin's Press, 1980), pp. 369–379.

Joseph Wood Krutch, *Human Nature and the Human Condition* (New York: Random House, 1959).

READING

Joseph Wood Krutch

NATURE AND THE HUMAN CONDITION

The words we choose to define or suggest what we believe to be important facts exert a very powerful influence upon civilization. A mere name can persuade us to approve or disapprove, as it does, for example, when we describe certain attitudes as "cynical" on the one hand or "realistic" on the other. No one wants to be "unrealistic" and no one wants to be "snarling." Therefore his attitude toward the thing described may very well depend upon which designation is current among his contemporaries; and the less critical his mind, the more influential the most commonly used vocabulary will be.

It is for this reason that, even as a mere verbal confusion, the use of "normal" to designate what ought to be called "average" is of tremendous importance and serves not only to indicate but actually to reinforce the belief that average ability, refinement, intellectuality, or even virtue is an ideal to be aimed at. Since we cannot do anything to the purpose until we think straight and since we cannot think straight without properly defined words it may be that the very first step toward an emancipation from the tyranny of "conformity" should be the attempt to substitute for "normal," as commonly used, a genuine synonym for "average."

Fortunately, such a genuine and familiar synonym does exist. That which is "average" is also properly described as "mediocre." And if we were accustomed to call the average man, not "the common man" or still less "the normal man," but "the mediocre man" we should not be so easily hypnotized into believing that mediocrity is an ideal to be aimed at.

A second step in the same direction would be to return to the word "normal" its original meaning. According to the Shorter Oxford Dictionary it derives from the Latin "norma," which has been Anglicized as "norm" and is, in turn, thus defined: "A rule or authoritative standard."

The adjective "normative" is not commonly misused—no doubt because it is not part of that "vocabulary of the average man" by which educators now set so much store. It still generally means "establishing a norm or standard." But "normal" seldom means, as it should, "corresponding to the standard by which a thing is to be judged." If it did, "a normal man" would again mean, not what the average man *is* but what, in its fullest significance, the word "man" should imply, even "what a man *ought* to be." And that is a very different thing from the "average" or "mediocre" man whom we have so perversely accustomed ourselves to regard as most worthy of admiration.

Only by defining and then attempting to reach up toward the "normal" as properly defined can a democratic society save itself from those defects which the enemies of democracy have always maintained were the necessary consequences of such a society. Until "preparation for life" rather than "familiarity with the best that has been thought and said" became the aim of education every schoolboy knew that Emerson had bid us hitch our wagons to a star. We now hitch them to a mediocrity instead.

Unless, then, normal is a useless and confusing synonym for average it should mean what the word normative suggests, namely, a *concept of what ought to be* rather than a *description of what is.*

It should mean what at times it has meant—the fullest possible realization of what the human being is capable of—the complete, not the aborted human being. It is an *entelechy,* not a mean; something excellent, not something mediocre; something rare, not common; not what the majority are, but what few, if any, actually measure up to.

Where, it will be asked, do we get this norm, upon what basis does it rest? Upon the answer to that question depends what a civilization will be like and especially in what direction it will move. At various times religion, philosophy, law, and custom have contributed to it in varying degrees. When none of these is available poetry and literature may do so. But unless we can say in one way or another, "I have some idea of what men ought to be as well as some knowledge of what they are," then civilization is lost.

Teaching Students to Revise

Reta A. Madsen,
Webster University

One of the most difficult lessons the composition teacher must teach is the importance of revision. Most students, especially the ones in developmental composition, where I have used this technique, find writing so difficult and unpleasant that they are simply relieved to have filled the requisite numbers of lines or pages; the idea of changing anything so hard won appalls them. In addition to this natural reluctance to work any harder than they have to, many of them have also built up over the years of their schooling a sense of injury with respect to their teachers. They work as hard as they can (they think), and what they get back is a stubborn refusal on the part of the teacher to understand what they are saying. Their friends, pressed to read papers with grades on them, understand what they *meant* to say. Why can't the teacher also understand? These two attitudes are obviously related: If the students does not really believe that his work is not clear, he will not be moved to revise it. Using the following strategy, I have been able to attack this double-sided problem with some success. I see no reason why it should not work equally well with students at all levels of competence.

CLASS 1   A theme is assigned on a specific topic, say the description of a person. When the students come to class with their papers, I ask them to divide into groups of two and swap papers. Then, *without looking over the paper in his hands*, each of them reads it aloud to the other. This means that the student hears his paper read aloud by his peer, cold. What happens, of course, is that wrong punctuation and grammar cause the reader to stumble and read wrong. Poorly expressed ideas prompt the reader to ask, "What does this mean?" And the writer, sitting there agonized, hears his work as if it had been written by another. During this operation I circle the room, listening, commenting, answering questions, and settling arguments about right and wrong. At the end of the class, each student gets his paper back,

WRITING
ASSIGNMENT

and the assignment is to take it away and rewrite it: Both versions of the paper are to be turned in together, and woe be unto the student if they are not significantly different.

CLASS 2

When I return the papers I read aloud as many as time permits (anonymously) and the whole class engages in criticizing them. With developmental students I have introduced a third level of revision from time to time, especially at the beginning of the semester. In this case the theme is assigned as an in-class writing project first. The students have half an hour to write and then they divide into groups and read the papers as above. The advantage of this is that it gets students who find writing very difficult over the initial difficulty of sitting down to write. When they go home, they have something started instead of an intimidating sheet of blank paper.

Grading can be handled in various ways with this approach. I grade the final copy, that is, the copy on which the final revisions have been made, but with careful comparison of all earlier drafts. I annotate all versions of the paper as needed, praising good revisions and sometimes pointing out that the revision is actually worse than the original and giving the reason. Once the paper has been graded, I do not normally allow further revision. After all, the student has by this time rewritten his paper at least once and often twice and is probably tired of it. He has presumably learned from his errors and should be able to carry over this learning to the next theme. Developmental students, especially, grow depressed doing the same thing over and over. If assignments are made to build on each other and if errors are continually priced at a higher rate, it should not be necessary to assume that each paper must be perfected. By the end of the first few weeks of class, it should be possible to penalize sentence fragments, run-on sentences, comma splices, and subject/verb disagreements with automatic F grades. But each teacher will have his own way of dealing with such errors. The method of inducing revision is not dependent on any single grading system or rhetorical organization.

I have actually had a few testimonials from students who, after a semester of this, reported that they had never revised before and now were even revising papers for other classes. They had made a great discovery, that one can change the written word, and they were delighted. But even those who just ground on through the course learned to revise, and their writing improved accordingly—for the most part. There are always one or two who simply change things, since that seems to be what is wanted. Don't be discouraged by them. It works most of the time, and in composition that's not bad.

What Your English Teacher Wants

David Sonstroem,
University of Connecticut

There is a profound pain caused only by English Composition. Students can bear a C in history, a C− in economics, a D in mathematics, an F in physics. But anything less than a B+ on an English paper knocks—in one sophomore's felicitous phrase—the sails right out from under them. It does so because in most subjects there is a definite, mercifully limited reason for a low grade: "I did not study the right facts"; "I have no head for numbers"; "Dissecting frogs makes me queasy." In English, though, the standard is hard to grasp, and seems to keep shifting. On an English paper you mention the same details as your friend but do worse because, your teacher says, you fail to organize your observations. The next paper is a parade of Firsts and Seconds, but, you are told, it lacks a thesis. The next paper has a thesis but, you are sorry to learn, no train of thought. The next is guilty of wordiness, imprecision, and inflated diction. The next is inconsistent in its treatment of the reader. The next, unacceptably punctuated. The next—little wonder—simply a sloppy job. By now you have decided that nothing will work: Your teacher pulls objections out of a hat, no matter what you do. In short, in any other course a grade measures a specific skill or operation; in an English course a grade seems a verdict on your whole personality, your very soul, and an outrageously arbitrary verdict at that.

It is not such a verdict—at least it should not be. It is neither a judgment of your basic self nor an arbitrary judgment. Let's consider each half of this painful assumption separately.

First, a grade on an English paper is the teacher's judgment not of you, but of what might be called a paper self. The teacher is evaluating a performance, much as a drama teacher evaluates a student's singing. Needless to say, the actor, singer, or writer pours a good deal of himself into the performance. But what is judged remains a performance: as only one of many, none of them definitive.

And second, let's consider the second assumption: that the English teacher's criteria are infinite and arbitrarily applied. Like any other ambitious performance, an essay includes quite a few components. A teacher may

57

stress now one, now another of them but will eventually expect you to attend to them all. The number of components—of standards or expectations—is large, but it is not infinite. Let's see if we can make up a list that includes all the standards that an English teacher might require.

(Note: When students see that essays are not evaluated capriciously but judged according to a manageable number of comprehensible criteria, they are more likely to take grades less personally, to gain an organized overview of the minimal criteria that constitute good writing, and to feel that improvement is definable and possible. What follows is presented through class discussion rather than through lecturing. I keep in the back of my mind the following Ten Commandments and have always managed to suit my students' offerings to the list. I put the Commandments on the board as they are mentioned. The order of the items is not crucial, although there is some logic to the order given here.)

1. *Facts.* Display your thorough knowledge of relevant material—often, the assigned material.

2. *A main point of your own.* Oddly enough, although teachers like to see the assigned facts returned to them, they seldom enjoy seeing them arranged in the original wording or order, or supporting the original conclusion. Instead, teachers like to see students make their own sense of the facts. Therefore study the material until all or most of it makes your *own* main point. Be able to express that point in one sentence.

3. *Organization of ideas.* Arrange your facts and observations to show how they are related to one another and to set off your main point to best advantage.

4. *Train of thought.* If the ordering of your ideas has been fairly complex—expressing itself in a network, say—translate that order into a sequence that a reader could best follow.

5. *Truth.* A notion, however well ordered, may be wrongheaded. Examine your main point critically, with an eye to faulty reasoning and damaging contrary evidence.

6. *Conventions of written language.* There are many conventions (punctuation or spelling, for instance) to be observed in writing. There are many more (diction, for instance) to be observed in using formal (academic) English. Learning to write in formal English is, in fact, learning a language different in many ways from that which you already know. Meeting this expectation may well take a considerable effort.

7. *Precise language.* Careful choice and arrangement of words and word groups are essential: Have you said exactly what you mean and have you placed your emphases according to the relative importance of your ideas?

8. *Consistency.* Examine your prose for consistency of argument, of tone, of imagery, of portrayal of yourself.

9. *Attentiveness to the reader.* Is your point clearly and persuasively presented? Have you looked at the topic through the reader's eyes?

Have you established the extent of agreement between you and the reader and been otherwise diplomatic? Are your points forcefully and vividly advanced?

10. *Painstaking preparation of final draft.* Meet all requirements regarding format. Submit a document that implies that you have worked hard and are proud of the results.

WRITING
ASSIGNMENT

This lesson leads to a written assignment (1–2 pp.) in criticism. I find that it is initially easier for students to evaluate another student's paper than one of their own. I hand out a ditto of a faithfully reproduced, anonymous, middling three-page paper abandoned by a student of some earlier semester. Students must evaluate the paper according to two or three of the Ten Commandments. I divide their responsibilities so that each commandment is considered and so that each is considered by more than one student. The second class of the course is a discussion in which the specimen paper is evaluated thoroughly.

Students Write Their Own Writing Textbook

Peter G. Beidler,
Lehigh University

One of the more deflating discoveries I have made in the course of more than twenty years of teaching is that most of what we teachers tell students the students will forget. On the other hand, what we can get students to tell us they may remember. I want to describe an experimental freshman composition course I built around that discovery. In building that course I tried to take pedagogical advantage also of another discovery I have made about students: They have an almost intuitional ability to recognize good writing when they see it.

Most courses in freshman composition are taught with the aid of a textbook on writing. The textbook has lots of rules and advice about writing—grammar, paragraphs, transitional devices, introductions, and so on. There are hundreds of such textbooks on the market, and I have tried a number of them down through the years. I have not, however, had much luck with these textbooks. The students read the textbook diligently enough, and the principles of good writing the textbooks set forth are sound enough, but few of these textbooks seem actually to improve student writing much.

Dissatisfied with the standard textbook approach, I decided not to use any textbook in a freshman course I taught recently. On the contrary, my students and I wrote our own textbook for use in the course. In previous classes I had often distributed to students mimeographed copies of themes students in the class have written. I would ask my students to tell me which of several themes was the best. Then we would take a closer look at that theme and try to determine what was good about it and why it was better than the other themes I had distributed. Almost invariably, the collective view of the students about which themes were best agreed with my own view, even though I never told the students in advance which themes I preferred. Individually, of course, some students missed the mark, and even those students who were best at distinguishing good writing from bad often had difficulty finding the words to explain why one theme was better than another. Still, I sensed that there was something to build on in the fact that even freshmen could, at least collectively, recognize good writing. I decided that there might be enough there to form the basis of a freshman-written textbook on writing. Accordingly, I asked for, and received, permission to teach an experimental section of freshman English.

A key feature of my method was that we tried never to talk abstractly about the principles of good writing. Rather, we would try to talk only about specific pieces of student writing. We would take the inductive approach, working from specific examples to general rules and principles.

In the first regular class period I had my students write a little essay on "The Loneliness of the Lehigh Freshman." I had at that point given them no instruction in writing, no information about "what I wanted" in their themes. Before the next class I mimeographed—anonymously, of course—six of their themes, selected more or less at random.

I distributed those six themes in the next period with the instructions that the students were to rank-order them from best to worst according to any principles of good writing that made sense to them. After we had computed the class average and determined the class rankings for the themes, we discussed the theme that the students liked best. (It was, incidentally, the one I liked best also.) We tried to determine what principles of writing made it better than the others. When someone in the class mentioned a principle of good writing that he or she had applied in choosing the best theme, I had one of the students—a kind of class stenographer—write that principle down. We had items like the following on the list: "Uses examples"; "Makes a single point"; "Supports the main point"; "Orderly movement from beginning to end"; "Interesting introduction."

At the end of the class I collected the list of principles from the stenographer and took it home, where I started a master list, with some examples, on my word processor. The next class period we discussed two other themes and wrote down some other principles: "Bold thesis"; "Organizes by topic"; "Active voice, not passive." For some of these, of course, the students were using terminology they had picked up in high school. That did not bother me as long as they were able to describe what the terms, such as *active voice*, meant.

After we had accumulated a number of principles I printed out copies of these principles and gave them to my students. We went through the list and tried to eliminate duplicates and sharpen our way of expressing the principles. We decided to put them in the form of parallel imperatives (in the manner of Strunk and White): "Be bold"; "Avoid exaggeration"; "Use transitions"; "Use concrete words"; "Organize." Then we talked about how best to organize our list of principles and came up with eight major categories: selecting a topic, focusing on a main idea, developing a thesis, supporting it, organizing the evidence or examples, writing solid paragraphs, being clear, checking words carefully, writing grammatically, and so on. In doing all that, of course, we were engaged in precisely the kind of thinking, shifting, and organizing that I wanted my students to do when they wrote their themes. I printed out and distributed copies of an interim list of principles, and we used it to evaluate other student themes, adding and rephrasing as we went.

Of course, I never entirely gave up control. Leading a discussion is, after all, *leading* a discussion. I could direct it in ways I wanted it to go ("Jay, what about that introduction?"), emphasize good points ("April, write what he said on your list! We don't want to forget that."), de-emphasize minor points ("Yes, it is misspelled, but even if it were spelled right, is that the best word he could have used?"), rephrase creatively ("I see, David. You think this writer might have used a stronger example? I agree."), and so on. The students knew what I was doing, of course, and seemed to welcome what direction I did give to our discussions. Still, our little textbook was very much a collaborative effort, considerably different in style and scope from what I would have written myself. The students knew that they had had a major role in writing it.

In the end we had our little textbook of rules and principles of good writing. Perhaps *pamphlet* would be a more accurate term, because what we ended with—a dozen or so pages—was not long enough to call a text-book. Nor was our little booklet any better than the hundreds of professionally written ones. But it was *ours*. Near the end of the semester I gave each student a copy of the final version, as edited by one of their classmates, and told them that I would grade their last themes—the ones that counted the most—solely on the basis of the principles of good writing that we had formulated together and written down in our textbook. My hope was that because my students had told *me* what makes one theme better than another, had told *me* what the principles of good writing were, they would be more capable of applying those principles to their own writing.

Was my hope fulfilled? Was my experiment a success? I think so, though it is impossible to be scientific about such things. Helping my students to write our own textbook worked at least as well as anything else I have tried. And I will also say that my method had one small advantage I had not anticipated: In commenting on and grading a student's theme I could use terminology the students were familiar with and point out that the theme did or did not measure up to the standard that the students themselves had established. As a result, my grading appeared to my students to be less arbitrary. Ours were not rules and principles passed down from on high, from some ancient writing master in the sky. They were not rules and principles that some ivory-tower English professor dreamed up and put into an overstuffed and expensive textbook. On the contrary, the rules and principles came right out of the class itself.

I sensed that my students were more willing to support our rules and principles because they themselves had had a hand in formulating them. Getting a C on a theme discourages most students these days, but at least that semester they knew they got the C because they did not observe all the principles of good writing that they had had a hand in discovering and articulating.

READING

HOW TO WRITE A SUPERIOR THEME

Introductory note: This brief booklet about how to write a superior theme was written by the students in Professor Peter G. Beidler's section of English 1 in the fall semester, 1984. Particular credit is due to two students in the class: April Pompa, who served as class stenographer as we hammered out the advice and principles contained in this booklet, and Kurt Ehresman, who served as a principal editor and reviser. The other students in the class, all of whom helped to develop these principles, were David Best, Carolyn Bromley, David Carlson, Laurel Casten, Richard D'Angelo, Brian Duddy, Gregg Fedus, Steve Heffernen, Keith Holcomb, Terri Jones, Charlene Jurasinski, Meighan Meeker, Patric Moran, Scott Rizza, Michelle Robertson, Kathy Smith, Paul Solomon, Jay Steinberg, and Diane Weibel.

The advice contained in this booklet was designed to help students write clear and forceful themes. The principles were designed in part to guide the teacher when he graded themes written in the course. Both the pieces of advice and the principles of good writing were set down in the full recognition that good writers sometimes quite rightly violate most of them.

—Peter G. Beidler

A. *Select an appropriate topic.*

1. *Be narrow.* In selecting a topic, think small, not big. The more specific your topic is, the more convincing your examples will be. If the topic is "Campus Transportation," for example, you might want to write about "Why Students Hate Busses" or "The Bicycle: The Most Practical Way to Get to Class."

2. *Be original.* In selecting your topic, think about your own experiences and point of view. Your own personal insights and personal experiences will enable you to write a theme that stands out from the pack.

3. *Be honest.* Never fake a point of view simply because you think it is the expected one. Using false examples to prove your points will detract from your credibility and make your theme sound stilted and insincere. Do not say roommates are wonderful if you hate the smelly one you drew.

4. *Be bold.* Take a clear stand on a topic. If you settle for the "wishy-washy" approach, your paper will be as boring to write as it is to read. Do not wander on about how "living in a freshman dorm is good for some people but not good for others." Say, instead, that "living in a dorm teaches people to cope with their peers" or "dorm life deprives students of their sense of dignity."

B. *Focus on a main idea.*

1. *State the main idea.* Put into your opening paragraph a one-sentence declarative sentence stating clearly and simply the main idea of your theme. This sentence is often called the "thesis sentence." It constitutes a kind of promise about what will be the central focus of your theme.

2. *Exclude extraneous information.* Every thought, sentence, and paragraph in your theme should serve to advance your main idea by offering clear support for it. You should rigorously exclude information that does not clearly and directly support your main idea.

C. *Support your main idea.*

1. *Be convincing.* Your theme fails if your reader is not convinced that your idea or thesis is a valid one. You must present logical proof of your thesis if you wish to gain the support of your reader.

2. *Be specific.* The best themes contain details so specific that only the writer of the theme could supply them. Avoid general statements such as, "Out of all the friends you make, the most important will be your roommate. The two of you will do everything together." Instead, say, "My best friend at Lehigh is my roommate. We go to parties together, drink together, and puke together."

D. *Organize the support for your main idea.*

1. *Have a plan.* Make sure you have and announce a plan for developing or proving your main point, a pathway through a forest of details you will be referring to. Once you get on that path—that is, once you have promised to take your reader to a certain place by a certain route—do not waver from it or both you and your reader will get lost in the woods. If, after beginning to write, you discover a better plan or route, make sure to go back and change your promise and get on the new pathway at the right place. Your reader must not know that you have changed your plan—only that you have a good one.

2. *Begin, bodybuild, and end.* Give your theme an effective beginning or opening—sometimes called an "introduction." Spend most of your time and effort planning and writing the central portion of your theme—sometimes called the "body." Give your theme an effective ending or closing—sometimes called a "conclusion."

3. *Organize by topic, not chronology.* Your points will be clearer and more convincing if your plan emphasizes subpoints rather than time scheme.

    a. Chronological example: "When I first entered the bar, I felt cautious and frightened. . . . Later, as I was thrown out the window. . . ."

    b. Topical example: "My first reason for going to bars is that. . . . My second reason is that. . . ."

4. *Use transitional devices.* Transitional devices knit together the points you are making in different parts of your theme and help it to "flow" gracefully.

    a. Simple example: "One reason is. . . . A second reason is. . . . A third reason is. . . ."

    b. More sophisticated example: "The most obvious reason. . . . This brings up a second reason. . . . The most powerful reason, however, is one most freshmen never think of until it is too late. It is that. . . ."

E. *Write solid paragraphs.* A theme is a collection of related paragraphs all of which serve to develop a main idea.

1. *Avoid one-paragraph themes.* A one-paragraph theme is merely a paragraph, not a theme. A paragraph is a collection of related sentences all of which serve to develop a single idea. Each paragraph in the theme, therefore, should focus on and develop a central point, and each point should offer direct support to the main point or thesis of the theme.

2. *Avoid very long and very short paragraphs.* A paragraph is a unit of length

as well as meaning. If a paragraph begins to get too long, you should consider whether you may not perhaps be developing more than one point, or whether the single point you are developing could not be developed more conveniently by subdividing it into two or more points, and therefore two or more paragraphs.

3. *Give each paragraph a topic sentence.* The topic sentence serves to summarize the main point of an expository paragraph. The rest of the paragraph is made up of detailed and specific support for that sentence.

F. *Be clear.* One of your primary jobs as a writer is, by being absolutely clear about what you are saying, to make your reader's job as easy as possible. Here are ten suggestions that will help you to do that:

1. *Provide a thoughtful title.* An interesting and fitting title carries your reader directly into your main point.

2. *Include all necessary information.* Put into your theme all that your reader needs to know. Learn to make a distinction between what is obvious to you and obvious to another.

3. *Avoid sarcasm and irony.* Do not say, "He was wonderful!" if you mean that he was awful.

4. *Explain fully and carefully.* Do not replace full explanations with phrases like "as you know," "as you can readily see," or "it is obvious."

5. *Avoid exaggeration and sweeping generalization.* Do not say, "Everyone hates English," or "A college degree is a guarantee of a good job" or "A freshman's roommate is a freshman's best friend."

6. *Repeat your main ideas.* It is good to remind your reader of your main idea from time to time: "Lehigh needs a new center for the arts for still another reason." Do not, however, use repetition as a form of padding. See point 7, below.

7. *Avoid needless redundancy.* Do not keep saying the same things over and over and over again in the same way. Do not repeat things unnecessarily or be repetitious. It makes your reader weary, tired, somnolent, heavy-lidded, and sleepy.

8. *Use the active voice.* Do not say, "Security was felt" when it is clearer to say, "He felt secure." Do not say, "Richie's voice was heard by us all" when it is more direct to say, "We all heard Richie's voice."

9. *Use parallel form.* Instead of saying that you like cats, find dogs appealing to yourself, and as for horses, you think they make interesting pets, just say that you think cats, dogs, and horses make good pets. Instead of saying that Charles likes drinking champagne, to eat steaks, and does not mind all-night nocturnal engagement in terpsichorean activities, say that he likes to drink champagne, to eat steaks, and to dance from dusk to dawn.

10. *Use examples.* Instead of saying that you approve of democracy, say that you like following a leader you helped to elect, like being able to publish a letter criticizing him in the newspaper, and like knowing that you can get rich.

G. *Choose your words carefully.* Themes can be no stronger than the words that make them up, just as a building can be no stronger than the bricks that make it up. Here are ten specific suggestions about choosing your words:

1. *Use concrete and specific words.* Say "generous" and "funny" or "gentle to stray cats" rather than "nice." Call something a "brick" or a "tree" or an "IBM personal computer" rather than a "thing."

2. *Use precise words.* Do not assume that "homesick" and "lonely" mean the same thing, or that "lost" and "frightened" mean the same thing. If you have a thesaurus, put it aside in favor of a dictionary. The former gives you inexact and often unfamiliar synonyms; the latter gives you precise meanings.

3. *Avoid big words.* When you have an equal choice between a big word and a little one, use the little one. To do otherwise is to write pretentiously (a big word) and to confuse readers. Use (rather than utilize) the simplest, most familiar words that will convey your thought. Do not let fancy words call attention to themselves when simple ones will call attention to your ideas.

4. *Avoid chatty, slang, dirty, or trendy words.* Fer sher, dude. Catch my drift? Awesome. Wicked. He had snot on his socks.

5. *Use strong verbs* rather than adverbs and adjectives. Do not say, "He went swiftly on his horse" when you can say, "He galloped." Do not say, "I was annoyed" when you can say, "I pounded the table, stomped on Mom's purse, and drop-kicked the cat."

6. *Avoid contractions* in formal writing. Write "he had" or "he would" instead of "he'd," and "I am" instead of "I'm." This principle does not apply, of course, when you are writing dialogue or direct speech.

7. *Avoid sexist language.* Do not use "he" to refer to people of both sexes, as in "When a freshman gets his grade in English 1, he despairs." Usually the plural is a convenient substitute: "When freshmen get their grades in English 1, they despair." In this case, of course, you are better off avoiding the false generalization to begin with: "When I got my grade in English 1, I despaired."

8. *Do not use "myself" when you can use "me" or "I."* It is all right to say, "I cut myself" or "I saw the accident myself," but it is not a good idea to say, "The teacher praised Sally and myself" or "John and myself went to town."

9. *Avoid awkward locutions.* Use "I" rather than some awkward phrase like "the present writer" (unless you wish to make a distinction between her and a past writer, or between him and a writer who is absent). And why use fancy words like "locution"?

10. *Avoid the impersonal "you."* Unless you are writing instructions (as we are in this booklet), it is better not to use "you" in formal writing.

    a. Weak example: "You feel awkward at first."
    b. Better: "One feels awkward at first."
    c. Better yet: "Freshmen feel awkward at first."
    d. Best: "At first I felt awkward."

H. *Write grammatically acceptable sentences.* Rules of grammar are not divinely given. On the contrary, they are made by people for people. If you ignore them, you may be misunderstood. Even if your meaning is clear, ungrammatical writing makes you look ignorant, sloppy, or lazy. Can you afford to make that kind of impression on your reader? Here are ten of the most important rules educated men and women have agreed to abide by:

1. *Do not write sentence fragments.* Bad idea. Will regret it. You in trouble. Being misunderstood.

2. *Do not write comma splices.* A comma splice is a joining of two complete sentences with a comma, this is an example. Two sentences can be joined by a comma if there is also a coordinating conjunction ("but" and "and," but not "however," "therefore," or "yet").

3. *Make your subjects and verbs agree in number.* Freshmen do not makes many errors like this, but it are wrong when they do.

4. *Do not use adjectives when adverbs are called for,* and vice versa. Students who do it write improper and ungrammatical. It does not make for well writing.

5. *Keep to a consistent point of view.* Instead of "A person who takes their money out of the bank should have your head examined," write "People who take their money out of the bank should have their heads examined."

6. *Keep the reference of pronouns clear.* Instead of "Tom and Jim went to the play and he enjoyed it," write, "Tom went to the play with Jim and enjoyed it," or, better, "Tom enjoyed the play he saw with Jim."

7. *Keep opening "-ing" phrases under control.* Instead of "Going to town in the train, the trees whizzed past our window," write, "Going to town in the train, we saw the trees whiz past our window."

8. *Punctuate carefully.* Use punctuation to clarify the meaning you intend to convey. "I like purple Christmas trees and sneakers" is not at all the same as "I like purple, Christmas trees, and sneakers."

9. *Spell out numbers of ten or under.* Instead of "We had 6 guests," write, "We had six guests."

10. *Learn the difference* between "then" and "than," "accept" and "except," "effect" and "affect," "lets" and "let's," "its" and "it's," "your" and "you're," and so on. Spell such words correctly.

Questioning Authority: Rules That Are Made to Be Broken

Samudra Haddad,
Washington University

Teaching composition has taught me faith in the ability of every student, under the right sort of duress, to say something intelligent and original. By the right sort of duress I mean the intellectual vacuum created when we have made him reject clichés and abandon verbal posturing but continue to expect essays from him. Once he stops trying to sound like *Time* magazine, CBS News, and assorted congressmen, administrators, and teachers—all the voices of Authority—he begins to hear his own voice. His sensitivity to development, organization, and other matters of form evolves with his attempt to explain his own insight. In my classroom, education often means de-education, all essays are subject to revision, no word is final, and all rules are formulated in order to be judiciously broken. I use shock tactics to jar students into thinking for themselves as soon as possible.

Teacher: How many of you have been taught that you should *never* use *I* in an essay?
Students: (*Show of several hands.*)
Teacher: That isn't true.
Students: (*Expressions of disbelief.*)
Teacher: Think about it. If you read something written in the first person, what's its effect on you? How does reading "I heard heavy footsteps at the end of the hall" make you feel, compared to how "He heard heavy footsteps at the end of the hall" makes you feel?
Student: Well, I identify more with the writer when he uses *I*.
Teacher: Not really with the writer, but with the person telling the story.

At this point we take a few minutes to discuss the notion of the author's *persona* and the writer's relation to his audience. Eventually I bring the discussion back to the pronouns and we identify the effect of every pronoun on the distance between writer and audience; we conclude that the choice depends on what the writer is saying and to whom, and on his attitude toward his subject, and what he wants his audience to think and feel. As we reach this conclusion an enormous sense of relief usually begins to fill the classroom.

Teacher: How many of you have had teachers who told you never to repeat words, but to find a synonym in a thesaurus?
Students: (Show of several hands, not necessarily the same ones.)
Teacher: Wrong again. There are no synonyms in the English language. Do *grin* and *smile* mean the same thing? What's the difference?

This point leads to a discussion about denotation and connotation and about the right way to use a thesaurus. This is also a good time to plug the *O.E.D.*

Teacher: What teachers were no doubt objecting to was careless repetition, repetition that slips out because the mind is repetitive and you weren't paying attention. But sometimes repetition serves a useful function in an essay. (Pause.) Now what function could repetition possibly serve in an essay?
When we finish discussing the use of repetition to increase coherence and supply emphasis, we proceed.
Teacher: How many of you have had teachers who wouldn't let you begin a sentence with *And* or *But?*
Student: Mine wouldn't let me begin with *Because.* (*Nods of agreement.*)
Teacher: Your teacher was probably concerned that you'd forget to finish the sentence. *Because* introduces a dependent clause, which must be connected to an independent clause if the thought is to be complete.
Student: I'm not quite sure what a clause is.

Most of them aren't, so we talk about clauses until students understand the difference between independent ones and dependent ones. We will have to return to this question in subsequent classes, but for today we say only enough to justify beginning with *And* or *But.*

Teacher: Of course if you begin every sentence with *And* you'll bore your reader, and sometimes you really won't want to begin with *Because,* because sometimes it makes more sense to describe the effect before the clause—but not always. So. How many of you were told never to end a sentence with a preposition?
Students: (Show of hands, laughter.)
Teacher: Outdated. It used to be a rule, but times change. What's a rule anyway?
We talk about language as a set of conventional agreements subject to change and refer again to the *O.E.D.*
Teacher: Actually, it usually is more graceful not to end a sentence with a preposition, so it's a good rule to keep in mind, but often you'll find that

in order to avoid ending with a preposition you have to make your sentence noticeably longer or more roundabout, and if that's the case you're better off forgetting the rule.

Student: How could it be that other teachers we've had imposed these rules?

Teacher: One reason—for example, with the rule against using *I*—might be that your teacher let you take the easy way and apply the rule instead of making you decide in every individual instance what worked and what didn't. Or in encouraging you to use a thesaurus, he or she might have been less interested in seeing you write a coherent essay than in increasing your vocabulary on the sly. If your school district couldn't finance new textbooks, the grammar book may actually have said never to end a sentence with a preposition. Or maybe your English teacher majored in political science and wanted to teach political science but was the only person in your school at all qualified to teach English. Also, if you took a survey, you'd probably find a smaller percentage of teachers pursuing their own writing, and it takes a writer to understand a writer's problems.

All those reasons you could change by changing the system. A more insidious problem threatens all of us who speak and write at any level of education. Do you know Orwell? Read "Politics and the English Language" for part of your homework assignment. Words like *analyzation* and *prioritize* and *aggress against* show an inability to connect new information with old, a sort of intellectual rootlessness. And I think that when people feel ignorant, or powerless, they use abstract language and passive sentence construction as a way of evading responsibility for what they think. It takes courage and intellectual security to say "I think" instead of "It is this writer's opinion that. . . ." And it takes constant vigilance and hard work to avoid slipping into this kind of language when we hear it around us all the time. I myself find garbage in my typewriter every day, and it's a daily effort to rescue what's valuable and throw the rest away. So don't be hard on your old teachers. And don't be hard on yourselves when you catch yourself slipping into jargon and Newspeak. Just scratch it out; remind yourself that your audience is composed of human beings who breathe, laugh, and cry; and try again to say what you have to say in words that will touch them.

WRITING ASSIGNMENT   For the rest of the homework assignment, I ask them to revise a page or two of an essay they wrote for high school and bring both original and revision to the next class for comparison; or if they don't have a high school essay with them, to write a page as they would have before this class, then to rewrite as they would after this class.

LESSON READING

George Orwell, "Politics and the English Language" in *Shooting an Elephant and Other Essays* (Orlando, FL: Harcourt Brace Jovanovich, 1950).

Dispelling Myths About the Writing Process

Leonard A. Podis,
Oberlin College

My lesson aims to correct several misconceptions that most students (particularly first-year students) have about the writing process. Since these myths are perpetuated in most high school English courses, my material might alternatively be titled "Questioning Authority: Rules That Are Made to Be Broken, Part II," with reference to another lesson in this collection (Samudra Haddad, pp. 68–70). While that lesson talks mainly about questionable rules of usage that interfere with a student's authentic voice, this lesson attempts to dispel three interrelated myths about composing: (1) that writing is easy for others, presumably those who follow the rules in composition textbooks, and difficult only for oneself; (2) that writers must know what they wish to say before they write (one of those textbook rules that supposedly make writing easy for those hypothetical others); and (3) that revision is a kind of superficial copy-editing activity (since good writers get it right the first time through, having been certain about a thesis before writing).

I begin this lesson by confessing to students that I, a practicing writer of many years (and in fact the author of a writing textbook I have shamelessly made them buy for the course), often have a hard time writing. But, I tell them, I would never have admitted to such a weakness when I was their age, because twenty years ago it wasn't the kind of thing that one talked about: Nearly everyone then subscribed to the myth that writing was easy if you followed the textbook rules. So if you had a problem with writing, as I did, you hid it. For example, in high school English and freshman composition, unable to write the outlines for my research papers in advance of writing the paper as one was supposed to do, I stealthily wrote the outline *after* writing the paper and handed the whole package in, careful not to reveal my inadequacy.

At this point, many students in the class will begin vigorously nodding

71

in agreement about the impossibility of doing those kinds of outlines that they were asked to do in high school. I call on some of these people and ask them to share their experiences with the class. After some discussion of this issue, I suggest to the class that there are enough real difficulties in writing without creating more for ourselves, such as that posed by the artificial outline task. I then distribute a handout on which I have reproduced the opening few lines of three successive versions of an essay I myself wrote. Leading them through the handout, I call their attention to the uncertainties, false starts, and tentative phrasings of the earlier versions and stress how much things changed as the piece developed. I also inform them how long it took for this process to unfold (nearly two years) and how often I sought advice from colleagues, relatives, journal editors—anyone who would listen to or read what I had produced. Lest such talk become too discouraging, I distribute a second handout on which is reproduced the first page of the essay when it finally became a published article. We pause then to talk about some of the rewards that students have experienced from their efforts to write. Students often mention such things as understanding their experiences better through journal keeping, entertaining themselves and their friends with letters they write, or gaining a sense of accomplishment from a course paper well done.

To conclude this phase of the lesson, I distribute another handout containing passages that express the anguish of writers trying to write. For example, Joseph Conrad complains:

> I have written one page. Just one page. I went about thinking and forgetting— sitting down before the blank page to find that I could not put one sentence together. . . . I am frightened when I remember that I have to drag it all out of myself. . . . Other writers have some starting point. Something to catch hold of . . . they know something to begin with—while I don't. I have some impressions . . . and it's all faded. . . . I am exceedingly miserable.[1]

And E. B. White observed, on the occasion of his seventieth birthday:

> All I have to do is one English sentence and I fly into a thousand pieces. . . . I wish instead I were doing what my dog is doing at this moment, rolling in something ripe he has found on the beach in order to take on its smell. . . . His is such an easy, simple way to increase one's stature and enlarge one's personality.[2]

Again students freely concede that they have felt discouraged at times too but assumed that other people knew how to write more easily. Everyone

---

[1] From Joseph Conrad, "Letter to Edward Garnett," in *The Writing Art: Authorship as Experienced and Expressed by the Great Writers*, eds. Bertha W. Smith and Virginia C. Lincoln (Boston: Houghton Mifflin, 1931), pp. 104–105.

[2] Israel Shenker, "E. B. White: Notes and Comments by Author," *New York Times*, 11 July 1969.

experiences satisfaction on learning that the anxiety-ridden writers in question were Joseph Conrad and E. B. White.

The second phase of the lesson builds on the first phase by undercutting the traditional belief that a writer must always develop a paper's thesis statement before attempting to write the paper. I ask the class how many of them were given such advice in high school, and most raise their hands. We stop and talk about the difficulties some of them had in doing this, and by this point two or three students feel comfortable in relating an anecdote or even a horror story about some abortive attempt to create a paper by forcing themselves to generate a thesis and then trying to come up with the material to support it.

I then remind the class about our earlier discussion of the difficulty in writing a perfectly predictive outline for a paper before writing the paper and point out the similarity between that issue and the thesis-in-advance issue. Invariably, some students ask whether indeed one *shouldn't* try to write a thesis before composing, and at that point I assure them that it's perfectly all right to *try* to write a thesis in advance but that one should think of it more as a probing device to get things started than as a constraining factor. So often, I tell them, we simply *don't know* what to say until we have waded into a paper and started to try out different ways of saying what's in our heads.

To reinforce the idea that writing can serve as an aid to discovery (not just as a tool for expressing what we knew to begin with) I distribute a final handout featuring excerpts from an article by Donald Murray. Included are brief quotations from many famous writers, which we take turns reading aloud. The common element in these quotations, we soon realize, is that the person speaking (in all cases a professional writer) uses writing to discover what needs to be said, not to say something he or she knew prior to the act of writing. (A typical quotation is E. M. Forster's "How do I know what I think until I see what I say?")

When we finish reading the quotations, I ask the students whether they have ever approached their writing in this frame of mind. Students who volunteer a response generally say that they haven't tried to write for discovery but have occasionally found themselves changing their ideas as they proceeded with a paper, sometimes feeling guilty for doing so. In some cases they may have discovered their thesis only after writing the whole paper, but either it never occurred to them to rewrite the paper, or they didn't have time to do so. We briefly discuss what options a student in this position might have.

Now we move to the final misconception: that revision is a superficial matter involving mainly copy-editing and proofreading. "How much time do you usually give to revising a paper you've written?" I ask. Answers vary, but the time is usually minimal. "What kinds of changes do you usually make when you revise?" Again answers vary, but the changes are also usually minimal: mainly looking for better ways of saying things at the word and sentence level. "How often were you asked to revise a paper substantially after you had submitted it to a teacher and received it back with comments?" Here the answers seldom vary: "Hardly ever" is the consensus.

I tell my students that they are by no means alone. Nancy Sommers's study of the revising practices of student and professional writers showed that students revise their work much less than professional writers and that the revisions they make are much more superficial than those of the professionals. Why do professional writers revise so often and so substantially? If writing is a discovery process, then writers need to redo their papers to incorporate and present more effectively what they have just begun to learn in their earlier drafts. In other words, the need for *substantial* revision results in large part from a writer's realization that his or her knowledge of the topic has grown in the act of composing a rough draft. The tentative idea with which the writer began may have changed into a new, perhaps more complex, idea as the writer sought the most appropriate words and phrases and as he or she considered the alternatives for arranging and organizing the thoughts. Such changes in a writer's knowledge require that he or she go back and revise in order to communicate the new ideas in the best way possible.

Why, then, do student writers so seldom revise? Generally, they have been taught a method that de-emphasizes true revision. Because they have been told that they should always know exactly what they will say before they compose, they justifiably expect that revision will involve only superficial, cosmetic adjustments in the language. Moreover, revising is hard work, as we saw earlier in the case of my own essay, which was two years and many revisions in the making. Students are seldom given the time necessary for substantial revision. Often the only revision they are expected (or allowed) to do is that which can be done to their first draft the night before their paper is due. They are not generally taught or encouraged to revise substantially in light of instructor or peer responses to their work.

At this point, I briefly list all three misconceptions on the board and we discuss how they fit together and reinforce each other, and we speculate on what implications our new understanding about these matters might have for how we should approach writing and revising.

WRITING ASSIGNMENT Since this is really a lesson in the *process* of writing, the actual topic students write about following the class is probably less important than the mentality with which they approach their work. The writing assignment I give allows students two options:

1. Search your files for a previously written paper that might profit from *substantial* revision and write a revised draft to submit along with the original; or

2. Write an essay in which you discuss a problem from your earlier years that once caused you a good deal of anxiety but that you can now, through time and distance, see in a clearer, *revised* perspective, one that enables you to

understand the experience more completely. The problem may be something that was of genuine importance or something trivial—in which case you may want to treat it humorously.

I encourage those students who can find a suitable paper to revise to choose the first option. The second option provides an accessible assignment for those students (and there will always be some) who insist that they have absolutely no previously written papers on which to draw. Students who choose option 1 will automatically confront the notion of writing as a process of drafting and revising that takes place over a period of time. Students who write on the second option should likewise be enjoined to revise their essays substantially at least once after receiving comments from instructor and/or peers.

FOR FURTHER READING

Anne Tyler, "Still Just Writing," in Janet Sternburg, *The Writer on Her Work* (New York: Norton, 1980), pp. 3–16.

COPIA: Personal Description

Steven Justice,
University of California, Berkeley

This lesson makes best sense following a long section in which the students learn about economy of style and argument, when they are as convinced as they ever will be that concision is a virtue. It is meant to suggest how the practical problem of finding things to say can become a resource for observation and expression. The discussion can be done at a pinch in a single class, although the readings provide enough for two; the assignment, however, falls necessarily into two parts.

I ask the students whether they sense, in our lessons on revising and concision, that any basic problems have been passed over. If no one has the courage to say (in a well-behaved class, usually no one will) that the real problem they face is the problem of filling the page, I suggest it, to expressions of relief that their unspeakable anxiety has just been spoken. "We have been working at getting rid of all the junk, paring down the prose to where it can't be pared any more. But why should we stop there? Why not pare away everything but the sentence that states the argument of the paper?" Someone who has been listening carefully will object that the argument would not then be an argument, but an unsupported assertion. "Fair enough; you have to argue any assertion. But if we were really paring down to the essentials, why not state the argument in syllogisms?" At this point I take a recent paper, a good one that has been discussed in a workshop and that the students therefore know, and reduce it to a series of syllogisms on the blackboard. "Why not do this instead of writing prose?" Comments suggest that it is too schematic, that it will not hold the reader's interest.

"But should it hold the reader's interest? Are we just catering to weakness by making writing attractive? Would human beings be better off if they didn't need to be attracted and entertained?" Here a discussion of what is necessary in life—food, clothing, and shelter—is useful. I get the students to reduce life to the essentials and then ask what a life made of essentials alone would be like; all that we look forward to, even in the essentials (pleasure in food, for example), is extra. We talk for a while about what makes something interesting, how the everyday can be either tedious or entrancing according to the quality of attention given to it. (Since my sections on argumentation usually deal with politics and are for many students their first exposure to political thought, I mention how the attempt to see something interesting in politics has made it interesting to some of them.)

At this point I explain the rhetorical concept of *inventio:* the problem of finding something to say. It is the students' problem every time they face the blank sheet of paper. But that practical problem is also a problem of inventiveness, a challenge to discover possibilities of interest in the material of their daily life and thought. I explain also the concept of *copia* (with its even greater potential for cynicism)—the process of expanding and developing the essay—as a specific version of this inventive prowess, the ability to return again and again to the object of discussion with new questions suggested by the ones already posed.

We take personal description as a test case for this process and Chaucer's description of the Prioress as an example of the genre. I explain what they need to know—that the office of prioress is one of both spiritual direction and practical decisions in a convent, that Madame Eglentyne is not a nun's name, that "milk and wastel breed" is better food than most peasants would eat, that entry to the cloister meant a repudiation of worldly status and pleasure—and show that the Prioress is wholly inappropriate for her office. "What is the difference between saying, 'The Prioress is too worldly for her office' and offering this description?" Generally, the answers will indicate that the students *like* her. The disjunct responses—moral disapproval and personal affection—can then serve as an index to the prioress's own ambiguities, a vacuous, quasi-religious earnestness co-existing with aristocratic ambitions and a hint of unrecognized sexual desire. Then we consider how the particulars of the description create our sense of the Prioress.

Roger Angell's essay on Steve Blass is a description of a different sort, a narrative. Why does he begin with the picture? Why end with the simulated inning? This introduces the question of how Angell might have conceived of and proceeded in this essay. We assemble a hypothetical history of its writing: He realizes Blass's departure; in speaking with him, sees the philosophy with which Blass has accepted his failure; considers the story of his failure in the light of the joy of competent performance; sees that he feels the sorrow of its loss in a way that Blass himself does not, and that that loss suggests the gratuitousness of the gift in the first place; uses the story as a way of exploring how the pressure that produces competent performance and the elation that follows can also destroy them.

WRITING ASSIGNMENT   The assignment falls into two parts, with the eventual purpose of producing a description of someone the student has known for at least a year. The first part is notebook work; the student should turn in a photocopy of it at the next class. The directions are to prepare for the writing by finding everything that is available to be said:

Begin by assembling all the observations of physical detail, remembered incidents, tics of behavior you can. Write them down. Use these to suggest some central observation about that person, something that some of the details suggest. Write *that* down in a sentence or two. Now reverse the process: Thinking of the person through the lens of this idea, try to discover other characteristics that had escaped your notice the first time, characteristics that exemplify or qualify the angle you have found. Write them down as well.

At the next class, a three-page description of the chosen subject is assigned.

LESSON READINGS

Geoffery Chaucer, The General Prologue, *The Canterbury Tales*, ll. 118–162.

Roger Angell, "Gone for Good," in *Five Seasons: A Baseball Companion* (New York: Simon and Schuster, 1977), pp. 223–259.

A Local Habitation and a Name: Specific Detail in Definition and Description

Judiana Lawrence,
St. John Fisher College

Early in a composition course I focus on the value of being specific in writing by conducting a couple of workshops in which the students discover the precept for themselves. Although I assign appropriate readings from whatever text we happen to be using, I concentrate in these workshops on the students' writing. During the previous week I assign an essay topic that draws on their immediate experience so that they will have plenty to say. A topic that works well reads as follows:

WRITING ASSIGNMENT 1
Write an essay of three or four pages in which you describe the best *or* the worst job you have had. Your audience is made up of your peers and your aim is to explain in detail why the job was either good or bad.

CLASS 1
For the first workshop I choose one of the better papers so that the class will not be distracted by numerous errors, so that the author will not feel singled out for ridicule (although I also protect his or her anonymity), and so that we can focus on the merits of the essay while at the same time discovering ways to improve it. The following essay, "A 'Good' Job," has worked well. I give each student a copy of the essay with the instruction to come to the next class ready to discuss it. What follows the essay is essentially an account of how two actual classes went, although I regularly use the method with a variety of materials for a variety of purposes.

79

READING

A "GOOD" JOB
••••••••••••••••••••••••••••

[1]   Summer vacation should be an enjoyable, relaxing break from an exhausting nine months of school. Unfortunately, most college students cannot afford to spend their entire summer relaxing, free from all responsibilities. Because of the high cost of college tuition and the fact that most students contribute a large portion of this cost from their own earnings, it is necessary for them to spend their summers working to earn this money. Like many other students, I have found that any job is hard to find, and that a good job, one which pays well and is interesting, is especially scarce. Over the years, I have held many summer jobs, including working in a church, in a construction office and, in a moment of extreme desperation, even in a factory, but none of these qualified as a "good" job. Finally, last summer, after months of depressing, degrading, frustrating job-searching, I landed what was truly a "good" job.

[2]   Early in the spring, a friend of the family gave me an application for a job at People Express Airlines where she worked. Because, after a few months, I did not get a reply one way or another, I decided to look for another job. This, however, proved extremely difficult and by the end of June I had just about given up. Just then, Joe Barnello of People Express called me to come out to the airport for an interview. I was excited but decided, from my previous experience, not to count on anything. Surprisingly, Joe opened the interview with, "Can you start Thursday?" Although my job title made me a little nervous (What exactly does a "Baggage Assistant" do?) I decided to take the job, after considering the attractive pay, the number of hours I would work and especially the unlimited free flights to which I would be entitled.

[3]   My job as a baggage assistant did not involve, as I had first assumed, being clad in coveralls and crawling into the bellies of 727s to load and unload luggage. Rather, it consisted mostly of tagging and carrying passengers' bags and dealing with people whose baggage had mysteriously disappeared, as well as doing anything else that needed to be done, such as deplaning and boarding passengers, helping older or disabled passengers, taking reservations, and even making sure the planes were neatly groomed inside before the passengers came aboard.

[4]   From working at People Express, I learned a lot about the technical side of the airline industry. I now know about the importance of the weight distribution of a plane's cargo, how to open the hatches of both 727s and 737s, the seating capacity of each plane, and even the code names of dozens of airports in cities in both the United States and Europe.

[5]   Perhaps more important, I learned a lot about people. I learned that they can be extremely nice and helpful as well as intimidating and hostile. I realized that in order to work successfully with the public, you cannot take anything people say or do too seriously or personally. Often, something would happen where I had to bear bad news and thus had to receive the reactions. Most people are less than complacent when you tell them that they cannot get to West Palm Beach because the plane taking them there is snowed-in in Chicago.

Similarly, breaking the news that the last Newark flight of the night has been cancelled due to snow usually results in thousands of screaming Syracuse University students preparing to hurl duffle bags at you because they cannot get home to Long Island for Christmas and have to spend the night in the Syracuse airport.

[6]   However, along with the many hostile passengers, there were equally as many pleasant and amusing people. There were always people who complimented my co-workers and me on the good job we were doing, who offered us tips, who brought us Christmas cookies, and who even offered us cold drinks on hot summer days. These were the people who were easy to help and with whom you liked to spend time. There were also a great number of very funny people every day to offset the irate ones. Once, for example, I was helping an older Southern man with his bags, and on the way to the elevator he started questioning my religious convictions. He believed his mission in life was to travel around trying to convert airline personnel. As fate would have it, the elevator got stuck; this, according to the man, was a sign that I needed to be saved. Luckily, the car started up again and I *was* "saved."

[7]   As well as the passengers with whom I dealt so closely, the other People Express employees were enjoyable. Because the company is less than four years old, most of the people who work for it—baggage assistants, reservationists, and customer service managers (who serve both as the airline's managers at each airport and as flight attendants)—are all relatively young. No one I worked with was over the age of thirty-five and many of the employees were college students like myself. The fact that everyone was close in age seemed largely responsible for the feeling of equality that was present. Often, because of weather conditions, it was necessary to remain at the airport until long after midnight. It would have been extremely difficult to work twelve and fourteen-hour-days if the other employees were not, for the most part, enjoyable. The job's disadvantages, such as working long hours, carrying bags in ninety degree heat, and boarding and deplaning in sub-zero temperatures were outweighed by the advantage of working with good people.

[3]   When I returned to People Express at Christmastime to work, I realized what a "good" job I had had the previous summer. Even though I learned a lot about the airline business and about dealing with people, I did not fully realize the value of my job until January 6, when I left behind a snowy, sub-zero Syracuse and landed, free of charge, at Palm Beach International Airport, where it was a balmy eighty degrees. It was then that I really understood what a "good" job was.

I begin by dividing the class into groups of four or five students and ask them to make a list of the reasons why this was a good job. After about ten minutes we have a general discussion that goes something like this:

Teacher: Well, why was this a good job?
Student 1: The pay was good.
Student 2: You learn about the airline industry.
Student 3: You learn about working with the public.
Student 4: The employees were enjoyable to work with.
Student 5: Fringe benefits, like free trips.

Teacher: All right. This student gave us five good reasons why this was a worthwhile job. At the same time we also learned quite a bit about what the job entailed. What did we learn?

Student 1: You don't have to crawl in the bellies of 727s, but you tag and carry passengers' bags.

Student 2: You have to trouble-shoot when flights are canceled.

Teacher: That's fine, but let's take a look at how specific the information in the essay is. For example, what was the pay?

The writer doesn't tell us, and from here on, I point out that much of the information given in the paper is general rather than particular. We now make a list of things we do *not* know by reading the essay:

How many times did the student have to work twelve- or fourteen-hour days? (Paragraph 2 cites "the number of hours I would work" as an advantage of the job.)

What is the importance of the weight distribution of the plane's cargo?

How do you open the hatches?

What *do* you do when a flight is canceled?

The next step is to determine how much more specific the essay needs to be. I point out again that it does contain specific information and ask the class to identify those instances when they, as readers, felt that they needed to know more. For example, we decide that knowing how to open the hatches is not as important as knowing what the airline personnel do to pacify irate passengers when a flight is canceled, or what the pay and working hours actually are. I finish the lesson by drawing some conclusions about the difference between general and particular information, and the reasons why specific detail is important. The object of the exercise, then, is to have the class discover the precept for themselves before it is spelled out, since this way round their own experience of the specific reinforces the meaning of the generalization: "Be specific." (Incidentally, the class also discovered that, although the essay is clear and coherent, the writer needs to specify in the introduction that she returned to the job during Christmas vacation because the references to snowbound flights in an essay about a summer job were confusing—a confusion not clarified until the final paragraph in the essay as it stands.)

CLASS 2   I now use "A 'Good' Job" in a second workshop to teach definition. At the next class meeting, I point out to the students that they have been advancing on several fronts: In addition to discovering the need to be specific, they have learned something about unity, coherence, and organization. To illustrate, we briefly examine the essay's strengths in these three respects, and I show them how the writer uses topic sentences and transitions to achieve clarity. I next ask the class to identify the kind of exposition that the topic calls for. With a little prodding, we establish that they have written an analysis of a good or bad job and that analysis involves discovering the component parts of the topic. I remind the class that the component parts in the student essay we read were the reasons that the job with People Express was a good one. My next objective is to teach the difference between the abstract and the concrete in order to prepare the class for writing a definition of an abstract term. I ask the class to look at paragraph 7 of "A 'Good' Job."

> *Teacher:* What is being analyzed in this paragraph?
> *Student:* Good employees.
> *Teacher:* What are good employees, according to this writer?
> *Student:* Young people.
> *Teacher:* Do you agree?

(When I taught this a lively discussion ensued about the relative merits of working with one's own age group, about "ageism," and about the youth culture in America.) I return to paragraph 7.

> *Teacher:* Why did *this* writer like working with young people?
> *Student:* Because it gave a feeling of equality.
> *Teacher:* Would a feeling of equality have been equally important if you were a manager?

(This question elicited an anecdote from one of the students: promotion to a position of authority in her job—from salesperson to supervisor—had entailed an unexpected loss, since she now felt isolated from the easy-going camaraderie that went along with the former lack of status.)

I had intended to focus on *equality* as an abstraction in need of definition, but, as often happens, the discussion veered off in an unexpected direction, and I went along. I pointed out to the class that in the process of describing a good or bad job, they had begun to discover what the term *job satisfaction* means to them and that the next assignment would be to focus on this abstraction in order to define it.

WRITING
ASSIGNMENT 2

I put the new topic to be defined on the chalkboard: "Job Satisfaction." The class divides into groups as before, and each group prepares a list of essentials for job satisfaction. After ten minutes, we pool our requisites and classify them. The topic has divided into two categories of jobs: occasional work (part-time, summer jobs, temporary jobs, internships) and careers. Since undergraduates' sense of what a career entails is more theoretical than practical, I suggest they confine themselves to their own experience and write a definition of "Job Satisfaction" as it pertains to occasional work. For the prewriting stage, they use their essay on the best or worst job they have had as a draft, revising it as radically as necessary and building on it to focus on the question, "What contributed to, or detracted from, making this a satisfying job?" I suggest that their answer to this question should lead them to discover from three to five essential ingredients of job satisfaction, ingredients that clarify the meaning of the topic by making it more concrete. Next, they should illustrate what they mean—the final step toward concreteness—with examples from their own experience.

Most college composition texts have good examples of definition essays to supplement the work in our second class. I have found the following useful:

W. H. Auden, "Water of Life," in *Forewords and Afterwords* (New York: Random House, 1952).

E. H. Carr, "The Historian and His Facts," in *What Is History?* (New York: Knopf, 1961).

Bergen Evans, "Sophisticated," in *Comfortable Words* (New York: Random House, 1962).

Lester Thurow, "A Zero-Sum Game," in *The Zero-Sum Society* (New York: Basic Books, 1980).

E. B. White, "Democracy," in *The Wild Flag* (Boston: Houghton Mifflin, 1943, 1971).

A Lesson in Organization

Elray L. Pedersen,
Brigham Young University

Teacher: I am going to read to you a list of ten items. Listen carefully to the list of items as I read them. Do not take notes. When I have completed the reading of the list, I will ask you to list as many items as you can remember, in the same order I read them. Ready? OK, here is your list:

Steel . . . belt . . . stockings . . . iron . . . necktie . . . shoes . . . shirt . . . lead . . . pants . . . hat. . . .

Now write as many items as you can recall. (*Students write.*) Check your answers with the ones I now read. (Read list from above, saying "1, *steel;* 2, *belt;*" etc.) By the show of hands, how many of you got ten right? Nine right in order? (*Continue down to one right.*) Why did so few of you get just over half of the items even though I told you you would have to list all items after I read them?

Student: The list was too long and the list had too many different items in it.

Teacher: Yes. Any other comments?

Student: Yah. Let me give you a list and see how many items you remember. I'll bet you won't do any better.

Teacher: Let me give you the ten items on the list all over again. Then try to list each item, one through ten, after I have finished giving you this new list.

hat . . . necktie . . . shirt . . . belt . . . pants . . . stockings . . . shoes . . . iron . . . lead . . . steel. . . .

Now try to list as many of the ten items as you can in the order they were read to you.

Check your own answers. Remember, items are in order. Here is the list as I gave it to you: *hat, necktie, shirt, belt, pants, stockings, shoes, iron, lead,* and *steel.* How many got a higher score this time?

Students: (*Almost all raise their hands.*)

Teacher: What factors do you think helped you to do better the second time?

Student: Well, one thing, we had heard the list before, and we were familiar with some of the items on the list.

Teacher: Yes, but knowing what items were on the list would not help you to know in what order to list the items. Did any of you recognize a pattern, a system, an order?

Another Student: I noticed that at the end metals were mentioned. I used the alphabet to remember which metal came first and which came last.

Teacher: We have some very perceptive students in this class.

How many numbers are there in an average telephone number?

Student: Seven.

Teacher: George Miller, a psychologist, wrote an article called "Seven, Plus or Minus Two" in which he shows that most people are able to recall up to seven items, sometimes more, sometimes fewer. It is interesting to know, however, that if the items are combined according to a system or code of some kind, we often can remember more than six or seven in a row. Often this system or code is called *organization.*

(Writes on the board the following five words: *book, numbers, lists, that, telephone.*) What do the five words on the board mean?

Students: (*Different guesses, all suggesting confusion.*)

Teacher: What would you say if I said that the first two words are *that book*? Could you make a sentence then?

Student: Yes, you would be saying, "That book lists telephone numbers."

Teacher: Yes, notice how the Subject/Verb/Object pattern of organization in English sentences helps us to convey an idea rather than a jumble. Using patterns or systems of ordering or grouping items is called *organization.* Organization helps us to see relationships among things. Organization helps us to put similar things into categories so that we can remember the parts and the items that form the parts instead of trying to remember or deal with every single thing at once.

Three hundred and fifty years before Christ, Aristotle, the Greek scholar and philosopher, began breaking all areas of knowledge into various subjects: *music, rhetoric, mathematics, logic,* and so on—all to help us systematize and organize knowledge into parts.

(*Taking out a large bag filled with groceries.*) Let's look at what is in this shopping bag. (Placing all items on the desk.) Suppose for a minute that we wanted a single word to talk about all of the items I have placed on this desk. What single word might be useful to talk about the items on the desk?

Student: How about *things*?

Teacher: Of course *things* might work, but *things* is so general that we could use the word for almost anything in the class or outside the class. Try another word. . . .

Student: Groceries!

Teacher: All right, let's accept *groceries.* All of the things on the desk are groceries. Now let us break the term *groceries* into two different words. If I chose *perishables* for one category, what would the other word be?

Student: Perishables and *non-perishables*. *Non-perishables*.

Teacher: OK. Are these two the only categories we might use to talk about groceries? What do you think?

Student: How about canned goods and non-canned goods or milk products and non-milk products. Anything that might be meaningful. . . .

Teacher: Already you are grasping two key points about organization. First, we must know what the idea or concept is that we are dealing with; second, we must be able to break that key idea down into a few meaningful parts—often only two, three, four, or five parts. Remember Seven Plus or Minus Two? Sometimes having too many parts weakens the unity and relationships of our ideas.

Suppose we want to break the term *groceries* into three parts instead of two. Suggest three appropriate terms.

Student: Fruits and vegetables.

Teacher: Dairy products.

Student: Meats.

Teacher: Good. These are as good as any, but there are no right ways to divide something into categories. There are only appropriate and effective ways to establish categories.

We could easily make a *topic outline* out of our *groceries* exercise by doing the following (moving to the board, writing *groceries* at the top of the board.)

After writing *groceries* at the top of our outline, we can list two or three or four Roman numerals for meaningful categories that we want to list as parts of *groceries*. Let's list now some categories for the groceries on the desk.

Groceries

I.   Canned goods
II. Non-canned goods
III. Meat products

IN-CLASS
EXERCISE 1 What we have just created is a topic outline. Sometimes we write outlines briefly by just naming the ideas. This is a *topic outline*. Sometimes we write our ideas down in complete sentences. This is a *sentence outline*. Read the following five sentences, think about them, and then determine which of the five is the overall idea that is being discussed. Write that idea as the *thesis statement* in the following *sentence outline*. Then list the four other statements logically in the outline as points I, II, III, or IV.

Roses and Children

THESIS STATEMENT:
I.
II.
III.
IV.

Like childhood diseases, diseases of roses can be treated through proper examination and care.

Growing prize roses requires much care and attention, like the rearing of children.

Proper training of roses, like the proper training of children, helps the flowers to stand tall.

Good nutrition helps roses and children grow properly.

Timely cultivation enriches the growth environment of both roses and children.

Teacher: This handout presents the problem of finding the best possible sequence for the statements given; the next handout presents an exercise in summarizing in a thesis statement.

IN-CLASS
EXERCISE 2

(Handing out a copy of the following *sentence outline* directs the students to look at each point in the outline, carefully noting what is being said.)

Outline

THESIS:
I.   Poor leadership hindered the efforts of the Donner Party.
II. Poor decisions hindered the efforts of the Donner Party.
III. Internal bickering hindered the efforts of the Donner Party.
IV. A feeling of fatalism hindered the efforts of the members of the Donner Party.

Teacher: Now based on the four points of the outline, write a *thesis statement* that summarizes the key points of the outline. Realize that at different times, for different reasons, we use one of several devices for organizing our ideas: *time* (chronological order); *setting* (spatial arrangement); deduction (thesis first, then key points); *induction* (a buildup to the main idea at the end); *comparison* (showing similarities between two things), and *contrast* (showing differences between two things); *defining* (saying what something is and is not); *logic* (using such things as cause-and-effect reasoning); *process* (using a sequence of steps or events); and *analogy* (discussing something unknown in terms of something known).

WRITING
ASSIGNMENT

You are to practice *organization* and *outlining* by completing a 500–1000-word paper for which you go to the library and dig up newspapers covering local, national, and international events that occurred on or around the day of your birth. To help you organize and present the material you may use either a Topic or a Sentence Outline, which should be turned in at the same time.

At a later point in the term we read and analyze E. M. Forster's "My Wood" as a striking example of clarity in organization.

LESSON READING

E. M. Forster, "My Wood," in *Abinger Harvest* (Orlando, FL: Harcourt Brace Jovanovich, 1936).

How Do You Know? Show Me

Tracy S. Flood,
University of Texas

This series of lessons addresses the problem I find most vexing in student writing: a frequent and nearly exclusive reliance on generalities, which strand the reader in the puzzling and unsatisfying realm of abstraction. This often translates as "needs development," or "be more specific" in my comments, which the students can respond to when they revise. But the most important thing I can do as a teacher is to help them "hear" editorial comments throughout the writing process, not just after they've turned the essay in. These lessons, by concentrating on concrete evidence in both reading and writing assignments, help students cultivate an internal voice, a questioning voice that demands full and specific development *as they compose.* At the end of class 2 they will also have generated material for a personal narrative essay.

CLASS 1 In class I ask the students to list ten or fifteen memorable events from their own lives—not necessarily monumental ones, but events they would include in a notebook if they had one. I remind them that Joan Didion in "On Keeping a Notebook," writes about rather small events, significant for what they tell her about herself or other people. Then, while we turn to the reading, we set aside this first bit of prewriting.

To begin discussion I write "shipping heiress" on the board and ask what we know about her; student responses go on the board: "She's rich," "self-centered," "selfish." Now we have generalities to work with.

Teacher: These are good *general* summaries; now let's be *specific.* (Write both words on the board.) How do you *know* she's like this?
Student: Didion says so.
Teacher: Where? Show me. (*Never be satisfied with unsupported answers; this will show the students that supporting an answer must begin here—at the thinking stage.*)
Student: Well, she didn't really come out and say so.
Teacher: Then how do you know? Show me.

Student: Well, the heiress sits in a room full of orchids and doesn't even know that it's snowing outside.

Teacher: Good. So Didion doesn't *tell* you the heiress is "selfish," she uses specifics, concrete details, and lets you draw your own conclusions. Why is that more interesting reading than "she's selfish" would have been?

We continue listing the concrete details that brought us to our general conclusions and do the same for Mrs. Minnie S. Brooks and even for Didion. I continually emphasize the effectiveness of specific writing, writing that gives the reader something solid to latch on to. My repeated "How do you know?" and "Show me" become such a common refrain that the students begin to take it up without prompting. But they'll need more work on using specific detail in their own writing. I write *person* on the board.

Teacher: Is that specific or general?
Students: General.
Teacher: How about *short woman*? (*I add this to the board.*)
Student: Better, but still pretty general.
Teacher: OK. How about *petite, red-headed woman*? (*Students like this, but I encourage them to make her even more concrete.*)
Student: Let's say she's impatient.
Teacher: Let's not say it; how can we show it?

After many suggestions, revisions, and continued proddings to "show me," we have:

Absent-mindedly smacking her pink bubble gum, and rapidly tapping her pencil against the table top, the petite, red-headed waitress shifted from one foot to the other and sighed loudly, practically daring the man to order breakfast.

A bit unwieldly and overwritten perhaps, but we're beginning to create a one-of-a-kind portrait. I underline the adjectives, adverbs, nouns, verbs that help specify this particular person. Now I ask the students to take their list of personal events home, choose the one that seems most promising as a paper topic, and list thirty-five to forty specific facts about it.

WRITING ASSIGNMENT

For the next class I assign Alice Walker's "When the Other Dancer Is the Self" and ask students to write one paragraph (and *only one*) in response to the following:

Choose one concrete image from Walker's essay and explain its effect in the story. Why is it significant?

CLASS 2

When they come to class, I ask two or three volunteers to put their paragraphs on the board. Typically, some will still focus on generalities: "Her happiness as a child is one concrete detail I found effective." Rather than being disappointed, I now have new material for again distinguishing abstract/general from concrete/specific. With my now predictable "How do you know?" I push the student to pick out the details that drove her to such a conclusion about "happiness." With luck you'll also have a paragraph that focuses on one concrete detail from the story, like the sample paragraph I've included at the end. The "crimson curtain" simile from this student's paragraph lets us talk about similes and metaphors as effective ways to make a point clear, to develop it for the reader. Describing an event, object, feeling, or person in terms of something else surprises the reader with the unexpected. As in the student example, an accurate simile can evoke an "Aha! So, that's exactly what she means!" or "Wow! I hadn't ever seen it that way before." And that's what accurate, concrete writing is all about. Encouraging student writers to *use* metaphors improves their writing for the same reason—the element of surprise. Having to search for just the right comparison pushes students to see something very familiar to them in surprising new ways, to abandon clichéd thinking, and to move beyond simple adjectives and adverbs without abandoning concreteness. *Any* student paragraph, however, provides material for re-emphasizing the general–specific distinction, as well as for pointing out the specific support needed to develop the paragraph itself. If a paragraph needs more development, we revise it as a class.

As one more board exercise I'll ask a general question:

Teacher: What is Ms. Walker like at the end of the piece?
Student: She's neat. You know, she's come to terms with her eye. I write the response on the board, in a slightly edited form, and ask, "How do you know?"
Student: Well, you know, she had that dream.
Teacher: What was the dream about? Be specific.
Student: About dancing with her other self; I guess the other self is the part of her she never liked—her eye. And now she can dance with it.
Teacher: Formulate that as a sentence.

Together, we edit for the board, adding to the first responses. I ask more questions:

Teacher: How does that contrast with the way she used to be?
Student: She hated her eye.
Teacher: How do you know?

The students are learning that I want evidence—not just abstractions. We put relevant information on the board, working out the sentences together. When we exhaust the subject, I announce, "Look, you've written the first draft of a paragraph here. One main idea, specific support, lots of development. Concrete evidence." They're surprised, pleased; and they're learning that my questions are the same ones they need to ask as they write: How do you know? Can you show me?

Now I ask them to evaluate their personal event "fact list" (see Class 1) for concreteness, as I circulate and offer suggestions. Someone will invariably be listing facts about "the last summer of my childhood" or something equally vast. Every item demands a separate paper, so I suggest that they "choose one and start over." This suggestion elicits groans—many people are trying to cover too much and will write too generally as a result. We talk about the importance of writing about a small event from an abundance of detailed material, rather than trying to skip superficially through many events. They are learning to be specific but need more encouragement. One student may list "hot day" among his bits of information.

Teacher: Is that a concrete detail? Can the reader see, feel, experience, share that hot day? How did you know it was hot?
Student: I could feel the asphalt through my sneakers.
Teacher: What else?
Student: My cheeks were red; perspiration kept dripping down my back.
Teacher: And what did you see?
Student: I could see trees in the distance; they looked wavy because of the heat radiating off of the parking lot.

We continue working as I press for specific details and put them on the board; everyone finds these tidbits more interesting than "it was hot" could ever be. I continue to circulate, plucking generalities from several lists for development on the board. A statement like "he was the best friend I ever had" may become an entire scene or series of scenes in which the student recounts concrete shared experiences with this friend. As the students begin to see what it means to write more specifically, I ask them to finish their lists at home, increasing the number of specific details until they've satisfied that now-demanding inner voice. With such a list of abundant material, they can begin to draft a paper.

WRITING ASSIGNMENT 2	In a 500-word essay tell the story of an event that has special significance for you. The event can be as life-changing as Alice Walker's eye injury, or it can be very small, as some of the events in Joan Didion's notebook were. In either case you should tell the story so that your audience will know why it's important to you. Perhaps it taught you something, changed the way you see yourself, or gave you a new perspective on a familiar person, place, or situation. You should not, however, explicitly spell out the "moral" of your story, but should let the story speak for itself. As we saw in our reading, small details and concrete images usually speak louder than long explanations and vague generalities; so be sure to pay special attention to the kinds of concrete images that will help your reader see and understand what you want to say.

Sample student paragraph (see Class 2):

I think one outstanding concrete detail from Walker's essay is "I watch as its trunk, its branches, and then its leaves are blotted out by the rising blood." It stands out because it describes *how* she last saw the tree before she was blinded. First, the trunk disappears, then the branches, then the leaves, as if a crimson curtain is rising over her right eye, fading to black. The detail is effective because it helps your imagination picture this event.[1]

LESSON READINGS

Joan Didion, "On Keeping a Notebook," in *Slouching Towards Bethlehem* (New York: Farrar Straus Giroux, 1966, 1967).
Alice Walker, "When the Other Dancer Is the Self," in *In Search of Our Mothers' Gardens* (Orlando, FL: Harcourt Brace Jovanovich, 1983), pp. 384–393.

---

[1] Used with student permission

Theme and Variations: The Concept of Audience

George D. Gopen,
Duke University

Since most students instinctively change their rhetoric to fit their audience, our task is to make them conscious of what they have been doing all along. Once aware of the concept, they can learn to become skilled at it. This assignment brings on that awareness and opens the door to any number of further exercises.

CLASS 1 Hypothetical: You are a junior, pre-med. (This is a particular bit of role-playing that many of them welcome.) You have been a biology major from the start, intent on getting into medical school because, well, because you have been intent on getting into medical school. Your freshman advisor was an interesting and interested man from the Psychology Department who, from the start, has been counseling you that your real interest and aptitude is in the social sciences, probably in psychology, and that you have been pursuing a pre-med course out of peer and parental pressure. As a junior, you now see the light and recognize he has been right all along. You decide to change your major to psychology and give up the pre-med courses.

IN-CLASS 1. Write a note of about four sentences to your advisor, informing him of
EXERCISES   your decision to switch fields. This should take about five minutes.

2. (after five minutes): Write a second note, same length, same information, to the chairperson of the Biology Department.

3. (after another five minutes): Write a third note, same length and information, to your favorite biology professor.

4. (after another five minutes): Write a paragraph of a letter to your parents informing them of your decision.

5. (after another five minutes): Write a paragraph of a letter to your best friend back home telling him or her about it.

95

This writing has posed little threat to any of the students. They are in control of the substance and are familiar with the styles. I am careful not to mention the concept of audience at any time before this assignment, so they have no idea why I am having them do this. There tend to be groans at the announcement of the third task, laughs at the announcement of the fourth. I take care to let them know that the fifth is the last. Then I have them vote:

1. Which of the five was the hardest to write?
2. Which of the five was the easiest to write?
3. Which of the five do you consider the best written?
4. Which of the five do you consider the worst written?

I record their votes on a large grid on the blackboard. Typically, several zeros appear. No one finds a best friend the hardest to write to, and only an occasional student admits to his or her parents' getting that vote; no one finds the favorite biology professor the easiest communication task; and so forth.

Students tend to be intrigued but not fundamentally surprised that so many large numbers and so many small numbers or zeros appear. As a group they have voted some generalizations into being. At this point I try to get them to articulate those generalizations by asking "Why?" of all the interesting numbers. Why did no one think the note to the chairperson was the best writing of the five? Why did no one think the paragraph to the best friend was the best writing? Why did so many think this paragraph the easiest? They begin to understand that instinctively they differentiate between audiences: Here is the same information being transmitted five times, but in five styles and of five qualities, all by the same writer. This is the moment to make explicit the concept of *audience* and to show them not that they *should* do it but that they *already* do it.

CLASS 2   Then I break the class up into groups of four or five students and have them read to each other their versions of note 1 (the one to the advisor). I ask them to analyze the stylistic similarities between these versions, attempting to get them to see what tone or approach a particular audience led them to adopt. We are progressing at this point from the realization *that* they took note of their audience to an understanding of *how* they did it.

When the conversation in the small groups begins to die down, I have them move on to reading aloud their individual versions of note 2 (to the biology chairperson). I ask them to repeat the process of the paragraph above, but this time they are to go further and compare the stylistic similarities engendered by the chairperson as audience with those engendered by the advisor as audience. They often discover, for example, that when they are faced with the more formal task of addressing the chairperson, they tend to shift the action from the verb, where it belongs, to nominalizations; or they take twice as long to get into the substance of a sentence;

or they consistently write sentences of the same length, either markedly short or markedly long; or they use longer, more latinate words in profusion. The details may vary from group to group, but the patterns are distinct enough for freshmen to be able to perceive them.

The students continue this process until they have covered all five writings. The cross-referencing can become quite complex by the end.

WRITING ASSIGNMENT   The gate is now open to all sorts of further assignments. They are now ready to try their hands at audience analysis of published prose, or at peer review of their most recent out-of-class assignment for the purpose of identifying audience-influenced stylistic decisions. After this initial exposure, the concept of audience can easily become a leitmotif threaded through the rest of the course.

The Writer's Character Is Always Artificial

Richard A. Filloy,
University of Oregon

This lesson is designed to help beginning composition students become aware of the creation of ethos (a writer's implied character in nonfictive discourse) and how they can begin to gain control over the personalities they project when they write. Before they can achieve these two goals, however, many of them must become aware that what we perceive about a writer's ethos is not an accident or something "natural," but the result of craft. To introduce this idea in a way that will catch their attention, I begin the lesson by proposing to them that a successful ethos is always artificial and that if they want to become really accomplished writers, they must learn to create an artificial personality too.

Of course this proposition usually elicits some protest, which gives us a chance to consider the meaning of the word *artificial*. Once we have established that the original meaning of the word is not *false* but *made by art* (useful cognates are *artifice* and *artifact*), the general point can be made that writing is always artificial and can only succeed with awareness and practice of the art. Students usually agree that letting others know what sort of person you are with words alone is a task requiring some art, even if you want to tell nothing but the truth. They can also readily see that it's even harder to establish what you are like when you are talking about some topic other than yourself and come into the discussion only indirectly.

At this point it's useful to illustrate these ideas by discussion of a short essay in which the writer gives us a clear sense of character. Many essays work well for this purpose, but for best and fullest effect a second essay by the same author showing a contrasting character is necessary. Among those authors I've used successfully for this assignment are Joan Didion, Virginia Woolf, G. B. Shaw, and E. B. White, all of whom exhibit contrasting sides of themselves in fairly short essays. My favorite starting place for this lesson, however, is George Orwell's "The Sporting Spirit." Orwell's anti-sporting stance is usually a shock to student unfamiliar with the essay and invites them to consider what sort of a person would hold such opinions.

One characteristic students readily perceive is Orwell's skepticism about

98

received opinion and his confidence and fearlessness in opposing it. With prompting, they can usually discover a number of key sentences in which he establishes this trait. Here are a few examples:

- "I am always amazed when I hear people saying that sport creates goodwill between nations. . . ." (Note how *always amazed* establishes a tone of utter confidence where a more cautious character might write, "It isn't clear that sport creates . . ." or, "I've never really believed that sport creates . . ." or, "I've often wondered whether. . . .")
- "Instead of blah-blahing about the clean, healthy rivalry of the football field and the great part played by the Olympic Games in bringing nations together, it is more useful to inquire how the modern cult of sport arose." (Again we can see the scornful dismissal of common opinion in the use of *blah-blahing* and *cult of sport.*)
- "it is possible to say publicly what many thinking people were saying privately. . . ." (This particularly ingenious little clause not only proclaims Orwell's courage in speaking publicly and his status as a thinking person but also implies the agreement of other thinking people with his position.)

To dispel the idea that what Orwell has done here is "natural" or accidental, we can begin by considering how alternative phrasings of these sentences convey other characteristics. It can be a valuable exercise to ask students to suggest how the sentences might be rephrased and consider the different effects produced. To reinforce this point, Orwell's character in this essay can be usefully contrasted with his much less confident and less skeptical character in "Some Thoughts on the Common Toad," where he defends his devotion to nature against those who consider it sentimental and apolitical. The tone is distinctly cautious and conciliatory, with none of the abruptness and insistence of "The Sporting Spirit." Here are some examples:

- "I mention the spawning of toads because it is one of the phenomena of spring which deeply appeals to me. . . . But I am aware that many people do not like reptiles or amphibians, and I am not suggesting that in order to enjoy spring you have to take an interest in toads." (Note the almost embarrassed confession of an attraction to toads and the rush to reassure the audience that he recognizes this as an idiosyncrasy and does not demand their agreement.)
- "The other idea seems to me to be wrong in a subtler way. Certainly we ought to be discontented, we ought not simply to find out ways of making the best of a bad job, and yet if we kill all pleasure in the actual process of life, what sort of future are we preparing for ourselves?" (Note how *seems wrong* softens the disagreement and contrasts with the certainty of Orwell's disagreement with opponents in "The Sport-

ing Spirit." The second sentence offers further concession to the expected opposition before introducing Orwell's own point.)

- "I have always suspected that if our economic and political problems are ever solved, life will become simpler instead of more complex. . . . I think that by retaining one's childhood love of such things as trees, fishes, butterflies and—to return to my first instance—toads, one makes a peaceful and decent future a little more probable. . . ." (Again *suspected* is crucial in establishing the cautious tone, which is reinforced by *I think* in the following sentence. Both these assertions could be much more forcefully put simply by omitting everything in the introductory clauses and stating the main ideas as independent clauses. We know Orwell is capable of such force, so he must have chosen to be more gentle here.)

Once students see the difference in these two characters and the choices of expression which bring them about, the teacher can quickly make several important further points:

1. The differences in character result from different assessments of the audience (who they are and what they are likely to accept) and from differences in the intended effect (shock, agreement, sympathy, etc.) of the essay. So a writer's character is ideally created with the audience and the aim of the essay in mind.

2. Although the characters in these essays are different, there is no reason to believe that either of them is false or deceitful. They simply result from Orwell's expressing different facets of himself in different contexts, something we all do. Thus conscious control of the characters we project is not a dirty trick but a legitimate part of communicating fully and effectively.

3. The most effective indications of a writer's character are often indirect and may depend on fairly subtle choices of words or expressions. Diction is a matter not simply of "What am I trying to say?" but also of "What am I trying to do?" and "How can I do it?" Therefore control of the characters we project as writers depends on careful attention to how we express ourselves and often requires adjustments to our first efforts. These adjustments are an important part of the revision that changes a rough draft to a finished essay.

With these points in mind, I make a series of related assignments:

1. Take home a photocopy of another student's essay (students will have each brought in a photocopy of a previous essay) and read it closely to discover the characteristics of the personality projected. Mark any passages that convey these characteristics. Why and how do they convey them? To give students the idea of what sort of thing they are looking for, the teacher should draw their attention to a passage and ask, "What kind of person would put it this way?" and, "What about this passage tells you something about what kind of person this writer is?" and,

"Why do you think the writer decided to appear this way?" After this guidance, students can be asked to find their own examples and supply their own answers to the questions.

WRITING
ASSIGNMENT

2. When next you write an essay, turn in a brief (three- or four-sentence) description of the important characteristics of the personality you have tried to assume and show why these are useful, given the aims of the essay and your expectations concerning audience. (*Note:* I read the essay first and the description afterward and then comment on how successfully the piece conveys the personality intended. I also offer suggestions about the appropriateness of the personality the student has chosen for this essay and for the projected audience.)

3. Rewrite the essay responding to the teacher's comments. The original essay should accompany the revision and be clearly marked to indicate where changes have been made so that the teacher can easily compare the two versions.

LESSON READING

George Orwell, "The Sporting Spirit" and "Some Thoughts on the Common Toad," in *The Collected Essays, Journalism and Letters of George Orwell*, Vol. IV, eds. Sonia Orwell and Ian Angus (Orlando, FL: Harcourt Brace Jovanovich, 1968), pp. 40–44, 141–145.

Capital *I:* The Joys of Egocentricity

Frederick K. Lang,
Brooklyn College, City University of New York

What has already been said on the subject is undoubtedly true. To write autobiographically is to risk being monotonous, self-absorbed, dependent on resources that may prove limited. Many editors and writing teachers recommend that the first person singular be used only occasionally. Yet that advice clashes with other advice of more immediate use. How to generate rich material? Write from experience; begin with deep personal concerns. How to develop a clear, forceful style? Use the active voice; rely on specific verbs to express actions and conditions. If the writer's own self comes first as subject, then it will be the likeliest grammatical agent. And attempting to camouflage the first person singular is usually a messy business. Solidifying each action or condition into a noun, then gluing the chunks together with the verb *to be* is a familiar ploy that results in vagueness, pompous diction, or sheer incoherence. Just as familiar and just as awkward are the pronominal substitutions. *One* sounds affected; a generic *you* causes confusion. Particularly with inexperienced writers, *we* can encourage banality, make it very difficult to get beyond popular opinion, common knowledge. Often students understand a prohibition against the first person singular to mean that they should look to other sources, including published ones. The result is recycled ideas and phrases, whether innocent borrowing or systematic plagiarism.

In freshman composition the continual use of the first person singular must be the first course requirement. An inexperienced writer has to begin with himself or herself, the subject on which he or she is an authority. By constantly, systematically writing sentences that begin with *I*, he or she becomes an even greater authority, gets to know much better the person being signified. And this "author" soon finds relevant the primary sense of the word *authority:* he or she has gained more control over the material, acquired the power to develop it, even transform it. Casual autobiography, a promiscuous use of the first person singular, tends to bring on the risks I mentioned at the outset. I am advocating structured autobiography, an almost programmatic use of *I.*

Teaching inexperienced writers to do research papers is considered so difficult that the attempt is usually put off until near the end of the semester. And that usually means too little too late. The research paper should be introduced the first day of class, the day on which the students learn their teacher's name, and he or she tries to learn as many of theirs as possible. Even this familiar ritual can be transformed into an occasion for writing. Students can be assigned the task of doing research on their names: They must find out what their names mean and how they originated. There are books on the subject, but dictionaries are just as useful. Once students have the information, they can respond to it. I have found that the best way to present such an assignment to writers who have yet to learn how to organize material is to give them a list of questions. As they answer the questions in sequence, they simultaneously compose and organize the essay. (The signals I give here result in very short paragraphs. However, not only are such paragraphs appropriate in an essay that is almost journalistic in its compressed presentation of fact and response, but indenting often gets writers who don't know what a paragraph is used to paragraphing. When, later in the semester, students must develop ideas rather than just provide information, they feel the need for longer paragraphs, and so produce them; but having had to indent repeatedly in earlier assignments leaves them with a vivid sense of the paragraph as a discrete unit of prose.)

"As his name is, so is he" (I Samuel 25:25):
What does your first name mean? Why did your parents give it to you?

Is there a traditional way of naming children in your family? Are you named for a relative or family friend? after a biblical figure, saint, historical personage or celebrity? What do you find most interesting about your name's original bearer? What do you have in common?

How do you feel about your first name? Does it suit you? How has it influenced the development of your personality? affected the way people treat you? If it hasn't, how did this miracle come about?

What nicknames have you had? How have they suited you? affected you? What nickname would you choose for yourself? Why?

(Take my questions about your first name and apply as many of them as you can to your middle name. Forget those about "influence" and "nicknames.")

Do you like to use your middle name? your middle initial? Does your middle name add to or detract from your first?

What does your last name mean? Is it taken from the name of a trade? a geographical area? a master or feudal lord? What do you find interesting about the source of your family name? (Please find something.)

How did the name pass to your family? Has it ever been changed? Does it suit your family?

How do you feel about your last name? How has it influenced you? affected the way people treat you? If it hasn't, how did this miracle come about? Have you ever encountered prejudice because of your name? Do people ever mispronounce or misspell it? (If so, please give me examples.)

What first and last names would you choose if you had to change your name? Why?

How would you feel about using your husband's family name? about your wife's using her family name instead of yours? about using both family names in combination?

What would you name your children? Why? (Please try to imagine yourself having at least one boy and one girl.)

What do you think now about the quotation from Samuel?

It is not necessary to have students read up on the psychological significance of names. But giving them even a brief article can enhance the assignment. They will then be able to offer more developed and sophisticated responses to some of the questions. A class of advanced or particularly promising students can be required to consult more, and more complex, sources. There can be greater sophistication at the other end of the process as well. Students can be asked to use one of the techniques for acknowledging sources: notes or parenthetical references. And the subtleties of paraphrase and quotation can be explored. With very inexperienced writers, though—a remedial class, for example—it is best just to have them weave material from sources into their own prose, mentioning titles or authors as they proceed.

WRITING ASSIGNMENT 2

Students can then be given another list of questions, this one pertaining to their education. Now they are being asked to discuss their "educational roots":

What do you think I'll find most fascinating, or at least unusual, about your educational experiences? (Don't go into detail here; just get me interested.) What aspect of your education has affected you the most? Why? the least? Why? How would you sum up your entire educational experience? (The answer to this last question is your *thesis statement.*)

How would you sum up your experience in elementary school? (The answer to this question is your *topic sentence.*) Where and when did you go to elementary school? (Be specific: name, location, dates.) What was your elementary school like? What did it give you? What did it fail to give you? How did you leave your mark on this school? If you didn't leave your mark, why not?

How would you sum up your experience in junior high school? (Right: your *topic sentence.*) Where and when did you go to junior high school? (Again, be specific: name, location, dates.) What was your junior high school like? What did it give you? fail to give you? How did you leave your mark on this school? If you didn't leave your mark, why not?

How would you sum up your experience in high school? (Right again: your *topic sentence.*) Where and when did you go to high school? (Yes, be specific once again.) What was your high school like? What did it give you? fail to give you? How did you leave your mark on this school? If you didn't leave your mark, why not?

How would you sum up your experience at this college? (Of course it's your *topic sentence!*) What is it like? What is its history? (Here's where the college bulletin will come in handy.) What is the college giving you? failing to give you? What contributions are you making to the college? If you aren't making any, why not?

How would you sum up the influence that your education has had on you? How would you sum up the influence it's failed to have? What's one important aspect of your education you would change? Why? What important insight into your educational experiences has doing this paper given you? If you haven't gained any insight, why not? What do you want your education to be like in the near future? (Be general here.) Why?

Indicating in parentheses the function of particular sentences is optional, but it is an easy way to introduce students to rhetorical patterns. In this assignment too the research is minimal, the organization rudimentary. Yet such a paper is quite an accomplishment for inexperienced writers, and in writing it they acquire both important skills and much-needed confidence. There are also fringe benefits: Probably for the first time the student will consult the college bulletin. Most important, students are both displaying themselves and moving outside themselves. That is, they are making connections between their own lives and institutional histories, and evaluating both the institutions and their performances with respect to them.

WRITING ASSIGNMENT 3   Though not the last of my "exterior" assignments, the following is the last I present as a list of questions. It is offered here in its complete form, but I want to stress that it can easily be subdivided or expanded, depending on the preference of the instructor, the abilities of the students. The focus can be narrowed to just a single aspect of selfhood: "family history," for example. On the other hand, students can be required to do more extensive research: to consult other sources besides family members, neighbors, and similar "oral historians." And, again, the presentation of the essay will be as casual, or as formal, as the instructor deems fit. I call this assignment the "self-portrait":

Family History

Who makes up your immediate family? What are they like?

What is the history of your family on your mother's side? on your father's side? (Go back as far as you can.)

Are there documents (letters, diaries, official record, etc.) that relate to your family history? What do they tell you? If there aren't any, why not?

Besides your mother and father, who in your family has been an important influence on you? Why? Of all the relations who died before you were born, who do you find the most interesting on your mother's side of the family? Why? on your father's side? Why? (Go back as far as you like.)

What is the last place where your mother's family lived before the place where your mother was born? where your father's family lived before the place where your father was born? What are these two places like? What are their histories? How do these two places compare?

How did the place leave its mark on your mother's family? How did the family leave its mark on the place? (Apply these questions to the other place and your father's family.) If there was no mutual influence of any sort, why not?

How does your mother's family compare with your father's, past and present? (Mention economic background, occupations, attitudes, specific relatives, and so on.)

The Day You Were Born

When were you born, and where? What was the place you were born like? (Describe the hospital and the neighborhood it's in; also describe the town or city if you weren't born in New York City.)

What of significance was happening in the world the day you were born? Which events have had some sort of effect on you and your life? How so? If there have been no aftereffects, why not?

According to astrological sources, what is the destiny the day (and time) of your birth determined for you? How does what has happened compare with what should have happened?

What is the religious significance of the day you were born? (Even if you're not religious, please study the "calendar" of at least one religion.) Has the religious significance of the day you were born touched on your life in any way? If not, why not?

Where were the members of your immediate family the day you were born? What were they doing around the time of your birth?

Where You Live

What is your neighborhood like? What is its history?

If you've lived in another place—what is it like, what is its history, and how does it compare with where you live now?

How has your neighborhood left its mark on you and your family? How have you and your family left your mark on the neighborhood? If there has been no mutual influence of any sort, why not?

If you've lived in another place—how did it leave its mark on you and your family, and how did you and your family leave your mark on it? If there was no mutual influence of any sort, why not?

How does where you live now compare with where your mother's family lived (the place you described in the "family history" section)? with where your father's family lived?

What would be different about you and your way of life if you lived in the first place? in the second? If nothing would be different, why not?

Introduction

What do you think is most fascinating, or at least unusual, in your self-portrait? (Don't go into detail here; just try to get me interested.)

What area (family history, name, etc.) are you emphasizing most in your paper? Why? least? And why?

Which of my questions are easy for you to answer? difficult to answer? impossible? Why, why, and why? Which of my questions are you unwilling to answer? Why?

What particular problems did you run into while doing your research? What are some of your ingenious solutions?

Conclusion

Looking back on your self-portrait, do you find people, experiences, and situations that have been major influences, for better or for worse, on the course of your life? If so, who or what are they, and why have they been so influential?

What "substitutions" (environment, schooling, and so on) would you like to have been able to make in your life? Why?

Has doing this self-portrait paper made you see yourself differently, at least a little? If so, how? If not, why not?

In a few sentences how would you best describe yourself at this point in your life?

Putting the sequence of questions for the introduction just before that for the conclusion makes students aware that an effective introduction cannot be written until the body of the essay has already been composed. A writer must be completely familiar with his or her material before it can properly be introduced. And, again, the more advanced the students, the more advanced the research they can be required to do. They might, for example, be asked to go back generations with respect to both family and geographical area. Even if they respond just to the questions I have listed, students begin to "find themselves"—to see how they have come to be the people they are, how the world around them has both shaped and inhibited their development. They move from pure egocentricity to a kind of "concentricity": They begin to see and evaluate the forces that encircle the self, that form its boundaries and potentials.

WRITING ASSIGNMENT 4   At this point I have students analyze short excerpts from the works of writers adept at first person narration. I find Raymond Chandler's fiction particularly helpful in this regard, though Orwell's essays run a close second. The assignment I give in conjunction with this analysis requires students to use the tactics the analysis brings to light. When adept professional writers use the first person singular, they are quite selective about writing *I*. To avoid monotony they generally reserve it only for sentences where the speaker is describing an action. To render sense impressions they tend to make the stimulus the subject of the sentence, use the active voice, and animate the sentence with a strong verb. Since the stylistic maneuvers involved are somewhat subtle for inexperienced writers, I provide a "revision" that demonstrates a less than cunning manipulation of the *I*. The scene referred to here is the murder of Harry Jones from Chandler's *The Big Sleep:*

Write your own scene for Philip Marlowe and include at least *three* of the following: an attractive, but unconscious girl; a revolver recently fired; a hammer with blood on it; a Mafia hit man; a ransacked bedroom; a hotel lobby; a trunk with a body in it; a college classroom on fire.

Keep Marlowe within a single setting (a room, an alleyway, and so on) throughout the scene and include dialogue.

Even though you are writing in the first person, use *I* only when you are having Philip Marlowe describe one of his actions, not when you are having him describe another character or what he sees, hears, smells, and touches.

Not: "I saw Harry Jones's body on the other side of the desk. I heard a street-car bell from far off. There was a brown half pint of whiskey on the desk. Besides the odor of bourbon I smelled another odor, the odor of bitter almonds. It was cyanide."

But, as Chandler writes: "Harry Jones looked at me across the desk, his eyes wide open. A street-car bell clanged at an almost infinite distance. A brown half pint of whiskey stood on the desk with the cap off. Behind the charred smell of the bourbon another odor lurked, faintly, the odor of bitter almonds. That made it cyanide."

Of course, the danger is in becoming overly dramatic, as in, "The stench of rotting garbage assailed my nostrils as I pushed my way toward the cans at the end of the alley." Preferable would be something shorter, simpler, and easier to take: "The stench of rotting garbage drifted from the cans at the end of the alley."

Avoid *was* and *were* whenever you can, even if it means writing a sentence fragment. Notice how Chandler twice gets around *was* in the sentences I quoted above.

WRITING
ASSIGNMENT 5

Later in the semester, I give assignments that are more adventurous structurally:

The Struggle

I'd like you to write a short "feature story" on yourself. First, choose the struggle in your life that has the greatest significance for you. (Please keep in mind that a "struggle" may be completely private, dramatically public—like a prize fight, let's say—or it may have both private and public dimensions.) Second, elaborate on that struggle: keeping your verbs in the *present tense,* describe everything you can remember—what you do, feel; what's said, left unsaid; and so on. Be sure to focus not only on the struggle itself, but on what leads up to it and what ensues from it. Also provide the necessary background: at what point in your life the struggle occurs, where and in what style you are living. Don't worry about chronology; the idea here is to bring to light as much information as you can.

The next part requires you to select and arrange. Go through what you have written and look for the sentences that contain the most valuable information, the most telling facts. Write each sentence on a separate index card. (Index cards usually come in packs of fifty; you should allow yourself to use up an entire pack.) Then put the cards in an order that is roughly chronological.

Now you're ready for the first draft of your story. The trick here is to find a way to organize all the material you've gathered, to deal out the cards in your hand. In other words, you have to find a form, a way of organizing your story. When I talked about arranging the index cards, I asked you to put them in an order that was only roughly chronological—"only roughly" because I want you to have a hold on your material before you begin your story; but I don't want you to be bound by strict chronology, to use a beginning-middle-end arrangement. I want you, instead, to contain all your material within your description of the struggle itself. Open your story where your struggle begins; end it where your struggle ends. But as you describe your struggle, continually "flash back" to the events leading up to it, and before you reach its end, briefly "flash forward" to the aftermath. Because this sort of manipulation can become quite complicated, you will have to work hard to maintain control of your material. To get a head start, impose a simple, emphatic structure on your description of the struggle. Your struggle may be so clear-cut that an outline or arrangement can be readily discerned: perhaps it has distinct stages or "acts"—planning, preparation, presentation—or perhaps it consists of a single action repeated with variation—first draft, second, final version. If you're not so lucky, you will have to find a metaphor for your struggle and impose that instead. Perhaps your struggle resembles a boxing match, a horse race, or a perilous voyage on the open sea.

Whatever structure you discern or contrive, you will have to divide your index cards into piles: description of the struggle itself, flashbacks, flashforward. Then you will have to divide your description pile into separate piles, one for each part of your structure. You must also divide your flashback pile: it's probably a good idea to limit yourself to four flashbacks. Finally, you will have to "fix the deck": description of the struggle, flashbacks at appropriate points throughout, flashforward at an appropriate point near the end. Remember, your story will open where your struggle begins. And you'll describe that struggle in the *present tense*. You'll signal a "flashback" by switching to the *past tense*. When you describe what ensued from the struggle, you'll also use the *past*.

Use captions to reinforce your structure, your arrangement of the material. A three-unit structure isn't mandatory, but anything too complicated won't be useful. Besides, there's something pleasing about units of three, and you are aiming for *three* pages.

Making Yourself Look Good

1. Choose a situation that shows you behaving in one way while another person or group of people is behaving in a very different way. Focus on that situation in your writing. Write in the *present* tense, and record as much information as you can, including background and specific incidents. Be biased; make yourself look good.

2. Select sentences that make you and your way of behaving look *very* good and that make that other way of behaving look *very* bad. Select many more sentences of the first sort than of the second. (I'm reluctant to specify a ratio here, but if pressed I might say 10:1.) Underline these sentences. I would also recommend the "card trick" I mentioned in the previous assignment. Once again you'll be needing a lot of "maneuvering room."

3. Find two people who are familiar with the situation you've chosen and who are on your side. Have each of them do a piece of writing that focuses on the situation; the idea is to make you look good. (I would have each person write for at least twenty minutes and use the *present* tense.)

4. Go through the same selection process with these two pieces of writing that you went through with your own. Again, the "card trick."

5. Write an "article" based on the material you've selected. First you have

to arrange that material. Everything you use from the writing done by the two other people will be given to me in the form of quotations. The trick here is to find a design that will help make you look very good and the "other side" very bad. Beginnings and endings are particularly important. So is variety, and that can be achieved by interweaving your words and those of the two people who have written on your behalf. The quotations should be strategically placed and the writers should be identified. But please don't quote too much or too often.

6. When writing your "article," try to give me the impression that you are simply being factual, that all you care about is objectivity. Never come out and say that you are right, that your way of behaving is better. Demonstrate it, make me feel it, by weighting the evidence in your favor—by allowing me to see and hear only what you want me to. (When you choose the situation and your way of behaving, keep in mind that you're going to want me to identify with you, even empathize with you. So you should show me behavior that I'll immediately approve of, "naturally" condone.)

7. Though your original writing will be in the present tense to assist recall, you should use in your "article" whichever tense or sequence of tenses seems most logical.

WRITING
ASSIGNMENT 7

As the "educational roots" assignment and the neighborhood section of the "self-portrait" help students to find connections between themselves and a place, so an assignment inspired by E. L. Doctorow's *Ragtime* helps them to find connections between themselves and a specific segment of time. Students need to read only a very small portion of the novel: I usually give them a copy of the first chapter.

> Write a *Ragtime*-style account of *one* day in your life. (Any day—as long as you go back at least *five* years. I'd be pleased if you go back further. The further the better, in fact.)
>
> Interweave events of "historical significance," events in the lives of the famous and the notorious, and events in your own life. Refer to yourself in the *third person*, but not by name: give yourself a short appellation that characterizes you at the time (the Sweet Young Thing, the Neighborhood Rascal).
>
> Keep your research to a minimum—the *New York Times* will probably provide you with everything you need. Be on the lookout for intriguing ragged bits of history, as well as coincidences, parallels, and path-crossings.
>
> A "helpful hint": If you don't find enough" world news"—or if you don't find interesting much of what you do dig up—concentrate on "passions" and "oddities" of the day. What were the current fads? What movies, and movie stars, were popular? Were there any strange news stories ("Man Divorces Dog—To Marry Cat," for example)?

As in the "make yourself look good" assignment, this one requires the writer to do research and to integrate source material into the essay. Here the research is of a more formal sort, though friends and family members can also be consulted. Transforming the *I* into the third person singular helps a writer to interweave history with narrative. That is, making the subjective component at least somewhat objective situates it on a psychological level closer to that of news items. Personal facts become more like other facts.

WRITING
ASSIGNMENT 8 I also give an "obituary assignment" that asks student to be both factual and inventive, both quite serious and somewhat playful. They are again asked to transform the *I* into the third person singular, to view themselves at a slight distance. As the assignments become more challenging, it is even more important for the instructor to "write" an assignment than to give it verbally or schematically. Not only do the students then have a clear blueprint, but the tone has been set. "Write your obituary" is such a morbid assignment that it would elicit very short, fearful responses. The teacher has it in his or her power to transform it, to make something morbid a great deal less so:

> Write your own obituary, pretending that you died today.
> Include in it as much of the following information as you can: vital statistics (date of birth and, of course, of death, date of engagement, marriage, etc.); brief descriptions and approximate dates of important "firsts" in your life (first date, first car, first kiss, etc.); family background (e.g., seventh son/daughter of seventh son/daughter); educational status at time of death (e.g., lower-about-to-become-upper freshman), as well as educational background; employment status at time of death (e.g., part-time tattooer), as well as employment record; your greatest pleasures in life (sex, food, a cold beer on a hot day, etc.); your strongest religious, philosophical, and political convictions (but don't feel that you must have convictions in all three categories—in fact, you might want to pass this one up); your most significant experiences (travel, summer camp, love relationships, etc.—include "formative" experiences as well, even if they were painful); characteristics that make you uniquely you (kindness, spontaneity, etc.—include any "paradoxes" you find, such as generosity with possessions, but stinginess with money); those you are leaving behind (include both lovers and loved ones, as well as just friends); the manner in which you died (choking on a twenty dollar bill, hit by a meteorite, etc.); and the manner in which your parting is being observed by those you are leaving behind (a "rock" funeral, a three-day orgy in a public telephone booth, five and a half seconds of silence, etc.).
> Please don't try to give the information in this order. Your "obituary" will constitute a short biography and should follow pretty closely the actual sequence of events in your life. (You can, though, lie whenever you want to cover something up.) You may not be able to give all the information on my list. But, while making your way from birth to death, select the "facts" of your life which you find most important and which you think I'll find most interesting.
> Since you are dead, your life story is being told by someone else. So be sure to write about yourself in the third person throughout your obituary. (For example: "Though a dedicated teacher, Lang enjoyed giving his classes bizarre assignments. One semester, he asked his students to write their own obituaries.")
> Read newspaper obituaries, particularly those of well-known people in the

New York Times, to get ideas for organizing your own obituary, but you don't have to be as solemn as the *Times* usually is. In addition, your "obituary" should be longer, more detailed, than those in the *Times.* Of course, you will be writing in the past tense except when you describe the funeral arrangements, survivors, and so on, but try to keep your prose as lively as possible—under the circumstances.

WRITING ASSIGNMENT 9

Kafka's *The Trial* and Hemingway's "A Very Short Story" were both begun in the first person. And there are the novels of Thomas Wolfe: autobiography in the third person. Having detached themselves from themselves somewhat, students are then more able to see their experiences as raw material to be shaped and manipulated. They can, for example, begin to free themselves from a chronological presentation, to find other, more interesting ways to organize their material:

Draw up a list of ten to fifteen important events in your life from your birth to the present. Then choose five or six that you consider very important and in some way related. (Yes: we'll be talking about how events "relate," or fail to.) For each event you've chosen, write a brief description; be sure to include essential information—time, place, and so on.

Now you have the raw material for a *story* of your life. Since this will be a story and not a history, there's no reason to present your material chronologically. Start with what you consider the most outstanding event and trace it back. (The paragraph describing this event will serve as your "introduction.") End with what you consider the second most outstanding event. (The paragraph describing this event will serve as your "conclusion.")

As you transform your raw material—your original five or six paragraphs—into a story of your life, you'll find that you must add and delete, play certain things up and others down, to achieve a sense of "relatedness." And I'd like you to revise your writing in two other ways. First, talk about yourself in the third person; that is, refer to yourself by name now and then, and say *he* or *she,* instead of using the pronoun *I.* Second, write both your first paragraph and your last, both your "introduction" and your "conclusion," in the *present tense,* the remainder of your story in the *past.* (I think you'll be surprised at the effects you'll achieve by this simple manipulation of tense.)

At the end of this sequence of assignments, the capital *I* seems to have been outgrown. But it is still behind and within the material, generating it and energizing it. In fact, switching to the third person in the manner I have advocated helps students to see that several *I*s are involved when we write: the *I* being written about, the *I* doing the writing, the *I* evaluating the process, the *I* who may see it all differently in the light of tomorrow morning.

Encouraging egocentricity leads students to "concentricity" and to a better awareness of just who they are. They see their own complexity, realize how rich and diverse life must be if just one self has such an intricate structure, such an adventurous evolution. According to Kierkegaard, "The more the self knows, the more it knows itself." Perhaps one way of summarizing the effect of this sequence of assignments is to reverse those two clauses. The more students learn about themselves, the more knowledgeable they become generally. The *I* of the latter essays denotes an informed and perceptive writer as well as an able one—a person singular indeed.

Transformations

This middle section is marked by a movement within each subcategory toward increasing self-consciousness and increasing mastery: from seeing to revision, from reading to imitation, from questioning to judgment.

Observation to Essay

The lessons in this section move from direct experience to interpreting and then to revising. We begin with direct reports of experience in which what matters most is a certain quality of attention together with accounting fully and precisely for what has been observed, whether through seeing (Randall, Chianese, Perrin, Krickel) or listening (Magnus). How can such experiences be rendered expressively for a reader (Sale, Crowe) and be made to yield meaning for oneself (Carnesi) and for others (Graver, Hunter)?

Critical Reading

Having asked students to pay closer attention to their experience of the world around them, how do we extend that quality of attention to the written word—in the form of a letter (Greenfield), story (Trimbur, Hilliard), essay (Fain), poem (Fain, M. Brown, Cain, Sharpe), historical document (Collette), political statement (Driskill), periodical (Summers), advertisement (Flowers), or comic strip (Rosenwasser)? Such close and conscious reading leads to a firmer sense of how writers get their effects, a sense confirmed by exercises in imitation (Robertson) and parody (Peterson and Strebeigh).

Argument

Here we begin with a lesson directed to complicated (and intriguing) situations in which multiple audiences must be imagined and addressed (Anson). How, in responding to a text, can students find a group of useful analytic categories (Coles)? How can they locate the center of an argument (Fahnestock and Secor)? What, in any argument, do writer and reader assume (Rottenberg)? How can students be interested in constructing an argument that takes the opposition into account (Harvey), in making considered judgments (Postlethwaite), and in seeing through words and images that mislead (Hughes, Wright, Eisenberg)? Finally, students as critical readers sift through, interpret, prosecute, defend, and judge in setting up a mock trial of an actual case (Kaufman) and in writing briefs for a hypothetical one (Haring-Smith).

Perceiving and Writing

Phyllis R. Randall,
North Carolina Central University

Many beginning students put their energies and enthusiasm into safe writing, using commonplace observations to make prosaic speculations, all free from error—and fresh air. Very early in the semester, usually the second or third class meeting, I introduce a set of exercises designed to bolster their confidence and their willingness to rely on their own observations and speculations, all with a view toward finding a voice of their own.

I bring to class a picture like Pieter Bruegel the Elder's "The Harvesters." (I happen to have that picture in a large print, but any number of pictures will serve. What I look for is a picture that is reasonably busy, so that answers to my questions come without much hesitation. The exercise should be straightforward, not tricky.) Then I ask them to report what they see. The discussion generally goes as follows.

Teacher: What do you see?
Students: A farm scene, out in the fields. People working and eating and resting. One is sleeping. A basket of food. A loaf of bread.
Teacher: What else?
Students: A field of grain, maybe wheat. A lake in the background. Lots of sky.
Teacher: Let me give you a chance to see it up close. Now what do you see?
Students: A small lake, maybe a pond. Some men appear to be fishing in it. Children playing in a field. Something that looks like a seesaw near them.
Teacher: What else?
Students: Birds flying up out of the field. Oh, a jug hidden in the wheat. (*A chorus of where's. Oh, yes, there it is.*) A church in the background.

When everyone has had a chance to make a contribution (though not all will have taken advantage of it), I ask them to come to some conclusions about this scene, to interpret what their sight tells them.

Students: It's summer (*the vegetation tells us*). The people are taking a mid-day break from their work (*lots of sun but no shadows*). The people are from long ago (*their clothes and eating utensils*). Their tools are old-fashioned too (*the scythes and pitchfork and ladder*).

Teacher: What is a ladder doing in a field of grain, I wonder.

Usually much animated discussion follows, a mixture of further observations about the picture (a wagon of hay on the road) and speculative interpretations (a ladder to climb to the top of the wagon?); the people are sitting under a pear tree (a ladder to get to the pears?).

Before discussion has a chance to wane, I make explicit my point. The raw material of ideas comes from our observations, our perceptions, which must then be integrated, interpreted to make sense of the whole set of observations. Since perception theory tells us that what we perceive is

"The Harvesters (July)" by Pieter Bruegel the Elder (mid-sixteenth century). [The Metropolitan Museum of Art, Rogers Fund, 1919]

based on our past experiences, knowledge, attitudes, and interests, and since we all differ in these characteristics, it follows that all of us look at the picture in our own way, a unique way.

Just as this uniqueness is true of the viewer of the picture, I go on, it is true of the painter. For it was Pieter Brueghel the Elder who gave us the material to observe, who used his own unique observations to present this picture of a relaxed moment in the life of some peasants in sixteenth-century Flanders. Like painters, writers too present their own unique vision of the world, and, like painters, they rely on their close observation of that world to create that vision. To learn to write effectively, then, requires, first of all, learning to observe closely and interpret convincingly, and, second, reconstructing that vision in words so that others may share it.

It is necessary to point out that seeing is just one of the ways we observe. Obviously with a painting, it is the primary sense we use, but the other four senses certainly may be involved as well. We return to the picture to see if it stirs any other senses, for example, sounds the peasants might be hearing (the flapping of the birds' wings, the muffled shouts of the children playing in the far-off field) or smells they must be experiencing (the strong, sweet odor of newly cut grain, mixed probably with their own sweat).

IN-CLASS
EXERCISE

Now I challenge the students to perceive with all five senses something that I will place before them, something they are all familiar with but have probably not paid much attention to. They are to touch it, see it, hear it, smell it, taste it, and then write a paragraph about their perceptions, all five of them. To each I pass out several pieces of candy—M and M's are ideal but virtually anything should work so long as it is edible.

Fifteen or twenty minutes later we are ready to listen to a sampling of the paragraphs. Student comments on the paragraphs generally begin with content, on what is observed. But after a few paragraphs, invariably someone will notice how the language makes a particular paragraph unique. One writer might have colorful, even onomatopoetic verbs; another, an arresting metaphor or simile. (Most of the students will know these terms, but a few minutes of review of figures of speech may be in order.) I always call for further examples of figures from paragraphs not yet read and have yet to be disappointed. In fact, I am usually pleasantly surprised by the variety and the ubiquity of figures in the paragraphs.

The exercise usually allows me to point out something else: An observation must ring true whether we readers have experienced it ourselves or not. A student once wrote of crunching into an M and M as a "benign explosion." Others in the class were quick to point out that they didn't bite into their candy, but allowed the outer shell to dissolve, so they had no explosion, benign or otherwise. Yet all in the class agreed that the observation was true and that "benign explosion" was good writing.

Is it possible, I wonder, for an observation to be true and personally experienced and still somehow be inauthentic? No, they usually respond in chorus. Then I ask how many included in their paragraphs something to the effect that the candy melted in the mouth, not in the hand. A few hands edge skyward. Why isn't this an authentic observation, even though experienced and true? The discussion that follows will point out that observations must not only be personal but also fresh as opposed to canned, unique as opposed to commonplace.

What we are looking for in writing, we conclude, are ideas, interpretations based on fresh and authentic observations that writers make for themselves by seeing and touching and smelling and tasting and hearing. This will be hard because so few of us bother to observe closely, and therefore have nothing fresh to say (and so fall back on the observations—and commercial slogans—of others). But it will be easy in a way, too, because each of us is the absolute authority on his or her perceptions, if we can only teach ourselves to be receptive to them. Once we have learned to observe closely, we must find the words to make those fresh, personal observations convincing to others. But these exercises have revealed that many are already aware of the importance of language, so we are off to a good start.

WRITING ASSIGNMENT   Remembering what you have learned in these exercises, write a paper not to exceed two and a half pages on something you observe between this classroom and your dorm (or parking lot, for commuters). Observe your object (person, thing) intently. Experience it through as many of your senses as are possible (or permissible). Using your perceptions, present your vision of the object so that we all can share it.

Describing Natural Motion: The Art of the Verb

Robert Chianese,
California State University, Northridge

This lesson involves a short assignment on the motion of natural objects and forces. It features practice in using action verbs and encourages students to break their dependence on abstractions linked by forms of *to be* as the basic structuring device for sentences. The lesson also raises key questions about the nature of seeing and the limits of language to convey what we see.

Any writer wishing to do justice to what he sees must depend chiefly on verbs. Ruskin, for example, sees the light that Turner renders in his painting as a living force, and in turn renders it in his prose through the brilliant and extravagant use of verbs and verb forms.

> There is the motion, the actual wave and radiation of the darted beam: not the dull universal daylight, which falls on the landscape without life, or direction, or speculation, equal on all things and dead on all things; but the breathing, animated, and exulting light, which feels, and receives, and rejoices, and acts,—which chooses one thing, and rejects another,—which seeks, and finds, and loses again,—leaping from rock to rock, from leaf to leaf, from wave to wave—glowing, or flashing, or scintillating, according to what it strikes; or, in its holier moods, absorbing and enfolding all things in the deep fulness of its repose, and then again losing itself in bewilderment, and doubt, and dimness,—or perishing and passing away, entangled in drifting mist, or melted into melancholy air, but still,—kindling or declining, sparkling or serene,—it is the living light, which breathes in its deepest, most entranced rest, which sleeps, but never dies.
>
> —*John Ruskin*, Modern Painters

Students need to practice such careful seeing and transcribing of natural forces, but they need to do it more simply and directly. This requires that they extend their facility in using verbs of action and motion. Consequently, they learn to write more precise, vigorous prose.

121

WRITING
ASSIGNMENT

For this particular writing assignment, I ask students to observe and describe in a two-page paper the motion of a single natural object, one typically stirred by the wind, such as a tree, a cloud, a blowing leaf, a wave or a rivulet of water, or identical objects moving together, such as grasses, flowers, or even butterflies. (This begs the Zen-inspired question of whether we watch the object move, the wind move, or the mind move.) The more focused their attention on details of the movement, the better, though they also have to characterize in most cases the large, interrelated movements and the overall motion, as well as the object itself.

In describing these large and small motions, we have to increase the total number of verbs in our sentences, to stretch our capacity for finding related verbs of motion, and to sharpen our use of gerunds and participles. As a consequence, we naturally correct some of the awkwardness and dullness that result from too many "isms" and "tions," and we shift emphasis to the inherently strong element of the sentence—the verb. Hence we turn up the voltage in our prose.

In class we practice transforming tame and repetitive sentences into "thing moves" ones, where the subject is a living or changing entity and the verb a verb of motion. For example:

> *original:* Crashing into the shore constitutes the last phase of the wave's existence. Its foam and spray are observed to spread out on the beach and become its final form.
> *revised:* The wave crashes onto the beach and dissolves into spray and spreading foam.

or,

> *original:* The buildup of flowing water over the drain, which is blocked, is what allows the circular movement to begin.
> *revised:* The flowing water gradually rises over the blocked drain and slowly begins circling above it.

By making sentences out of concrete objects and action verbs, we not only cut down on abstractions and the tortured search for still more abstractions, but also present the objects more directly, move "lovingly," one wants to say, unfiltered through pompous, empty, and distracting prose.

This exclusive focus on the details of an object and its motion might leave us little to say, and students often struggle to generate a few paragraphs of unalloyed description. We can produce more description by artificially generating a list of related verbs of motion in our head, or we can go to the dictionary and thesaurus; however, these reference tools define words only as they are ordinarily used or link words that have similar meanings. They usually do not provide help in finding imaginatively descriptive words that are not directly related to words one already has found. Returning to the object again and again for further scrutiny creates fresh insights and can suggest more verbs better than anything else.

When the object and its motions exhaust our capacity to find words to describe them, we tend to use analogies ("like a ballerina in the pond") or focus on the surroundings or on the observer. Resist these shifts of attention. Stay with the object and its motion; with the dedication of a naturalist painter, see it move and convey that motion to the reader in evocative words.

Some pointers and problems:

- Settle on any moving object to study; searching endlessly for the "right" one will not make the assignment work better.
- Avoid describing a big animal or a pet; we carry too many preconceived ideas about them.
- Aim at a clarity somewhere midway between the reputed objectivity of scientific records and the murky subjectivity of bad poetry. Avoid intruding on the object with your "impressions," though, of course, you will inevitably express them, especially through diction and tone.
- Use present tense, active voice.
- Search for Anglo-Saxon, monosyllabic verbs to balance Latinate ones.
- Vary syntax to add interest.

Once students begin composing, they encounter problems organizing their theme, which is really a "sketch." Since it has no formal thesis, it cannot begin with an argument and end with a conclusion. Nevertheless, we can organize the description in several ways:

- spatially, from top to bottom, for example.
- hierarchically, from the most moving part to the least, from the most independent to the most connected movement, and so on.
- by the inherent sequence of a cycle and pattern, such as a wave has, though one still has to stipulate where it "begins."
- by the sequence of the observer's experience of the motion, which, of course, shifts attention to the observer.

Students inevitably write on similar subjects and can therefore compare their results more fruitfully in class. One can then generate a discussion about the complexities of seeing and rendering motion.

LESSON READINGS

Theodore Roethke, "Big Wind," in *The Collected Poems of Theodore Roethke* (Garden City, NY: Doubleday, 1966).

John Ruskin, "Of Water, as Painted by Turner," in *The Genius of John Ruskin*, ed. John D. Rosenberg (New York: George Braziller, 1963), pp. 32–41.

Virginia Woolf, "Time Passes," in *To the Lighthouse* (Orlando, FL: Harcourt Brace Jovanovich, 1927), Chapter II.

Good Description Begins at Home

Robert Perrin,
Indiana State University

Good descriptive writing depends on choices of details, and students often have little sense of which details are important or interesting. When students read a good example of descriptive writing, they can recognize the details that make it effective, but they often cannot create detailed descriptions of their own—and they often need to in the course of writing exposition (comparison/contrast, problem/solution, and persuasive essays). One of my most successful lessons, or series of lessons, is what my students jokingly call "Better Homes and Descriptions."

CLASS 1   The lesson begins simply enough. I pass around the classroom some photographs of my house. Being something of a photographer, I have lots of stray pictures and try to include pictures of the outside of the house (front, back, and sides), living room, dining room, family room, kitchen, bedrooms, and garage. I encourage my students to ignore the people in the pictures; they don't. Most important, I ask them to notice basic features of the house itself and as many details as possible, then to list them.

Next I distribute to the class copies of the real estate listing for my house—one taken from the multiple-listing book prepared for realtors in my city. It includes all sorts of facts about the house: its age, lot size, number of bedrooms, kind of furnace, school district, room sizes, and other standard features that are of interest to potential buyers. I ask them to compare their list of important details about the house with the realtor's description, then to list the features they have noted but that weren't included on the multiple-listing sheet. The students share this second list, elaborating on what they have noticed. I ask why these features did not appear in the real estate description. What do the class's details say about the house that the listing doesn't?

CLASS 2   I distribute to the class a sampling of real estate advertisements taken from the classified section of the newspaper. Varied samples like these work best:

Price reduced on spacious country home near Fowler Park. 5 bedrooms. 2 full baths, 2 half baths, beamed family room with fireplace, living room, country kitchen, formal dining room with deck, den, plentiful closet space, large utility room, barn and work shed. 5.7 acres including pond. NOW $100,000. (2733)

A PERFECT PLACE TO RETIRE: Really, it's perfect for anyone, located southwest of the city on a lake. Recently updated with pegged wood floors in LR. Carpet in the 3 bedrooms, central air, screened porch and dock—oversized 2 car garage, too. Transferred owner needs to sell and will help you finance. Priced upper 40's. (0604)

ALLENDALE ESTATE w/picturesque hillside view and plenty of privacy. Quality built redwood family home designed for entertaining and fun. Has tennis court, jacuzzi, cathedral ceiling, great rm w/loft, frplc and wet bar. 4 BRs. 3½ tile baths, kit w/chef's stove and char grille. Cherry and redwood custom built bookcases and cabs. Separate chalet style guest house w/kit, 1½ baths, BR and upper deck. Acreage completely fenced.

IN-CLASS
EXERCISE

Using their multiple-listing sheet for my house and their own noted features, students then write a newspaper ad for the house. After students have written their ads, we read a few and discuss why certain features appear in most of them. I ask how they feel about omitting so many of the details about the house.

At this point I prepare the students to write a list for the next session. They are to think about their parents' home (if they are "traditional" college-aged students), or their own homes (if they are "returning" students), or any other, including apartments. They should prepare a list of important features of the house, including anything important or interesting: good neighbors, nearness to a swimming pool, closeness to shopping, landscaping, a good floor plan, traffic on the street, or the history of the house or neighborhood.

CLASS 3

I give the class blank multiple-listing sheets. (You can get a sample from a local realtor and have it photocopied—or photocopy this sample.) The students prepare the information sheet using the home they have described.

I expect some groaning because students will claim that they don't know anything much about their homes. I explain to them that good description often requires research of a general kind if writers don't remember important details. That means that they will have to do some "research" to complete the form, making sure that the information is accurate and complete. They are to bring the completed form to the next class session.

CLASS 4

I have students form small groups—three to four in a group is ideal—and discuss their lists of important features and their completed multiple-listing sheets. I encourage group members to ask questions and demand clarifications. Students should expand their descriptions based on group members' queries and comments. Before the groups break up, each student should note with asterisks or check marks the features of the house others found most interesting.

Sample Multiple-Listing Sheet:

| | | MLS NO. | Address _____ Street _____ City _____ County |

Type _____	Stories _____	Porch _____	Price _____
Ext. Const. _____	Rms. _____	Patio _____	Sq. Ft. _____
Basement _____	Bdrms. _____	Garage _____	Landscp. _____
Crawl _____	Baths _____	Drive _____	Firepl. _____
Slab _____	Yr. _____	Sew. _____	Range _____

	Story	Room Size	Floors Walls
Living Rm.			
Dining Rm.			
Kitchen			
Family Rm.			
Bedroom			
Bedroom			
Bedroom			
Bedroom			
Utility Rm.			
Basement			

Wat. _____   Disp. _____

Gas _____   Dish. _____

Elec. _____   Stm. Dr. _____

A.C. _____   Stm. Wind. _____

Htg. _____   Insul. _____

Htg. Cost. _____   Mtgee. _____

Other Property _____

Assess value $ _____   Tax w/ex. $ _____

Lot Size _____   Prof. Ser. _____

Schools _____

Reasons For Selling _____ Possession _____

Zoning _____ Showing Instructions, Comments, Directions _____

Occupant or Owner _____   Occup. Phone _____   Key Box _____

Listing Office _____   By _____   L.N. _____

WRITING
ASSIGNMENT

Write an essay of 500–750 words describing your chosen house. The essay need not present the house as if it were for sale, but it should describe the house with enough detail that someone *might be* interested in visiting the house or perhaps in buying it. Include major information that might make the house seem special in some way. The essay could be organized topically, including major features, special features, the neighborhood, and so on. Alternately, the essay could be arranged spatially, presenting a "walking tour" of the house: outside features, foyer, living room, dining room, hallway, bedrooms, and so on—suggesting what people would see if they walked through the residence.

These activities that lead up to writing a descriptive essay can help students learn more about selecting details. First, the activities show students what kinds of details are considered standard. Second, they show students that "standard details" are not always as revealing as unusual details. Third, the activities are built on a subject that students typically take for granted—their homes. This choice of subjects works well because students learn to observe details more carefully; by discovering what they often ignore in familiar surroundings, they can recognize how much around them goes unnoticed.

These activities are not miracle cures, and all students will not produce well-detailed essays. But the activities do sharpen students' powers of observing important details, which in turn leads to more effective descriptive writing.

This lesson in description and selection of details is, as the title suggests, only a beginning. It may also serve, if the teacher wishes, as an entryway to the art of description, exemplified by Hawthorne, Scott, Poe, Thoreau, Clemens, Dickens, Lewis, and Frank—all of whom go beyond the language and point of view of real estate to an exploration of human life in its relation to place.

FOR FURTHER READING

Excerpts from:

Nathaniel Hawthorne, *The House of the Seven Gables*
Sir Walter Scott, *Ivanhoe*
Edgar Allan Poe, "The Fall of the House of Usher"
Henry David Thoreau, *Walden*
Samuel Clemens, *The Adventures of Huckleberry Finn*
Charles Dickens, *Bleak House*
Sinclair Lewis, *Babbitt*
Anne Frank, *The Diary of a Young Girl*

Much in Little:
Observing as an Art

Edward Krickel,
University of Georgia

Ezra Pound recommended that students describe a tree on campus with such particularity that the other students would recognize it. Also, he told the anecdote of Agassiz sending a student back again and again to sketch a decomposing fish until he had mastered the appearance of the fish. (It must have been harder to drop a course then than now.) Rilke, a poet of quite a different temperament from Pound, studied a caged panther so closely that he perceived its nictitating optical function.

These masters got such results in their poems that one must acknowledge as valid their recommended or practiced disciplines. Of course, the chances of our having students of even budding genius is beyond any capacity to estimate. I wonder, though, how much the run-of-the-mill state university students I encounter, with their fantasies about their places in the technological future, would benefit from such disciplines. I have tried the tree assignment, and various adaptations of it, with poor results. There is no way for me to adapt the fish project to a composition assignment. My students more nearly see a tree for its timber potential than as an object of aesthetic contemplation. And panthers are exceedingly scarce.

How can I bring students out of their reveries of self long enough to respond to something and write it up in a way I can accept as a composition? At whatever level of skill, they *need* the ability to respond to the world with written words of sufficient accuracy that another person can re-create the objects of the original response, perhaps in a technological world more than any other. I regard this as self-evidently valuable. If I gave each student a mirror and asked for a description of the image seen, I might touch his main concern, but the results would be, I suspect, cloudy visions, every now and then recognizable, not of the students themselves, but of the movie, TV, and rock celebrities our commercial culture has trained them to revere and thus to imitate. What follows is my version of how to get some use from the next thing likely to interest them—people like themselves.

I read aloud the 300-word sketch "Birthday Party" by Katharine Brush, in which an unidentified narrator seated in a small restaurant observes from this fixed vantage a man and woman seated at another table far enough away as to be out of earshot but close enough for their appearance and actions to be clearly discernible. The narrator presents by means of well-selected details the progress of the emotional crisis they are in. The narrator describes the setting, estimates the ages of the couple, deduces the occasion and the failure of the gesture that the woman makes but that does not have the desired effect on the man. The sketch ends with the woman in tears and the narrator with averted eyes. Every detail is given with the barest sufficiency of words to make it real. If it is like an emotional scene in a soap opera, so much the better. The sketch is short enough for me to ask the students to validate each detail. Would they know the ages of the man and woman? They believe so. A round face is obvious enough, but a self-satisfied look on such a face? Easy enough, they say. Though the narrator is chiefly a frame, intruding into the last paragraph, they know it is a woman because only a woman would notice certain details. For example, even in this hatless age, the girls are sure that when the narrator recognizes that the woman is wearing her best hat, they would recognize it as the best too. I am much less sure but let the vanity pass. And so on with the other details.

WRITING
ASSIGNMENT

The assignment, then is to go and do likewise. Take up a fixed vantage point, observe at a short distance an action for which you have to deduce the truth, significance, or meaning. If it turns out to be commonplace do not worry about it; that is acceptable. Worry instead about finding the words, descriptive and otherwise, to bring the scene and action to life, as is done in "Birthday Party," with the revealing detail and the barest minimum of words. Leave yourself out of it except as frame.

Students seemingly get so caught up in the subject that they forget it is a hated English theme. Sometimes they even leave out the unnecessary commas and misused apostrophes (both too many and too few); their spelling is no worse than usual. True, I feel like a campus spymaster at uncovering so many lovers' trysts, guilty intrigues, betrayals (if I may borrow terms from old Howells), and other teeming phantasmagoria of the undergraduate mind that purportedly take place in libraries, student coffee shops, restaurants, city buses, or just wherever young people are. Students have an assignment that—as assignments go—they do not despise and that calls for close observation, consistent point of view, selection of details, and most of all, finding the right words for what is deduced. I get good results.

LESSON READING

Katharine Brush, "Birthday Party," *The New Yorker*, March 16, 1946.

Listening and Writing: The "Secret Music" of Talk

Laury Magnus,
The U.S. Merchant Marine Academy

I use Aksakov's phrase for a lesson intended to train students to attend to the language they hear or overhear, in other words to *listen*, to note accurately, to be mindful and alert. If they attend to the detail of what is being said when others say it, they will be more likely to attend to the detail of what they themselves write and say.

I also use the lesson to train students to interpret—to understand and perceive what is implied but unspoken, what is really meant: in other words, to discriminate between how things seem and how things are.

The written assignment is meant to train students to write as well as listen and understand, and when they write, to write as clearly and accurately as they listen and understand.

I use bits of dialogue from Ibsen, Chekhov, Hemingway, Pinter, and Grace Paley. The questions I ask sound like this:

Consider the uses of dialogue in these selections, but pursue the thread that runs through them all. What is actually being said? What is being left out? Why? What differences in meaning can you find between what is being overtly expressed and what is being suggested or implied? Why does a writer use quoted speech in, say, a story, instead of describing a character or commenting on his behavior or giving us a clear exposition of what is happening in a situation?

WRITING
ASSIGNMENT

I then ask the class to do the following assignment in two parts.

1. Make an effort—without being noticed, if possible—to overhear a conversation, argument, dialogue, dispute, etc., which goes on at home, on the subway, in the car, in the dorm, anywhere. The exchange should be one that interests or involves you. Try to listen as accurately as possible, noting particular characteristics of speech—and then, as soon as possible, transcribe the complete dialogue as accurately as you can.

2. From these notes write a brief composition (two to three pages) indicating the following things in the following order: (1) the background of the dialogue, including your relation to the speakers; (2) the *ostensible* subject of conversation and the reason for the conversation (for example, are two people arguing over who is going to take down the garbage?); (3) the *real* subject of conversation. Selecting appropriate parts of the conversation for purposes of illustration, try to locate the real, the concealed subject and/or purpose of the conversation—for example, a power struggle between husband and wife. For this reason it is suggested that the exchange you select be heated, humanly interesting, or involving for some other reason that you should make clear in your paper.

In addition to sharpening the students' observation of physical signals passing back and forth and inflections in tone of voice as well as the actual language used, the exercise also leads them to ponder why people don't just say what they mean, how language can be, as Orwell puts it, an instrument for concealing rather than revealing thought and feeling.

LESSON READINGS

Sergei Aksakov, *Years of Childhood*, trans. Alec Brown (New York: Vintage, 1960), pp. 62–75.

Robert Browning, "My Last Duchess," in *Complete Poetical Works* (Boston: Houghton Mifflin, 1895).

Anton Chekhov, *The Three Sisters*, in *The Major Plays*, trans. Ann Dunnigan (New York: New American Library, 1964), pp. 259–260.

Grace Paley, "Wants," in *Enormous Changes at the Last Minute* (New York: Farrar Straus Giroux, 1960), pp. 3–6.

Harold Pinter, *The Collection*, in *Three Plays* (New York: Grove Press, 1962), pp. 43–49.

Rebecca West, *The Fountain Overflows* (New York: Viking, 1956), pp. 91–92.

Describing Places for Yourself and Others

Roger Sale,
University of Washington

Perhaps the deepest understanding we have of ourselves, and of each other, places us in time and tells a story. Indeed, this understanding of character as story is so pervasive that we may overlook the understanding that can come from considering our relations to places. In different places we are often or usually happy or scared, open or tentative: in streets, in bed, in kitchens, churches, classrooms, beaches, other peoples' houses and apartments, Alaska, automobiles, mountaintops. There is a place in southeastern Oregon, another in the north of England, another in my home, another on campus, that I think of as the countries of my heart. If I could tell my relation to these places, and why they are the countries of my heart, I might come as close as any story can to saying who I am.

Toward the end of a thematic composition course in which students explore in writing a variety of familiar and unfamiliar places—from the local shopping center to places of historical significance to a great city they have never seen—I make a two-part assignment asking them to describe a place that is, for them, "fringed with joy." The phrase comes from Virginia Woolf's *To the Lighthouse*, in which, when Mrs. Ramsay tells her young son that he may be able to go to the lighthouse tomorrow, "To her son these words conveyed an extraordinary joy"; and, when he looks at a picture, "it was fringed with joy." We have all looked forward to going to such places only to be disappointed in the actual going; but the really magical places are those to which we go, and perhaps return many times, and whose very name can still convey "an extraordinary joy."

WRITING
ASSIGNMENT

In the first part of the assignment students are asked to describe such a place carefully, but to do so without writing about their own experience of it. Since they will choose the details, the tone, the angles of vision, the paper will of course be "theirs," but not personal to them. In the discussion that accompanies the making of the assignment, I am particularly concerned to show how many choices are available to each writer: I mention several sorts of places that are for me sources of joy even after repeated

132

visits; we discuss the use of mementoes (photographs are most likely for most people) in helping to summon details, and the way in which the "nature" of a place may suggest the best ways to write about it—a place of historic interest, for example, may more easily yield a story about someone else than would, say, a place of rendezvous for lovers. The form this description takes is up to the individual student: It might be a history, a story of what happened to someone else there, a guidebook account, a piece of atmospheric wizardry.

The second part of the assignment, made when the first description is handed in, is to tell the story of *their* own particular experience of this magic place. Again, they are free to do this in a variety of ways—a dramatic scene or series of scenes, spending much or little time describing the place itself, and so on—so long as they remember that the primary aim is to show how and why the place is *for them* "fringed with joy."

I try to discourage the idea that the first part of this assignment is necessarily to be "objective" and the second "subjective," or that the two must contrast sharply. To emphasize the variety of ways in which the second part might be done, I hand out copies of my own sample response to the first part, and ask everyone to spend ten minutes in class writing the beginning of a possible second part to go with it. When two or three of these are read aloud there usually is a good deal of variety, both in the stories being told and in their means of telling. In any event, it is not difficult to show that even when writing about a personal experience one need not abandon the means employed in the first part. If there is a single "point" to emerge from this assignment, it is that little is to be gained by abstracting an "idea" of writing from a situation and that there is much to be gained by letting the situation, the character of the place itself, help a writer to discover the best way to write about it.

Defining an Abstraction and Rendering an Experience

Janis Crowe,
Furman University

Early in the introductory composition course, usually while we are talking about description and narrative structure, I schedule one day for a concentrated look at abstractions and the temptations they offer the inexperienced writer, together with the related problem of slippery, vague diction. Students bring to class their own dictionaries, and I supply them with an armful from the English department so that we have represented a range from minimal paperbacks to standard, comprehensive desk dictionaries.

Without recourse to any of the dictionaries, I ask the class to define two abstractions: *hunger* and *heat.* They try, but they are also eager to see what the dictionaries have to say, and we note the varying definitions offered by our various dictionaries. We then compare the students' own definitions with those they have found. We note the reliance, in both sets of definitions, on other abstractions to explain meanings, and at this point I ask the class to define the word *abstraction.* They struggle with the problem, and we go again to the dictionary, where we find the etymology: from Latin *abstractus,* "removed from (concrete reality)."[1]

Next, I ask the students to *illustrate* the terms we have been discussing: *hunger, heat,* and *abstraction.* The illustrations the students offer demonstrate to them how much further they must go to render or convey as vividly as possible the actual sensation of being hot or hungry—or both—in order to communicate the specific experience to someone else. They must use, and they must choose well, the concrete details that will give their writing immediacy and power.

At this point I offer examples of abstractions defined in contexts by professional writers, and I point out that lexicographers have traditionally found their definitions in the particular contexts given by writers; I describe

---

[1] *The American Heritage Dictionary of the English Language.*

134

Dr. Johnson in his London garret with nine years' worth of pieces of paper containing quotations and definitions. *Writers* significantly influence the power words have.

With this introduction I offer examples by two professional writers: a passage from Richard Wright's *Black Boy* and one from James Agee's *Let Us Now Praise Famous Men.* Starting with the most general, most encompassing meaning of *discomfort,* we consider degrees of specificity between extremely general abstractions and those that impinge on the concrete by suggesting physical sensations or dimensions. We look at these passages to see how the particular contexts and points of view determine the conceptual language, intensifying the effect. Both writers leave us in no doubt about what it means to be hungry or too hot to eat.

We look at Wright's dramatic personification of "hunger" as a stranger who terrifies a child and robs him of his strength, and at Agee's definition of the sickening discomfort caused by trying to swallow food in a room too hot to breathe in. We note in Agee's static, spatially organized paragraph his interest in the physical construction of the kitchen, the shape, the materials, and the size—and his focus on the detached act of swallowing, without a narrative or a whole person visualized. In contrast, Wright's narrative is highly dramatic: The word *hunger* is repeated as the personification becomes more varied and threatening, and the profusion of verbs and verb forms suggests how painfully the boy is assailed. The paragraph is followed by a short dialogue that puts the matter in another key—ironic perhaps, but as baffling and disorienting to the boy as the phenomenon of hunger itself. No matter what their method, both writers use precise diction and concrete, well-selected details that communicate the experience. I ask the students to choose an abstraction, then to define it as clearly as they can as an epigraph (I explain the term) to a long paragraph in which they give an account of the concrete reality alluded to by that abstraction.

WRITING
ASSIGNMENT 1

WRITING
ASSIGNMENT 2

The discussion of abstractions provides a basis for two other assignments I make later in the term. One asks for a 400–500-word description of a person the writer knows well. Students must decide what characteristics they wish to emphasize and then figure out concrete, specific contexts in which their subjects can come alive. No abstractions allowed! (This assignment also entails discussions of the effectiveness of one point of view rather than another, that is, how best it can reveal the writer's understanding of his material.)

WRITING
ASSIGNMENT 3

Another assignment I use in connection with this lesson is to describe a room and its contents without relying on abstractions. Students must decide how to structure the description and what they want emphasized before they start writing. With concrete language they have to give the reader a sense of what it is like to be in this place and how it is important to them—or to anyone.

Long after we have left these assignments I continue to emphasize the power of concrete diction and selective detail, both in the anthology pieces we read and in the papers the students write. We look at abstractions as problems in definition: They say too many things; and we consider them in their more debased forms—the hackneyed, sentimental language of greeting cards that speak loosely and repetitively of love and happiness; and, more alarmingly, as the staples of political rhetoric that Orwell has definitively examined.

READING

Richard Wright

BLACK BOY

Hunger stole upon me so slowly that at first I was not aware of what hunger really meant. Hunger had always been more or less at my elbow when I played, but now I began to wake up at night to find hunger standing at my bedside, staring at me gauntly. The hunger I had known before this had been no grim, hostile stranger; it had been a normal hunger that had made me beg constantly for bread, and when I ate a crust or two I was satisfied. But this new hunger baffled me, scared me, made me angry and insistent. Whenever I begged for food now my mother would pour me a cup of tea which would still the clamor in my stomach for a moment or two; but a little later I would feel hunger nudging my ribs, twisting my empty guts until they ached. I would grow dizzy and my vision would dim. I became less active in my play, and for the first time in my life I had to pause and think of what was happening to me.

James Agee and Walker Evans

LET US NOW PRAISE FAMOUS MEN

There is a tin roof on the kitchen. It leaks only when the rain is very heavy and then only along the juncture with the roof of the main house. The difficulty is more with heat. The room is small: very little more than big enough to crowd in the stove and table and chairs: and this slanted leanto roof is quite low above it, with no ceiling, and half the tin itself visible. The outdoor sunlight alone is in the high nineties during many hours of one day after another for weeks on end; the thin metal roof collects and sends on this heat almost as powerfully as a burning-glass; wood fires are particularly hot and violent and there is scarcely a yard between the stove and one end of the

---

Richard Wright, from *Black Boy* (New York: Harper & Row, 1945), p. 21.

table: between the natural heat, the cumulated and transacted heat striven downward from the roof, and the heat of the stove, the kitchen is such a place at the noon meal time that, merely entering it, sweat is started in a sheet from the whole surface of the body, and the solar plexus and the throat are clutched into tight kicking knots which relax sufficiently to admit food only after two or three minutes.

James Agee and Walker Evans, from *Let Us Now Praise Famous Men* (Boston: Houghton Mifflin, 1941; rpt. 1980), p. 177.

Narration and Description: Rolling and Stopping the Camera

Mary Carnesi,
University of Texas

In the following sequence my first purpose is to teach students to narrate and to describe; my deeper purpose is to help each student to remember and re-create some event that changed him and made him see in a new way.

CLASS 1   I assign the reading on narration and description in John Ruszkiewicz's *Well-Bound Words*, and we discuss the main difference between them, namely, that although narration considers something as it moves in time, description depicts that same thing "as if it were frozen in time."

At this point I try to expand this concept from my own experience. For visual effect I draw a horizontal line on the blackboard and reflect on the fact that each of us has a beginning and an end but that between the points of birth and death we move through time and space living, acting, becoming. I then draw a vertical line straight through the horizontal and ask if anyone has ever had an experience in which time stops—for example, watching the sun set or being with a person one is in love with and coming to realize only after the fact that many hours have passed and one had completely failed to notice. Students usually recognize this phenomenon of the "timeless moment" full of intensity and meaning.

I go on to talk about the states of being and becoming and the existence in English of two main categories of verbs: the verb *to be* and the active verbs. To make the bridge from rhetorical terms (narration and description) to living terms (becoming and being) gives students a sense of the impor-tance of writing as an embodiment and further expression of life itself. I use the analogy of a camera rolling to depict narration and of a camera

138

stopped to depict description. I tell my students first to imagine that they have their cameras focused on a person running through time and space and then to imagine zeroing in on the face of the runner and stopping the camera to see the details: perhaps the fear in his eyes, the sweat rolling down his forever-bobbing face, the open, cracked lips crying for more oxygen. Though the runner continues to run, it seems as though he is stopped, suspended in a timeless moment in order that we might contemplate him, and through such contemplation experience the intensity and significance of his situation. One could ask students to share what each of them saw in that moment of stopping the camera of imagination.

I then assign a reading for the next class like Maya Angelou's "Graduation" or George Orwell's "Shooting an Elephant" and ask students to mark passages where the action slows down and the writer's camera stops to re-create an intense moment through a concentration of details.

CLASS 2
IN-CLASS
EXERCISE

I begin class with a journal assignment (or brief writing assignment if students do not keep journals), asking them to do one of the following:

1. Briefly tell about a significant event that changed you in some way, made you see something you had not seen before, whether positive or negative.

2. Think back on your experiences in the classroom sometime between first and twelfth grade. Briefly tell about an incident that you can never forget, one from which you learned something significant or that changed you, made you understand something in a new way or for the first time.

3. Think about your relationship with your mother or father. Now think back on some encounter you had with your parent that stays in your memory. Briefly write about that important moment when you perhaps saw your mother or father in a new way, penetrating beyond your illusions about her or him.

I give the students only five minutes to write, withholding the news that there will be a formal assignment on this journal topic. (I find that without the pressures of the formal paper students are much more spontaneous and that, in the majority of cases, the five minutes of writing yields the core of the coming paper.)

By this time I have both introduced the students to the concepts of narration and description and begun, through the short writing assignment, to get them thinking about their own significant experiences. Now the link between these parts of the lesson is provided by a full-fledged discussion of the reading. I find that reading out loud is often effective in stimulating discussion: If I read slowly and dramatically all sorts of comments usually emerge. Reading aloud brings a passage to life for those students who read it but "didn't get anything out of it." I ask questions like "Have you ever felt this way?" and "Have you had a similar experience?" Here I try to link the reading to their lives and their lives to the reading, and students often become deeply involved in the discussion.

CLASS 3   Next we deal with descriptive and narrative passages in the reading. I ask what places they have marked as particularly descriptive, where the writer has "stopped" his camera. Usually we agree on many passages, but occasional disagreements on whether a passage is more narrative or descriptive are also helpful. Our discussion firms up the concepts of rolling and stopping the camera, enables us both to perceive the powerful effects of the rhythm of rolling, stopping, then rolling again and to discover that the most intense moments of an incident are largely descriptive.

CLASS 4
WRITING
ASSIGNMENT   I make the formal writing assignment in writing to avoid misunderstanding or confusion. In the handout I try to formulate the assignment so that all the threads of our previous work [narration/description, the readings, and the significant event(s) on which the student will write] are pulled together. I hand out copies of the assignment, reading what I have written out loud, commenting and clarifying as I go:

> *Main purposes:* Self-expression & Exposition
> *Main modes:* Narration & Description
> *Audience:* myself & the people in our class
> *Length:* 750 words/3 typewritten pages
> *Date due:* one week after making the assignment (at the beginning of class)
> *Directions:*
> This paper will be about yourself so you will need to use the first person singular "I."
>   Basically, I want you to tell about an experience you have had in your life. It may have happened in your early life or in your more recent life. What is important is that you choose *an event which changed you,* made you *see* something, *understand* something, you had not seen before, you had not understood before.
>   Think, for example, of Maya Angelou and of the night of her graduation: a specific time and place and event. Or think of Orwell at the moment when he must decide whether or not to shoot the elephant as the crowd, as well as the imperatives of power and authority, press upon him.
>   In a similar way, you need to let yourself explore your memories, whether distant or close, for some experience you have had about which you felt strongly and about which you still feel strongly.
>   Perhaps it was a time when you felt oppressed, or faceless, or powerless— or a time when you felt anger, even rage, because you had been unfairly treated—or when you experienced revenge and/or forgiveness.
>
>   You need to *narrate* the event—re-create the action for your readers—as the camera of your mind moves through the scene. At this point, however, probably at the high point of your experience (*your* story), *stop the camera. Describe* your feelings as, for example, Maya Angelou does. She expresses her total loss of hope in herself and in all people through the image of the pyramid of flesh, which she describes in some detail. The image conveys her deep and utter distress and rage over her sense of being dominated and oppressed by uncaring white people (represented by the two token white men who show

up to "speak and run" at what was to have been her beautiful and joy-filled graduation). After Angelou has *re-created* her despair and her rage for us, after she has allowed us, her readers, to share the depth of her feelings, she moves the camera of her mind and heart over the rest of her graduation, moving from icy despair to a new and hopeful sense of who she is.

In brief, in this paper you need to *narrate and describe*, that is, to move the camera through the remembered action and to stop the camera when the *intensity* of the experience, of the feelings, demands to be recorded and re-created for your readers.

One reminder: Be as *honest* as you can be. And remember that good and great writing is born not of superficiality but within those human beings who have the courage to remember what really happened, to face the pain, but in the facing of their pain to find within the ashes that there is perhaps, after all, a young round bird singing of hope, and rising up, saying in her song that hope is stronger than any despair.

Your life is full of experiences worth writing about. You only need to find them and reflect on them to find that they are still speaking to you, still revealing to you who you were and who you are. Writing about yourself is, after all, one way of discovering yourself.

My criteria for evaluating your paper:

1. Have you *limited* the event enough and really focused your attention on a specific meaningful event, or have you tried to cover so much ground that you have ended up with a paper full of *vague generalizations*? Remember that generalizations are all right but that without *specific details* to flesh them out generalizations remain empty and boring.

2. Have you succeeded in *re-creating* for your audience the significant event that changed you—that is, have you made it *live again* in vivid color and power?

3. Have you *stopped the camera* at least once during your narrative?

4. Have you been *honest* and straightforward about what happened and about your responses to the event, or have you spoken only superficially, staying on the surface of things?

5. And, of course, spelling, grammar, punctuation, paragraphing, and so on are also important, since this is a formal paper rather than an informal journal entry.

LESSON READINGS

Maya Angelou, "Graduation," in *I Know Why the Caged Bird Sings* (New York: Random House, 1969–1970), Chapter 23.

George Orwell, *Shooting an Elephant and Other Essays* (Orlando, FL: Harcourt Brace Jovanovich, 1950).

John Ruszkiewicz, *Well-Bound Words* (Glenview, IL: Scott Foresman, 1981).

Personal and Analytic Essays: Bridging the Gap in Two Steps

Suzanne Graver,
Williams College

My basic composition courses follow a familiar pattern. They begin with writing assignments based on personal experience and then move on to the more objective and analytic forms of writing that tend to be characteristic of college essay assignments. Opening with the personal experience essay has the advantages of engaging the students and probably reducing their anxieties about writing. The confidence and skills that students develop in these first essays, however, do not easily carry over into their analytic expository writing. The following two paper assignments are designed to bridge this gap between personal and analytic writing.

During the third week of the term, by which time they have already written two personal experience essays, students read George Orwell's "Shooting an Elephant" and Richard Rodriguez' "Going Home Again: The New American Scholarship Boy." Both essays use autobiographical material to make a larger point about competing cultural values. Both writers explore how cultural pressures lead to self-conflict and generate ambivalent responses. Together these essays create a context for the following writing assignment (the third in the semester):

WRITING
ASSIGNMENT

Orwell, in "Shooting an Elephant," conveys his ambivalence toward the Burmese whom he both sympathized with and hated. Rodriguez explains in "Going Home Again . . ." the conflicting and contradictory feelings he experiences as a "scholarship boy." In an essay of about three pages (approximately 750 words), write about the mixed responses you have had toward an individual or a group, an institution or an idea (belief, concept, ideology). Choose a subject that has not only personal but also cultural implications.

In thinking about ways to develop your essay, review the organizational (thesis and progression of paragraphs) and rhetorical (description, narration, analysis) strategies used by Orwell and Rodriguez. Review as well how Orwell and Rodriguez make their particular cases exemplary of wider cultural dilemmas.

CLASS 1   To prepare for this paper, we discuss the Orwell essay in one class and the Rodriguez essay in another. The students are asked to bring to class a sentence or two in which they state each essay's thesis or main point, and the discussion begins by comparing their various statements. Many students offer as Orwell's thesis his statement "that when the white man turns tyrant it is his own freedom that he destroys." We discuss why, if this is the main point, Orwell makes it in the middle of the account. We also discuss what else the style, details, and organization of the essay suggest, by discussing such matters as the highly metaphoric language, the many details about the Burmese, the function of the first three paragraphs and the closing one. This discussion leads students to perceive how Orwell's autobiographical narrative itself embodies and communicates his own ambivalence as well as the wider thesis that imperialism tyrannizes *both* the oppressor and the oppressed. For their own essay, I suggest that they follow either the conventional format of stating their thesis directly or Orwell's strategy of making the thesis implicit in the language, organization, and narrative or descriptive details. What the discussion stresses above all, however, is Orwell's use of the simple but time-honored strategy of giving abstractions relevance and meaning through many carefully chosen details.

CLASS 2   For the Rodriguez essay, we again begin by discussing the statements of thesis the students have written down. Rodriguez, unlike Orwell, states his thesis directly, but not until the concluding paragraph. We discuss the advantages and disadvantages of this strategy and consider also how Rodriguez structures the body of the essay to prepare for his thesis that education, by causing cultural dislocation, exacts "a large price in exchange for the large benefits it has conferred" on "scholarship boys." Rodriguez' strategy is different from Orwell's in other ways too. He uses narration and description primarily when he speaks of his family's Chicano culture, creating personal moments that are interlaced within the more dominant mode of explaining and analyzing the costs and benefits of an education that both separates and unites. Thus these two essays suggest different ways of combining narration with explanation and autobiography with analysis.

The next writing assignment reflects an effort to create a fusion between personal and analytic writing over the whole course. As such, it constitutes not so much a lesson as an approach to writing. The approach, which is described in the Course Guidelines and discussed on the opening day, involves journal writing of a particular kind. Here are the instructions the students are given:

WRITING   You are required to keep a journal which contains at least four entries written
ASSIGNMENT   over the course of a week. Date the entries and spend about 20 minutes on each. The notebook you keep them in will be collected periodically. The

purpose of the journal is two-fold: to make writing a virtually daily activity; to make writing a tool for learning. Your journal entries may be related to many different kinds of intellectual activities: understanding and remembering what you have read; analyzing or evaluating readings; responding to a lecture or preparing for a class discussion; understanding a topic, concept, or event; analyzing, synthesizing, and evaluating ideas, practices, attitudes (your own or those of others). You might, for instance, select an important statement from something you have read recently and explain it: rephrase it, explain what it means to you, point out problems you might have in understanding its meaning and discuss its implications or why it is important. Your discussion of a particular matter need not be restricted to one entry.

I generally collect the journals at three- to four-week intervals, and when I collect them I ask the students to note any entries they especially want me to read. Then, at some point during the last third of the course, and sometimes even at the end (depending on the progress of the group), I ask the students to write a paper in which they do an analysis of their journals. The paper (three to five pages in length) requires a coherent thesis, structured around the major preoccupations they wrote about in their journal and the revelations of character implicit in them. This assignment tends to take the students by surprise, and often their first response is that the entries are so disparate as to make impossible a unified essay. To help them, I suggest the following "Before Writing" guidelines:

1. Classify the entries: Note what they have in common; see what major groupings evolve; reduce the groupings to no more than half a dozen.
2. Look at the random entries (i.e., those that don't fit into your major groupings) and consider whether they have anything in common.
3. Consider things important to you that are not reflected in the journal entries. Generalize about them as well and about your reasons for leaving them out.
4. Consider the extent to which your journal is bound by time and place. How different does it seem from one you might have kept in the past?
5. Look over the results of your analysis (1–4): What do the emerging topics and generalizations reveal about the person who wrote the journal?
6. Formulate a central thesis.

The essays this assignment produces often turn out to be the best in the course. A number of students, moreover, who had never kept a journal before have reported to me that they continued to keep a journal after the course was over. Writing had indeed become for them a daily activity.

LESSON READINGS

George Orwell, *Shooting an Elephant and Other Essays* (Orlando, FL: Harcourt Brace Jovanovich, 1950).

Richard Rodriguez, "Going Home Again: The New American Scholarship Boy," in *The American Scholar* 44, Winter 1974–75.

On the Road to Wigan Pier: From Journal to Essay

Jefferson Hunter,
Smith College

This is a sequence of assignments about a sequence of writing tasks: reviewing notes, seeing the significance of apparently minor points, developing an idea fully, finding corroborative detail, putting phrases in order. It teaches a lesson wearisomely familiar to us but unknown to our students—that writing, as an activity carried on by real people in the real world, involves repeated rewriting and that rewriting involves expansion, not just correction.

CLASS 1   I begin with an announcement: Suppose you're a journalist commissioned to write an article on poverty in one of the hard-hit industrial cities of the North. Your editor has given you a list of questions to think about: What does prolonged unemployment or underemployment do to workers and their families? What are the effects of slum housing and an inadequate diet? Do the poor get used to conditions or just keep on suffering? And so on. To find answers you've been traveling through working-class neighborhoods, keeping your eyes open, listening to people talk, recording observations. Here [handout] is an excerpt from the notebook you've been keeping:

> Passing up a horrible squalid side-alley, saw a woman, youngish but very pale and with the usual draggled exhausted look, kneeling by the gutter outside a house and poking a stick up the leaden waste-pipe, which was blocked. I thought how dreadful a destiny it was to be kneeling in the gutter in a back-alley,[1] in the bitter cold, prodding a stick up a blocked drain. At that moment

---

[1] Two words ("in Wigan") are omitted from the original at this point. I don't want my students confused by an unfamiliar place name; they handle the passage better if they assume it describes an American scene.

145

she looked up and caught my eye, and her expression was as desolate as I have ever seen; it struck me that she was thinking just the same thing as I was.

Next you must work this passage up into a paragraph for your article. Take a few minutes right now, in class, to do that—revise the passage, improve it, expand it if you like. Keep phrases that work and cut out ones that don't. Keep, cut out, or add details, making free use of your imagination.

After twenty minutes or so I ask the class what problems in the passage they noted and tried to fix. They begin talking, invariably, about phrases (e.g., the piled-up adjectives in "usual draggled exhausted," the limping rhythm of the last line), but they can be encouraged to discuss such larger issues as the adequacy of visual detail (what does *youngish* mean?) and the propriety of using *I* in writing like this. They can be asked what the passage means as a whole—not an easy question to answer, because it has no progression, no emphasis. At the every least I want my students to see that the passage, however ineffectively, describes two people, observer and social victim, and that it has a narrative as well as descriptive purpose, but I am careful to keep a variety of interpretative possibilities open, because the students' work is not yet over. I conclude the first meeting by telling them to take the original passage home and revise it further, or anew. Their goal is a 300-word paragraph with expressive details and a clear main point.

Before class, each student has written her paragraph, made multiple copies of it (omitting her name), delivered the copies to a central rendezvous, and read the paragraphs of all the other students (a routine procedure in my writing courses). In class, I get them to tell me which paragraphs seem most "interesting" (a vague word, advisedly used), and after we single out two or three we proceed to analyze, reread, and mark up the copies before us. I ask them what makes these revised paragraphs work. What different lessons have been drawn from the woman's plight? What new relations between the woman and the reporter have been dramatized? If discussion turns on journalistic ethics—can it be right to imagine a scene, invent details, in what claims to be nonfiction?—all the better. Good students always raise this issue. Even better ones note prejudices about poor people we all seem to share. (Student revisions often make the woman black.) Toward the end of class I reveal the truth. The passage they've been working on comes from a real notebook kept by a real (and distinguished) journalist, George Orwell, who in 1936 was commissioned to study conditions in the depressed industrial towns of northern England. Furthermore, Orwell expanded his notebook entries into the opening chapters of a book, *The Road to Wigan Pier.* Their last task is to study Orwell's own 300-word revision of the passage. I have sometimes simply provided them with the relevant paragraph:

The train bore me away, through the monstrous scenery of slag-heaps, chimneys, piled scrap-iron, foul canals, paths of cindery mud criss-crossed by the prints of clogs. This was March, but the weather had been horribly cold and everywhere there were mounds of blackened snow. As we moved slowly through the outskirts of the town we passed row after row of little grey slum houses running at right angles to the embankment. At the back of one of the houses a young woman was kneeling on the stones, poking a stick up the leaden waste-pipe which ran from the sink inside and which I suppose was blocked. I had time to see everything about her—her sacking apron, her clumsy clogs, her arms reddened by the cold. She looked up as the train passed, and I was almost near enough to catch her eye. She had a round pale face, the usual exhausted face of the slum girl who is twenty-five and looks forty, thanks to miscarriages and drudgery; and it wore, for the second in which I saw it, the most desolate, hopeless expression I have ever seen. It struck me then that we are mistaken when we say that "It isn't the same for them as it would be for us," and that people bred in the slums can imagine nothing but the slums. For what I saw in her face was not the ignorant suffering of an animal. She knew well enough what was happening to her—understood as well as I did how dreadful a destiny it was to be kneeling there in the bitter cold, on the slimy stones of a slum backyard, poking a stick up a foul drainpipe.[1]

I think it preferable, however, to send students to the library and let them find the passage for themselves. (It comes on page 18 of *The Road to Wigan Pier*, so not much work is required.) Their formal assignment runs as follows:

WRITING ASSIGNMENT

Read the opening chapters of *The Road to Wigan Pier* (on reserve in the library), locate the revised paragraph about the woman with the stick, and write a two-page essay on Orwell's changes. How does he extend and clarify his point, establish a consistent tone, control his reader's response? How does he, in short, improve the passage? Compare his version with your own, if you like, but keep the emphasis on Orwell.

CLASS 3

We discuss Orwell's paragraph, and with it general notions of revision. Sometimes I begin provokingly ("Are you sure this passage is really improved?"), but the question that seems to work best, to help students see Orwell's achievement most clearly, involves the added detail of the train. Why should Orwell distance himself from the woman in this way? Examination of *"The Road to Wigan Pier* Diary" (this document too can be put on reserve) suggests that Orwell was on foot when he made his original observation. Why does he fictionalize the scene? For that matter, why does he alter "She looked up and caught my eye" to "I was almost near enough to catch her eye"? Students can of course answer these questions best if

---

[1] From *The Road to Wigan Pier* by George Orwell. Reprinted by permission of Harcourt Brace Jovanovich, Inc. and the Estate of the late Sonia Brownell Orwell and Secker & Warburg Ltd.

they have read a certain distance into *The Road to Wigan Pier* and understand the larger purpose of the book—one reason to assign it to them, rather than give them the paragraph on a handout.

Revision   The essay handed in at the third meeting is the only one I collect, mark, and—eventually, after it has been revised once more—grade.

LESSON READINGS

George Orwell, "*The Road to Wigan Pier* Diary," in *Collected Essays, Journalism and Letters of George Orwell*, ed. Sonia Orwell and Ian Angus (Orlando, FL: Harcourt Brace Jovanovich, 1968), Vol. I, pp. 170–214.

George Orwell, *The Road to Wigan Pier* (Orlando, FL: Harcourt Brace Jovanovich, 1958), p. 18.

Who Is Speaking and to Whom?

Tia Greenfield,
City College of San Francisco

My purpose in the following series of assignments, which I use early in the term, is to help students develop a keener awareness of audience. Although this particular letter to the editor of the *San Francisco Chronicle* (April 8, 1983) usually produces spirited reactions, any provocative or controversial letter could be used. The idea is particularly useful for students with writing blocks.

EDITOR—If I ever saw my wife on television protesting anything, she wouldn't be my wife much longer. A woman's place is in the home.

What women shouldn't be: police officers, lawyers, judges, bus drivers, behind the wheel of a car, pipefitters, machinists, carpenters, golfers, or politicians.

I think you get the drift.

George M. Hall,
Vallejo

WRITING
ASSIGNMENTS

1. "Freewrite" your honest reaction to this letter (five minutes).

2. Who is George M. Hall? What does the M. stand for? How does he look? How old is he? What are his hobbies? What is his educational background? What kind of work does/did he do? What does the inside of his house look like? What does he like to eat and drink? What kind of clothes does he wear? What are his favorite entertainments? Where does he spend his vacations? What is his family like? Does he have any children? How does he treat them? What do they think of their father?

Write a character sketch of George M. Hall. You may use these questions as a guide, and add any other information you think important.

3. Write him a letter commenting on his views.

4. Write a character sketch of his wife. Be sure to give her a name. (You may refer to the questions in item 2.)

149

5. Write a letter to her.

6. Pretend that you are George. Write his reply to your letter to him (item 3).

7. Pretend that you are his wife. Write her reply to your letter to her (item 5).

8. Write your own letter to the editor of the *San Francisco Chronicle* in response to George's letter.

When the writing is turned in, some of the responses may be read aloud and discussed. Students may be asked to comment on whether or not particular Georges described could have written the letter to the editor, on how he would react to particular letters to him, on how his wife might respond to letters to her, on whether their letters to students seem consistent with particular character sketches, on how various readers might react to students' own letters to the editor, and so on.

Students learn that in order to communicate with someone who looks at the world as differently as George M. Hall, they must make a serious attempt to understand him: Is he merely Archie Bunker? Is his wife necessarily an Edith Bunker? Can you see why he might have written such a letter? I think you get the drift.

Story: Perspective and Purpose in Narrating

John Trimbur,
Worcester Polytechnic Institute

Storytelling is an ancient art, reaching back to the earliest human cultures. To be able to recognize a story, the archaeologist Alexander Marshack says, is to be able to act in time and space, to plan and carry out cultural practices within the patterns and periodicities of nature. The stories we tell—from the unwritten narratives painted on the walls of Paleolithic caves to the Bible and the latest episode on *Dallas*—structure our perception of the world, of how we fit into the ongoing flow of events, and of what it means to be human.

The following sequence of writing assignments grows out of my dissatisfaction with the treatment of narrative in most composition texts and with my own teaching practice. I used to assign narrative as an exercise to bridge the gap between personal experience and wider public issues. Since narrative appeared to be a "natural" mode of development (relying on the natural category of time), I thought it was "easier" than other rhetorical modes, and thus a good place to begin. I asked students to tell stories based on important events in their lives and then derive the larger issues implied in the stories.

After experimenting with various exercises, I still think narrative is a good starting place. I have come to see, though, that narrative is richer and more complex than I had allowed—not just a way to generate and sort out material by arranging it in temporal sequence but, more important, a way to construct meaningful patterns of thought through the artifice of fiction, of creating stories as "made up" things. For this reason I have found it useful to take a cross-cultural approach to narration—to tell and analyze stories from different cultures—in order to emphasize the "made up" quality of a narrative and to raise the issue of fiction and truth. I want students to see that what we think of as true or factual is really a story, that the "facts" depend on cultural and conceptual beliefs and assumptions that can give them considerably different meanings.

And I have found it useful to ask students to look at an event not only from different cultural perspectives but with different purposes of their own as writers. For this reason I ask students to write about the story of Columbus' discovery of the New World (though many other events could substitute here) with various aims in mind—expressive, informative, literary, and evaluative. In short, I try to engineer a sequence of writings to show how the story and its meaning change according to the perspectives of the characters in the story and the purpose of the writer.

CLASS 1   *The Plot of the World*

At the beginning of class, I tell students we are going to read two stories—one of them familiar and one not so familiar. I hand out copies of Genesis I and Jaime de Angulo's version of a northern California Indian creation myth. Then I ask students to form groups of five or six to discuss the following questions and to prepare responses to share with the rest of the class:

1. What happens in each story? List the sequence of events.
2. What is the plot? That is, what force or power causes the world to come into being in each story?
3. What differences in cultural beliefs and values do you see when you compare the two modes of creation?

After discussion, each group reports, and I write the responses on the board without comment. Students see rather quickly that the mode of creation in these two myths implies a good deal about cultural differences. They see that in Genesis God the creator is above and outside creation, calling the world into being out of a void through the power of his word. In the Indian tale, on the other hand, they see that Fox and Coyote are part of the natural order and that they create the world through the magical power of ritual. By comparing the two accounts, students typically conclude that Genesis describes a hierarchical world, created systematically by the centralized authority of God's word, whereas the Indian tale describes a communal world, created spontaneously by the authority of collective song and dance.

Once the class has agreed, or agreed to disagree, about their responses, I initiate a discussion about how stories recount inaugural events in the life of a culture and how cultures derive their aspirations and sense of destiny from the stories they tell. I ask students to think of stories that shape the purposes and hopes of the communities they belong to—the life of Jesus, the American success story, the Holocaust, Rambo, soap operas, and so on.

CLASS 2   *Inaugural Events (Two Classes)*

I open by recalling our discussion of how cultures record inaugural events. Then I write "Christopher Columbus," "Discovery of the New World," and "October 12, 1492" (all in quotation marks) on the board. I ask students to "free-write" whatever comes to mind in response to the name, event, and date. When the students finish writing, I ask why I put the name, event, and date in quotes—and we discuss the sense in which each term is problematical and depends on a cultural framework to be meaningful. Students usually see right away that the "Discovery of the New World" is a Eurocentric view that does not take into account the perspective of the native people already living in America. It takes them a little longer to see that the date "October 12, 1492" depends on the Gregorian calendar, which reckons years from a primary mythic event, the birth of Jesus. And they may need help to see that "Christopher Columbus" is the anglicized version of the Italian navigator Cristoforo Colombo (and that he's known in Spanish accounts as Cristóbal Colón).

WRITING
ASSIGNMENT 1 I ask students to go to the library, look up some information on Columbus (encyclopedias or history textbooks are adequate sources for this assignment), and write a one-page account of the "Discovery of the New World" on "October 12, 1492."

CLASS 3 I ask students to form groups to discuss their accounts, using these guidelines:

1. Where do they agree?
2. Where do they disagree? What omissions, differences, discrepancies are there?
3. How do you account for these discrepancies?

The groups report, and I steer the discussion toward the problem of facts and interpretation. At this point, students usually begin to see that the significance of facts and details depends on the interprctive framework in which they're located. Students see too that there is more than one interpretation of Columbus in the historical record and that the way he is portrayed—as an expert navigator in the Age of Exploration, as an emissary of Spanish imperialism, or as a visionary mystic—determines which facts and details are meaningful. Then we talk about what interpretations students have implied in their own accounts of Columbus.

CLASS 4 *The Event in Fiction (Two Classes)*

At the beginning of class, students "free-write" for ten minutes about what they think was going on in Columbus's mind when he stepped ashore in the New World. I tell the students to pretend they *are* Columbus and to imagine how he would talk about what he saw and experienced. When they have finished, I ask a few students to read their writing aloud. Then I ask the class to "free-write" for ten minutes again, this time about what was going on in a native's mind when Columbus stepped ashore. Again I ask a few students to read aloud.

WRITING
ASSIGNMENT 2   I ask students to write a fictionalized account of October 12, 1492, taking *either* Columbus *or* a native as the main character. I suggest they begin their fictions *in medias res:*

> Start the story just before the event happens. Give details that will create a living experience for the reader. Then, at the end of the paragraph, anticipate what is to come. Cue the reader to the point of the fiction—what the character realizes or how the event affects the character.

CLASS 5   I ask the students to exchange their stories for written peer response:

1. Does the story account for the change? Does anything seem left out? Is there anything you want to know more about?
2. How would you describe the writer's attitude toward the event?
3. What is the significance of the story? What does it mean to you?

CLASS 6

Evaluating the Event (Two Classes)

I begin class by asking students what differences they see between writing an informative account and a fictionalized version. I point out that their fictions have already started to interpret the event, to draw out its significance. Then I ask students to reread all the writing they have done so far and to form groups of five or six to discuss these questions:

1. Have your perceptions and/or attitudes toward Columbus changed? If so, how? Explain the change.
2. What issues emerge from the writing you have done about Columbus? List as many as you can.

After talking about the changes in perceptions (and these are often considerable), I list issues on the board. These usually include Eurocentricism, a culture's need to record and commemorate inaugural events, the usefulness of cross-cultural perspectives, the irony of history in Columbus' attempt to find a passage to India, the misnaming of the "Indians," and so on.

WRITING
ASSIGNMENT 3   I ask students to write a short essay (300–500 words) on one of these issues or any other that comes to mind. For this essay the students need to take a stand and make and support an evaluative statement about the significance of the issue they have chosen to write about.

CLASS 7   Students read their essays aloud and then exchange them, preferably twice, for peer response, using such commonly accepted guidelines as:

1. What is the main point of the essay? What sentence or sentences best express the point?
2. How does the writer support the point? What reasons, arguments, evidence, and so on, does the writer use?
3. What did you like about the essay?
4. Did you feel lost or confused at any point? If so, where and how?

CLASS 8   *Conclusion*

By this point each student has assembled a considerable packet of writing. I have been responding to (but not grading) each of the assignments, often framing my comments as a response to the peer response. In the final class in this sequence I ask students again to look over what they have written and to form groups of five or six to discuss these questions?

1. How do the various accounts you have written resemble one another? How do they differ? How did your perspective change from one writing to another?

2. Characterize your purpose as a writer in each of the writings. What were you trying to do? How did you approach your readers?

This exercise leads to a discussion of the various overlapping aims—expressive, informative, literary, and evaluative—that I have embedded in the various assignments.

REVISION   Finally, I ask students to revise *either* Writing Assignment 2 *or* Writing Assignment 3 to turn in for a grade. I point out that in either case, whether they choose to revise their stories or their essays, the students will be involved in an interpretive reconstruction of the event. I want the students to see that their essays are just as much "made up" things as their fictions and that the task for a writer is not simply to record events straight from the past but to represent these events according to the writer's perspective and purpose.

This sequence helps students see there is more than one way to tell a story. Through group and class discussion, students learn to talk about the perspectives and purposes they have adopted as writers. In a preliminary way, the sequence raises a theme I pursue in the next sequence of writings—when I ask the class to read and compare professional interpretations of historical events and literary texts. And the sequence introduces them to storytelling as a technique humans use to explain how things came to be the way they are.

LESSON READINGS

Genesis I
Jaime de Angulo. *Coyote Man and Old Doctor Loon* (San Francisco: Turtle Island, 1973), pp. 21–22.

FOR FURTHER READING

Ford Madox Ford, The *"Half Moon"* (excerpt) in *The Ford Madox Ford Reader*, ed. Sondra J. Stang (New York: The Ecco Press, 1986), pp. 18–28.
William Carlos Williams, "The Discovery of the Indies," in *In the American Grain* (New York: New Directions, 1956), pp. 7–26.

Writing a Critical Essay Together: The Connection Between Thinking and Writing

Raymond F. Hilliard,
University of Richmond

This lesson, normally requiring five or six class periods, engages students in the largely *collective* writing of an essay on D. H. Lawrence's short story "The Horse-Dealer's Daughter." The class works under my guidance: I lead discussion, write suggestions on the blackboard, prepare machine copies of work in progress. My role is delicate. I have to keep the project moving at a seemly pace while resisting the urge to make specific suggestions of my own. The class occasionally fails to detect what I see as a problem—unsuitable diction or an awkwardly constructed sentence, for example; in such instances I point out the general nature of the problem but let them solve it. Much of the value of the lesson derives from the continuous give-and-take between students, one student suggesting a sentence, say, and others responding with criticism or alternative suggestions.

The lesson has three overarching aims: (1) to show students—rather, to have them show each other—*how to think their way into a topic* and, once there, *how to achieve conceptual clarity, coherence, and precision*; (2) to demonstrate the *organic* nature of effective writing (how the parts can be made to fit the whole); and (3) to teach students about the problem of *evidence* (how much is needed, for example). A definite benefit of the lesson is that, for the remainder of the two-semester course, the class has a concrete frame of reference, a common vocabulary—for instance, a student will understand what I mean if I note in another paper that a point is "conceptually imprecise." Throughout the lesson I emphasize the intimate connection between language and thought, both in the story itself and in the paper we are writing.

Other stories would serve as well—Faulkner's "Dry September," for instance, or Hemingway's "The Short Happy Life of Francis Macomber"—but I often use "The Horse-Dealer's Daughter" because it has thematic density appropriate for my purposes. Though a not-so-incidental result of the lesson is that students find it much easier in later assignments to write about literary works, I insist throughout that I am not concerned with literature as such, that what they are learning about the relationship between thinking and writing is applicable to their work in other courses. By the end of this lesson students typically say that they had never previously understood how much effort should go into writing an essay; they claim that no earlier English course had ever gone so far beyond *telling* them *about* writing to *showing* them *how* to do it.

The lesson contains the following steps, which I briefly explain in advance:

CLASSES 1 AND 2   1. I have announced our topic—"Lawrence's notion of love as made apparent in this story"—at the previous class meeting, when I assigned the story itself. During the first in-class session we do an exhaustive conceptual survey of the story, using a version of the method known as free association and ending with a list of all the possible ideas we may eventually want to include in our essay. We do not, at this point, worry about how precisely the ideas are stated.

2. We organize the ideas from our random list into logical categories. Beginning with as many as thirty or forty items, we usually end up with five or six categories to which we affix such labels as "Mabel Pervin's unhappiness" or "the social setting" or "strange outbursts of passion." We then re-examine the items in each category and try to be more precise in our phrasing both of the items themselves and of the general heading. We might, for example, begin with "Mabel's unhappiness" but then proceed to "Mabel's loneliness and depression," and finally to "Mabel's sexual and emotional frustration." We notice that such changes in our wording go hand in hand with an increasingly deeper understanding of the story. I tell the students that, for all practical purposes, a thought is only as good as the language that expresses it. Accordingly, I also tell them that we should not hesitate, during the remaining steps in our lesson, to tinker without phrasing so as to make it reflect more accurately the concepts we are dealing with.

Steps 1, 2, and 3 are likely to consume two class periods. Beginning with Step 2 I require students to prepare written suggestions between class meetings. Only a few of these suggestions are shared in class, but I collect all written work and return it with comments at succeeding meetings. This becomes especially important by Step 4, when students are preparing entire sentences.

We often discover in Step 2 that some items in our original list are inconsequential or irrelevant enough to be thrown out. This discovery entails discussion of evidence, a matter to which the class will return in Step 8. (I find that literary works are particularly useful in teaching students about evidence because the instructor has considerable—if not complete—control over the evidence, knowing when and how much evidence—or counterevidence—has been overlooked.)

3. We discuss the conceptual relationship between one group of ideas and another. For instance, we talk about the social circumstances of the two main characters in relation to their thwarted emotions. The students see more of the significance of—the "ideas" behind—many of the apparently trivial social details in the story (Ferguson's being a "foreigner," for example). I point out that we are discovering patterns of meaning (inter-related concepts) implicit in the factual data provided by the story and that this activity of conceptualization is essentially the same that occurs when people work with data in any discipline—history, sociology, and so on.

Historians, for instance, studying the activities of European powers in Africa and elsewhere in the late nineteenth century, find it useful to employ the omnibus term "imperialism," which brings the separate facts together in a single conceptual category. I mention that when students take a history course they are likely to be introduced to the concept of imperialism before being given concrete instances of it, but that historians themselves move, at least in principle, from the facts to the concept. In practice, I tell them, thinking and interpreting are never so simple, in part because people are likely to interpret new data in the light of established categories, which have heuristic value. For example, in trying to understand a story like "The Horse-Dealer's Daughter," readers are at an advantage if they are already familiar with the concept of emotional repression, including the notion that such repression can entail displacement (Mabel's attachment to her function in the family as a substitute for personal relationships). As the course goes on I use such examples as these to stress the relevance of our efforts to interpret and write about stories to problems that arise in other areas of intellectual inquiry. It can be particularly useful to have students talk about why parts of certain stories resist interpretation (some readers are apt to have trouble with the aftermath of the pond incident in Lawrence's story, for example).

CLASS 3
AND FF

4. With the topic and the several categories in mind, we formulate a thesis. I stress that the thesis should not be a mere restatement of the topic ("D. H. Lawrence writes about love in his story.") but a statement *about* it, and that it must be carefully worded so as to do justice to the complexities of the story as we have come to understand them. That is, our thesis must point as precisely as possible to Lawrence's idea of love as dramatized in the story and yet be *inclusive* enough to allow us to deal in the paper with the several dimensions of the topic that we have identified as important.

5. Keeping the thesis steadily in view, we prepare a topic outline; we use the categories, both headings and itemized contents, defined in Step 2, though we sometimes see a need to combine or reorganize some of the categories. After the analysis involved in Steps 1, 2, and 3, the students

produce the thesis and the outline with remarkable dispatch; in fact, they are surprised at how readily a good argument suggests itself.

COLLECTIVE WRITING ASSIGNMENT

6. We compose an introductory paragraph that begins with our thesis statement. I tell them that the introduction we are usually three weeks into the course and, for the time being, I impose simple, somewhat mechanical notions) should indicate as specifically as possible the overall direction of the essay.

7. We turn the major headings of our topic outline into complete sentences, with a view to using each sentence as the topic sentence of a paragraph in the essay. Remembering that an essay is a series of ideas related to each other and to a controlling idea, we make sure that each sentence is conceptually related to the one that precedes it and to the thesis. We work very carefully on these sentences, as well as on those in the introductory paragraph, talking at length, again, about how to make each one *inclusive* and *precise*. I know no better method of getting students to attend to diction and sentence structure—to the connection between what is being said and how it is said, and between a particular sentence and its context. Students often smile in wonderment at what they can accomplish simply by transposing the parts of a sentence or by subordinating one part to another. Since analysis of the topic inevitably means discussion of similarities between the two main characters, we invariably experiment with parallelism as well. We talk also about the desirability of semicolons, colons, and dashes in particular situations; I point out that each of these punctuation marks signals a special kind of relationship between one thought and another.

INDIVIDUAL WRITING ASSIGNMENT

8. Having collaborated on the conceptual skeleton of the essay, students work individually (out of class) to flesh it out with textual evidence—in other words, to develop each of the paragraphs that follow the introductory one. In the end, the class as a whole has written every sentence in the introductory paragraph and the topic sentence in each of the succeeding ones, and individual students have completed the paper on their own.

LESSON READING

D. H. Lawrence, "The Horse Dealer's Daughter," in *England My England and Other Stories* (New York: Thomas Seltzer, 1922).

FOR FURTHER READING

William Faulkner, "Dry September," in *Collected Stories* (New York: Random House, 1950).

Ernest Hemingway, "The Short Happy Life of Francis Macomber," in *The Short Stories of Ernest Hemingway* (New York: Modern Library, 1938).

READING

UNCORRECTED STUDENT PAPER[1]

In "The Horse Dealer's Daughter," D. H. Lawrence shows that love is a powerful emotional need which, if repressed, can explode in an act of passion. He focuses on the developing love relationship between two characters: Mabel Pervin, whose feeling of unfulfillment comes mainly from her family's failure to show her love, and Jack Ferguson, whose need for an intimate relationship has been frustrated by his situation as a foreign doctor in an English working class community. The characters' repressed need becomes completely obvious at the pond when Jack saves Mabel from suicide and the two of them discover an uncontrollable love for each other.

Because of her brothers' failure to recognize Mabel's emotional need, and because of her father's second marriage, Mabel is continually depressed; therefore, she can feel love and devotion only towards her money and her dead mother. The only remaining daughter in the family, Mabel is unable to relate to her coarse, unsympathetic brothers. In her mother's death, Mabel lost her greatest source of love, and when her father remarries, she feels that he too has deserted her. With the absence of both parents, she must rely on her money and social status for a sense of self-worth. Yet this works against Mabel in alienating her from the working class community. She finds herself alone in the world, without female companions or male suitors. When the horse-dealing business falls into ruin, she even loses the security of wealth and status, and the final remnants of the family break up altogether. Deprived of love and security, Mabel seeks escape from her unfulfilling life in a suicidal reunion with her last object of affection, her dead mother.

Jack, isolated by his background and profession, is like Mabel in lacking an affinity with the townspeople. Being of Scottish origin, he is a foreigner in the English community. In the same way, he possesses an "alien" occupation. While the other inhabitants of the town are colliers and ironworkers, Jack holds the title of doctor's assistant. As with Mabel, this higher social status works to alienate him from his neighbors. He cherishes his working class patients because they are "strong-feeling people," but his foreign identity and his profession prevent him from expressing his own feelings and being a real member of the community, which he calls "the hellish hole." Like Mabel, he is alone in the town, having no extraprofessional relationships.

When Jack symbolically rescues Mabel from her attempted suicide in the pond, the two recognize a passionate need for one another. Since both have had to repress their feelings for such a long time, this revelation of passion

---

[1] I have italicized the sentences written by the class as a whole. The rest was written by the best freshman student I had that term.

takes the form of a spontaneous explosion. Seeing that she may still have a reason to live, Mabel violently clings to Jack's leg, "clutching him with a strange, convulsive certainty," while reassuring herself that she has finally found a lover in repeating, "You love me." Unable to resist Mabel's pleading or his own built-up need, Jack leaps over professional barriers and passionately expresses his newly found love. When Mabel becomes fearful that her strong behavior may seem "awful" to him, Jack reaffirms his devotion by promising to marry her as soon as possible. Lawrence implies that in their mutual desire for each other, Jack and Mabel discover a permanent outlet for their long repressed love.

Redefining "Research": Becoming a Better Reader

John Tyree Fain,
University of Florida

"Word Echoes in Carlyle's *Past and Present*," the article on which this lesson is based, is one of the illustrations I use in my classes to discuss the elementary research paper. In this kind of paper, "research" is fundamentally what *you* find in a work of literary art, not a hodgepodge of what others have to say about the work.

WRITING ASSIGNMENT
Select a single volume of a good writer. The ideal way is to get a copy of your own so that you can mark up the margins. As you read, put an *x* by the side of an idea, a word, an image that you consider worth remembering. Then when you run across the same idea or motif again (as you well might in the language of a work of art), put the *x* beside that too. As you continue to read, you may find another idea or word or image that seems significant to you. Put a *y* in the margin beside that one, and continue the process as you continue to read. You may find that one or two of your alphabetical symbols turn up often whereas others fade out; and you would then eliminate those that do not persist. Of course, if you use a library book for your project, you would use cards with your quotations on them and marked with your alphabetical symbols.

This process will be your attempt to formulate what seems to occur when we read a work of literary art. As we begin to read, many things may be said that seem to convey little to us. We file them away close to the threshold of consciousness, where they lie until the literary artist, by a series of echoes and recapitulations, brings them to life for us, gives them meaning.

The meanings that you derive from your series of quotations are dependent on your own imagination and judgment. You have probably been told, or will be told, not to write impressionistically. Don't believe a word of it. Your own impressions will be the lifeblood of your writing. But be as sure as you can be that your impressions are supported sufficiently. "Just impressionism" *is* bad, but your impressions supported by the best evidence and logic you are capable of is good. Don't be afraid to get yourself out on a limb, but be sure that your limb is strong enough to hold you up!

Once you have become aware of a particular idea or word or image and how it is used in a particular work, try to generalize from your specific readings—that is, keep asking yourself "What does all this mean?"

Some of the things that you find in such a study may have been noticed by other writers, and maybe you could see if such findings have been published. But don't try to find out *before* you make your own investigation. If you do, you will destroy the benefit I believe you will derive from the discoveries made on your own.

You could take a volume of Emily Dickinson and make a study of her language. Emily Dickinson never did go anywhere much, so her poetry is full of the things she saw and did around home. She helped with the housekeeping, cooking, cleaning up, dusting, making beds, putting things away in drawers, mending, and sewing, and she uses the words and "pictures" connected with such things—words like *bonnets, hats, shoes, needles, thread, tattered seams,* and so on. She was in the garden behind her house a good deal, so her poetry is full of things she saw there, linnets, snakes, butterflies, bumblebees, and all the colors in the garden. Or every time you see religious language in her poetry, make a note of it and say what it refers to in the Bible, how she uses it in the poem, words like *heavenly Father, devil, iniquity, deity, Eden, sacrament, resurrection, Tabernacle, divine, doom, heresy,* and all the biblical names she uses. She just talked to people in the family, and her father and brother were lawyers. Every time you run across something that looks like a legal term, make a note of it, words like *briefs, clauses, codicils, emolument, proviso, estates.*

But I believe this time it would be better for you to use a volume of good nonfiction prose, and it would be hard to beat Carlyle.

LESSON READINGS

Emily Dickinson, *The Complete Poems of Emily Dickinson,* ed. Thomas H. Johnson (Boston: Little, Brown, 1960).

Thomas Carlyle, *Past and Present* (Boston: Little, Brown, 1843), Chapter 1.

John Tyree Fain, "Word Echoes in Carlyle's *Past and Present*," *Victorian Newsletter,* August 1955.

READING

John Tyree Fain

WORD ECHOES IN CARLYLE'S *PAST AND PRESENT*

Past and Present has perhaps been accorded too little attention as a work of art. A study of Carlyle's repetitive devices is particularly rewarding. For the work is full of key words and phrases that echo like bells struck now and again in the impassioned prose, producing the effect of refrain and playing their part in the integration of the several themes. In one of his favorite repetitive patterns Carlyle takes an incident from history, mythology, or the daily press and uses it as an illustration or as a symbol in the development of a social theme. While presenting the incident, he repeats a certain word or phrase often enough to enable it to act as a vehicle for its context. Then when he wishes to refer to the same theme again, the echoed word or phrase calls up the whole imaginative, emotional manifold of the first treatment. For instance, in the first chapter, which develops the Midas legend as a symbol of the condition of England, the exposition is built around the word "enchanted." England is full of wealth but no man can touch it, for it is enchanted fruit. "Twelve hundred thousand" workers sit enchanted in their "Poor-law Prisons." Master workers and master unworkers are also subject to the "baleful fiat as of Enchantment." In the six pages (Centenary Edition) of the first chapter "enchanted" and "enchantment" occur eleven times. Then they are available throughout the book and are used dozens of times; their impacted meaning also exerts influence on a cluster of words such as "phantasm," "phantasmagory," "chimera."

In the meantime other words are being developed in a similar manner. In the first chapter itself Carlyle tells about the Stockport Assizes case in which parents poison three children to collect burial fees. Thereafter merely the name Stockport holds within itself as it reverberates through the pages the images and details of the initial narrative: "Yes, in the Ugolino Hunger-tower stern things happen. . . . And now Tom being killed, and all spent and eaten, is it little starveling Jack that must go, or poor little starveling Will?—What a committee of ways and means!" (p. 4)

Thus the process of building and utilizing a vocabulary continues. One can feel some of the pulsing life of the book by calling to mind typical instances: the sphinx as a symbol of justice and nature's law, the widow who died of typhus and proved her sisterhood by infecting the whole neighborhood, the men of the Dead Sea changed into apes, payment by forfeiting a grinder tooth, the horse hair and iron body of the Pope riding through the streets of Rome, Igdrasil, the champion of England encased in tin, the seven-foot hat. Of course, not all of the words and phrases that form repetitive patterns are built up by the process outlined. Some of them are just taken from the press or popular parlance and used so often that they acquire added power merely from the echo itself, for instance, "Corn-Laws," "Sliding-Scale," "Useful Knowledge

Published in *Victorian Newsletter,* August 1955.

Society," "Supply and Demand," "Morrison's Pill," "bribery elections," "gig-man." These words and phrases, then, however they may have become charged with additional power, interweave in the formation of the rich Carlylean texture: "Two million shirtless or ill-shirted workers sit enchanted in Work-house Bastilles, five million more (according to some) in Ugolino Hunger-cellars; and for remedy, you say,—what say you?—'Raise *our* rents!' I have not in my time heard any stranger speech, not even on the Shores of the Dead Sea." (p. 171)

The most frequent echo in *Past and Present* depends upon the words "si-lent" and "silence." The workmen of England sit silent. Abbot Samson's best quality is his "talent of silence." Even Plugson of Undershot is ennobled by the "force of silence" in him. Silence is a medium through which man com-municates with God: "There shall be a depth of Silence in thee . . . a Silence unsoundable; known to God only." (p. 200) In fact, "silence," which is used in so many senses that it is not definable as a concept, is one of the devices that enable Carlyle to maintain the level of the sublime in parts of *Past and Present*. Of the dictum "Work Is Worship" he says:

> He that understands it well, understands the Prophecy of the whole Future; the last Evangel . . . its litany and psalmody the noble acts, the heroic work and suffering, and true heart-utterance of all the Valiant of the Sons of Men. Its choir-music the ancient Winds and Oceans, and deep-toned, inarticulate, but most speaking voices of Destiny and His-tory,—supernal ever as of old. Between two Silences:
>
> > 'Stars silent rest o'er us,
> > Graves under us silent!' (p. 233)

That is, "silence" is one of the means by which Carlyle is enabled to consider man in his sublime aspect. And *Past and Present* is therefore, among other things, a sort of paean to man: "Ye are most strong, ye sons of the icy North, of the far East,—far marching from your rugged Eastern wilderness, hitherward from the gray dawn of Time." (p. 276) This fact accounts for some of its impact on the age, for it is one of the two or three most influential English books of the nineteenth century. Men were yearning for an antidote to scientific in-vestigations which gave them a smaller and smaller place in the universe.

The passages quoted suggest another device which helps to maintain the sublime level—the repetition of words indicating vast stretches of time and space, the infinite, the innamable, the unfathomed, the unspeakable. But this seems sufficient to point up an approach that some students of Carlyle may not have emphasized sufficiently. *Past and Present* is a remarkable social document, as all commentators agree. It is more remarkable as a work of art.

Definished Poetry in the Composition Classroom

Mary Brown,
Marion College

Because composition teachers also think of themselves as humanists, they constantly strive for effective ways to integrate the teaching of literature and composition. Although teachers see the connection as obvious—almost inevitable, their students usually find it vague—forever frustrating. We have begun to realize that when students are presented with polished, published poems, short stories, and novels, they fail to see the relationship between these "museum pieces" and their own tentative, sometimes error-laden drafts. In an attempt to help them make the connection, teachers show them Xeroxed copies of the early drafts of famous authors, expose them to professional writers' explanations of their own writing processes, and assure them that every piece of literature began with a human mind, a pen in hand, and a blank sheet of paper. Still, for inexperienced writers, the connection often remains academic. My attempt to make the connection more real for my students has taken many forms, but one approach that seems to work well is to present my students with "unfinished" literature. (Perhaps I should call it "definished" literature, since I undo part of what an author has done before presenting it to my students.)

It seems to me, for instance, that there is no better way to teach the concepts of deliberate word choice, connotation, and denotation than in the context of good poetry where word choice is often pivotal, economy and precision most crucial. Although the act of writing is actually an intricate web of many decision-making processes, students often become so overwhelmed with the breadth and depth of their options that they exercise few of them, relying on old patterns, clichés, comfortable but ineffective (and sometimes incorrect) habits. They don't recognize and so don't use the power available to them. Rather than lecture on the importance of a writer's choices, however, I allow my students to experience a focused kind of literary decision making that is admittedly contrived, but effective, nevertheless. I employ some of the principles of a reading teacher's technique known as the "cloze procedure," in which students are required to supply words deleted from a passage to demonstrate their understanding of text content and structure. Many good testing tools are also good teaching tools, and an adaption of the cloze procedure has been useful to me in teaching the relationship between content, structure, and word choice.

IN-CLASS EXERCISE

I select a good poem with which I am fairly confident my students are not familiar. I type the poem, omitting words that are crucial, perhaps not always to the gist of the poem, but certainly to its depth and power. (I break a bit here from normal cloze procedure, which calls for words to be deleted at regular intervals.) I divide my twenty-five composition students into groups of five and hand to each student a sheet of paper that looks like this:

After great pain, a _____ feeling comes—
The Nerves sit _____, like Tombs—
The _____ Heart questions was it He, that bore,
And Yesterday, or Centuries before?

The Feet, mechanical, go round—
Of Ground, or Air, or Ought—
A _____ way
_____ grown,
A Quartz contentment, like a _____—

This is the Hour of _____—
Remembered, if outlived,
As Freezing persons, recollect the Snow—
First—Chill—then _____—then the letting go—

—Emily Dickinson, c. 1862[1]

Giving the groups an entire fifty-minute period, I ask them to work collaboratively to fill in the blanks of the poem with appropriate, powerful words. The puzzlelike quality of the exercise challenges and appeals to students, and before too long they begin to look for cues and clues within the poem, to discuss the poem's meaning, and finally to debate the word choices that have been offered in their group. Seldom are poems returned to me with unfilled blanks; students work enthusiastically and begin to

---

[1] From "The Complete Poems of Emily Dickinson," edited by Thomas H. Johnson. Copyright 1929 by Martha Dickinson Bianchi. Copyright © renewed 1957 by Mary L. Hampson. By permission of Little, Brown and Company. Reprinted by permission of the publishers and the Trustees of Amherst College from "The Poems of Emily Dickinson," Thomas H. Johnson, ed. Cambridge, Mass.: The Belknap Press of Harvard University Press, Copyright 1951, © 1955, 1979, 1983 by the President and Fellows of Harvard College.

see that choicemaking is a practical, not only theoretical, principle of composition.

At the end of the hour, the exercises are handed in, and the following day students are given a copy of the poem as it was published. (Depending on the scope of the class and the particular poem used, this might be an appropriate time to discuss various published versions of the poem.) When students see the published poem, they are sometimes amazed, sometimes disappointed, sometimes smug. I am repeatedly surprised at how often students decide on the same word the poet actually used. We compare and contrast the poet's choices and the students' choices for their effectiveness, their inventiveness, and their power. Students sometimes explain, or apologize for, or blush over their choices; more often they defend them fiercely. Occasionally, the students insist that one of them has chosen a word that works even better than the one Emily Dickinson, Edwin Robinson, or Theodore Roethke chose, and, even more occasionally, I agree.

WRITING ASSIGNMENTS   The poetry exercise works productively as preparation for a number of writing assignments. First of all, it is an extremely helpful prewriting assignment if the students' next assignment is to write about the poem. The cloze exercise forces students to do the kind of detailed analysis that inexperienced poetry readers so often are unable to do on their own, and it pushes them to give the poetry the careful consideration it requires to be understood and appreciated. Similarly, the exercise can work well to prepare students to write on diction and imagery in another poem—perhaps one on a similar theme and employing some of the same words used in the exercise poem. Finally, the exercise helps to prepare students to write a definition essay in which the strategies of connotation and synonym are so important. After working with the Emily Dickinson exercise, one of my students wrote an interesting, pointed essay defining the mourning process in her family.

The more I use the cloze-poem procedure in my composition classroom, the more possibilities it seems to contain. It encourages better writing and a better understanding of poetry. It forces the serious analysis and contemplation of words and meanings, a process central to improving both reading and writing. It substantiates my humanistic conviction that literature and composition *can* and *should* work together in the classroom to create a dynamic process that enriches both disciplines.

LESSON READING

Emily Dickinson, "After Great Pain," in *The Complete Poems of Emily Dickinson*, ed. Thomas H. Johnson (Boston: Little, Brown, 1960), p. 162.

Acts of Choice in Writing: Ben Jonson's "On My First Son"

William E. Cain,
Wellesley College

Throughout the semester, and especially in the first couple of weeks, I stress "acts of choice" in writing. I encourage students to think about the kinds of choices that writers make in crafting a poem or piece of prose and urge them to become self-conscious and explicit about these choices—about why writers "choose" to do what they do in their words, phrases, and sentences, and how they might have chosen differently.

Often I find that the basic shortcoming of my students in their writing is a loose, slack, inattentive response to language. They have trouble, to be sure, with big matters such as topic, thesis, and organization, but they seem to suffer even more from an inability to be really sensitive to their own and others' uses of language.

Early in the semester, then, I highlight intensive reading of short passages, passages usually keyed to a common subject. I want to get my students to ponder, become keenly interested in, and able to talk about the acts of choice that writers make in their shaping of language, and to see, in addition, how careful reading and careful writing reinforce each other. The more alert the student is to what she reads, the more skillful and self-aware she will be in what she writes. Another way of putting this is to say that I want the student to grasp writing as something she "does," and as something she should be doing, hard as it may be, with pride and pleasure. Writing well is not something that somehow happens by fortuitous accidents.

One of the best texts for my purposes is Ben Jonson's poem "On My First Son." The situation is a highly charged one—Jonson describes here his feelings about his son Benjamin's death—and students readily acknowledge why the choices in this text carry special significance for the writer. Sometimes I work through this poem in class, posing questions to the students and developing and clarifying their responses, always slanting the discussion toward Jonson as a self-conscious writer engaged in acts of choice. On other occasions, I distribute the text of the poem and ask students to write fifteen or so questions (a sentence or two in length) of their own that focus on choices that Jonson has made. We then discuss the questions together in class, the great variety and range of the students' questions demonstrating Jonson's precise concern for each word and phrase. As a third option (varying my plan helps keep this lesson fresh and interesting for me), I distribute both the poem and my own list of questions, and I ask the students to write two or three sentences in reply to each one.

Here are examples of the kinds of questions I ask (obviously there are many others that teachers and students could add):

1. Jonson could have written "On My Son." What is the significance of singling out this son as "my FIRST?"
2. What kind of word is *farewell*? Why does Jonson address his son as "child of my right hand?" What is the effect he produces by using the word *joy*? What other words might he have chosen?
3. Why use the word *sin*? Isn't this an inappropriate choice? Doesn't it give the poem a puzzling tone? Why would Jonson want to see his hope for his son as a sin?

(*Note:* In at least a few questions, such as this one and 9 and 10, I want students to inquire into both the gains and losses of Jonson's choices. I aim to provoke some skeptical thinking about Jonson's crafting of the poem, and, I hope, eventually to lead students to argue about and defend the choices Jonson makes.)

4. Why does Jonson use financial terms in lines 3–4? Why does he employ the present tense *pay*?
5. How does Jonson get from line 4 to line 5?
6. In the standard edition of Jonson's works, the editors, Herford and Simpson, print *loose* rather than *lose*. What are the differing implications of each of these words? Which seems better?
7. Why is the sentence from the end of line 5 through lines 6–8 relatively general in meaning? How do these lines fit together with the preceding lines?

(*Note:* The purpose of a question like number 7 is to counter any tendency of my own or my students to think in exclusively "local" terms about aspects of the poem. I want us to discuss words and phrases, but also want to keep attending to Jonson's attempts to relate and connect the specific parts of his poem as a meaningful whole. One of the advantages in using short poems is that I can generate valuable discussion about specific choices while not losing sight of the whole work.)

8. Why *rage*? Look up this word in the *Oxford English Dictionary* and explain why it fits Jonson's meaning so well. What does Jonson imply— and in what tone—when he says "WORLD'S and FLESH'S rage"?

(*Note:* I frequently emphasize to students how useful the dictionary and thesaurus can be in enabling them to perceive the specific choice the writer has made in relation to other choices he might have made. This is another valuable lesson for early in the semester—regular use of dictionary and thesaurus—that my assignment underscores.)

9. Isn't *soft peace* too abstract? Shouldn't Jonson have chosen a different, more concrete phrase?

10. What is the significance of Jonson's reference to Ben Jonson in line 10? Isn't he confusing the reader here? Shouldn't he have made his point more lucidly and directly? What *is* his point?

11. Why *all* his vows? What exactly is a vow?

12. Here are several general questions that will help us to integrate our response to Jonson's poem as a whole. What is the distinction Jonson makes between *love* and *like* in the final line? Can such a distinction be maintained? Is Jonson making a good choice in closing his poem in this fashion? How does this line follow from what Johnson has said in the earlier lines?

WRITING ASSIGNMENT   The questions listed above for lines 11–12 frequently serve as the basis for a writing assignment (two to three pages in length). After discussing lines 1–10 of the poem with the students in class, I ask them to articulate and examine the choices with which Jonson concludes. My assignment usually takes the following form:

> In our class discussion of "On My First Son," we have stressed Jonson's many acts of choice in writing. In your paper (2–3 pages), I would like you to focus on the final two lines of the poem, explaining both the specific choices that you see Jonson making and the relation between the concluding lines and lines 1–10. You might find the following questions helpful in developing your insights: What is the distinction between "love" and "like" in line 12? Can such a distinction be maintained? Is Jonson making a good choice in closing his poem in this fashion? How does this line follow from the earlier lines?
>
> Good writers are especially thoughtful about the choices they make in their conclusions. They do not simply repeat what they have said before—this would be a waste of words. They also know that readers do not want to read the same thing a second time. How does Jonson manage to conclude his poem effectively without repeating himself?

I want my students, as I have said, to recognize the kinds of decision making that skillful writers practice and, in addition, to feel the reinforcing connection between intensive "close reading" and careful, self-conscious writing. But I hope also that my assignment will get them, even at this initial stage of things, to think particularly about conclusions. I find that students usually conclude their papers badly, largely because they see the conclusion *not* as a part of the paper that involves deliberate choices but, instead, as a block of prose that mechanically summarizes what has already been said. More than anything else, the conclusions to student papers reveal the lack of self-consciousness with which most students write. When I tell them that it is in fact quite odd to write a final paragraph, especially in a two- to three-page paper, that basically repeats what has already been said, they generally grasp my point right away: They see that what they have been doing is silly and, even more, insults the intelligence of their reader. But because they have not learned to be alert to the nature and impact of their choices and have grown habituated to writing unself-consciously, they have committed themselves in their conclusions to doing something that mocks simple common sense.

After working with "On My First Son," I often proceed to Jonson's "On My First Daughter." It is very stimulating to consider the differences between these two poems, and to explore why Jonson chooses to treat the two deaths as he does.

There are, of course, other poems that group nicely with Jonson's, and that give me lots of variations, in texts, classroom exercises, and writing assignments, as I underscore "acts of choice" in these early stages of the semester. Examples include: Dryden, "To the Memory of Mr. Oldham"; Johnson, "On the Death of Mr. Robert Levet"; Wordsworth, "There Was a Boy"; Emily Brontë, "Remembrance."

LESSON READING

Ben Jonson, "On My First Son" and "On My First Daughter," in *The Complete Poems*, ed. George Parfitt (New Haven, CT: Yale UP, 1975).

READING

ON MY FIRST SON
····································

Farewell, thou child of my right hand, and joy;
My sin was too much hope of thee, loved boy,
Seven years thou wert lent to me, and I thee pay,
Exacted by thy fate, on the just day.
O, could I lose all father, now. For why
Will man lament the state he should envy?
To have so soon 'scaped world's, and flesh's rage,
And, if no other misery, yet age!
Rest in soft peace, and, asked, say here doth lie
10   Ben Jonson his best piece of poetry.
For whose sake, henceforth, all his vows be such,
As what he loves may never like too much.

ON MY FIRST DAUGHTER

Here lies to each her parents' ruth,
Mary, the daughter of their youth:
Yet, all heaven's gifts, being heaven's due,
It makes the father, less, to rue.
At six months' end, she parted hence
With safety of her innocence;
Whose soul heaven's queen, (whose name she bears)
In comfort of her mother's tears,
Hath placed amongst her virgin train:
10 Where, while that severed doth remain,
This grave partakes the fleshly birth.
Which cover lightly, gentle earth.

Ben Jonson, "On My First Son," "On My First Daughter," in *The Complete Poems*, ed. George Parfitt (New Haven, CT: Yale UP, 1975).

Sweeping Away Preconceptions

William Chapman Sharpe,
Barnard College

How can we introduce our students to the challenges and surprises of literature when they already know what they'll find there? Complete critical objectivity may be an impossible (and even undesirable) ideal, but very often preconceptions about what a text is *likely* to say restrict the complacent reader's understanding of it. In order to read and write with accuracy, students must learn to recognize that they have biases that may lead them to draw precipitate conclusions.

I developed the following combination of two classes and a writing assignment to encourage a "poverty" of prejudice among students in a traditional freshman English program, where composition and introduction to literature are taught together. Close analysis of two poems by William Carlos Williams—classwork on "The Red Wheelbarrow," followed by a writing assignment on "The Poor"—succeeds at the start of the semester in encouraging careful reading, self-awareness, and the use of supporting evidence. The exercise is also valuable to pair with an assignment on Orwell's "Politics and the English Language" because it reveals how we are as likely to be victims of our own unexamined ideological assumptions as we are to be taken in by political newspeak and government euphemisms.

CLASS 1   *"The Red Wheelbarrow" (Discussion)*

The first class period is designed to open discussion about the nature of literature, criticism, and exposition and to provide a relaxed way to begin writing about poetry, a topic that often seems intimidating. First, I copy Williams's short poem "The Red Wheelbarrow" onto the board. After a student reads it aloud, I ask the class to write a ten-minute essay, not to be graded, on the meaning of the poem. I remind them that they should be able to back up any assertion they make with a quotation from the text. Having collected the papers (for my future information on their critical orientation and expertise), I start the discussion by asking *what* depends on that wet red wheelbarrow beside the white chickens. I arrange the responses on the board as the students talk and am shortly in a position to point out how their interpretations fall roughly into three groups. They are either economic (the wheelbarrow is an important tool, a means of livelihood); personal (the wheelbarrow has special associations for the poet); or aesthetic (the look of the wheelbarrow, in its juxtaposition to the white chickens, is visually appealing). Some students take the third idea a step further and say that the poem itself, as an aesthetic object, also depends on the existence of such a wheelbarrow: Since the whole poem describes it, without it there is no poem.

This last observation—that a poem can be about itself—allows the students to consider the idea of form *as* statement and helps me to introduce the different strategies of communication employed by a poem and an expository essay (which they are going to write about it). In the poem the way in which a thing is said is paramount to its meaning, whereas in the essay, direct statement of certain ideas usually takes priority. The poem tends to emphasize the medium; the essay, the message—though not always. Backtracking for a moment, I have the students consider *how* they arrived at their interpretations of "The Red Wheelbarrow" and I suggest they bear this process in mind when doing the coming assignment. What are their methods for finding meaning in poems, and how do these depend on what they expect a poem to say? How would they lead others to the same conclusions? By the time the class ends we have established that writing about a work of literature involves developing a thesis about the text's meaning and supporting the thesis with a series of paragraphs that examine the text's often indirect method (images, rhythms, juxtapositions) of conveying it.

WRITING
ASSIGNMENT

I ask the students to read William Carlos Williams's poem "The Poor" (1938) with care. Their assignment is to employ what they've just learned about formulating and supporting a thesis by writing a two- to three-page close analysis of the poem. Since the poem comprises only twenty short lines, they can say something about almost every line if they desire. They are warned specifically to leave aside their own personal feelings about the poem's subject (not about the poem itself) and to concentrate on just the words and ideas that the poet uses in the poem. (The warning may be omitted, but I find it is more valuable for students to discover how many preconceptions they bring to the text even after they are asked to be as objective as possible.)

CLASS 2

"The Poor" (Discussion)

After the students hand in their papers, I give them the chance to present their overall conclusions about the text. Comments tend to focus on the poet's concern for the ragged children and the old man in the poem and, depending on the interpretation of the last stanza, the pride of the poor, or the futility of their struggle in an uncaring world. Here I point out that no adjectives or descriptions in the poem specifically support any of these verdicts. A thesis, I emphasize, is only as good as the evidence that supports it.

Then I ask two central questions: (1) What *is* the "anarchy of poverty" *as Williams defines it*? (2) What is the meaning of the "delight" that the poet says he takes in it? Clearly, the poem—written during the Depression, no less—violates the political expectations that the title prompts. By revealing in the opening stanza that he takes an *aesthetic* view of poverty, the poet compels the alert reader to abandon the stereotypical attitudes toward poverty that he has come to expect from literature or the media and that he may share himself. He must ask himself whether the poet's surprising attitude—he likes the way poverty looks—can be justified either artistically or socially.

Further analysis shows that Williams has built "anarchy" into the very structure of the work, his broken syntax and unorthodox punctuation reinforcing the content. The poem proceeds by contrasts; every aspect of poverty the poet mentions triggers an opposition that makes it into a symptom of disorder—and variety. Wooden houses sit among brick tenements, the sidewalk sweeper works in a fitful wind, fences remain "in an unfenced age." These contraries prompt the reader to ask a series of more probing questions: Does the old sweeper represent the dignity of poverty or its futility? What is the relation of social order to "disorders" like poverty? Does the "anarchy of poverty" provide a measure of freedom from the "system"? Or is it part of the system? Is the wind that the sweeper disregards and that has "overwhelmed the entire city" in the final line a symbol of the inherent anarchy of things or of the challenge the poet faces in shaping the random materials of life into art?

From here the discussion can shift to how the students have organized the "anarchy" of their own ideas on paper. First, how sensitive were they to the actual words and structure of the poem when they formulated their theses? Objectivity and critical acuteness are the product not just of the students' knowing their own predilections, but also of their testing their theories against the text itself. If they can't back up their ideas with a quotation, perhaps the ideas need modification. Second, they must also make an important strategic decision: Is it better to structure the paper thematically or to proceed chronologically through the work? What are the implications of following one route or the other? By the end of the class the students should have started to grasp the nature of the decisions they need to make in order to present their ideas clearly and convincingly.

The impact of "The Poor" depends on the reader's expectations—and on their violation. The poem anticipates the reader's assumptions, but succeeds in challenging them only if he restrains his impulses to replace the poem's meaning with his own. Thus the assignment demonstrates to students both the need for careful interpretation and the value of having some detachment while doing it. As the students reconsider their initial emotive responses, they begin to recognize the necessity of close reading, especially in situations where preconceptions—either in attitude toward the topic or in expectation of what a literary work might say about it—can deflect the understanding. "Know thyself" is the chief focus of the lesson, but close behind should come the realization that use of supporting evidence not only renders an argument more convincing, but also helps keep the writer honest. Finally, the poem itself provides training in subtlety of analysis: Is there a shift in tone and social concern in the last phrase? Does it imply a dawning social consciousness on the part of the poet? Class discussion of these topics, *after* they have written their essays, makes the students more receptive to suggestions for revision while helping them acquire the self-awareness necessary for future interpretation, writing, and editing.

LESSON READING

William Carlos Williams, "The Poor" and "The Red Wheelbarrow," in *The Collected Earlier Poems* (New York: New Directions, 1938 and 1951).

The Children of Pride: Deducing Character from Family Letters

Carolyn P. Collette,
Mount Holyoke College

In conjunction with a college-wide curriculum review, the English department at Mount Holyoke College has reformulated its approach to teaching English at the freshman level. As a result we have developed courses whose goal is to link the study of English more directly and more fundamentally to the other arts, sciences, and humanities that students will study during their years at Mount Holyoke. We believe that the skills we develop to read works of imaginative literature are useful in reading works commonly thought of as belonging to other academic fields, and vice versa. Reading a poem, reading an essay in political philosophy, reading a scientific article—although each act of reading may call for specialized knowledge—all involve comprehending both text and subtext, recognizing hidden analogies, identifying the writer's point of view, and sorting out underlying assumptions and biases.

The following assignment, based on the one-volume abridgment of *The Children of Pride,* a collection of letters among the members of the Jones family, a well-to-do, religious, slave-owning family from Georgia during the Civil War, provides an opportunity to read analytically through a series of letters, to try to uncover the metaphors and images that governed the writer's sense of the world, and to face the problem that manifestly good people often do evil, either wittingly or unwittingly.

Student Guidelines for Reading *The Children of Pride*

This collection of letters may well be unfamiliar territory to you, especially within the context of an "English course." Remember that this course is designed to acquaint you with the techniques of close analytical reading that will open up many kinds of texts, not just literary texts. As you read *The Children of Pride,* ask yourself the following questions:

1. Can you distinguish voices among the letters? If so, can you de-

scribe a personality on the basis of what he or she writes? Select one of the characters who particularly interests you and follow him or her through the volume.

2. The people who wrote these letters were all educated in a Christian, classical culture. How does that culture affect their perspective on what they witness around them and what they experience? Again, focusing on one favorite character would be a good way into this subject.

3. How can we judge these people? Shall we judge them as slave owners? as Christians? as American patriots? as appropriators of other people's goods and labor? Where, and on what grounds can you take a stand?

WRITING ASSIGNMENT 1

To accompany this reading unit I assigned a journal in which the students were to record within twenty-four hours of each class whatever they recalled as significant, interesting, or provoking about the class discussion and the reading. I then directed them to the journal excerpts in the text; these, although full of facts, also revealed the writer's perspective and feelings. In them students could find reflections at times thoughtful, at time impassioned. (Our class discussions reinforced my suspicion that, in a misguided effort to avoid *I* in formal writing, students had become used to filtering themselves out of their writing. They forgot, or never knew, that good writing comes from people's actively responding to ideas, events, books, to other people.) The problem of what to put in a journal led us nicely back to a major theme of the course, that good writing presupposes an interested—and hence interesting—writer. I urged the students to write what they "felt" in the hope that over several weeks they would discover a unifying theme in their own reactions. I encouraged them to use the journal as a means of talking to themselves to discover what they really thought about the material. By the end of the month they had at least glimpsed the idea that serious writing is not always public writing and that some of the best "public" writing often comes out of private writing.

For the sake of argument and initial order we began discussion by focusing narrowly on personality, the students accounting for why one of the Joneses rather than any other interested them. Charles, Jr. seemed an obvious romantic, because he wrote in such a flowery style. My response was to ask which came first, the style or the romantic. I could then ask them to penetrate behind the surface of the prose to try to understand what motivated the writer to express his thoughts about the world in the way that appeared on paper. Why, I asked, does Charles, Jr. keep referring to the Old Testament when he speaks of the Civil War? Before they could address this question the students had a burning issue of their own: They repeatedly criticized the formality and the conventions of letter writing, particularly of salutation and closing. We tried to compare our own forms of communication, especially the phone call, to the letters. Students were reluctant to see the parallels between our own formulaic phrases and the Jones's. In fact, the style and content of Charles, Jr.'s letters provoked a lot of discussion about what sort of man he was. This discussion in turn led to questions about the content of his education and the culture it reflected. What did it mean to him to be educated? How far was his sister educated? To what purpose? In what ways was the Bible important to Charles? How could he be so apparently "religious" and yet not a communicant of Midway Church?[1]

Mrs. Jones, too, sparked a good deal of interest. We noted that Mrs. Jones, although somewhat in her husband's shadow, was a capable and strong woman. Along the way our discussions of her raised such broader issues as women's role on plantations. Mrs. Jones was clearly a full partner with her husband in running their plantations; this fact led us to talk about the Miltonic conception of Adam and Eve as two halves of one whole and its possible influence on a family acquainted with the devotional, religious tradition in English literature, with the classics and with Protestant theology. We were also able to dispel the myth of the fragile Southern belle and to discover the real importance of women in plantation society.[2]

The Reverend Mr. Jones's outrage at the debauching of one of his female slaves by a house guest, himself a clergyman, at first seemed evidence of Mr. Jones's probity and compassion. As we discussed culture and education, as we moved on to the issue of judgment, we came back to the letters on this subject, and to our conclusions, each time sharpening our sense both of what the Reverend Mr. Jones meant when he said the accused clergyman had insulted him and of what he assumed about his relationship to the slave. In the course of our exchanges on this topic it became clear that the Reverend Mr. Jones was most concerned with saving a soul entrusted to his care. Whom, we asked, did the insult most afflict? What was a slave to him? Was owning a slave a privilege or a heavy responsibility? How human were slaves to any of the Joneses, anyway?

Eva B. Jones's letters evoked the most lively class discussions by far. Initially, students were unable to recognize the difference in tone and style between her letters and those the other women wrote. Once we hit on reading the letters aloud, though, the students began to hear the difference and to laugh at what was a unique and lively humor. We asked ourselves what it meant that Charles, Jr. married her during the war; what it meant that she needed a Northern climate to restore her health when the South lay in ruins; what it meant that she called her august and upright husband "Charlie"; what it meant that she read so much history. Students were

---

[1] In all these discussions we relied solely on our text; a teacher who wants to go outside the text on the specific issue of the culture of nineteenth-century Southern gentlemen can consult Richard Beale Davis's *Intellectual Life in the Colonial South*, 3 vols. (Knoxville: University of Tennessee Press, 1978). Chapters 1 and 2 of Raimondo Luraghi's *The Rise and Fall of the Plantation South* (New York: New Viewpoints, 1978) are also helpful. Sacvan Bercovitch's *Typology and Early American Literature* (Amherst: University of Massachusetts Press, 1972) is very helpful on the use of the Bible.

[2] To supplement the text I referred students to Jean Friedman's *The Enclosed Garden* (Chapel Hill: University of North Carolina Press, 1985) and to Catherine Clinton's *The Plantation Mistress* (New York: Pantheon, 1982).

quick to see her as a symbol of enterprise and pluck and to understand her illness as at least as much psychological as physiological. Our most intense discussions revolved around the triangular relationship we perceived among Eva, little Ruthie, and Mrs. Mary Jones. Students saw Eva as removing Ruthie from Mrs. Jones's life and affections.

In these discussions we reminded ourselves that we were reading real letters written by real people. Interpreting their actions and reactions, making a story out of the fragments we were reading led us to question how narrative urges shape our lives, to think about how we make up stories about the events of our days.

WRITING ASSIGNMENT 2

By this time students were drafting a paper based on both class discussions and their journals, facing in writing the problem we had been facing all along, namely, how the order within the mind of the beholder—the witness of historical events, the reader of *The Children of Pride*—mirrors or distorts the order of the "real" world. Each student was to write a paper (six to ten pages), choosing one of the members of the Jones family who particularly interested her and using the evidence of what that person says as well as what others say about him or her in order to interpret that person's character and relation to the culture. How, finally, can that person be understood, given the very different assumptions we now make about human conduct?

LESSON READING

The Children of Pride (excerpts), ed. Robert Manson Myers (New Haven, CT: Yale UP, 1972).

Vote for Me: Winning Votes with Style

Linda Driskill,
Rice University

This lesson is about style and about how readers interpret such features as organization, sentence structure, and word choice in the statements of candidates for campus offices. The lesson begins by speculating on the personalities of five writers and reports students' conclusions as "rules" for revising the style of such statements. (Naturally, these examples could be replaced by others from one's own campus newspaper.)

Whether you run for office, I tell my students, or apply for a job or for admission to graduate school, the impression you make depends largely on your style. College students who are given separate grades for "content" and "style" (with the "content" grade counting for more) sometimes think that style doesn't matter or that the two can in fact be separated. But outside the classroom style often does matter a great deal.

Several candidates have declared for the office of vice-president of the Program Council, the organization that sponsors all campus-wide social events. Who would get your vote? Look at the opening paragraphs of each candidate's statement (the first candidate is really two persons offering to share the job) and decide what kind of person each candidate is.[1]

Mike Lester/Bob Ruschinghaus (the Blues Brothers)

They just let us out. They're not going to catch us now. We're on a mission from God—we're out to have a good time and make sure everyone else does too. Our primary goal is to rock the whole campus.

Lily Sams

The Program Council is a fundamental organization for campus activities. I want to contribute to the formation and development of events such as Beer-Bike, TGs, Springfest, and various other social functions that are such an integral part of university life.

---

[1] All the candidates' names have been altered, and some of the statements have been altered to clarify or to add needed information. The statements were taken from the campus newspaper over a four-year period.

John Waters

Whoever becomes the new PC vice-president will have really big shoes to fill. Kyle Durr has given the PC not only his time and energy but also his good humor and joie de vivre. No one can replace him, but I hope that I can contribute as much of myself.

Kevin Sonderson

My name is Kevin Sonderson and I am running for the office of vice-president for the Program Council. I am a hardworking student, but I believe that students should have fun, too. That is what the office means to me—an opportunity to make good times happen for other students.

Ralph Rich

It is with a great deal of concern that I, Ralph Rich, look at the present Program Council. The general apathy with which the school has greeted these elections (there are many positions that are not contested), coupled with the resignation of the current vice-president, has caused a dark shadow over something I feel to be very important to all of us. Furthermore, two concerts had to be cancelled last year, which severely reduced the operating budget, concerts that should never have been offered. It is with this thought that I implore you to think very clearly about your vote.

You probably have already formed some ideas about the personalities and characters of these candidates, without ever having met them. The content of the candidates' statements is important, but the writing style also affects students' votes. The Blues Brothers' breezy, wide-open style, Rich's gloomy and moralistic accountant's view of the situation, Sam's elevated and abstract (even wordy) generalizations, and Sonderson's earnest "My name is . . ." tone give clues to who these people are, their motivation, and their way of handling problems.

In analyzing the impressions the candidates made through their writing, the students agreed that content must not be vague. In each statement, they wanted the candidate to mention:

1. The usual responsibilities or functions of the office.
2. Problems (if any) that needed solution.
3. What the candidate would do to solve these problems or meet the challenges of the office.
4. The candidate's qualifications or experience.

When the office was "chairman" or "president" of the entire organization, they thought that discussing the aims and problems of the organization as a whole would be appropriate.

The students concluded that once the content was set forth specifically, it was the style of the statements that affected their willingness to vote for that person. The students in this class wanted candidates to be dedicated to serving the school rather than self-centered; they wanted candidates to be forthright and specific rather than evasive and ambiguous; and they wanted candidates to be good problem solvers.

Candidates' Character: How It Makes Itself Known in Writing

The students in this writing class wanted the candidate to be concerned with performing the duties of the office, not with the ego gratification of being an officeholder. "Campus politicos" were suspect. When candidates made *I* the subject of most of their sentences or spent much time talking about personal attitudes, students felt the writer was preoccupied with himself or herself. In the following excerpt, the candidate seems to be recording a monologue:

Candidate A

In anticipating a few of the questions you might like to ask me if you could, I suppose the first I should answer is "why?" If I only wanted to be involved, a myriad of other student activities are available, and most are less time-consuming, less serious, and less difficult—and then there is always home-work! If I needed only interaction, just to be part of something, the residential college system, the intramurals, the interest clubs would be more effective. But I feel a position on the Honor Council is more than these. For me, it would be the relevant activity, the one that makes the difference around me— in my school work, in the academic atmosphere of the university, in the general uniqueness of the university.

Candidate A seems to believe that voters are more interested in why he would choose the office over all others than in what he would do if elected. Candidates who seem more interested in themselves elicit a less favorable response than candidates who seem more interested in results, as excerpts from B and C illustrate:

Candidate B

The Student Association President's job is multi-faceted; however, one main function is representing the students' views to the administration. All too often the SA president has represented the administration, trying to justify the university's actions to the students. As president, I will not only express student views, but I will also stand up for them. As the main and possibly only effective student link to the university administration, the SA president must impress upon the administration the worth of student views; the administration must not continue to ignore the ideas and concerns of the students.

Candidate C

My name is Ellis Evans and I am running for the office of Student Association external vice president because there are specific things I would like the SA to do. The external vice-president has several responsibilities, many of which could be expanded.

The job with the most tangible impact on students is the telephone directory. With conscientious planning, there is no reason why it has to come in late, or over budget, or with too few copies, as has often happened in the past. I have been in charge of various publications for the last five years. I was editor of my high school yearbook and edited the Wilson residential college section of the university yearbook for the last two years. I was also editor of the Wilson Handbook, a typeset, illustrated booklet sent to three consecutive years of freshman classes at Wilson Residential College. I am familiar with various printers, and through experience, know the importance of ads, budgets, organization, and deadlines.

A second major responsibility of the external VP is to promote good relations with the city and with other universities. . . . To accomplish this major task, I would like to see the SA start a volunteer community service program. Not only would this help the university's reputation in the community, but if organized properly. . . .

In the last example, mentioning one's accomplishments and experience was judged to be evidence of Candidate C's competence, not self-centered preoccupation. The students derived the following rule:

I. Including statements of experience that demonstrate you can do the job; delete statements that show you thinking about your own concerns.

A second personality trait conveyed by style was forthrightness or directness. The candidates most admired stated clearly what they meant, showing some care in choosing their words and in constructing "who does what" sentences rather than opaque and entangled ones. As one student remarked about a particularly confusing paragraph, "If she doesn't know what she's saying, how can she know what she's doing as an officer? It isn't my fault that the sentence doesn't make sense."

The students' second rule was:

II. Make the meaning of sentences clearer by:
   a. Identifying the subject and the main verb of the sentence and seeing whether they make sense together.
   b. Recasting the sentence after asking "Who does what?" (And if necessary adding the *who* in a sentence using the passive voice.)
   c. Replacing "low-content" verbs such as forms of *be, do, have, seem, make,* or *give* with "high-content" verbs.

IN-CLASS EXERCISE   The following sentences were judged neither direct nor precise. Try applying the students' second rule to improve the directness of the sentences.

1. These are the reasons that I should be voted for.
2. It is the need of the Student Association for hard-working, experienced leadership that is required.
3. I would like to see some other things done, including building up the films shown and expanding the ballet and opera tickets.
4. Filling the Program Council's prescribed role "to offer an opportunity for students to participate in programs of social, cultural, recreational, and educational value" can be filled by the residential colleges' realizing what the Program Council has to offer.
5. There are five things that the Student Association should do.
6. It has been my experience that too often what the university rule is is not understood and we need to have better orientation for students, which would avoid many cases in the first place, and I want the university court to try this.

The class then looked critically at a *paragraph* from a candidate's statement:

"The Program Council? What's that?" In my three semesters here I have heard this asked quite a few times. I think people at this school generally feel the Program Council doesn't do a good enough job. Concerning this I talked to several seniors and graduate students and looked through some old yearbooks. I was stunned to find this was true about the feelings toward the Program Council almost from the beginning. The basis of judgment of a good Program Council has always been how well it handled films, homecoming, and the spring festival but new ideas were seldom experimented with.

Some of the sentences are ambiguous because of their structure. Notice that the last sentence uses *but* to contrast two clauses. The student readers asked each other: "What kind of contrast is he making here? Does he mean that innovation or use of new ideas has never been a basis of judgment? Or does he mean that new ideas have never been tried?" The sentence structure doesn't provide any answers.

Furthermore, the placement of some prepositional phrases makes some sentences hard to understand. For example, "of a good Program Council" is placed after the subject of the sentence, "The basis of judgment," where possessive phrases are usually placed—for example, "the policy of a good teacher" usually means "a good teacher's policy." However, the students believed that the writer did not mean "the good Program Council's basis of judgment" but something like this: "Students rate a Program Council's work highly when. . . ." This last paraphrase shows the "who does what" technique at work. When a reader is trying to figure out what is meant, he often asks, "Who does what?" The students also noted the vague use of pronouns such as *this, which,* and *that,* and the distracting ambiguities they cause.

Coherence of Argument

The readers also decided that this candidate did not build a coherent argument. He switches subjects several times:

What is the program council?

Most people don't feel the Program Council's performance is adequate.

I talked to several seniors and looked through old yearbooks.

The basis of evaluating performance has always been X, Y, and Z, but new ideas were seldom tried.

What is the candidate's point? His point might be that "Although the Program Council's performance has never been rated high, a good program could be offered if new ideas were tried." If this were his main point, he could build a better path to that idea in his opening paragraph:

> The University Program Council is responsible for the all-school films, concerts, and special events such as homecoming. I found in conversations with senior and graduate students that the Program Council's performance has never been rated high. After examining the records, I concluded that programs offered were unsatisfactory because innovation was rare. A good program could be created if new ideas were tried.

In this revised paragraph the subjects are easier to follow: What the council does, how well it has done its job in the past, why it failed, why it could succeed in the future. The result of an easily followed arrangement of subjects within the paragraph, students decided, made the speaker seem intelligent, capable of analysis, and therefore able to solve problems. Their third rule was:

III. Review the sentences in the paragraphs to make sure the evaluations flow from evidence and that recommendations or conclusions fit the analysis or evaluation.

Word Choice and Personality

Some of the candidates chose impersonal, abstract terms to discuss both the office and their own qualifications. Latin derivatives such as *integral, institution, endeavor, prestigious,* and *experience* gave an elevated and serious tone to their statement. On the other hand, such statements seemed more impersonal, less vivid, and rather stodgy. Students who primarily used contractions and slang terms seemed less serious and responsible, although they were judged to have more informal and approachable personalities. Contrast the two sets of phrases from two candidates' statements:

Candidate X	*Candidate Y*
moved back a week	rescheduled
had a hand in it	instigated
passed judgment	mandated
cut off	isolated
nixed	vetoed

In addition, the use of specific events, details, and actions made promises and claims much more convincing.

The rules derived from these analyses can be used directly to edit the statements of other candidates, and may also serve as the basis for the following assignment.

WRITING
ASSIGNMENT

Claim a Vote for Yourself

Choose an office on campus and write a statement about why you should be elected to that office. Be sure to answer the following questions:

- What does this officer or organization do?

- What problems have been experienced in the past?

- What do you think should be done to solve these problems or to meet the challenges of the office?

- What experience or qualifications do you have that would enable you to take the necessary actions?

Review your statement and revise, following the three rules we have developed for editing candidate statements.

I. Include statements of experience that demonstrate you can do the job; delete statements that show you thinking about your own concerns.

II. Make the meaning of sentences clearer by
a. Identifying the subject and main verb of the sentence and seeing whether they make sense together;
b. Recasting the sentence after asking, "Who does what?" Sometimes you will have to supply the *who* for the sentence.
c. Replacing "low-content" verbs such as forms of *be, do, have, seem, make,* or *give* with high-content verbs.

III. Review the sentences in the paragraphs to make sure that the evaluations flow from evidence and that recommendations or conclusions fit the analysis or evaluation.

Ask another student in the class to read your statement and to make any suggestions necessary for a clearer and more effective style.

The Periodical Room as a Source for Reading and Writing: Analyzing Magazines

U.T. Summers,
Rochester Institute of Technology

Nowhere can students get a better idea of the concepts of *audience* and *purpose* than in the periodical room of a good college library. It is both a temple to American freedom of speech and a bazaar of ideas and products— a suitable place to learn about the presentation of ideas for different audiences and purposes and the meaning of "Let the buyer beware."

After the work we do early in the term devoted to close reading and the analysis of short pieces, I like to remind students of what can be learned by an overall look at the heterogeneous grouping of materials in a contemporary newspaper or magazine. At the same time I hope they will become aware of the richness of resources in the periodical room.

A discussion of audience or of purpose in writing can proceed naturally to a discussion of which periodicals students read: the local daily paper, *The New York Times, USA Today, The New Yorker, Playboy, Mademoiselle, MS., Mother Jones, Scientific American*, hobby magazines? From the question of which periodicals the students read, the discussion proceeds to *why* they read them—entertainment, desire to know what is going on in the world, the latest information in science or politics for a term paper, practical information on fashion and travel, information on "how to" in many areas? Students will probably be surprised by the range of interests fellow students already have. The teacher also has an opportunity to bring into class copies of magazines students should be aware of.

To provide the students with a good sampling of magazines, I divide the class into several groups, each of which will study a particular kind of periodical; within each group each student selects a publication for analysis. Some possible categories for the groups are newspapers, news magazines;

magazines of opinion; magazines for men, for women, for different ethnic and religious groups; magazines directed toward specific subjects such as sports, science, hobbies. Although I hope that students will consider periodicals that are unavailable on newsstands (i.e., to be found only in the library), I encourage them to buy, if possible, a current copy of the magazine of their choice and to bring it to class, having familiarized themselves with their magazines so that we can use class time efficiently in the attempt to discover how a given magazine can be scrutinized analytically. I leave class time for students looking at magazines in the same category to pool their observations.

WRITING
ASSIGNMENT 1

I ask for an essay of 750–1000 words that analyzes the "book" (whatever is not advertising) and the advertising of one issue of a newspaper or magazine in order to discover the orientation and purpose of the periodical and, insofar as possible, to define its readership.

The following questions have proved helpful to students both in the class discussions and the written work at home:

Facts About the Periodical

Look and feel of the publication? Size? Quality of paper, typeface, ink, reproductions? History of the publication? (A reference book such as *Magazines for Libraries*, published by R. R. Bowker Company, can be useful here.) When was it founded? How often does it appear? In what areas of the country? How many readers? Cost? Publisher? (Note whether it is the official publication of any particular organization.)

Content of Book

Note categories (articles, stories and poems, departments) and subjects (as you can judge them) in the table of contents. What do you notice about the style or styles of writing? Personal, informal, practical, academic, technical, scientific? (These do not exhaust the possibilities.) Is the periodical directed toward experts and students in a given field, amateurs, the general reader, other? What attempts are made to convince the reader of the reliability and authority of the information? What are the values presented in the "book"? Is the reader urged to adopt any particular attitude or to take any particular action? Who are the heroes? the villains?

Advertising

Categorize the types of advertisements used. What do these tell you about the economic status, aspirations, and values of the readers.

Here I offer my students a comparison of my own between two magazines with similar interests in order to demonstrate the range of relevant observations. Most teachers will feel that a careful written analysis of one magazine is enough for a week's work, but others may wish to use this occasion to assign papers comparing and contrasting two comparable magazines.

Two Nature Magazines

Readers of both *Field and Stream* and *Audubon* would probably all call themselves nature lovers. A comparison of the March, 1986, issues of the two magazines gives an idea of what different conceptions nature lovers have of nature and their own attachment to it, not to speak of their activities.

Both magazines are monthlies, founded during the same half-decade: *Field and Stream* in 1895 and *Audubon* in 1899. They are about the same size; *Field and Stream* is 8 by 11 inches and *Audubon* is 8¼ by 11 inches. (Both are indexed by the *Reader's Guide to Periodical Literature*, and *Audubon* is indexed as well by *Biological Abstracts*.)

Available on almost any magazine stand at $1.95, *F & S* claimed a circulation of 2.1 million in 1982, "by far the largest circulation hunting and fishing magazine in the world."[1] *Audubon*, with a circulation of 350,000, comes as one of the "benefits and privileges of National Audubon Society membership," which costs $30 annually; but the magazine can also be purchased for $3 at well-stocked magazine stands throughout the country.

Most of *F & S* is printed clearly on a fairly good grade of magazine paper, with a heavier and shinier grade used for some sections of advertisements. *Audubon* consistently uses the same excellent quality of heavy paper, suitable for reproducing the nature photographs for which the magazine is famous; the same paper is used for advertisements.

It would be difficult to say which magazine gives the reader more "book" for the money. The copy of *F & S* examined has 194 pages; *Audubon* has 130—each with three columns to the page. *F & S* has eight feature articles with a four-article "Canadian Fishing" section, a seven-page "Northeast" section, and twenty-one "departments" or signed columns, including an editorial. Advertisements are run throughout the magazine so that both features and departments must often be continued later in the magazine. The fact that both are relatively short, two to three pages, makes them easy to follow. *Audubon*'s eight feature articles, with their many illustrations, run straight through the magazine from p. 41 to p. 110 without interruption by the advertisements. The first feature is a twenty-seven-page article, "The Decadent Forest," illustrated by thirty-eight photographs, in-

---

[1] Bill Katz and Linda Sternberg Katz, *Magazines for Libraries*, 4th ed. (New York: Bowker, 1982).

cluding the wraparound photograph on the cover. An editorial, "The Endangered Forest," reinforces the political implications of the argument of the article, namely: "Congress and the Forest Service must develop a long-term strategy that will ensure the survival of the last old-growth forests." Unfolded proofs of the photographic cover are available for ten dollars. The names of the illustrators of the feature articles are written in the same size of type as those of the writers.

It seems reasonable to assume that *F & S*, owned by CBS, Inc., expects advertising to pay much of the cost of the magazine's production and that many readers are as interested in the information offered by the advertising as they are in the material in the "book." The advertising department of *F & S* has eight members; more than half the magazine, ninety-seven pages, is devoted to full pages of advertising. It seems equally likely that *Audubon* is paid for mostly by the dues of the National Audubon Society and other society sources of income.[2] About one quarter of this issue is given to full-page and smaller advertisements. The most striking section of *F & S* is the eight full pages, on heavily coated paper, of Nissan trucks, mostly red, plowing through rough terrain. *F & S* has twenty pages of advertising for automobiles and automobile equipment versus three in *Audubon*, ten for motorized boats and boat products versus none in *Audubon*, eleven for cigarettes versus none in *Audubon*. Surprisingly, of the full-page advertisements in *F & S*, only two are given to guns and ammunition. Advertisements related to fishing, including K-mart Sports Center's twenty full pages on "The Fish America Sale" and many small advertisements for lodges and outfitters, have the most space in the magazine. *Audubon*'s largest number of advertisements are for travel agencies and trips and cruises, some as expensive as $20,000, and for bird lovers' collectibles such as a porcelain vase decorated with portraits of male and female bluebirds at $120.

The feature articles in *F & S* are written mostly as true first-person narratives. They are about equally divided between hunting stories—"For Deer, Whistle Dixie," "The Last Buck," and "Stag Party"—and fishing stories—"Drifting Bait for Trout," "Spinnerbaits for Pike." The fishing stories emphasize "how to do it" in beautiful surroundings; the hunting stories, adventure and romance. A hero reminiscent of Faulkner's Sam Fathers in "The Bear" figures in a story on the grizzly, "The Wraith That Roars": "It was his sincere conviction that no real sportsman with any sincere regard for the future has a moral right to kill more than one grizzly in a lifetime." Good sportsmanship is the primary moral value emphasized in stories, editorial, and the "Conservation" department. The "bad guys" are those who indulge in any hunting that involves "shooting from roads, baiting of waterfowl or doves, the use of 2-way radios, or any willful flaunting of the principles of fair chase. . . ." Of the twenty-one departments, two are called "How It's Done"; most are given to practical suggestions in specific areas

---

[2] Smaller advertisements in *Audubon* mention summer camps, trips and cruises sponsored by the society, as well as life annuities available through the society.

such as "Vehicles" and "Gun Dogs." An article on Canada is illustrated by a photograph of a father fishing with a little girl, but there are few pictures of women in either articles or advertisements. In the Camel ad, a blond curly-haired young man stands behind his outboard motor with his sleeves rolled up; he suggests an ideal for both younger and older male readers.

Although one usually associates both the magazine *Audubon* and the National Audubon Society with birds, among the eight feature articles in the March issue, only one, "Ravens on My Mind," focuses specifically on birds. Others are on manatees, the prairie sphinx moth, and tree frogs; the value of gravel pits as wildlife habitats; highway carnage of all kinds of animals; the old-growth stands of forest in the Northwest and in Alaska; and "Inland Island," the 37-acre nature preserve that the writer Josephine Johnson has allowed her Ohio farm to become. The eight regular departments have articles on fairy wrens, cranes, and cormorants, but also on eels, the feeding of big game in winter, the poisonous water hemlock, the general topic of crowding, and conservation policy in Canada.

Since the days when it was called *Bird-lore*, the interests of *Audubon* have broadened to take in whole ecosystems and narrowed to consider all forms of life, including lichen and insects. Some articles are largely descriptive and historical (notably the one on eels—the American appetite for them being too small to endanger the various species in our waters). Most articles offer some specific appeal, prohibition, or warning to the reader: Don't allow those at the political appointee level of government to sell off the great old Douglas firs; save the gravel pits as wildlife preserves; don't eat water hemlock. The first-person true narrative is the favored literary form as with *F & S*, but instead of telling us where to go to hunt and fish in what vehicle and with what lure, the writer of an *Audubon* article takes us into obscure marshes and drainage ditches as well as on mountain tops to tell us what to observe and conserve in America and all over the world. A villain is a collector who pays $2000 for a prairie sphinx moth. A hero is an amateur herpetologist who spends rainy evenings during spring migratory season carrying buckets of frogs across a state highway so they will not be squashed by cars.

The National Audubon Society, made up of clubs and affiliated organizations in 500 communities, is also frankly a national lobbying force for environmentalism, primarily interested in preserving the natural heritage of the nation. It is effective partly because it unites some of the very wealthy who can afford to take trips to New Guinea to see the fairy wren with those whose chief investments in their hobby have been binoculars and walking shoes. *Field and Stream* appears to be a successful commercial enterprise which meets the needs of many readers for entertainment and practical information. Morally and politically, it concentrates on the behavior of the individual sportsman—"Hunt fair, fish fair"—rather than on the effects of such activities on the environment. It glamorizes the four-wheel-drive vehicles and the motor boats that have been such effective aids to man as predator and polluter of forests, beaches, and waterways.

WRITING
ASSIGNMENT 2

A further assignment that grows out of this sequence enables students to apply what they have learned about audience, tone, purpose: I ask them to decide on a typical article in the magazine or magazines they have studied and to imitate that article, choosing a subject appropriate to the magazine and using a style the editor would recognize as right for his readers.

A Lesson in Logic: Advertising Fallacies

Linda Flowers,
North Carolina Wesleyan College

CLASS 1
WRITING
ASSIGNMENT

This assignment is designed to follow immediately on a paper written as an argument. For a three-to four-page paper analyzing a selected advertisement, I talk about particular ads both the class and I bring in. Discussion is at first quite general. It is enough that the ads engage our interest. Without any overt preparation, I simply hold up a magazine—*The New Yorker* seems to work especially well (perhaps because, even if they have not seen it before, students recognize and are caught up in its moneyed look)—and turn from one ad to another, the class readily joining me in discussion. We will have just completed several sessions on logic, as a necessary basis for writing and analyzing an expository argument. At first, students will likely not see the connection between the two: syllogisms and logical fallacies and their argument paper, on the one hand, and pictures of Bayer aspirin and Buicks, Apple II computers, Cabbage Patch dolls, and Chivas Regal on the other.

I allow the discussion to proceed more or less as it will until—as always happens—certain students begin to point out that *"That"* (a languorous model predictably) "doesn't have anything to do with *that"* (a Ford pickup or a cigarette); "the scene doesn't really go with what they want you to buy"; and so forth. Once such conclusions are drawn, discussion sharpens, and our previous work with the logical fallacies, syllogisms, enthymemes, and the like can be driven home. My point, here and for the next one or two class periods, is that advertising is manipulative, illogical, shrewd— and enormously effective: It too has a thesis; it too makes an argument. Even students who earlier have had trouble recognizing equivocations, non sequiturs, fallacious appeals to authority, red herrings, and other fallacies typically are intrigued to discover them now deployed so knowingly and deliberately and to such telling effect. What may have been merely a dull list of terms bewilderingly set forth has now some chance of seeming relevant enough to be taken seriously. I ask students to bring to class next time two or three ads about which they have something to say and which they "like" and to read Orwell's "Politics and the English Language."

195

Class 2   During this second (and often third) class period, I repeatedly use such terms as *implication, premise, assumption, association*—as well as the names of the fallacies—and ask such questions as, "But what is, in fact, being sold? the car? or the idea that by buying the car, you will have as glamorous a life as you see in the picture?" "Which fallacy do you spot? equivocation? improper authority? both?" I urge students to use the vocabulary thus developed in class (and in their textbook), prodding them to be as precise and concrete in their oral analysis as possible. Orwell's essay, of course, provides explicit reinforcement. Such discussion leads into considerations of audience, appeal, intention, context; hence the point of my working from a whole magazine, rather than from an ad without regard for its context (although students may bring in single ads). Students quickly develop a sense of the kind of ads run in particular publications, and what they have in common is often a theme in their essays.

The students and I work together to define the criteria by which they will select their ad. Since by now they know they have a paper to write, yet are still in the process of choosing their ad, it is important for them to realize that not all ads are ideally suited for discussion in logical terms. (In general, the more print in an ad, the less interesting the ad is logically.) They will need to spend time finding an ad appropriate to their own skills and interests, as well as to the assignment: Some ads are too bland, others provide too little ground for developing a full-length essay. Most students come to realize that I expect every paper—no matter the particular ad—to be fleshed out, and in specific ways: The picture will need to be described as well as the layout and the relation of the print to the picture. Such details, necessary in and of themselves (though subordinate to the main topic), lend the necessary concreteness to the more abstract discussion of logic.

Class 3   By the third class period, I pass around copies of both successful and not-so-successful papers from previous semesters. Discussion now centers on development: how an initial impression of an ad can become the basis for a more substantive consideration, which is, after all, the problem the students must face in the papers they are to write. The fact that even the simplest picture will require several sentences of description will not have been apparent to many. It is helpful, therefore, to take fifteen minutes or

In-Class Exercise   so now and have the class write a three-sentence description of an ad you hold up. Accept no more than three sentences, and insist that they include all that truly matters in the picture: arbitrary rules, of course, but your purpose is to encourage economy (as well as sentence effectiveness). Repeat the exercise with different ads as often as possible prior to the day the paper is due. Stress that even though the ad is submitted with the essay, the essay itself ought to be self-explanatory; that a reader needs to be able to visualize the ad solely from what the essay tells him. Finally, you and the class together list on the board the main topics of their papers: logic, word choice and connotation, layout, audience (and magazine), appearance (colors), print, and so forth. Be careful to maintain that although every paper is of course different from every other, they all will have these concerns in common.

Variations: Television ads work as well as those in magazines, as do billboards, some political mailings, and the like. Different ads for the same product are especially useful for showing how ads are slanted for placement in different kinds of publications. Comparison of a recent ad with one for the same product but a year or so old may also be revealing.

LESSON READING

George Orwell, "Politics and the English Language," in *Shooting an Elephant and Other Essays* (Orlando, FL: Harcourt Brace Jovanovich, 1950).

Looking Skeptically at the Funnies

David Rosenwasser,
Muhlenberg College

I believe that there are two prerequisites to writing successfully: You have to know something, and you have to figure out what you think about it. Hence the primary problem in teaching composition: Most freshmen, however intelligent, don't know how to think and don't know anything to think about. The challenge in freshman composition lies in inducing students to look closely, to perform active rather than their customary passive mental operations—in short, to accept English 1 as a course in epistemology rather than one in procrustean formulas and exercises in correctness.

If freshmen do know anything, it's popular culture; and the following assignment attempts to build on that knowledge. It is an assignment in analysis, but also in the formulation of a point of view; it shows how, by looking closely (and preferably, skeptically) at something, we can begin to have ideas. This assignment has generated good essays. I think that it works because it provides sufficient freedom within the imposed form and because even students know the funny pages—in most cases they've just never thought about them critically before.

I distribute some version of the following five paragraphs at the end of a class.

WRITING ASSIGNMENT

We all have read the funny pages in the newspaper. Select one comic strip you read (or have read) regularly and discuss it as an expression of American culture. In order to anchor your generalizations, locate one or two examples of the strip—a paradigm—and cut it out of the paper or duplicate it. You will need to think through this topic to arrive at the big point you want to make. Then focus all your attention on the twin goals of articulating what cultural values or messages the strip conveys and how it conveys them. As you begin your analysis, you should probably keep two facts in mind. First, remember that strips come and go: The cartoonist makes a living by producing his work for daily consumption by (a segment at least of) the American public. His success depends on his ability to give that public what it wants. How does the comic strip you choose define and satisfy its

audience? Second, remember that nobody takes the funny pages very seriously; we consume them without thinking. Well, what in fact are we
consuming? How does the strip in question give us the quick fix we seek
as we grab that first cup of coffee and unfold the day?

You know my bias, that everything in the culture implies more than it
says. Therefore you will probably find it useful to distinguish between the
values or cultural messages that the strip overtly espouses and its covert—
often unintentional—implications. For example, "Mary Worth" overtly documents the struggles of its benign, grandmotherly heroine to save an endless
stream of wayward characters from their immoral impulses, from the lures
of sex and money and power. Covertly, I'd argue, the strip revels in this
moral seediness: We read not to see this old moral dinosaur maneuver
others into doing what *she* wants them to do with *their* lives, but rather
to watch how these seedy types operate, how they almost get the innocent
victim whom Mary has decided to protect, until our heroine somehow
saves the day. I doubt whether the cartoonist would agree with my interpretation—he probably doesn't intend this message—but the evidence is
there.

In a consciously ironic strip such as "Doonesbury," on the other hand,
Trudeau clearly intends that we see through the overt meaning to the covert
cultural critique. And then some strips are hard to call. Overtly, "Blondie"
laughs at the frailties and foibles of American domestic life; covertly (perhaps), it portrays the ceaseless frustrations of that life—a wife who spends
all her husband's money on showing off her hourglass figure (usually taking
the money for her next compulsive shopping spree from his wallet as he
naps on the sofa); a tyrannical pipsqueak of a boss who physically and
verbally abuses his employees; a life in which, at least for Dagwood, the
undisturbed bath is an utter impossibility.

In short, there is more to the funny pages than commonly meets the eye,
and I want you to excavate the unseen or embedded cultural assumptions
that all strips contain. The idea for this topic originated in an analysis of
Walt Disney's cartoons that I found in a novel entitled *The Book of Daniel*
(1971) by E. L. Doctorow. You might find a brief look illuminating:

> The animated cartoon itself ... came to express the collective unconscious
> of the community of the American Naive. A study today of the products of
> the animated cartoon industry of the twenties, thirties and forties would yield
> the following theology: 1. People are animals. 2. The body is mortal and
> subject to incredible pain. 3. Life is antagonistic to the living. 4. The flesh
> can be sawed, crushed, frozen, stretched, burned, bombed, and plucked for
> music. 5. The dumb are abused by the smart and the smart destroyed by their
> own cunning. 6. The small are tortured by the large and the large destroyed
> by their own momentum. 7. We are able to walk on air, but only as long as
> our illusion supports us.

You need not share Doctorow's viewpoint or use any of this information in your own analysis; but his critical attitude should offer you a useful model for your analysis.

In closing, I want to stress the importance of integrating specific details with generalizations in all effective argumentative prose. Although your evidence need not be limited to the strip that you cut out and staple to your essay—indeed, you will need to provide the necessary context, to show how this strip *is* representative—you should devote most of your analysis to its specific details, both visual and verbal. I can see two traps to avoid. On the one hand, don't be too general: don't focus on what *you* think of the housewife of the 1980s (say); focus on what the cartoonist seems to be saying about her. On the other hand, avoid unnecessary plot summary: We don't need to know what's happened over the past six months in "Apartment 3-G" to appreciate your analysis of the strip. Aim for two to four pages of engaging prose. Please staple the strip to your essay.

I prime the class for this assignment by leading discussion of a strip or two, but the real preparation has occurred in previous sessions, where I have introduced the notion of using what I call paradigms in composing analytical essays. As I define it, a paradigm is a really great example, an example so rich in detail and implication that it embodies—can represent and anchor the treatment of—a larger idea. By forcing students to find a paradigm (in this case, one or two examples of the same comic strip), the teacher closes off the usual escape route from analysis through plot summary, while imposing a limited focus. As I phrase it, the rule for paradigms is that "it is usually better to make ten points about a single issue or example than the same basic point about ten similar issues or examples."

Two paradigmatic examples of "Momma" by Mell Lazarus follow [on page 201]. I have received essays on each of these strips; both discussed the authoritarianism of the mother, which each strip ends up ridiculing. Yet as one of the essays pointed out, the kids repeatedly go home to report to momma, to seek her approval, even as the strips document their attempts to subvert her authority and their refusal to change their ways sufficiently to win that approval. When we laugh at "Momma," perhaps we laugh at the hopeless complexity of relations with the mother.

LESSON READING

E. L. Doctorow, *The Book of Daniel* (New York: Random House, 1971).

FOR FURTHER READING

Thomas S. Kuhn, "The Route to Normal Science," in *The Structure of Scientific Revolutions* (Chicago: U of Chicago P, 1962).

Momma

By Mell Lazarus

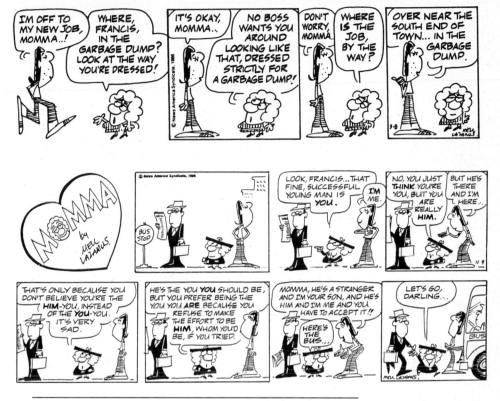

Momma by Mell Lazarus. Courtesy of Mell Lazarus and North America Syndicate.

Style and the Man: Using Imitation to Teach Writing

Michael Robertson,
Princeton University

Let this then be my first precept, that we show the student whom to imitate, and to imitate with greatest care the most excellent qualities of his model.

—Cicero, De Oratore

About this time I met with an odd volume of the Spectator. *It was the third. I had never before seen any of them. I bought it, read it over and over, and was much delighted with it. I thought the writing excellent, and wished, if possible, to imitate it. With that view I took some of the papers, and, making short hints of the sentiment in each sentence, laid them by a few days, and then, without looking at the book, tried to complete the papers again by expressing each hinted sentiment at length, and as fully as it had been expressed before, in any suitable words that should come to hand. Then I compared my* Spectator *with the original, discovered some of my faults, and corrected them. . . . By comparing my work afterwards with the original, I discovered many faults and amended them; but I sometimes had the pleasure of fancying that in certain particulars of small import I had been lucky enough to improve the method or the language, and this encouraged me to think I might possibly in time come to be a tolerable English writer, of which I was extremely ambitious.*

—Benjamin Franklin, Autobiography

A few years ago I happened to be reading Benjamin Franklin's *Autobiography* during the same semester I was teaching composition. When I came across the passage just quoted I decided, in the I'll-try-anything-once mood common among instructors teaching freshman English for the umpteenth time, to have my students follow Franklin's advice. I added an extra step, though, to Franklin's exercise and asked them to go on to write an original essay, on a topic of their choice, in the style of another author.

WRITING
ASSIGNMENT

The assignment sheet that I gave to my students included the passage from Franklin, a list of twentieth-century writers with a distinctive non-fiction prose style, and five steps for students to follow:

1. Read at least fifty pages of your author's work, enough to get a sense of his or her style.
2. Choose a passage of at least 250 words that you particularly like and that is typical of the writer's style. Copy it word-for-word. Though this may sound like a penmanship exercise, it is the best way for you to become aware of a writer's style.
3. Make a brief outline of the passage, using your own words. Set the outline aside for at least two days.
4. Then do as Franklin did and try to re-create the original passage by referring to your notes. When you compare your passage with the original, don't worry too much about word-for-word accuracy. The important question is, Does your passage have the same sound, the same style, as the original?
5. Now write an essay of at least six hundred words in the style of your chosen author. The topic is up to you, but your choice will, of course, be influenced by the kinds of topics that your author typically chooses.

The essays that resulted from this assignment were the best set of student papers I had read in ten years of teaching. A student whose papers had been timid and jargon-filled, full of passive constructions and locutions like "In the opinion of this writer it has been demonstrated that . . ." had chosen to imitate Nora Ephron. Influenced by the informal, confessional tone of such essays as "A Few Words About Breasts," this student wrote a fascinating essay about her experience as one of a handful of women engineering majors, an essay that skillfully combined first-person narrative with a thoughtful analysis of male and female roles in our society. A physics student whose essays had an almost mathematical rigidity imitated Tom Wolfe and wrote a piece about college parties that shared Wolfe's playful experimentation with prose style and point of view. Another student, imitating *The Autobiography of Alice B. Toklas*, wrote an autobiographical essay that not only reproduced perfectly Gertrude Stein's style but that was also deeply moving in its account of love and friendship, themes central to Stein but of an immediacy and power that the student had never come close to before.

IN-CLASS
EXERCISES

There were also some notable flops along with the many successful essays. A couple of students clung to their original model as if to a lifesaver, simply reproducing one of their author's essays with a few changes in wording. Another couple abandoned their models completely and wrote essays in their usual prose style with only the slightest of stylistic nods to the writer they were supposedly imitating. To counter these problems, I now meet with each student while the essay is in progress, and I preface it with two in-class warm-up exercises. First, I give students the opening of a novel or short story written in the first person and ask them to continue the story for another few paragraphs. Students enjoy imitating the stylistically distinctive vernacular narrators of such works as *Adventures of Huckleberry Finn, Catcher in the Rye,* "Why I Live at the P.O.," and *The Color Purple.* Next, I hand out a particularly flamboyant passage from Tom Wolfe; the opening of "The Last American Hero" works well. After discussing Wolfe's style, we brainstorm as a group for subjects suitable for Wolfean treatment. Each student then chooses one and writes about it, following Wolfe's syntax fairly closely. This exercise is more difficult than the previous one; up to half the students may have trouble with it. So I ask them to divide into pairs and have each pair choose the imitation that they think is more promising, then revise it together before reading it aloud to the class. By the time they have completed this in-class work, almost all the students have a good sense of how to imitate prose style.

As I've indicated, however, my students' imitative essays have turned out to be much more than exercises in style. Frequently, they are better organized and more perceptive than anything the students have written before. Why does this general improvement occur? My attempts to answer that question have led me to reconsider not only my students' conception of the act of writing but also the history of imitation.

There is, of course, nothing novel about using imitation to teach writing. In ancient Rome, imitation of the best Greek and Latin authors was an essential part of the curriculum. In England, schoolboys from the sixteenth to the beginning of the twentieth century spent much of their time imitating Latin writers through exercises such as translating a passage of Cicero into English and then back again into Latin. Although the classical tradition was not so strong in nineteenth- and early twentieth-century America, the teaching of composition was still heavily based on imitation, with Daniel Webster and Abraham Lincoln serving as prose models in place of Cicero and Horace.

Only within this century has the teaching of composition through imitation fallen into disfavor and an emphasis on originality, reflecting Romantic notions of the artist, taken its place. During the Renaissance, the artist was expected to rely on his predecessors. A literary commonplace, taken from Quintilian, held that "Language is the dress of thought"; that is, style was seen not as an expression of the individual personality but as a form in which we clothe our ideas. But a competing notion of style as a *mentis imago,* an image of the individual mind, gained strength throughout the eighteenth century and received definitive expression in Buffon's phrase, *Le style c'est l'homme même*—"style is the man himself." During the Romantic era, artistic approbation shifted from the often witty transformation of classical models—as in the poetry of Ben Jonson or Pope—to the Wordsworthian ideal of the spontaneous overflow of powerful feelings.

It seems to me that Romantic ideas of creativity and individual style dominate our culture, and certainly dominate the thinking of most students of freshman composition. Our students have absorbed the notion that writing—writing even an essay for one's freshman English class—is a dangerous exposure of the private self to the public world. The result of students' self-consciousness about revealing their personality through their prose, combined with their natural desire to avoid mistakes, is that young writers frequently confine their prose to the clichéd terrain they have traveled before. Imitating another writer freed my students from their self-conscious fears. In the guise of another writer's voice, they could make stylistic experiments they would never have dared on their own, and they could deal with topics of deep personal importance that normally they would have regarded as taboo. Imitation served as a carnival mask, allowing them to behave linguistically and thematically with a new-found *élan*.

Imitation is certainly no cure-all. But the stylistic and thematic freedom it provides can help some students, as it helped young Benjamin Franklin, on their way to becoming tolerable English writers.

FOR FURTHER READING

Tom Wolfe, "The Last American Hero," in *The Right Stuff* (New York: Farrar Straus Giroux, 1979).

Mark Twain, *Adventures of Huckleberry Finn*, ed. Sculley Bradley et al. (New York: Norton, 1977).

Gertrude Stein, *The Autobiography of Alice B. Toklas* (New York: Vintage Books, © Gertrude Stein, 1933).

William Carlos Williams, "Poor Richard," in *In the American Grain* (New York: New Directions, 1956), pp. 144–157.

Teaching Humorous Writing

Linda Peterson and Fred Strebeigh,
Yale University

Librarian to Professor: "You'll find 'Teaching Methods That Never Fail' listed in the card catalogue under 'Humor.'"

Students often ask for the chance to write humorous essays—as a break, they think, from the difficult work of writing expositions and arguments. Too often, however, their attempts at humor produce dull or, at best, sophomoric writing, and both they and their instructor feel disappointed that a potentially pleasurable assignment has failed to please or amuse.

To prevent such disappointment and to integrate humorous writing with the goals of the composition course, we have developed a method that almost never fails: It gives students accessible models for writing humor, it produces genuinely amusing essays, and it fits, moreover, within a theoretical framework of teaching writing through the understanding of prose conventions. In teaching humor we focus on two basic types, which we call *parody* and *travesty*. We introduce these forms not by giving abstract rhetorical definitions, but by showing students examples of each and asking them to analyze and imitate the strategies that humorists use.

Parody

We begin with parody, a mode of humorous writing that closely mimics a serious form but exaggerates (or deflates) its content. We give students short examples of parodic humor, paired with the "straight" forms on which these parodies are based: for example, Nora Ephron's "Dear Frequent Traveller" along with a frequent-flyer brochure from TWA; Veronica Geng's "Partners" and a page of wedding announcements from the *New York Times*; or Bruce McCall's "Order Toll-Free from Briefcase House Today" and a fashionable mail-order catalogue such as *The Sharper Image*.[1]

---

[1] Other recent examples include Polly Frost's "Turbotome," a parody of computer software packages, Bruce McCall's "Current Listing," a parody of *New York Times* real estate ads, and Frank Gannon's "The Price You Gotta Pay," an "update" on the new 1040 form from the Internal Revenue Service. Since short parodies appear frequently in *The New Yorker*, we can update our examples easily as fads and fashions change. We have found that parodies based on written texts (rather than oral or visual products) work most effectively.

CLASS 1   In class we first analyze the format, style, and content of a "straight" piece. When we discuss TWA's frequent-flyer brochure, for instance, the students quickly notice the dominant features of its format: (1) the bold headlines (GET A FREE GIFT WHEN YOU TAKE FLIGHT 760), (2) the gushy exclamation points (!), and (3) the multiple markers and small-print notes (*Quantas Southern Cross and New Zealand routes must include travel to . . .) They also notice distinctive features of style: (4) the breezy, conversational tone and (5) the direct address in the second-person ("If you're headed from Los Angeles to London on Friday, October 12th," as if this were a personal letter from a friend who thought you just might be heading his way for a little Columbus Day excursion). Finally, we discuss content: (6) the flight upgrades and bonus deals, (7) the airlines we've never heard of (Dash Air, Jetstream International), (8) the odd mileage transformations, and (9) the bizarre contests (TWA promises to "raffle off separately" (one Ballantyne sweater and one bottle of Ballantine's scotch on Flight 760).

After we've looked closely at the original form (and laughed at its inherent absurdities), we turn to the parody. Students are usually surprised to discover how closely the parody resembles the original, how little the humorous writer has needed to exaggerate. This point is worth emphasizing, since inexperienced writers most often fail to produce humor because they try too hard and exaggerate too much. Other points we emphasize include these:

1. In parody, the format closely mimics the original. Nora Ephron, for instance, uses the same bold headlines, the same gushy exclamation points, and even more asterisks and small-print notes (* * * * * * * *Wednesdays only) than appear in the TWA brochure.

2. Style, too, closely mimics the original. The opening sentences of Ephron's "Dear Frequent Traveller," with their breezy, conversational tone, might almost have appeared in an actual TWA brochure: "Global Airlines is once again happy to bring you its monthly update on the most innovative Frequent Traveller Program in existence. It's been three years since we first introduced our Frequent Traveller Program for a limited period of time, and two years since we extended the limited period of time for an additional limited period of time, and a year since we decided to do it forever."

3. Humor builds from the mildly amusing to the completely absurd. Students should discover that the parodist rarely attempts a laugh in the first line; rather, exaggeration begins once the writer has established the basic target. The parodist seeks plausibility at the outset, drawing the reader into a recognizable rhetorical world. After that world has been invoked, the parodist explodes it through humorous distortion—as in Ephron's final section: "Frequent Travellers, there are more reasons than ever to stick with Global! In the months ahead, we will be offering bonus mileage credits any time you buy a loaf of Pepperidge Farm raisin

bread, a major appliance you already own, or ten thousand shares or more of stock in any Fortune 500 corporation."

We try to allow these points to emerge during discussion, giving the class plenty of time to discover them and to analyze Ephron's purpose in writing parody. Like many humorists, Ephron exposes the absurdities of a current fad: the American mania for special deals and free gifts gone berserk. But Ephron goes beyond the merely humorous in the final paragraphs, when she awards bonuses for such serious things as "a short stay in the hospital" or a "separation, divorce, or remarriage." Here she exposes the wishful thinking that underlies our mania: We all hope to get something more—and more pleasant—than life ordinarily has to offer.

WRITING ASSIGNMENT 1

Even before we suggest subjects for their own parodies, students have begun to identify possible targets: ads in newspapers or magazines; local campus posters or brochures; letters of appeal from publishers, political organizations, even charitable groups. We've had particularly good luck with magazine ads and with direct-mail contests and sweepstakes. But students have written brilliant parodies of such seemingly unamusing forms as the academic textbook, the course syllabus, and the university's catalogue of undergraduate courses.

As students discover such targets of humor, we reiterate the rhetorical strategies that parodists use, but we also raise questions about the serious purposes of humor. While it is true that parody sometimes seeks merely to amuse the reader and momentarily expose an absurdity of modern life, parody can also intend a serious criticism of a social or political institution. In "Partners," for instance, Veronica Geng parodies the form of wedding announcements in the *New York Times,* with their concern for the social status of the bride and groom. Her parody does more, however, than amuse; it exposes the economic structure on which marriage depends:

> The marriage of Nancy Creamer Teas, daughter of Mr. and Mrs. Russell Ruckhyde Teas of Glen Frieburg, N.Y., and Point Pedro, Sri Lanka, to John Potomac Mining, son of Mr. Potomac B. Mining of Buffet Hills, Va., and the late Mrs. Mining, took place at the First Episcopal Church of the Port Authority of New York and New Jersey. The bride attended the Bodice School, the Earl Grey Seminary, Fence Academy, Railroad Country Day School, and the Credit School, and made her debut at the Alexander Hamilton's Birthday Cotillion at Lazard Freres. She is a student in the premedical program at M.I.T. and will spend her junior year at Cartier & Cie. in Paris.
>
> The bridegroom recently graduated from Harvard College. He spent his junior year at the Pentagon, a military concern in Washington, D.C. He will join his father on the board of directors of the Municipal Choate Assistance Corporation. His previous marriage ended in divorce.

We Americans like to tell ourselves that marriage represents the union of two hearts and minds. What Geng suggests, however, is that marriage still represents the union of money and class and that the media cooperate in (perhaps even encourage) this commercialization of the personal life. Discussing parodies such as Geng's helps students understand that their humorous writing can simultaneously have a serious purpose, that humor can make an argument as effectively as more logical, straightforward forms of writing.

Travesty

In our experience, parody is the easiest form of humor to teach student writers. For instructors who have advanced students, however, or who want to offer a second mode of humorous writing, we recommend the travesty. We use the term *travesty* because this form of humor presents its subject (usually serious) in a verbal dress intended for a different kind of material (usually not serious). Literally, *trans* means "over or across" and *vestire* means "to clothe or dress," and one way to help students recognize this form is to invoke the term *transvestite*, which similarly carries the sense of dressing up a subject in an inappropriate garb. We sometimes add the term *take-off* because the form "takes off" from some actual fact, event, situation, or quotation.

CLASS 2   Although *travesty* and *take-off* can easily be defined, in class we find it preferable to focus on examples: for example, Garrison Keillor's "U.S. Still on Top, Says Rest of World" or Russell Baker's "One Very Smart Tomato." As with parody, we begin with the "straight" news source on which the humorous piece is based. Keillor's essay originates, for instance, in a quotation from then-President Richard Nixon: "America today is Number One in the world." We ask students to imagine why such a quotation might have caught Keillor's attention: What does it mean to be Number One? What kind of competition is the United States in? With whom are we competing—and how? and why? and for what? Then we look at Keillor's opening paragraph to see how he exploits the metaphor of competition and makes Nixon's words seem absurd by reporting them as if they were the final standings of a sports competition:

> The White House is very, but unofficially, elated over America's top finish in the 1971 Earth standings, announced yesterday in Geneva. The United States, for the twenty-eighth straight year, was named Number One Country by a jury of more than three hundred presidents, prime ministers, premiers, chairmen, elder world statesmen, kings, queens, emperors, popes, generalissimos, shahs, sheikhs, and tribal chieftains who hold voting membership in the Association of World Leaders.

Students quickly see how Keillor continues the travesty throughout the essay: how he re-creates the presidential press conference as a sports event, how he makes the response in the White House parallel to locker-room bedlam after a key victory, how he dresses Nixon in a victor's costume ("wide silver-blue necktie, with the inscription *El Numero Uno*"), how he gives special awards to the competing countries (China gets "population honors"; the European Community, the "Top Bloc"; Japan, the "exports prize"; and so on).

WRITING
ASSIGNMENT 2

Although students can readily analyze such examples of travesty, we have found the transition from analysis to composition more difficult with this form than with parody. We thus spend more time helping them identify news stories or quotations that might provide the basis of their own travesties; we also help them generate "inappropriate" forms of verbal dress for their chosen subjects. On the day we last taught travesty, for example, the *Times* "Quotation of the Day" came from a man who, about to receive an artificial heart, declared: "Let's go for it." Like Garrison Keillor, we imagined treating a serious operation as a sports competition. We studied newspaper articles to grasp the language of sports reporting, and as a class, we generated sentences about the heart operation as if it had been a football game (thus implicitly exploring the competitive spirit that pervades even humane professions like medicine).

This approach to teaching humor, as instructors quickly discover, is no less rigorous than any other form of teaching writing. Our practical rationale for suggesting it, however, is that students enjoy it and succeed: they make their classmates laugh and make serious points at the same time. We can also offer a more theoretical rationale for our approach. One of the most important strategies a writing instructor can teach is that of analyzing a piece of prose—not only for its aesthetic merits, but for how it works. That strategy can enable students to expand their own repertoire of writing styles and modes, whether the modes be "serious" argument or "serious" humor.

LESSON READINGS

Russell Baker, "One Very Smart Tomato," *So This Is Depravity* (New York: Congdon & Lattès, 1980), pp. 70–72.

Nora Ephron, "Dear Frequent Traveler," *The New Yorker*, 5 March 1984.

Polly Frost, "Turbotome," *The New Yorker*, 22 July 1985.

Veronica Geng, "Partners," *The New Yorker*, 16 June 1980.

Garrison Keillor, "U.S. Still on Top, Says Rest of World," *Happy to Be Here* (New York: Penguin, 1981), pp. 150–152.

Casebook Writing Assignments for Students . . . and by Them

Chris M. Anson,
University of Minnesota

Students usually have little opportunity to say much about what assignments we give them. We expect them to invent material, discover new insights, and produce interesting and informative essays on topics in which they may have little interest. We restrict fields of inquiry ("you can't write on abortion; it's too broad, and too controversial"); we mandate structure ("be sure to include arguments both for and against the issue") and length ("I want no more than four pages, but it has to be at least four"); and, often, we even restrict the students' choice of audience or purpose ("remember, this paper will be for people who are clearly opposed to your solution and your purpose will be to change their minds"). In short, many of our assignments all but straight-jacket our students, perhaps because we have learned our lessons about granting freedom in the past, or perhaps because, deep down inside, we think we know what good choices make a good paper, and we want to make those choices for our students.

Students, too, have learned to play the game; as William Perry has suggested in his important study *Forms of Intellectual Development in the College Years*, young college students tend to be "dualistic" in their attitudes toward knowledge and learning. For everything there is a right and wrong answer, a correct or incorrect way of proceeding. If they can figure out what the teacher believes is right, they'll succeed. They, too, are hungry for mandates, however dulling and constricting these make the task of writing.

In my own teaching, I want to free both myself and my students from the dangers of this mechanical view of writing. Early in my courses, I do make the assignments for my students, but I help them to ask *themselves*

211

questions, instead of relying on their teachers to give them all the answers. And frequently I find myself turning their questions back on them: How long do you think this essay should be, given what you're trying to accomplish? What do *you* think about using that sort of language for that audience? How did the members of your revision group feel about that part of your paper? What *would* someone opposed to your solution say about it?

WRITING
ASSIGNMENT

Toward the end of my courses, however, I like my students to design writing assignments for each other. To keep them away from "stock" assignments they have seen (or even responded to) in the past, I ask them to work together in groups of three or four to design elaborate rhetorical "case assignments." In these cases, the students invent (and fully document) a problem or situation that culminates in one or more writing tasks. I give the students about two weeks to design their case, and on the due date the group must come prepared to distribute copies of their case to three or four other class members. Each student thus contributes to the design of his or her group's case, and responds to the case assignment of another group.

In the early stages of the case building, the students respond to sample cases which I distribute in class. Unlike most published cases for writing, however, these assignments are "deep," involving complicated and interesting situations. They are also supplemented by dozens of "specimens," which, like exhibits in court proceedings, give the students a fuller sense of the context they are writing in. In having the students work their way through one of these "deep cases," I hope to show them the value of providing as much "context" in their own cases as possible.

One of my cases, for example, places you, the writer, in the role of a veterinarian working at a small clinic in Denver. Recently, a brand new animal hospital has opened up near the clinic, boasting three veterinarians and a large support staff, beautiful new buildings, a free "pet-limo" service to pick up animals at their homes and return them after treatment, and all the best in modern technology. One by one, your clients have been asking you to send their pets' records over to the new hospital, and business is dwindling. But one of your clients, elderly and wealthy Mrs. Thompson, has kept her faith in your services, and your only *new* clients since the competition moved in are friends of Mrs. Thompson. In short, she is extremely important to your business.

To make a rather long story short, Mrs. Thompson travels to her beach cottage in the Turks and Caicos Islands to recover from the loss of her husband, who has died several months before. She boards her aging English spaniel, Beckett, at your clinic, asking you to contact her immediately should anything happen to the dog. Soon after she leaves, Beckett develops a urinary blockage caused by bladder stones. You try to treat the stones with injections, but are eventually forced to operate. The dog dies a day or two after surgery. Because Mrs. Thompson can't be reached by phone, the writing task in this case is to send her a letter explaining the circumstances surrounding the dog's death.

Unfortunately, these circumstances are rather complicated—Jim Tufts, your kennel cleaner, turned down the thermostat in the boarding kennels after surgery because he was hot, and forgot to turn it back up again. The cold temperature may have contributed to the dog's death. Other supporting documents include all sorts of business agreements—clinic statutes, in effect—which you established several years before with your partner, Mary Johanssen, about the payment of bills and the denial of "special exceptions" for friends or important people. There are recent letters from the Colorado State Board of Health reminding veterinarians about the incineration deadlines for animals that die in your care and are not taken away by their owners. There's a note from Jim Tufts, who, overcome with guilt, has quit—and you can't be sure he hasn't apologized to Mrs. Thompson about his error, too. And there are many other specimens, some important, some not—pictures of Beckett, Mrs. Thompson, Jim Tufts, Mary Johanssen, and the competing clinic; a copy of the dog's medical chart; lists of costs for treatment; a tentative bill up to the point of death; a postcard from Mrs. Thompson informing you that she has decided to stay another week at her beach cottage; and so on.

Discussion of this case (and the students' first drafts) focuses on the need for rhetorical balance between "self" and "audience"; some students, for example, overcompromise their professional positions in an attempt to appease Mrs. Thompson, whereas others are far too cold and clinical, as if insisting on their authority. We also look at the effect of certain stylistic, structural, and substantive decisions. (Do you mention the dog's death as an opener or work your way up to it? How do you deal with the Colorado incineration law? Do you include the $550 bill with the letter? What sort of language do you use to describe the surgery and its complications?) After the students have turned in a rough and final draft of their letters, they receive a request from the Hartford Mutual Insurance Company: Beckett was insured against accidental death, and Mrs. Thompson has begun a claim. The company wants to know what happened. Now the new writing task seems more legalistic, and the process begins again . . . but not without making an important point about the power of written language.

Soon after the students work their way through this (or one of several other) case assignments, we begin talking about what makes a successful and interesting case. A good case should, of course, require writing as the central means of solving a problem or exploring ideas. It should be challenging, immersing the writer into a world of people and conflicts. It should not assume technical expertise or knowledge. (Everything you need for the vet case, for example, is included, and it does not demand any specialized knowledge or terminology.) Ideally, its further specimens should create new knowledge or dissonance in the writer to encourage revision. And, whenever possible, it should bridge the gap between the process of writing and the process of making personal decisions in a world where language has consequences—both to writers and readers.

Over several years of experimenting with this group case assignment, my students have taught me much about their own learning processes and the principles that underlie growth in written literacy. Of chief interest to me are four things that I see happen, again and again, in the students' work designing and then responding to the cases:

Language Diversity

Like many, I used to think that young students have "only one voice," that they can write only "freshmanese," that they are insensitive to the tremendous variety of discourse in the world around us. Because the cases include "attachments" or "specimens," however, the students often show that they are quite attuned to the different sorts of written language emerging from diverse situations or contexts. The case assignments give them a chance to tap into those different kinds of discourse because good cases are realistic. When the cases includes a letter from a lawyer as a specimen, for example, that letter does, indeed, read very much like a letter from a real lawyer. And to the pleasure of the students who read and respond to the case, such letters are usually typed on realistic "legal" letterhead that the students have produced on a word processor or obtained from a law firm.

Successful Collaboration

Writing is often thought of as an individual, solitary activity done in the cloistered privacy of one's room or study. In fact, writing is a highly social, collaborative activity, and writing classes should likewise become a community of learning. And I have found few better ways to motivate students to work hard, and to share responsibility, than the group case assignments. Because they are designing an assignment for their own peers, the members of each group take their roles seriously, often going far beyond my own or the other class members' expectations.

Enjoyment and Motivation

Writing is hard. but the more fun it is, the more willing we are to work at it. Unanimously, my students report putting in more time on the cases than any other assignment, and feeling most pressured by the constraints of time. Unanimously, however, they also tell me that the case assignments are the high point of the term, something they will "never forget," something that "really makes the course." Ironically, they praise me . . . but it is they who have done all the work.

Learning from Within

Finally, the cases throw the responsibility for the students' learning back on the students themselves. I am no longer like Dickens's schoolmaster, gazing out over rows of students waiting like little vessels to be filled with knowledge. Instead I am a facilitator, a guide, helping them to assemble assignments for each other. And when they finally distribute their finished cases among their peers, there are still groans. But now they are groans of amused agony as they eagerly glance through the case they have received, watching its rhetorical dilemma unfold.

There are, of course, still problems with the case approach—how to evaluate the cases, what to do with the responses to poorly designed cases, how to avoid too elaborate or confusing assignments, how to handle sexist or racist or ethically questionable ideas or situations. Solving these problems is where we once again step in as teachers, using the sort of judgment and experience our students have come to trust us with. And so we have the first and last word on the case assignments—but to the benefit of our students' learning, they must put a lot in between.

Addendum: Descriptions of Some Typical Student Cases

"The Neighborhood Eyesore Case"

You live in a nice, middle-class suburban neighborhood where householders take good care of their property. Recently, some new neighbors have moved into a house at the end of your cul-de-sac. In the past week or so, the owners have been hauling all sorts of junk and debris into their back yard: old refrigerators, tires, pieces of automobiles, scrap metal. You soon discover that Edson and Samantha Williams, the new neighbors, are both artists, and they like to construct huge sculptures from "found objects." They intend to make their back yard a repository for junk they can use in their work.

You happen to be the head of the neighborhood association. The association has suggested you write the Williamses a letter asking them to do something about the mess. The case includes many supporting documents and pictures, including material from the Health Department on what can and can't be kept in one's back yard. The case continues to build, so that several further tasks are required later on.

"The Riceland Boy Scout Trip Disaster"

You are the scout leader of Troop 66. Each summer, the troop goes on a camping trip to a wilderness area near the Canadian border. The troop is usually divided into different "patrols" that have their own short treks into the woods during the camping trip. This year, John Pendleton—an extremely wealthy businessman and a generous benefactor to the Boy Scouts—has persuaded you to take along his thirteen-year-old son Dean (even though he is slightly underage for this kind of trip).

During the trip the "rat patrol," which has a bad reputation among the scouts, wants to take a half-day hike toward the Canadian border. Dean wants to go with them, and puts up a fuss. Against your better judgment you give them permission to go. By the end of the day disaster has struck the unruly patrol: The young boy was mauled to death by a grizzly bear just over the Canadian border.

The task in this case is to write a statement for the courts explaining what happened on the trip. Supporting documents include journal entries by Dean (he was keeping a diary of the trip), a short history of the scout troop, two newspaper accounts of the accident, a picture of the grizzly, a parental permission and release form signed by the boy's father, a transcript of the news bulletin on the local TV news show, letters from the Pendletons' attorney, and U.S. and Canadian police reports.

"The Martha Dithers Case: Rights of the Aged"

Martha Dithers is a seventy-nine-year-old woman residing in a health care center. Recently, she's had several car accidents, and people are starting to question her right to own and operate a motor vehicle. Principal documents in the case are letters from Mrs. Dithers's insurance company, testimonials about Mrs. Dithers's abilities from a priest at the St. John's Catholic Church and the Head Nurse at the health care center, a recent medical report, several traffic accident reports, a short article on the rights of the elderly, and some information about automobile accidents caused by senior citizens. There are several possible roles; in one, for example, you are the judge at the Jefferson County Traffic Court; you must decide whether to revoke Mrs. Dithers's license. The task is to write an editorial for the local newspaper explaining why you made your decision.

Writing About Reading: Responding to a Text

Nicholas Coles,
University of Pittsburgh

Across the curriculum, too much of students' writing about their reading is devoted to reporting the contents of texts and not enough to responding to them. This is perhaps the legacy of the way schools have traditionally used writing to test what student have "learned" from their reading. Most of us, though, have come to believe that writing can itself be a process of learning—not just of restating or summarizing what has been learned—and have adapted our composition teaching accordingly: using multidraft writing and sequenced assignments, for example, through which students explore what they can say about a subject and discover what they can then claim to know about it, describing and accounting for what they think of, what they feel, and what connections they make when they read.

WRITING ASSIGNMENT

The course from which this lesson comes is a version of the University of Pittsburgh's Basic Reading and Writing course that was designed especially for returning adult students. It uses a sequence of assignments on the subject of working—something these worker-students know a good deal about. About half of our class time is typically spent in discussion of our students' own writing, which is primarily of two kinds: narratives about and analyses of their own work experiences, and essays in response to the assigned readings (which include Studs Terkel's *Working*).[1] The following lesson in developing strategies for writing about reading occurs early in the term, when we discuss our students' work on their first assignment. We

---

[1] The course and the following lesson are the result of a collaboration with my colleague Susan V. Wall. The design of the course and the conception of the lesson owe much also to the work of David Bartholomae, Anthony Petrosky, and William E. Coles, Jr. For a full account of the course on which ours is modeled, see Bartholomae and Petrosky, *Facts, Artifacts, and Counterfacts: Theory and Method for a Reading and Writing Course* (Montclair, N.J.: Boynton/Cook, 1986).

had asked them to read an article, "The Secretarial Proletariat" by Judith Ann,[2] and to write a paper addressing these questions: "What do you understand to be the most important point or points Ann is making about working?" and "How do you, as someone who has also had some experience with work, respond to what Ann is saying?" Ann's article recounts her experiences working for an insurance company, a bank, a bridal magazine, focusing on the boredom and isolation of this typically female clerical work, and especially on the sexual discrimination which, she argues, makes the myth of a better job just that for most women. She concludes with a call for collective action by women workers to overcome their exploitation.

CLASS 1   For this class session we have dittoed a pair of contrasting papers to hand out to the class. They contrast, by the way, neither in their overall quality (we don't want to confirm any sense of sure-fire technique for one writer or damage the confidence of another) nor in their position on Ann's argument (we don't want to debate whose "opinions" are right or wrong, nor what Ann "really says"), but rather in their differing ways of coming to terms with the article. Our aim is to recognize and affirm a wide range of "strategies" that seem fruitful in enabling writers to articulate and elaborate their responses to what they read.

After reading the papers aloud and taking a few moments to note first reactions—parts we liked, sections that worked—we begin the discussion with questions like: Where do you see the writer saying how s/he responded to Ann's article? What is the writer doing here with what s/he has read? As the class works through, identifying what we call "strategies," we ask students to come up with labels for these strategies and we write them on the board: What could we call it when a writer does this? How could we label this kind of move? We feel it is important to use students' own labels—provided we can agree on their appropriateness—rather than teacherly ones, so as not to confound what they are able to see happening in their writing with some anxiously misremembered "rules" of composition. These are some of the labels that I copy on the board, with examples reproduced, largely uncorrected, from student papers. (And since some labels are idiosyncratic to the vocabulary of this particular group of students, I have provided [in brackets] some conventional explanation.) These are at this stage in no particular order, and many clearly overlap. For now, though, we want simply to locate and label as many strategies as we can.

bringing yourself in: "I myself feel the same way as Ann does. Basically we have the same problem—which is men."
typing [generalizing]: "Most people are afraid because they feel they have no alternatives, so they continue to struggle & accept it."
labeling: "The men are male chauvinist"; "It's a game and the rules are the same."

---

[2] Robin Morgan, ed., *Sisterhood Is Powerful* (New York: Random House, 1970), pp. 86–100.

changing labels: "She calls it rebellion but I call it laziness."

strong emotional statement: "No one, yet no one, should have to experience the disgrace of not getting a job, because of sex, color, age, etc."

issualization of the subject [political/economic/social analysis]: "All they're really concerned about is whether or not they'll make a profit or not at the lowest possible input & for the highest returns."

telling your own story: "For what I do on that job and some of the abuse I take that I am not paid for it. . . . We are supposed to get a 15-minute break, but we don't . . ."

same but different/different but same [comparison/contrast]: "There are jobs that men hold that they are looked down at. It may not be discrimination because their boss is a man also, but it is the same feeling."

using imagination/metaphor. "Whatever job you have you shouldn't be treated like you're in prison"; [metaphors of robots, machines, master/slave]

statement against [the writer's ideas are against what most people think]: "Myself, I do and will always think that men are higher and better than women."

make own point: "If a lot of men give an equal chance to women to prove themselves, I think there's going to be a lot of disappointed men. Because some men can't face the fact that women are equal to men."

putting it in a historical era [for distancing]: "Well, responding to Ann is kinda hard to do because that was back then in the 1960's and this is the 1980's and things are much better now"; [for qualification]: "Ann's points are still present in today's working world. They are much more subtle, however. Women are starting to become less of a token. . . ."

philosophizing: "I think most heads of businesses have a bad habit of forgetting that we all are God's children and just travelers that must give up our jobs and lives someday."

judging the writer: "Judith Ann is a very independent, sensitive type of woman who knows what she wants and what she really deserves from society."

Norma Rae syndrome [comparing to well-known figure]: "She reacted like a bra-burner, like people who carry signs around for the ERA, a Norma Rae type of woman."

giving advice [to the author]: "If Judith Ann would have pulled herself together and finished college she might not have been discriminated against at all"; [to oneself or generally]: "Sometimes you don't like your job, but it is a job. Stay there until you find something better."

different angle: "From the point of the bosses they worked hard to get where they are and they're not going to give it up. . . ."

fantasizing: "If I was in her shoes I would come in the night and padlock the mensroom."

These represent ways that readers can go about relating themselves and what they know to the texts they read. Some, clearly, will be more useful than others in the context of a university classroom: "different angle," for instance, will serve an academic reader, such as our students aim to become, much better than "giving advice." Nevertheless, we will type up the whole list and turn it back to the class as a reminder of the wide array of what they already have available. These are only the starting points of the more developed responses to texts that we want to foster.

CLASS 2   Our next step, in the following class session, is to sort and order this random list, connecting strategies according to how they might be made to work together in developing a line of argument. The class could see, for instance, that merely *telling your story*, by itself, did not constitute an adequate response: We had a paper that, after a strong start, trailed off into a personal work narrative and never came back to use it as the basis for an informed comment on Ann's argument. But a series like *telling your story/ same but different/make own point* took one further, as we could see from another (uncorrected) paper:

> What Ann has stated I can somewhat relate to in that I worked in a bank as proof reader and as a file clerk. I started these jobs believing to climb the latter of success, but found I was growing numb to thinking skills. I was told what to do never alowed to give imput that I would receive glory for, Management would always keep the glory while I continued to try to find honor in employment. The only difference is that I am a black man minority and Ann a woman minority, Ann struck back by speaking out, I'm stricking back through seeking New Career through education.

This is the kind of paragraph we can initially praise because in it the writer articulates his reading of Ann in terms of his own experience of the workplace and, in doing so, establishes some authority of his own vis-à-vis the text. It is also the kind of paragraph that allows us to make the general points about reading and writing to which our class discussion has been leading: that reading is an active relation, as much a matter of what readers bring to texts and do with texts as of what texts "say" to them; and that composing a reading is as much an act of putting together one's own responses and working out a coherent attitude toward a text as of communicating the information found in texts.

REVISION   At the end of the second class session, we give the students back their papers, marked with our written comments and questions, and ask for revisions in which they will use some of the strategies they came up with in order to explain more fully, for themselves and the rest of us, how they responded to Ann's article and why they read it as they did.

LESSON READING

Judith Ann, "The Secretarial Proletariat," in *Sisterhood Is Powerful*, ed. Robin Morgan (New York: Random House, 1970).

FOR FURTHER READING

Michel de Montaigne, "To Philosophize Is to Learn to Die," in *Essays*, trans. Donald M. Frame (Stanford, CA: Stanford UP, 1948).

Studs Terkel, *Working* (New York: Pantheon, 1972).

Lewis Thomas, "On Natural Death," in *Medusa and the Snail* (New York: Viking, 1979), pp. 83–86.

Finding a Workable Argument

Jeanne Fahnestock, University of Maryland
and
Marie Secor, Pennsylvania State University

Though many course outlines isolate "argument" as a separate assignment at the end of a semester, arguing is in fact not a new mode of writing or thinking that suddenly requires teacher and students to shift gears. But unfortunately, an isolated argument assignment often makes students think they must do something radically different, taking on one of a few currently controversial topics—abortion, capital punishment, legalizing marijuana— and supporting extreme views on it. Of course these are important subjects, but every teacher is wearily familiar with the kind of stale writing they too often inspire. Even if students are warned away from such topics, they are still likely to approach the argument assignment with a general, foggy sense of an unwieldy, amorphous subject and a confused notion that the assignment requires them to be polemical, even strident in tone. But there is a way to work from this unpromising beginning by showing students how any subject, whether public or personal, breaks down into an ordered set of potential issues, a series of fundamental questions that follow from each other, questions concerning facts, definitions, causes, value judgments, and proposals. To teach this logical order of the issues is to link the contemporary practice of argument with a classical tradition of invention and to give students a set of constructs that will serve them in any subject area. This single assignment may well be the most important in the course.

CLASS 1   *Finding an Argument in a Broad Subject*

On the first day of the assignment the teacher has to demonstrate to students how any subject can be resolved into a series of possible arguments that have their own inherent logic. The best technique for demonstrating this is, as always, to do it live, on stage, with student participation. The teacher begins by introducing a large, amorphous subject of public interest, say terrorism, and asks students to express their opinions or make claims about it that the teacher writes on the board as quickly as possible. In our

221

experience, students are most likely to volunteer statements like, "We shouldn't negotiate with terrorists," "We should bomb terrorist countries," "The media should not give air time to terrorists." In other words, they usually begin with proposal statements, recommendations of what should or should not be done. But if you press a bit, or cross-examine, some other kinds of claims will emerge. If you ask, for instance, how refusing to negotiate in a particular instance would be a response to unofficial terrorism rather than to an official act of war by a recognized government, you will bring them back to two fundamental questions: "What actually happened in a particular situation—that is, what are the facts and how reliably can we know them?" and "How do we define *terrorism* so that we know it when we see it?" If you pursue these issues in class discussion, even briefly, students will realize that answers to these primary and fundamental questions about facts and definitions also require argument and that policy recommendations must be based on facts and definitions. At this point you may want to ask students for tentative definitions of key terms in the subject under discussion, definitions that the class can then challenge and refine.

To continue with our example, if students are fixed on a particular instance of terrorism and an adequate response to it, then another fundamental question arises, that of cause or responsibility. After all, before any government can retaliate, it must identify a responsible agent, not always an easy matter in the tangle of events and evasions that surround such incidents. Furthermore, questions of cause include not only who did what and how they did it, but why they did it as well, what immediate or long-term goals were served by the act. Answering such questions requires causal argument to establish chains of intention and result.

From the beginning of a class discussion on a broad subject, some students will respond with immediate judgments: "Terrorism is barbaric," "Terrorists are thugs." Statements like these may look like definitions, but they are actually value judgments. They convey an attitude toward or an evaluation of the subject, inevitable in the case we are considering here where the very name *terrorism* connotes judgment. The best way to get students to unravel a value judgment is to play the devil's advocate and contradict them. "What," you may ask, "is so barbaric about the politically powerless taking action?" or, using the "so-what" response, you may ask, "Why should the fate of a few people be so important to a government or the press?" To defend their challenged evaluations, students will again have to back up to the fundamentals of fact, definition, and cause: for example, "Terrorism is barbaric because it harms innocent people," or, "Terrorists are thugs because they act outside the legitimate channels of political protest." This particular example probably does not lend itself to interesting evaluation arguments addressed to fellow Americans because our contemporary cultural values predetermine judgment. In order to justify terrorist actions, an arguer must establish a perspective outside that of the victimized culture.

The live blackboard discussion of a large, chaotic issue such as terrorism helps students resolve it into its fundamental components, questions of fact, definition, and cause. Answers to these questions can themselves become the theses of extended arguments. Or students who still want to evaluate actions or propose remedies will at least see what they have to build on. This is where audience, always a factor, becomes especially critical. If an arguer can assume that an audience knows the facts, agrees on the causes and consequences of an action, and is likely to share the same definitions of key terms, then it makes sense to go on to argue for forceful evaluations and specific recommendations; the shared assumptions may or may not be articulated in the written argument. It is more likely, however, that audiences are not in perfect accord about facts, definitions, causes, and effects. In that case, any argument that wants to push on to policy recommendation must back up and first argue its basic assumptions into place.

This is an introductory lesson, and students need not, probably should not, write on the topic discussed in class. But they must learn to take their own self-generated topics through the same series of questions. The value of the lesson comes from generalizing the procedure, applying it to a wide range of subjects, public or private, current or historical, national or local. When repeated several times, or led by students, this kind of analysis can teach students a habit of mind, an ability and an inclination to disentangle complex issues into their component questions of fact, definition, and cause before they jump to evaluation and proposal. It will certainly lead to fuller and more cogent written arguments.

CLASS 2   *Finding an Argument from a Reading*

The method of analyzing a topic into its component issues or questions, which is illustrated in the preceding section, also works on arguments that have already been formulated. In this lesson we will discuss a short, frequently reprinted essay, Paul Goodman's "A Proposal to Abolish Grading,"[1] to show how it can be broken down into separate components of fact, definition, cause, and value judgment making up the proposal. When students see how a readily comprehensible essay like this one can be understood as an argument, they will find the task of responding to written arguments a little less formidable. Furthermore, they can use such analytical skills to generate topics and arguments of their own.

Goodman announces unambiguously in his title and in his first sentence that he is arguing for a course of action, a policy that should be instituted at all colleges and universities: the abolition of grading. When first assigning this essay, which gives away its thesis immediately, ask students what supporting arguments they would expect to find. They will probably predict

---

[1] Paul Goodman, *Compulsory Mis-Education and the Community of Scholars* (New York: Vintage, 1964).

that the essay will contain a negative evaluation of grading (one rarely argues to get rid of something good), some positive consequences to follow from its removal, and some consideration of how such a drastic change might actually be brought about. Thus common sense has already taught the average college student the minimum essentials of the proposal argument: a bad situation to be corrected, the promise of improvement, and a nodding acknowledgment of the demand for feasibility.

Students will find all these constituents and more in Goodman's argument. The bad consequences of grading can be found in paragraphs 2, 7, and 9; good consequences of its abolition are mentioned in paragraphs 10 and 11. Students may not at first notice the very brief consideration of feasibility in the first sentence, the suggestion that a few prestigious universities could set a trend that others would follow and the implied practical argument mentioned later that professional institutions should be able to take care of their own testing and certification.

What students are less likely to predict and what the teacher can point out are the many arguments from definition that Goodman uses. In a very short space he probes the nature of a university, arguing that it is best defined as something like a guild that helps young people move from apprenticeship to mastery; it is not, in Goodman's view, a gatekeeper for the professions. If it were, grades would be necessary to weed out the unworthy. By grounding his argument in a definition of the university as a place where people are taught rather than a place where they are penalized for failing to learn, he can also employ certain causal arguments about how grading itself creates failure (paragraphs 11, 12, 13).

Like any astute debater, Goodman argues against as well as for, anticipating and answering the objections his readers will naturally raise to so radical a proposal. After students have read the essay, ask them to extract all the passages containing Goodman's refutations and then orally re-create the arguments he is answering. When they do, they will find themselves exploring the causes of students' success, failure, and motivation to learn. No matter which side they take, this exercise will expose the roots of Goodman's argument in certain assumptions about the causes of human behavior.

WRITING
ASSIGNMENTS

Once students have learned how to analyze an argument into its structural components, facts, definitions, and causes leading to value judgments and hence to proposals, they can respond to it in more varied and sophisticated ways than simply accepting or rejecting its thesis. Students working with Goodman's essay could first do some research about the facts: Have any schools abolished grading, and if they have, what have been the results? Contradicting Goodman on an assumption of fact, some might argue that most or many students are not grade grubbers, concerned only with what the final exam will cover. Or they might concede Goodman's characterization of students, but argue a different value judgment from it, defending competitiveness and pragmatism as useful survival strategies in preparation for life after college. They can argue with Goodman's definition of the university as analogous to the medieval guild, or they can insist that it is a better gatekeeper than an employer or professional school could be. Turning to causes, students could dispute Goodman's causal model for student success and failure. Or they could predict the actual effects of abolishing grades, effects that might be different from those Goodman assumes. And of course students could return to those constituents of the typical proposal argument that they identified in the first place, perhaps arguing that it would not be feasible for any institution, let alone a highly prestigious one, suddenly to forswear grading.

The point is that even so brief an essay as Goodman's can yield a rich array of possibilities to the student who reads analytically with potential issues in mind. We have indicated only some of the directions a spin-off argument could follow. Our brief analysis demonstrates that teachers who want to use reading assignments to generate written arguments need not worry that student invention will be limited to a pro or con response to an overall thesis. Furthermore, they can feel confident that the activity of analysis itself will be directly related to the students' growing power to invent and construct arguments.

READING

Paul Goodman

A PROPOSAL TO ABOLISH GRADING

[1] Let half a dozen of the prestigious Universities—Chicago, Stanford, the Ivy League—abolish grading, and use testing only and entirely for pedagogic purposes as teachers see fit.

[2] Anyone who knows the frantic temper of the present schools will understand the transvaluation of values that would be effected by this modest innovation. For most of the students, the competitive grade has come to be the essence. The naïve teacher points to the beauty of the subject and the ingenuity of the research; the shrewd student asks if he is responsible for that on the final exam.

[3] Let me at once dispose of an objection whose unanimity is quite fascinating. I think that the great majority of professors agree that grading hinders teaching and creates a bad spirit, going as far as cheating and plagiarizing. I have before me the collection of essays, *Examining in Harvard College*, and this is the consensus. It is uniformly asserted, however, that the grading is inevitable; for how else will the graduate schools, the foundations, the cor-

From *Compulsory Mis-Education and the Community of Scholars* by Paul Goodman (New York: Vintage, 1964), pp. 127–130.

porations *know* whom to accept, reward, hire? How will the talent scouts know whom to tap?

[4] By testing the applicants, of course, according to the specific task-requirements of the inducting institution, just as applicants for the Civil Service or for licenses in medicine, law, and architecture are tested. Why should Harvard professors do the testing *for* corporations and graduate-schools?

[5] The objection is ludicrous. Dean Whitla, of the Harvard Office of Tests, points out that the scholastic-aptitude and achievement tests used for *admission* to Harvard are a super-excellent index for all-around Harvard performance, better than high-school grades or particular Harvard course-grades. Presumably, these college-entrance tests are tailored for what Harvard and similar institutions want. By the same logic, would not an employer do far better to apply his own job-aptitude test rather than to rely on the vagaries of Harvard section-men. Indeed, I doubt that many employers bother to look at such grades; they are more likely to be interested merely in the fact of a Harvard diploma, whatever that connotes to them. The grades have most of their weight with the graduate schools—here, as elsewhere, the system runs mainly for its own sake.

[6] It is really necessary to remind our academics of the ancient history of Examination. In the medieval university, the whole point of the gruelling trial of the candidate was whether or not to accept him as a peer. His disputation and lecture for the Master's was just that, a master-piece to enter the guild. It was not to make comparative evaluations. It was not to weed out and select for an extra-mural licensor or employer. It was certainly not to pit one young fellow against another in an ugly competition. My philosophic impression is that the medievals thought they knew what a good job of work was and that we are competitive because we do not know. But the more status is achieved by largely irrelevant competitive evaluation, the less will we ever know.

[7] (Of course, our American examinations never did have this purely guild orientation, just as our faculties have rarely had absolute autonomy; the examining was to satisfy Overseers, Elders, distant Regents—and they as paternal superiors have always doted on giving grades, rather than accepting peers. But I submit that this set-up itself makes it imposible for the student to *become* a master, to *have* grown up, and to commence on his own. He will always be making A or B for some overseer. And in the present atmosphere, he will always be climbing on his friend's neck.)

[8] Perhaps the chief objectors to abolishing grading would be the students and their parents. The parents should be simply disregarded; their anxiety has done enough damage already. For the students, it seems to me that a primary duty of the university is to deprive them of their props, their dependence on extrinsic valuation and motivation, and to force them to confront the difficult enterprise itself and finally lose themselves in it.

[9] A miserable effect of grading is to nullify the various uses of testing. Testing, for both student and teacher, is a means of structuring, and also of finding out what is blank or wrong and what has been assimilated and can be taken for granted. Review—including high-pressure review—is a means of bringing together the fragments, so that there are flashes of synoptic insight.

[10] There are several good reasons for testing, and kinds of test. But if the aim is to discover weakness, what is the point of down-grading and punishing it, and thereby inviting the student to conceal his weakness, by faking and

bulling, if not cheating? The natural conclusion of synthesis is the insight itself, not a grade for having had it. For the important purpose of placement, if one can establish in the student the belief that one is testing *not* to grade and make invidious comparisons but for his own advantage, the student should normally seek his own level, where he is challenged and yet capable, rather than trying to get by. If the student dares to accept himself as he is, a teacher's grade is a crude instrument compared with a student's self-awareness. But it is rare in our universities that students are encouraged to notice objectively their vast confusion. Unlike Socrates, our teachers rely on power-drives rather than shame and ingenuous idealism.

[11]   Many students are lazy, so teachers try to goad or threaten them by grading. In the long run this must do more harm than good. Laziness is a character-defense. It may be a way of avoiding learning, in order to protect the conceit that one is already perfect (deeper, the despair that one *never* can). It may be a way of avoiding just the risk of failing and being down-graded. Sometimes it is a way of politely saying, "I won't." But since it is the authoritarian grown-up demands that have created such attitudes in the first place, why repeat the trauma? There comes a time when we must treat people as adult, laziness and all. It is one thing courageously to fire a do-nothing out of your class; it is quite another thing to evaluate him with a lordly F.

[12]   Most important of all, it is often obvious that balking in doing the work, especially among bright young people who get to great universities, means exactly what it says: The work does not suit me, not this subject, or not at this time, or not in this school, or not in school altogether. The student might not be bookish; he might be school-tired; perhaps his development ought now to take another direction. Yet unfortunately, if such a student is intelligent and is not sure of himself, he *can* be bullied into passing, and this obscures everything. My hunch is that I am describing a common situation. What a grim waste of young life and teacherly effort! Such a student will retain nothing of what he has "passed" in. Sometimes he must get mononucleosis to tell his story and be believed.

[13]   And ironically, the converse is also probably commonly true. A student flunks and is mechanically weeded out, who is really ready and eager to learn in a scholastic setting, but he has not quite caught on. A good teacher can recognize the situation, but the computer wreaks its will.

Examining Assumptions

Annette Rottenberg,
University of Massachusetts–Amherst

When arguments go wrong, that is, when claims or propositions are weak or unconvincing, students will first point to a lack of factual proof. Even in informal arguments, they may be quick to ask, "Where's the evidence?" But they are less likely to detect and identify the weaknesses when the premises, the assumptions on which the claims are based, are doubtful. One definition of assumptions—"beliefs taken for granted"—underscores the problem. If arguers or readers take these beliefs for granted, they may ignore the necessity for examining them. As beginning writers, freshman students need practice in asking questions about the assumptions that underlie the arguments they read and write.

My objective is to give students an opportunity to discover for themselves that no argument can be stronger than its assumptions. I begin by suggesting a familiar claim to be defended by data about which there will be no dispute since we want to concentrate attention on the soundness of the basic assumption.

IN-CLASS
EXERCISES
Without informing students of the purpose of the assignment, I ask them to take a few minutes to list the characteristics—one sentence for each trait—of the best or worst teachers they can remember having had in high school or college. (As an alternative assignment, I sometimes ask students to write out in paragraph form descriptions of these teachers. After reading them, I extract the evidence and duplicate it for discussion in class.)

While students are writing, I make an outline on the board. On one side of the board I write:

Claim: He/she was a good teacher.
Evidence: *Assumption:*
1.
2.

On the other side I repeat the outline, using a different claim: He/she was a bad teacher.

At the end of the allotted time, I ask each student to produce one sentence from his or her list. On the board I write down the descriptive statements in the columns marked *Evidence*. I omit repetitions. When all the descriptions have been exhausted, we go through them, one by one, as I ask, "What are your general beliefs about education, about the relationship between teaching and learning, that caused you to describe a good teacher or a bad teacher as one who _____?"

Here are some of the statements about good teachers that emerged in one class:

1. He showed a personal interest in me and tried to help me solve my problems.
2. She taught us not only how to handle psychology but how to handle life. She would sense a personal problem and seek you out and try to help.
3. He was very entertaining.
4. I felt relaxed in her classroom.
5. The teacher called me by name in a crowded lecture hall.
6. I did the work because the teacher tried so hard to be effective (even though he was not).
7. He organized a class basketball team which played after school.
8. Perhaps the most important reason he was a good teacher was his commanding voice.
9. Most of all, what I liked about this man was his looks and personality.
10. She taught in an interesting way.
11. He made it clear that he would be strict and that we were expected to work very hard.
12. Hers was the first class in which I felt like an adult.
13. She was young, and I was not affected by the student–teacher gap that exists in so many classrooms.

To ask about assumptions is to make clear to students that I am asking about the relationship between evidence and claim. In other words, how does the fact that the teacher is entertaining prove that he's a good teacher? My objective is not, at this point to quarrel with their assumptions, although students may challenge each other, but rather to encourage examination of the validity of the relationship.

When the discussion begins, not all students will be able to answer the question, "How does the teacher's personal interest in you (or sensing that you have a problem and trying to help) make her a good teacher?" But a few students will see the connection, and in the column headed *Assumption* I will write: "A good teacher must take an interest in the student's personal life." Or "Students can learn best in a classroom where the teacher tries to help students solve their personal problems." As we go on to discuss the rest of the descriptive statements, students find it increasingly easier to express the assumptions and evaluate their soundness.

The assumptions do, in fact, tell us a good deal about what students regard as the significant elements in the educational experience. One thing that is almost never mentioned by freshmen—although it is sometimes offered by upper classmen in a composition course—is the teacher's mastery of the subject. Nor do freshmen suggest that good teachers are those who impart skills or knowledge. Perhaps freshmen are incapable of judging either the teacher's academic competence or their own acquisition of skills. They do, however, make reference to strategy: "She taught in an interesting way." But clearly students associate "good" teaching primarily with a bright personality, attractive appearance, friendliness, good will, the personal approach. A discussion based on analysis of these assumptions can be lively and enlightening—for both students and teacher.

Descriptions of "bad" teachers are equally revealing—and sometimes more unsettling. Here is a list of comments about bad teachers:

1. He was a teacher who couldn't earn the respect of the students because we all knew about his messy life.
2. Miss S. had no ability and no desire to control the class. Above a steady hum of conversation, and despite a constant barrage of papers, pens, and pencils being thrown across the room, she would begin her lecture. Miss S. expounded on the wonders of the Westward Expansion while the class dozed, daydreamed and doodled until the bell finally freed us.
3. His inability to control the class disrupted his teaching. The class could see that they could get away with almost anything and thus paid no attention, did no assignments, would fight, yell, and even rip up the detention slips in front of his face.
4. His clothes were always dirty with chalk and wrinkled.
5. He had many nervous and annoying mannerisms that distracted us. He was mimicked and picked on mercilessly.
6. He looked like a scared puppy. He always thought that the class was laughing at him and ridiculing him.
7. He tried to be friends with the boys by saying he'd go out drinking with them.
8. He didn't seem to care about teaching.
9. He was boring.

Under *Assumption* I will write:

1. Knowledge of a teacher's unsavory personal life influences adversely my ability to learn.
2. A teacher's unattractive appearance and mannerisms influence adversely my ability to learn.
3. A lack of respect for the teacher prevents students from learning.

And so on. Not surprisingly, the most provocative assumption, the one that occasions the most spirited discussion—and defense—is this one:

4. Students are not responsible for their conduct in class. Its the teacher's responsibility to impose order.

In reviewing these beliefs about the relationship between teachers and education, I am alternatively amused and distressed. For many high school students and college freshmen, teachers are perceived as parent surrogates, just as they were in elementary school, judged according to the same personal criteria by which adolescents continue to judge their parents. (Are they kind to me? Do they care about me? Can they control me when I misbehave? Would I be proud to show them to my friends?) Of course, I don't press this conclusion in a class discussion, but thoughtful students will often pick up the resemblance.

WRITING
ASSIGNMENT

Having recognized the relationship between these usually hidden assumptions and their claims about teaching, students can be asked to write essays that support or reject one or more of their stated beliefs. I urge them to consider one hard question above all: How much responsibility do students have for their own education, even with boring and unattractive teachers?

LESSON READINGS

John Holt, "How Teachers Make Children Hate Reading," *Redbook* (© McCall Corp.) Nov. 1967; *The Under-Achieving School* (New York: Putnam, 1969).

Bertrand Russell, "The Aims of Education," in *Education and the Good Life* (New York: Boni & Liveright, 1926).

Constructing an Argument Together

Bruce Harvey,
Stanford University

In this exercise the class splits into several small teams, with each team developing either the pro or con sides of a controversial issue. Afterward, I put the skeleton arguments devised by the opposed teams on the chalkboard and then discuss assumptions, support, rebuttal, and concession. The lesson engages the students in lively debate and prepares them to tackle their first written argumentative paper with greater confidence and skill.

CLASS 1   For the previous class the students read the chapters on argument in the required composition handbook (usually either Crews's *The Random House Handbook* or Barnet and Stubbs's *Practical Guide to Writing*), as well as a few professional essays taking opposed stances on a topic of controversy (last time I taught, a series of essays on "Lifeboat Ethics"—on whether the United States should take in immigrants or feed the hungry of third-world countries—in *The Borzoi College Reader*, 5/e, worked well). In class we examine the professional essays in terms of the argumentative strategies outlined by the handbook. I explain that most good arguments convince us by mixing rigorous logic and rhetorical persuasion. I especially emphasize the difference between fair and unfair emotional manipulation (the use of wit versus sarcasm or *ad hominem* attacks, for example) and lead the class to distinguish between personal ethics and logic as the basis for making assumptions. (The statement that "federal funding for abortion should not be legislated because society has no obligation to assist women who have been promiscuously careless" depends on the seemingly logical extension of a personal belief—that is, that individuals should pay for their mistakes. In and of itself, that moral belief cannot be logically assailed; but another, unstated assumption on which the argument relies can be logically disputed: Not all women with unwanted children have been careless—some have been the victims of rape, others simply lack the means of adequate birth control.)

CLASS 2   In the following class, the students divide into four small groups with four or five students in each group. I first let the students elect the side they prefer, but then reassign several if the sides are unequal. Having a few students take a stance contrary to their initial choice may, in fact, help the group to generate a more complex argument. Two groups are instructed to devise an argument for the "pro" side of a selected controversial issue; the other two groups work with the "con" side. I supply sheets (see below) with an argumentative skeleton (matching the terms used by our composition handbook). Each side must (1) clearly state its thesis, (2) come up with several points of support, (3) anticipate what the other side's main arguments will be, and (4) attempt to refute their position. I assign a "recorder" to jot down the ideas in their final form on the skeleton sheet. Usually, fifteen to twenty minutes suffice for the contesting groups to summon forth ample ammunition for their viewpoints. I let the students choose the topic of controversy from several canned ones I've worked out previously (thus allowing me to direct the exercise efficiently as it takes shape). The type and complexity of topic will of course depend on the interests and maturity of the class; I try to stay clear of issues ground to a bewildering mush in anthologies (nuclear energy, the death penalty) or issues on which the entire class will likely unite on the same side. Though it will eventually become outdated, the question (used below) of whether the president and his family should live in high style in the White House has consistently worked well. After the allotted time, the recorders from the two "pro" sides report the groups' ideas in turn, and I write them on the chalkboard following the format of the skeleton sheet. (Having two groups focus on the same side ensures a wide range of supporting points.) The same is done for the two "con" sides on the right side of the board.

In the time left (half an hour) we criss-cross between the "pro" and "con" sides now mirrored on the board. I start by asking each team to define its key terms. (Does *high style* mean mere ostentatious living? or style in the sense of dignified decorum suited to the highest public office? To what extent does or should the function of the White House shape the way of life within it? Is it just the residence of the First Family, or is it a national museum and national reception grounds for foreign dignitaries? (Do the different roles of the president—personal, public, symbolic—conflict with each other?) I encourage them to see that one of the problems resulting from fuzzy definitions is that we may end up arguing at cross-purposes. One side, for instance, may define "living in high style" as living in personal luxury; whereas the other side may define the phrase more in terms of public ceremony. If so, perhaps the two sides actually agree on basic points: It's fine for the president's wife to purchase expensive china for public receptions, but improper for her to spend thousands of dollars on designer dresses. We then focus on whether each side has supplied adequate supporting points, if the opposition's stance has been anticipated and plausibly refuted, if additional points need to be made, if some types of evidence would suit the argument more than others (examples of past presidents versus foreign leaders), if one structure would be more convincing than another (weakest argument first, strongest last), and so on.

By the end of the exercise, some students may feel the controversy cannot be resolved if they grasp the logical merits of both sides and that the proper response, therefore, is to straddle the fence. I explain that our positions on debated issues (especially moral ones) often don't follow from a chain of logical inquiry; rather, we believe in something and then try to use logic honestly to encounter and convince those who might disagree with us.

WRITING
ASSIGNMENT

The argumentative scrimmage sparks most of the class into active participation. The initial fifteen- to twenty-minute team effort elicits (often riotous) humor when one side overhears the opposed side's strategy in the making. I often assign a quiet student (if not too shy) to be the recorder, since the reporting back of collectively developed ideas is nonthreatening. The board provides visual emphasis and stimulates further debate and analysis (also many chances for student wit—"Your team says the president should live in the White House more like the average Joe. . . . Great! He pretends to sympathize personally with the average family, but socks it to them in his economic proposals!"). Finally, the exercise leads directly to the students' first argumentative essay (roughly three pages). Before tackling that assignment on their own, they have practiced analyzing assumptions, marshaling evidence in a persuasive order, and developing their own stance by doing fair battle with the opposition. The following is an argument skeleton I give to each side of the debate (I leave space between each heading in the actual handout):

THESIS
SUPPORT
OPPOSITION (May include opposition to above support plus additional points)
REBUTTAL
CONCESSION (optional)

And here are the results of one such session:

PRO	CON
THESIS	THESIS
President should live in high style in the White House	President should not live in high style in the White House
SUPPORT	SUPPORT
Impressive White House needed for foreign diplomats	We don't need to impress anyone
President deserves relaxing luxury	Relax yes; but with new china!
Image of what anyone in a democracy can achieve	Wastes money better spent elsewhere
Publicizes splendor of America	Insensitive to condition of common man
White House is a national museum (needs expensive upkeep and furnishings)	

OPPOSITION
  Wastes money
  Position holds enough dignity
  President is not royalty; insensitive
  to common man's plight

REBUTTAL
  Money is donated (issue of tax deductions insignificant; no favorit-
  ism shown to donors)
  President lives "royally" only in regards to the need for public, symbolic ceremony

CONCESSION
  Maybe insensitive; but other points
  outweigh our concession

OPPOSITION
  Image of what anyone can achieve
  in a democracy
  Impress foreign diplomats
  President needs luxury to relax
  Money donated

REBUTTAL
  Every penny counts; president
  should set an example
  Creates envy; not an instance of the
  American dream
  President can relax on his many va-
  cations
  Impress foreign diplomats more by
  living austerely

CONSESSION
  No concession!

Judging Judgments About Judgments

Diana Postlethwaite,
Mount Holyoke College

I teach Joan Didion's essay, "The Women's Movement," at the end of the semester, as we study the logical structure of argumentation and the persuasive use of supporting evidence. After analyzing Didion's argument, the students are given a writing assignment that invites them to make their own logical argument based on supporting evidence that they have gleaned from a familiar contemporary source.

The students will expect a polarized feminist debate. But Joan Didion will deliberately frustrate those easy expectations; she is neither Phyllis Schlafly nor Gloria Steinem. Where does she stand on the "women's movement"? How are we to interpret the tone of her title? seriously? ironically? In reading the essay in preparation for class discussion, I suggest that my students focus particular attention on the first two paragraphs. I also ask them to pay attention to everything Didion places in quotation marks and to look for any principles of structure around which the thirteen paragraphs of the essay can be organized.

We begin our class discussion with a close reading of the first and second paragraphs of the essay, which provide the foundation for the argument that follows. We've been discussing some of the rudiments of logic in previous classes; here we review basic definitions of *deduction* and *induction*. In a general way, we discuss the potential pitfalls of both forms of reasoning. Deduction can lead to an overinclusive premise, to oversimplification; induction can lead to false generalization from a particular, to the mistake of taking one part to stand for the whole. Didion opens by accusing revolutionary theorists of a deductive logical fallacy: Every oppressed person should be a revolutionary; every woman is oppressed; therefore every woman should be a revolutionary. But doesn't Didion herself commit some logical sins? For example, she asserts that the "tendency for popular discussion of the movement to center for so long around day-care centers is yet another instance of that studied resistance to political ideas which characterizes our national life." I ask the students whether this seems to be a fair conclusion. Is it an example of inductive reasoning? Or has Didion overthrown any real logic in order to achieve a rhetorical effect? Throughout our discussion of the essay, we want to be similarly alert to the local flaws and the rhetorical effects of both Didion and those she criticizes.

The second paragraph of the essay centers on two quotations, one from feminist theorist Shulamith Firestone and the other from a *Time* magazine special issue on women. We discuss why Didion picked those two statements, and the ways in which they epitomize the two groups around which she focuses her argument: the first stage of the movement, the radical theorists; and the second stage, the popularizers. We note how Didion manipulates and heightens the tone of her quotations by the manner of her presentation ("announced flatly," "musing genially"). She uses quotation marks in the first paragraph, too: "oppressed," "class," "idea." Why? How are those quotations different from the second paragraph's? This same line of inquiry can be followed throughout the essay, as we look at the sources Didion chooses, and the contexts in which she presents those sources.

Just what is Didion's argument? We try to extract it from the first two paragraphs. Does Didion sympathize with either Firestone or *Time*? What are the limitations of the radical theoreticians? of the popularizers? We move into a discussion of the overall structure of the essay, which falls into two parts, corresponding to the Firestone/*Time* dichotomy of the second paragraph. Paragraphs 3–6 address the reductionism of the theorists, and the American public's ultimate lack of interest in the "Marxist idea" (par. 3). But at least the theoreticians are "serious" (par. 7). Paragraphs 7–13 focus on Didion's version of the sad fate of the would-be revolutionary transformed into talk-show trivializer, as she lambastes the jargon and cliché that plague the rhetoric of contemporary feminism.

Throughout the essay, Didion suggests that she is concerned not merely with the "women's movement," but also with "that studied resistance to political ideas that characterizes our national life." But would the essay imply that Joan Didion is a political activist? I point out that Didion is a novelist as well as an essayist. She asserts that "fiction is in most ways hostile to ideology" (par. 6) and defines herself as one "committed mainly to the exploration of moral distinctions and ambiguities" (par. 7). *Does* she believe that women are different from men? (I hope the students will point to paragraph 11: "that dark involvement with blood and birth and death"). Do the Novelist and the Woman share any common perspectives? How are they different from the Feminist or the Political Activist?

Perhaps the trickiest part of reading this essay is defining Joan Didion's elusive voice. What does she reveal to us of her values and opinions? Is she a feminist? What tone does her argument take: reasoned? witty? impassioned? detached? snide? (all of the above?).

At this point, I encourage a lively verbal debate over the legitimacy of Didion's attack on feminists as "perpetual adolescents" (par. 12). But rather than allowing them simply to express their own opinions about feminism, I insist that my students address themselves to what they perceive as the vulnerable points of Didion's argument. I urge everyone to contemplate both the strengths and the weaknesses of that argument: its rhetorical effectiveness and its logical flaws; Didion's sense of humor and her smug superiority; her accurate social criticisms and her selective presentation (distortion?) of women's issues.

WRITING ASSIGNMENT

At this point, I ask the students to write a three-page essay on the following topic:

> In her essay "The Women's Movement," Joan Didion argues that the serious moral, imaginative, and cultural issues affecting women's lives have been debased by the cliché-ridden trivialization of popularizing feminists who are nothing more than "perpetual adolescents."
>
> Using the current issue of *Ms.* magazine as your source, what evidence do you find there which would support this argument? Do you find anything which would disprove it? Pay careful attention to the logical structure of your own argument.

In a single issue of the magazine, my students pointed to a moving letter to the editor describing the painful moral choice behind a decision not to have an abortion; an incisive survey of women in the military; a provocative indictment of child abuse in America. On the other hand, Didion herself would have had a field day with the travelogue of a feminist utopia in Santa Cruz: "Ahead of me was a Datsun truck driven by a young woman in ponytails. On its left side was a bumper sticker that read NO MORE PROFITS OFF WOMEN'S BODIES. On the right side another read I'D RATHER BE SMASHING IMPERIALISM." Another article solemnly memorializes the tennis contest between Billie Jean King and Bobby Riggs: "nothing ever equaled the drama of this match." A review of a book on American couples concludes glumly that "heterosexuals represent the least interesting research of the book."[1]

The latest issue of *Ms.* should yield many examples of both kinds and will give the students a sense of confronting the immediacy of current issues. Try to encourage a sense of humor on the subject, even as they consider the more solemn aspects of the topic. Encourage them to read *Ms.* from cover to cover, advertising and editorials as well as articles. This lesson can also be useful for alerting students to clichés and jargon. Of course, the field of investigation could be expanded from a single magazine into many contemporary media, but I find the magazine gives my students the opportunity to draw from a variety of secondary sources as supporting evidence, yet to do so within a workably small context. This lesson could also provide the opportunity for discussing the technical aspects of quoting from a variety of sources, and rules for the documentation of sources.

---

[1] Grace Lichtenstein, "Should You Move to Santa Cruz? A Tough Look at a 'Feminist Utopia,'" *Ms.* November 1983: 54. Meredith Freedman, "The Day Billie Jean King Beat Bobby Riggs," *Ms.* November 1983: 101. Christine Doudna, "American Couples: Surprising New Finds About Sex, Money, and Work," *Ms.* November 1983: 119.

LESSON READING

Joan Didion, "The Women's Movement," in *The White Album* (New York: Simon and Schuster, 1979).

FOR FURTHER READING

Any issue of *Ms.* magazine.

Engaging Students in Reason: An Argumentative Text and Its Context

Bradley Hughes,
University of Wisconsin–Madison

All writing teachers would agree that students need to learn to read an argument critically, to be engaged with its ideas, and to construct effective arguments of their own. Far too often, though, argumentation is limited in students' minds and experiences to two extremes: heated, often irrational, disagreements with family and friends, on the one hand, and, on the other, the lifeless abstractions of logical fallacies catalogued in writing handbooks. Student writers need to learn to take a stand on a controversial issue, to feel the power and force of written arguments, and to develop a keen skepticism and an appreciation for logic. Instruction in this fundamental use of our language can often best proceed inductively, not by requiring students to read a handbook chapter on argumentation, but by giving them a chance to read, discuss, and write in response to a controversial and lively argument.

One essay that provides abundant opportunities to bring argument alive in a writing course is Edward Bunker's "Let's End the Dope War: A Junkie View of the Quagmire," a piece that originally appeared in *The Nation* in 1977 and has since been frequently reprinted. Bunker's essay is ideal for engaging students: It is about a familiar subject; it is at once accessible and substantial; and its controversial stand demands a response—students react strongly to it, eagerly debating the merits of its proposition and method. The essay argues for what initially appears to be a shocking proposal, that the United States should abandon its war on narcotics and should license addicts, providing them, under supervision of physicians, maintenance doses of narcotics. In a very carefully structured manner, Bunker vigorously supports this proposal and refutes alternatives to it. The essay's surface of reason often appeals to readers, persuading many who initially recoil at its thesis. But careful analysis of the argument reveals that it skims over complex issues, throws statistics around carelessly, leaps over numerous logical gaps, and commits almost every logical fallacy imaginable. Discovering the flaws in this argument while still appreciating its power teaches students important principles about both reading and writing arguments.

IN-CLASS   Our class work on this essay extends over the last fifteen minutes of one
EXERCISE   class period and all of the next. During the closing part of the class *before* the students have read the essay, I distribute a sheet of paper to each student with the fundamental proposition of Bunker's essay presented in the form of a Gallup poll question and ask each student simply to agree or disagree with it. I then ask students to write out at least four points in favor of Bunker's proposal and the same in opposition to it. Having taken at least a tentative stand on Bunker's proposal and having developed some appreciation for both sides of the issue, students approach reading the essay and the class discussion of it with a clearer sense of purpose. They tend to read the argument more critically, for they now have a stake in the issue and thus can experience some of the satisfaction of having anticipated certain arguments and can eagerly challenge others.

Early in the class discussion of the essay, I am especially interested in finding out whether reading the essay actually changed anybody's mind, and if so, how. I want students not only to recognize how shallow the responses to pollsters' questions can be but also to experience firsthand how written arguments can have the power to persuade. We then begin to examine the essay's structure and strategy and extract from the discussion some principles of effective argument by asking questions such as these:

How is Bunker's argument structured? (It is, in fact, very carefully structured, following a classical argument form: opening statement of thesis; history of the failure of attempts to outlaw narcotics; arguments in favor; refutation of opposing arguments; recapitulation.) What are his main assertions in support of the proposal? Why is the essay so carefully structured? Why would he state such a controversial proposition as prominently as he does? How does he appeal for our support? (Through a purposefully wide variety of ways: through statistics and facts; through analogy—comparing the American system unfavorably with the British; through appeals to the reader's personal benefit—even if drug addition does not affect a reader directly, the street crime and burglary it necessitates do; through emotional appeals—by describing the suffering of addicts, and by claiming to be able to save our children.) Who is his audience? (Well-educated, upper and middle class, liberal; notice, for example, the classical allusions in the essay.) How does this affect the way he argues? What crucial issues does he fail to address? (Among many, the problems in the British system; the inevitable abuses of such a system; the social and moral implications of creating a group of permanent addicts.) And why? I then remind students of the essay's title, which leads to a discussion of Bunker's analogy between our approach to controlling drugs and fighting a war. (This analogy is, in fact, a central part of his argument: The war involves propaganda, demagoguery, reductive views of the enemy, and crimes of all sorts, committed by both sides; and, of course, Bunker's argument that we should not continue a protracted and ever-escalating war that we have no chance of winning would have had instant sympathizers in the 1970s, when this article appeared.) The subtitle too raises important questions about the authority of the author, about how Bunker's experience as an ex-junkie and ex-convict influences our reading of the argument.

We will then, usually because an answer has led us there, proceed to examine very closely the logic of a specific section of the essay. I will ask if there are particular assertions that are not adequately supported, or facts that we should doubt. In our discussion we inevitably discover numerous examples of Bunker's selective use of evidence; casual, even careless, use of statistics (see paragraph 10, for example); exaggerated claims; generalizations drawn from anecdotal evidence; *post hoc* logic; *ad hominem* attacks (see the comment about doctors in paragraph 5); and sarcastic shots aimed at various targets (usually politicians). The post–World-War-II section of Bunker's history of the war on drugs (paragraphs 6–9) provides several examples of arguments we should question. Bunker here attributes the geometric increase in drug addiction since 1953 solely to the Jones–Miller law, without even considering other possible contributing factors such as the dramatic increase in the population of young people and the general affluence following the war. In paragraph 9 Bunker takes the opinion of one unnamed Drug Enforcement Agency official as representing the entire government's position on heroin maintenance. Another spot where the argument clearly falters is Bunker's sympathetic portrayal of the misery addicts suffer (paragraph 12). After claiming that drug addiction has no deleterious effects whatsoever (a questionable assertion in itself), Bunker likens taking drugs to drinking milk, an inept analogy certainly, and his subsequent assertion that a narcotic may "contribute to longevity because it's the ultimate tranquilizer" leads one to ask if we should not all become addicts. During this close reading students will inevitably notice that Bunker gives no source for most of his facts—a particularly damaging indictment.

We conclude our discussion of the essay not by making easy criticisms of it, however, but by trying to determine how the argument remains persuasive and demands a serious response despite these shortcomings. Crucial to reading arguments carefully is recognizing the complexity of the issues involved and discovering that no argument is airtight, that there is always room for rebuttal.

WRITING ASSIGNMENT   The writing assignment that follows this reading and discussion gives students different ways to respond to Bunker's essay, each requiring them to improve on Bunker's logic and to create an argument aimed at a specific audience. I distribute the following assignment at the end of our discussion and ask students to choose their topic, or propose an alternative, by the beginning of the next class when we will have time to discuss the assignment further.

1. I ask those students who find Bunker's proposal morally unacceptable and logically flawed to respond in the next issue of *The Nation*. Their response can take the form of a letter that strictly refutes Bunker or it can be an article of its own, usually about half the length of his.
2. I ask those students who find Bunker's proposal appealing but logically flawed to rewrite a part of his argument, keeping the same proposal but arguing more persuasively for it.
3. I ask those who find both the proposal and the argument convincing to rewrite, in a condensed form, the argument for a different audience, such as one of these:
   a. a congressional committee investigating drug laws.
   b. a group of addicts.
   c. law enforcement officials.
   d. physicians and health care professionals who run a methadone clinic and believe that addiction can be cured.
   e. a neighborhood association.
   f. a group of sociologists.
   g. a rural or small-city newspaper.

A discussion of this argument also provides abundant opportunities for research, if it is appropriate at this point in the course. Students could do research and write about any of the following:

1. Learn more about the British system to see if Bunker has described it accurately and to find out why the British government has recently done away with its licensing system.
2. Check and update some of Bunker's facts. In the years following the essay's publication has the situation changed? in the ways he predicted?
3. Find out if a Gallup or Harris poll has been done on this subject. Conduct a small survey of their own and write up the results.
4. Contact a local methadone clinic and talk with its director about Bunker's proposal.
5. Find out if Congress or state legislatures have considered such proposals.
6. Find opposing arguments in print and analyze them or compare them with Bunker.

LESSON READING

Edward Bunker, "Let's End the Dope War: A Junkie View of the Quagmire," *The Nation*, June 25, 1977.

CAVEAT LECTOR, or How to Spot Hidden Persuasion

Steven Wright,
Williams College

WRITING
ASSIGNMENT
This assignment asks students to identify and explain the techniques and tricks (see the following partial list) that journalists use to persuade—or bully—readers. This paper (1500–1750 words) is the last (of nine) and longest assignment in a one-semester course in basic freshman composition. It has many of the advantages of a conventional research paper (students must find suitable articles and document the paper fully), but it exercises more sophisticated skills than the usual research paper and students find it far more entertaining.

During the preliminary lessons (to be described briefly) I help the students identify some common devices used by writers to present a persuasive— and perhaps slanted—case on one side of an issue. We discuss the use and effect of such techniques as:

- the use of loaded words, or the device of putting quotation marks around words or phrases.

- offering unfair, slanted comparisons or misleading, meaningless analogies.

- using apparent logic or logical terms (*therefore*) intended to sway a reader's judgment.

- indulging in mockery, sarcasm, or name calling.

- presenting unanalyzed facts, especially when the writer's failure to draw a conclusion from the facts cannot hide how the writer wants us

244

to interpret those facts, or combining facts in a suggestive way without comment.[1]

As students discuss these techniques, they come to see that this paper is *not* about the subject or issue itself, but about the coverage of that subject, and especially about the tricks and methods that can influence uncritical readers. Students soon see that virtually any subject that can support strong or opposing opinions will serve for this assignment as long as they can find roughly six articles to analyze. (Some students seek out articles on both sides of the question; some find articles representing only one side.) I have seen excellent papers on the coverage of subjects as diverse as John Belushi's death, National Basketball Association centers, the Mary Cunningham/ William Agee "scandal," and the Greensboro riot. One of the great advantages of this assignment over a straight research paper is that it produces interesting papers on the tired subjects of conventional research papers, such as "nuclear power" (for instance, a student might have to explain the effect on the reader of referring to technicians or scientists as "wizards"). Throughout the preparation for this paper, I stress that this paper should state the opposing viewpoints on the issue only very briefly. The real object of this paper is to point out devices intended to sway the reader's judgment and to analyze the way these devices work.

I require brief conferences with students (seeing a small number of students at the same time helps give all of them fresh ideas) after each student has collected copies of six articles (these copies must be submitted with the final draft). Students often ask about the best organization for this essay. They see that the general thesis for these papers is virtually a formula ("The point of view of a writer influences the way that writer will present his material") but that the actual thesis for a particular paper might reflect some pattern the student finds in the coverage ("The proponents and opponents of nuclear power use similar persuasive tricks, but use them to prejudice the reader against different groups," or, "While presenting the same facts, the coverage of John Belushi's death creates two distinct impressions of Belushi—damned druggie versus tragic and misunderstood young man"). Most students can point out at least that opponents on a certain issue tend to use many of the same devices to influence their audiences. A paper organized around such an insight tends to group the articles surveyed according to the positions those articles take up on the issue. Strategies of organization that sort the tricks or devices into categories can also be effective if the student can arrive at a thesis that argues that some tricks are more effective—perhaps because of their subtlety—than others. This method works well for papers based on articles that do not really take up opposing views on some issue. For instance, the student who examined a

---

[1] A text helpful in analyzing devices of rhetoric and as a source of examples: Howard Kahane, *Logic and Contemporary Rhetoric: The Use of Reason in Everyday Life*, 3rd ed. (San Francisco: Wadsworth, 1980).

series of articles on NBA centers sorted the persuasive devices he found into categories that he found most effective (such as the use of verbs such as *fly* for *run*). Sports coverage, because it is intended to excite, proved an excellent subject for this paper.

In preparing students to pick a subject and to collect copies of six promising articles, I first spend a seventy-five-minute period on how to analyze the ways the audience is manipulated, using first advertisements (pictures and text) and then selected pieces of prose, such as the second-from-last paragraph from John Updike's "Tips for a Trip" [pp. 95–98 in his *Picked-Up Pieces* (New York: Alfred Knopf, 1975)] or a snide attack on the Miss America Pageant from a newspaper. Then I teach a second class in how to find articles in which the writer is likely to employ persuasive tricks and techniques.

CLASS 1   Any visual material usually moves students to enthusiastic analysis; advertising is often good because it also introduces a brief and loaded text. (What effect is the familiar invitation to "Marlboro country" meant to have on us? What impression does it create that the picture of a cowboy strengthens?) In the piece on Miss America, what is the effect of combining the ideas shoved together by the title? What is the effect of planting the suggestion (in the final paragraph) that these contestants might prefer to take scholarship money in cash? The Updike piece is useful because his comic effects are often easy to analyze. Why, for instance, does Updike switch to a glaring passive construction in confessing "A divot the size of an undershirt was taken 18 inches behind the ball"? Throughout the class period, be sure to insist that students must offer close analysis of *why* and *how* certain devices create an effect.

CLASS 2   To help students grasp how to find promising material, I pick a sample topic, such as the coverage of the 1980 Olympic Boycott, and pass out copies of pages from the 1980 *Readers' Guide to Periodical Literature* (Vol. 40, pp. 1086–87). As the students examine the titles listed, they will soon pick out such articles as "Neo-Nazi Olympics" as likely candidates in which to find some loaded argument. I urge them to look at articles from magazines that appeal to strongly opinionated people—such as *The Nation* or *National Review*. In class we look at one or two articles that I have selected and duplicated in advance for some further practice in finding and analyzing these persuasive devices. On this topic, it is not surprising to find *Sports Illustrated* indulging in some inflamed argument.

This paper presents students with a chance to do some shrewd analysis of the coverage of subjects of their own choosing. It also poses a considerable challenge in organization late in the term. In addition, many students have told me that they leave the course scrutinizing what they read word by word after their work on this assignment.

Samples for analysis follow.

LESSON READING

John Updike, "Tips for a Trip," in *Picked-Up Pieces* (New York: Knopf, 1975). (Originally appeared in the *New York Times*)

READING

Peter Mattiace

MISS AMERICA TELLS OF HER RELIGION, DESIRE TO MAKE MONEY

The new Miss America, Susan Powell of Oklahoma, said yesterday she is a deeply religious person who has never used drugs, has no boyfriends and considers pre-marital sex "not right" for her.

The 21-year-old brunette from Elk City, Okla., crowned the 54th Miss America Saturday night, likened her victory to "a wild black stallion coming off the plains into the big city—very graceful and very much myself."

She attributed her victory to determination, positive thinking and hard work and said she wanted "to make as much money as possible (as Miss America)."

"Yes, $100,000 would be really nice," she said. "The epitome of success is doing something we absolutely love and being paid to do it," she said, repeating her statement of the previous night to pageant judges.

The senior vocal performance major at Oklahoma City University, defeated 49 rivals partly on the strength of her rendition of "Lucy's Aria" with an antique telephone.

"I felt my greatest asset is my singing. . . . My voice is a gift from God," said Miss Powell, who hopes to earn a master's degree in voice and become an opera star.

As a young girl, Miss Powell said, she always wanted to become Miss America. "I used to get a sheet and wrap it around my neck."

Miss Powell emphasized her small-town, "middle-class" background, implying that success has been difficult. On her official pageant résumé, for example, she underlined that she once "chopped cotton."

But Miss Powell's friends in Atlantic City said her divorced parents are well-to-do, thanks to her father's success in Oklahoma's booming oil and gas industry. Her family also breeds racehorses, and Miss Powell has had years of training in piano, trumpet, voice, theater, dance and acting.

She said she is a deeply religious person who can express "my love for Christ through my singing. Religion is my life."

Miss Powell said she has no desire to be married soon. "I will marry if I meet someone I can't live without," she said.

Of pre-marital sex, Miss Powell said, "It's not right for me at this time in my life, but I can't speak for every woman in the United States."

Miss Powell said she favors equal rights for women, but not the proposed Equal Rights Amendment. The issue, however, has "people talking more about women and thinking more about women."

Although she said she has never used drugs, she said marijuana should be decriminalized, but not legalized.

Asked about the "naughtiest thing you've ever done," Miss Powell hummed for a moment and waited for another question.

As for her presidential preference, she simply said, "I always pull a curtain on the voting ballot."

Miss Powell said she sees herself as an unelected representative of the country and she wants to "learn to love our country even more" during her year's travels.

As Miss America, Miss Powell won a $20,000 scholarship, which she may take as cash, and is guaranteed at least $50,000 in advertising and public appearance bookings during her reign.

ENGAGED. Garrison Keillor, 43, beguiling, bittersweet chronicler of U.S. small-town life on radio *(A Prairie Home Companion)* and in books *(Happy to Be Here, Lake Wobegon Days)* and Ulla Skaerved, a former exchange student at Keillor's Minnesota high school, who met him again when she returned in August for a 25th class reunion. The marriage, scheduled for Dec. 29 in Copenhagen, will be the second for both. Keillor had dedicated *Lake Wobegon Days* to Margaret Moos, his radio producer, with whom he shared a house in St. Paul; she has taken a leave from the show.

Time, *November 18, 1985*[1]

What is the effect of telling the reader about the dedication of Keillor's book?

---

[1] Copyright 1985 Time, Inc. All rights reserved. Reprinted by permission from *Time.*

☐ Enclosed please find my contribution to the restoration of the Statue of Liberty and Ellis Island. I understand both these irreplaceable American symbols are urgently in need of everyone's support.

☐ **No. I'm not interested in liberty at this time.**

Name_____

Address_____

City_____State_____Zip_____

The Statue of Liberty/Ellis Island Foundation,
P.O. Box 1992, Dept. C, New York, NY 10008.

This message created as a public service by Quinn & Johnson/BBDO,
Boston, Massachusetts 02116.
Photograph by Jake Rajs.

Time, *September 16, 1985. Reprinted by permission of Ingals, Quinn and Johnson.*

What is the effect on the reader of pairing these choices? Why is the second in bold-face print? What is the effect of not capitalizing the word *liberty*?

Signs of the Times: Reading Ads and Re-Viewing the Common World

Diane Eisenberg,
Princeton University

One way to encourage students to regard their writing as a process of discovery and reflection, and to take a fully engaged approach to it, is to have them re-view and re-engage aspects of their own experience that they usually take for granted. In *Ways of Seeing*, John Berger and his colleagues observe that advertising images confront us more frequently and more relentlessly than any other kind of image, yet we "are now so accustomed to being addressed by these images that we scarcely notice their total impact" (p. 130). The students we teach are, of course, favorite targets of advertising, and often what originates in the counterculture of their generation is eventually assimilated and manipulated by advertising; many television commercials for a variety of products, for instance, have adopted the style of rock videos. In his foreword to the second edition of *Brave New World*, Aldous Huxley predicted that the successful totalitarian states of the future would "control a population of slaves who do not have to be coerced, because they love their servitude." Students who are already attuned to the manipulations of political language are often not so savvy about other kinds of persuasion. Examining an accepted role, such as that of consumer, often leads to some widening of or shift in perspective. But consumerism is only an interesting example. Ultimately, I want my students to be able not only to think about different subjects, but to identify and question all the "givens" those subjects present, and then to re-think and re-view. Sometimes what the students see is totally new.

The following sequence of assignments includes several short writing assignments and one reading assignment which concerns advertising. The sequence can be compressed, expanded, or otherwise adapted according to the needs of the individual class and teacher; I spend three to four class days on it. I usually place this unit some time after the students have both analyzed and written full-blown argumentative essays; that is, usually during the latter part of the semester.

CLASS 1

I begin the first class by distributing copies of an ad for trainee copywriters that appeared in *The New York Times* in 1984 (see ad following lesson). The eight "assignments" furnished by the Thompson agency ad possess the virtues of coming from a "real-world" source, inviting creativity, and suggesting a connection between writing ability and employability. (In fact, the agency did hire a number of people with no previous experience in advertising on the basis of their responses to the ad.) Even though the lure of possible employment is no longer current, my students have been eager to take up

IN-CLASS
EXERCISE

the gauntlet. I ask each of them to choose and start working on one of the assignments in class—previous exercises in invention will demonstrate their worth now. About twenty-five minutes before the end of the class, we stop writing in order to listen to some of the students' drafts. I don't expect my students to finish the assignment or to produce something as accomplished as they could if they had more time; but then, it's not my intent to unloose a cadre of ingenious hucksters. Rather, in describing the strategies of even our rudimentary efforts, we start formulating some general notions about the appeals made by the ads. We discuss the feelings and images evoked by those efforts we find successful, as well as the ways in which they demonstrate an awareness of audience and fashion a language for their product or idea. Even the tasks that don't overtly entail selling a product can be discussed in terms of audience and effect. Our analysis of advertising thus begins inductively and issues from a focus on the students' own writing.

This class session also prepares for the reading and writing assignments. Students approach Chapter 7 of *Ways of Seeing*,[1] by John Berger and others, with the additional interest of already having been practitioners in both creating and analyzing ads. Berger's plainly written but highly provocative text argues that ads have more to do with the socially conditioned anxieties and desires of prospective buyers than with the real qualities of the products being sold and that, collectively, advertising constitutes a visual and verbal language that distorts the true picture of social dynamics. I ask my students,

WRITING
ASSIGNMENT 1

in addition to reading Berger, to analyze in a short essay (300–500 words) one advertisement from a newspaper or magazine.[2] Students should consider the following questions as they work on their essays: What image of product and buyer does the ad project? What is the ad's implied narrative— what illusion of the past does it promote, and/or what promise of the future? How does its overall design function, and what is the relation between picture and text? How is nature used? If the ad shows an interior, how does

---

[1] My thanks to Michael Robertson for recommending this book.

[2] There are several possible variations of this assignment. For example, as the basis of a more ambitious project, a teacher could ask students to find two ads for the same kind of product that employ seemingly different strategies or to compare a contemporary ad to one from fifty years ago. [This sort of comparison, developing into the history of the advertising of any single product, would, we think, be an excellent topic for a research paper.—*Eds.*]

each element—the furnishing, fabrics, accessories, spatial arrangement—contribute to the effect of the whole? Even though an ad's basic design on the viewer is relatively easy to read, inspecting a constructed image in this way reminds students that ads, texts, paintings, photographs, and so on, are not objective slices of life but rather constellations of careful choices, all made in hopes of engaging and influencing the reader or viewer.

CLASS 2   I ask the students to bring both ads and essay to the next class, and we scrutinize some of the ads brought in, to see how each one interprets or constructs its "world." Most of the ads brought in show human figures, and these generate the most interesting discussions. We look to see whether men and women are portrayed differently, and how they are presented in relation to each other. (A teacher interested in gender roles, and specifically in how female figures are portrayed in relation both to male figures and to the viewer, may want to read chapter 3 of *Ways of Seeing* and *Gender Advertisements* by Erving Goffman, which deal with oil paintings and ads, respectively. My students often discover for themselves, in the course of classroom activity, some of the ideas presented by Berger and Goffman.)

From looking at particular ads, we move to a discussion of some of Berger's larger claims about the relation of advertising to social, political, and economic issues. How do we evaluate Berger's concept of glamor? Does he make a credible connection between the tradition of oil painting and the practice of advertising? Does advertising merely reflect the present state of social relations, or can it change them? Is consumerism, as Berger contends, a substitute for true democracy? We rarely reach a consensus about these questions, and I am satisfied if my students continue to think about them outside the classroom.

Whether they agree with Berger or not, however, most of my students infer that some coherent and developed ideology underlies his argument, and this leads us finally to turn our critical focus back on the texts themselves—the ad and the chapter. I ask whether the ad represents only an unusual recruitment campaign or whether it also "sells" the J. Walter Thompson agency. Is its pitch only to would-be copywriters or also to potential clients? We compare the ad's perspective from within the industry to Berger's view outside of it.

WRITING   By now we have come to realize that there is much to reconsider and to
ASSIGNMENT 2   say about other things that, like advertising, we often accept passively and without being aware of their workings on us. For the final written assignment in this unit, I present my students with the categories of Food, Clothing, Shelter, Modes of Transportation, and Modes of Communication. I ask the students to choose one item or custom from one category that has become familiar enough so as not to seem strange, but that, when re-examined, reveals something significant about social mores or structures. What do high heels or the wearing of safari-style clothing signify, for instance? Why was it once a sign of good breeding to leave food on your plate at a restaurant, and why do the most expensive restaurants serve the small-

est portions? How have telephone answering machines affected social interaction? Students need not read Roland Barthes to undertake this assignment, and I have read many delightful and stimulating essays in response to it. These essays, which are usually between 300 and 500 words, make excellent workshop papers, as students are naturally curious to get a new slant on things they otherwise take for granted.

This writing assignment is also designed to draw upon faculties exercised in both the previous assignment and the class exercise. The assignments adapted from the Thompson ad are fun; they also give a sense of the discipline required to achieve specific rhetorical effects economically. In addition, the ad analysis allows students to hone descriptive and critical skills. The third assignment solicits both ingenuity and analysis and involves more of the students' own thoughts and experiences than the first two.

LESSON READING

John Berger, *Ways of Seeing* (New York: Viking Penguin, 1972), Chapter 7.

FOR FURTHER READING

Erving Goffman, *Gender Advertisements* (Cambridge, MA: Harvard UP, 1979).

READING

WRITE IF YOU WANT WORK

Have you ever wondered how you could get a job as an advertising copywriter? Have you ever wondered *if* you could get a job as an advertising copywriter? This is your chance to find out. With this copy test. Eight entertaining and involving assignments that should stimulate and challenge you to do the thing you do best. Write.

We're anxious to see clear, imaginative, and compelling answers to these questions. The completed copy tests will be reviewed by some of our Creative Directors, and the best respondents will join us as trainee copywriters at J. Walter Thompson, New York.

Like the best of you who will ultimately join us, we're good at what we do. This year, Ad Week named us Agency of the Year. And year after year, we produce memorable and compelling advertising for a host of diverse and stimulating clients. Burger King. Ford. Goodyear. Kodak. Nestlé. And more. Clients that you'll come to know and enjoy as we do.

Opportunities like this don't come along every day. So if you've ever wondered if you could write a great ad, stop wondering. Tear out the page. And get to work if you want to write.

Send completed copies to "Copy Test," J. Walter Thompson, 466 Lexington

---

"Write if you want to work" advertisement. Reprinted by permission of J. Walter Thompson.

Avenue, New York, NY 10017, Attention: Jim Patterson, Executive Creative Director. And please. No phone calls. We're interested in how you write. Not talk.

WRITE IF YOU WANT WORK.

1 You are the songwriter for hitmaker Poppy Putrid. She's just had three recent No. 1 hits. All love songs. For her next hit, Poppy wants a song about moldy pizza, rancid butter, and flat beer. Her agent is convinced it should be another love song. Make it both. (Don't worry about the music, or adapt a tune you know.)

2 Write a "Dialogue in a Dark Alley." (Not more than 200 words.)

3 You've just learned that the IRS is planning to lower the percentage ratio of income to medical expenses, thus lowering the tax deductions for dental, psychiatric, and medical expenses. You are the star reporter for the daily newspaper, The National Sensational. The editor wants to make this the banner story. Write your head and a two-column story.

4 A delegation of Martians has just landed in Central Park. They do not understand any Earth languages—only very basic symbols. Prepare a short speech (com-prised of pictures and symbols) to welcome them and to tell them just what kind of place Central Park is. (Please enclose a plain language version of the speech in an envelope, in case we are confused!)

5 Describe, in not more than 100 words, the plot of the last episode of "Dynasty."

6 You've heard the story about the man who made a fortune selling refrigerators to Eskimos. In not more than 100 words, how would you sell a telephone to a Trappist monk, who is observing the strict Rule of Silence? (But he can nod acceptance at the end.)

7 Design/draw two posters. One is for legislating strict gun-control laws. The other is in support of the NRA.

8 The ingredients listed on the tin of baked beans reads: "Beans, Water, Tomatoes, Sugar, Salt, Modified Starch, Vinegar, Spices." Make it sound mouthwatering.

J. WALTER NEW YORK

Your response to the copy test becomes JWT property and will not be returned.

© 1984 J. Walter Thompson USA

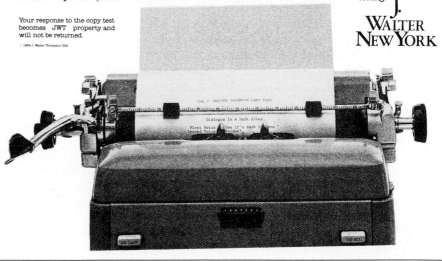

Trials Without Tribulations: The Composition Class as Court for a Short Run

Andrew Kaufman,
Hunter College

Last winter, in my otherwise somnolent remedial composition class, it took two words to ignite shouting matches: Bernhard Goetz. Although an issue that inspires such passionate disagreement presents great opportunities for writing classes, the difficulties here were especially daunting. Not only did the overwrought responses to this case threaten to polarize the class racially, but the students could hardly be blamed for the cacophony of clichés, misapplied generalizations, and misinformation, since their responses mirrored the local tabloid, television, and radio coverage of the story: Goetz was a hero because "it's time something was done about all the crime"; he was guilty because "white people usually get away with attacking black people."

CLASS 1   Not wanting to become what William Blake called a restrainer of energy or a dull and unwise "horse of instruction," and groping for a format that would fulfill the mission of English 100 while taking on all this media-supported illogic, I issued a challenge I hadn't fully considered: How many people want to set up a trial? Three students rushed to sign up as "prosecuting attorneys." Three insisted I let them be "defense lawyers." Three others wanted to be police witnesses. Someone wanted to be Goetz. The seven remaining students signed on for jury duty. Suddenly, I was barraged with offers and suggestions for doing research from a group that had been maddeningly indifferent to Composition.

CLASS 2   The next week I brought in copies of fourteen newspaper and magazine articles on the Goetz case, along with the section of the New York State

WRITING
ASSIGNMENT 1   penal code dealing with second-degree murder. Assignment 1: Read the articles and reduce all fourteen to a 400-word summary of the most central

255

WRITING
ASSIGNMENT 2

facts. Someone objected that the media were "totally biased." Assignment 2: Pick one article you think is slanted; summarize it, and then use specific examples to support your objections. By the time we went over these student essays in class, everyone could see the differences between how the *New York Times* organized and worded its stories and how the *New York Post* covered the same events. Because all the students had key responsibilities in the upcoming trial and had themselves chosen them, the students viewed these relatively conventional assignments as preparations for an important event or contest, rather than simply as homework for a required course.

WRITING
ASSIGNMENT 3a

Next, the "police witnesses" were asked to submit additional, more detailed summaries, each concentrating on a different segment of the case. One "officer" was responsible for a report summarizing the information that became available to police the day of the incident, such as eye-witness accounts and medical reports describing the wounds suffered by the youths. A second "police report" covered the information obtained by the police in New Hampshire from the confession Goetz made just after his surrender. A third covered statements Goetz made to reporters and friends, the previous police records of the youths, and more recent developments, such as the statements by two of the victims that they had intended to rob Goetz. Further, it was stressed that each of the "police witnesses" was to make clear the source of his information, so that its credibility could be evaluated.

CLASS 3

REVISION

Together, these reports were to constitute the body of evidence for the trial. Once they were distributed we convened our first hearing. "Jurors" sat in two rows along the side of the room; the defense and prosecution teams each had a "table" in the front row, while I presided from my desk as "judge." The police reports were distributed and read out loud; "lawyers" for each side were asked to challenge any wording they felt distorted their cases or any omissions they thought serious. "Jurors" were required to question any wording they found unclear. The sides were encouraged to argue back and forth, and, as "judge," I had the final word on admissibility of evidence. Successfully challenged passages had to be rewritten. Interestingly, the students wanted to impose more rigorous standards of clarity on the reports than I had been requiring of the class. As several of the "lawyers" kept insisting, "The evidence has to be clear." When placed within this judicial framework, the discussion of basic principles of good writing stimulated a great deal more interest and thought than the group had ever given to the job of writing.

WRITING
ASSIGNMENT
3b

Next, I asked the "lawyers" each to write a 400- to 500-word "brief" supporting their positions with reference to the facts in the police reports. Yet once we moved from summary to persuasion, I found that the chaotic logic pervading the students' initial response to the case had not disap-

CLASS 4   peared. But each side could now identify it in the other's arguments and could object to the types of irrelevant and inflammatory generalizations that had characterized their initial discussions of the case. Our work to this point had helped students recognize flaws in opposing positions more easily than in their own work. One paper stated Goetz was "approached," but someone wanted to know exactly what this meant. Goetz was "surrounded," but how close does this mean the youths were to him? He "felt threatened," but on what basis did he believe his life was endangered? The trial context made it clear that these weren't nit-picking, semantic objections, but that the entire case would depend on the replacement of vague language with specific formulations supported by facts. Further, it was becoming clear that imprecise language was working as a smoke screen to hide or muddle the central details of the case. Students on each side began to see that to prove their points they would have to improve the quality of their arguments. By the middle of the session they were pleading to know how they could make their briefs more effective. Students complained

CLASSES 5, 6, 7   about the frustration of having firm convictions that they couldn't support. For the next week, when we talked about the differences between general and specific statements, between relevant and irrelevant material, between opinion and fact, and the use of factual statements in implying and supporting particular arguments, we were working on techniques the students themselves wanted to learn.

WRITING ASSIGNMENT 4

EXERCISE   When I asked that the briefs be redone and that everyone in the class write one, the students were eager to improve their earlier efforts. The quality of the new work was surprisingly good, and we were nearly ready for the trial. The last assignment I gave to the "lawyers" was to write a list of every fact they wanted brought out in the trial, then to organize this list into the most effective sequence, and finally to turn each statement on the list into a question they could ask one of the police witnesses or "Goetz." There wasn't enough class time to provide members of each team a chance to go over one another's arguments; I was troubled about this until the day of the trial, when I found both teams had gotten together on their own for this purpose, as well as to organize a division of tasks. In the week before the trial students were asking me to go over their "briefs," and a member of the defense team made her way to the offices of the *Daily News* to do additional research in their files. A reporter whom she had asked for directions phoned me and asked if he could cover our "trial" and bring a photographer.

CLASS 8   The trial itself followed courtroom procedure as closely as was practical. Irrelevant statements and leading questions were disallowed, as was any evidence inconsistent with the reports prepared earlier. The prosecution presented its case by examining police witnesses. The defense cross-examined them, and then called "Goetz" to testify. The prosecution cross-examined him, and then each side presented a summation, which, as in actual court, could include only material that had been introduced previously. Even considering the amount of effort and energy that had been put into the project, I found the quality of the "trial" to be astonishing. The reporter said afterward that in one hour we had covered every issue he thought would prove important in the actual case. The department chairman had warned me that I would need to explain that this was a remedial class, but instead I had the opposite problem of trying to convince the reporter how poor the students' work had been before the Goetz project.

WRITING
ASSIGNMENT 5

CLASS 9

After the trial each "juror" was required to submit a summary of the arguments presented by both sides and to follow it with a verdict based on the facts presented. I announced that the decision of any "juror" would be disallowed if the opposing side could show that there were serious gaps in the summary of its position or in the logic through which the writer developed his conclusion. In the next class these papers were distributed one at a time and then discussed.

The final results: During the month the case had run (it was alternated with other exercises and presentations) everyone had written and many had rewritten essays requiring summary, narrative, persuasion, and analysis, and the students had spent a great deal of time criticizing, defending, and questioning one another's work. Many had worked collaboratively as well as individually. Virtually everyone produced his or her best work of the term. The oral format not only had provided incentive by offering a forum for class response to individual writing but had reduced the sense of intimidation the students felt about writing, since they came to think of the essays as part of the in-class proceedings. In addition, students came to recognize the effectiveness of carefully detailed, logical, relevant arguments. Many did more work than assigned, and most thought more carefully about their work than they had before. The competitive framework of the trial, together with the opportunity to argue a position they felt strongly about, provided great motivation, yet they had a sense of shared endeavor. Although some students initially said they thought the project would polarize the group racially, it ended up uniting the class in the shared effort to write and argue effectively and to base their responses on logic and fact rather than emotion. At the conclusion of the trial the "jurors" applauded both summation speeches. Students came away with the sense that the skills emphasized in Freshman Composition were not simply schoolwork, but the only means they had of moving from banality and illogic to an authoritative voice that commands attention. Half of them even had their names in the newspaper. Two were invited to appear with me on a local radio program to discuss the project and give their views on the case, and they had the satisfaction of realizing that they spoke about it with greater clarity and logic than most of the callers who phoned in to the show. But perhaps most important, the tasks related to the project created a confrontation or collision within the minds of most students between the uncritical or irrational thought processes underlying their initial responses to the case and the type of logic and documentation that the proceedings required. The "trial" format forced the students to confront the fact that their original ways of considering and arguing the case were inadequate, since positions based on clear reasoning and relevant details proved far more difficult for them to refute than those based on the forms of thought and argument with which they had begun. More important for the composition class than dramatizing the guilt or innocence of Bernhard Goetz, the "trial" and the work leading up to it thus dramatized the distinction between critical thinking and unsupportable emotional bias. As for the verdict itself, despite serious divisions among "jurors" before the trial started, each arrived independently at the same decision: guilty of attempted second-degree murder.

The Goetz case, with the variety of impassioned responses it evokes, lends itself especially well to this type of project. Yet the trial format itself, with its dependence on a wide variety of basic Freshman English skills and the considerable range of abilities it can accommodate, together with its dramatic and competitive nature, requirement for team work, integration of written and oral presentations, and power to involve students pleading causes for (or against) which they have strong feelings, has a place in the composition class that is worth exploring and refining.

Arguing an Obscenity Case

Tori Haring-Smith,
Brown University

The assignment described here is designed to teach advanced exposition students about persuasion and argumentation. Specifically, it helps them practice (1) adapting discourse to specific audiences, (2) balancing emotional and logical appeals, (3) sorting and weighing evidence, and (4) inferring generalizations from specifics. The assignment comes from a unit on legal persuasion, a topic of great interest to many of my students.

The students begin this unit by reading the six closing arguments of the Karen Ann Quinlan trial in the Superior Court of New Jersey.[1] They are asked to examine these documents carefully and to come to class prepared to discuss the characteristics of legal reasoning, as evidenced by these speeches. Having worked in a similarly inductive manner during our study of advertising and of political persuasion, the students are able to see that legal persuasion relies heavily on analogy and on a complex mixture of formal logic and blatantly emotional appeals. They can describe the persona adopted by the lawyers, the uses of both general and specific appeals, and the ways in which lawyers acknowledge the interests of the court. We discuss how the arguments address two different kinds of issues: questions of fact and questions of law. In order to demonstrate how these issues are related, we may analyze the arguments, using Stephen Toulmin's model for reasoning.[2]

After we have explored the features common to most of the closing arguments, we then examine each argument separately, looking at differences among the lawyers' strategies. We see, for example, that Mr. Einhorn's

---

[1] *In the Matter of Karen Quinlan* (Arlington, VA: University Publications, 1975), pp. 507–39.
[2] See Stephen Toulmin, *An Introduction to Reasoning* (New York: Macmillan, 1984).

I should make it clear that the inferences these students draw about legal reasoning are generally accurate. The objective of the lesson, however, is *not* to define specific rules of legal argumentation, but rather to teach students how to analyze written arguments and apply what they have learned to writing similar arguments of their own. The type of argument studied is irrelevant, but legal reasoning is effective because it intrigues so many students.

speech is very formal, pointing out technical objections to each of the precedents cited in Mr. Armstrong's brief. At the opposite extreme is Mr. Armstrong's conclusion, which is a blatant emotional appeal. Mr. Porzio mixes strong legal arguments with downhome realism and casual diction, and Mr. Coburn makes repeated ethical appeals.

Following this discussion, which may occupy us for one or two class periods, I present the students with the following assignment.

WRITING ASSIGNMENT 1

WRITING ASSIGNMENT 2

Read the account of the fictitious court battle involving the Town of Dullsburg and Artco Films [reproduced on pp. 262–266]. You have one week to prepare a five-page concluding argument for the prosecution. At the end of this week, bring in two copies of your argument, one for me and one for another member of the class. You will then trade papers and assume the role of the defense lawyer in order to develop a closing argument that responds to the prosecution's statement written by your classmate. Your job is to argue both sides as well as you can. Feel free to discuss the case among yourselves as much as you like, but please confine your argument to the facts and rulings cited in the materials I have given you. Keep the following guidelines in mind as you plan your arguments.

1. Analyze the case carefully to see which laws and facts are relevant.
2. Consider the limits and qualifications in each law or ruling. Under what circumstances does it apply?
3. Explain carefully how the laws and rulings that you cite are relevant to the facts of this case.
4. Always consider possible rebuttals.
5. Consider both the denotations and the connotations of your language.

This assignment could, of course, be altered to suit different kinds of courses and different levels of writers. If students needed help generating arguments, the class could debate the case in order to get some of the issues aired before they began to write. These concluding arguments might also serve as the basis for a research project if students were urged to supplement the information on the assignment sheet with additional legal precedent.

This assignment has been very successful because it combines critical reading and critical writing, while also reinforcing the connections between writing and speaking. Furthermore, students are motivated to complete the assignment since it draws on their competitive instincts and provides them with a real audience. When I first designed the assignment, I asked students to write arguments for both sides at the same time so that they were in fact arguing against themselves. As a result, they set up one lawyer as a straw man and demolished him with the answering statement. This kind of facile response to assignments was all too familiar. But when I asked the next semester's students to exchange papers and answer one other, I saw them really wrestle with the facts of the case and work at applying a variety of argumentative tactics, rather than one tactic in isolation. The assignment was no longer a "hot house" exercise that allowed them to respond without thinking.

READING

THE TOWN OF DULLSBURG
v. ARTCO FILMS

The Facts of the Case (not disputed by either side)

On Friday, October 11, 1979, the North Theatre in Dullsburg, Illinois, presented the X-rated film *Patty Does Providence* for one show only, beginning at 11 P.M. It offered half-price tickets to patrons with valid student identification cards from the local college, Fox College. The box office reported that 312 tickets were sold; the North can seat 500.

The film was advertised in the *Dullsburg Journal* and the *Fox Student* as "Shocking. Exciting. A movie you'll never forget," and the advertisement included a line drawing of a voluptuous girl of about 21, legs spread, wearing hot pants and a tank top, superimposed on an urban landscape. In addition to promising half-price tickets to Fox students, the ad included the obligatory notice: "X-rated. Those under 18 not admitted."

The film tells the touching story of an unhappy farm girl who runs away from home, leaving one morning on a Bassethound Bus for Providence. In Providence she realizes that her meagre savings have been stolen or mislaid, and she begins to weep. An older woman offers her assistance, and we soon learn that the woman is the matron of a local whorehouse. She teaches Patty the trade, and Patty practices it with relish. One of her clients, a university physicist, offers Patty a position as his "personal secretary." Telling the matron that she is going to New York City for the weekend, Patty leaves Providence forever, taking with her some "borrowed" funds. In New York she joins her professor. In return for a variety of sexual favors for him and his friends (singly and in groups), she meets important people, attends high-class social events, and makes a fortune. She becomes, in short, a member of the jet-set scientific community. As time passes, she grows more and more involved with a bachelor friend of the physicist's, a NASA engineer whom she sees frequently in Washington and Houston as well as New York. She believes that he loves her and fantasizes that he will marry her one day. But when he proposes to another woman and still expects Patty to continue as his mistress, she realizes that he can only think of her as a whore. Recognizing what she has done to herself, she resolves to return to the farm and support her aging parents with her savings. The film ends as Patty is boarding a Bassethound Bus for Kansas.

The film includes six acts of intercourse, three instances of oral sex, one case of bestiality, two occurrences of masturbation, one sexual encounter with a neutron accelerator, and innumerable cases of "physical flirtation."

THE TOWN.   Dullsburg, a town of 55,000, is located in central Illinois. The population consists of about 21,000 farmers, 22,000 factory workers and their families, 12,000 professionals and small businessmen, and 500 employees of the local college. The town suffers from a sharp town/gown split because the community at large is conservative and Republican, whereas the college faculty (and, of course, some professionals) are liberal and Democrat on the whole. The average income of a Dullsburg family is $26,623 per year. The town has one high school, two junior high schools, eight elementary schools, a dying downtown, and a thriving mall on its outskirts.

Fox College, founded in 1838 by Reverend Dull, who also founded the town, has been coeducational since 1860. A liberal arts college with high admission standards (average SAT composite of 1200), it now has 1323 students from 38 states, three foreign countries, and the Virgin Islands.

ARTCO FILMS.   Artco Films of Chicago, which produced *Patty Does Providence*, creates and markets a line of pornographic films and a series of sex education films. It is the parent company for Smartco Films, which produces experimental cinema. The company was established in 1955 and has been remarkably successful with films like *The Boom-Boom Babes*, *Pussy in Boots*, *Amazonian Amours*, and *Stan Stud, Quarterback*.

THE THEATER.   The North Theater, the oldest of three movie houses in Dullsburg, is located in the heart of downtown, five blocks from the college campus. It offers a wide variety of films from Walt Disney to *The Wild Bunch*, most rated PG or R. The last X-rated film shown there before *Patty Does Providence* was *Deep Throat*, presented on May 26, 1979.

The Judge and the Jury

Judge Richard Wentworth: 41; married; two children, graduate of the University of Illinois law school; active in local Republican politics; respected for calm, even-handed management of his courtroom; no previous decisions in obscenity cases.

Reginald Bosanquette: 27; tractor mechanic (carburetor specialist); high school education; single; hobby is making ashtrays out of old pistons.

Callie Calliope: 31; stock broker; single; recently moved to Dullsburg from New York to manage local office of Venal, Grinch, Fleece, Dunner, and Ramanujan.

Uriah Coffin: 48; married; 12 children, 9 still living at home; Rainbow the Clown on an early morning show for preschoolers; wife does his make-up and runs body-painting classes in her spare time; taped shows are used by the TV station while Uriah is on jury duty.

Jane Dough: 45; home economics teacher at Dullsburg High School; married to successful corn and pig farmer; one son, who is away at college.

Eugene Labriola: 53; head salesperson in large appliance department of local Sears store; married; three children in junior high and high school.

Ludwig Ludwigson: 74; retired soybean farmer who now spends his time playing the options market; widower; lives with daughter and son-in-law who now manage the farm.

Wolf Lupus: 29; veteran who has returned to college after three years in Army (two in Vietnam) and four years working at a Drug Rehabilitation Center for veterans in Chicago; not married, but apparently lives with his girlfriend; senior English major and aspiring poet.

Maxine Malchance: 23; waitress at coffee shop of local K-mart; separated from husband; one child, two years old.

Harry Mason: 56; IRS auditor; divorced; hair graying at temples and worn long; during trial has worn polyester leisure suits in a variety of pastel colors.

Laurie Salmon-Jones: 27; free-lance writer and director of Community Theater Workshop; married to geology professor at Fox (Fox's specialist on rox, as she likes to say); no children, but a small menagerie of pets.

Mildred Spinster: 63; unmarried; lives with sister Jezebel in apartment over the fabric store that they manage together; Mildred is heavily into chintz.

The Proceedings

PLAINTIFF'S CLAIM.   The town of Dullsburg contends that *Patty Does Providence* is a hard-core pornographic film that appeals to prurient interests and as such offends the community at large. It should, therefore, be banned from Dullsburg.

DEFENDANT'S CLAIM.   Artco Films maintains that its film has redeeming social value that outweighs its obscenity. Because of the film's X-rating, however, Artco's standard policy (adhered to in this case) is to recommend that the film be shown after 10 P.M.

WITNESSES' TESTIMONY.   John Rokesmith, speaking as chairman of the Board of Selectmen of Dullsburg, stated that he saw the film and was "shocked," that the film offended him and his wife. He later described the film in detail at a dinner party with other Selectmen and members of the community. Although the others had not seen the film, they, too, were "shocked." Rokesmith, 44, is vice-president of a local savings bank and his wife is a homemaker.

Officer Lawlis, night patrolman, reported that he investigated two sexual assaults in Dullsburg on the night of October 11, 1979. At 3 A.M., Minny Malmrose, a night nurse at John Deere, was attacked in the parking lot of the factory as she was leaving for home. According to Minny, the attacker tied her to a lamppost and kept talking about ships and neutrons. He told her he'd return for her and kissed her private parts before racing off in his pick-up. Minny was able to loosen her bonds, free herself, and run into the factory to call the police. Because it was dark, she had not noticed what her attacker's truck looked like. No suspects have been arrested in the case. Minny has since died of pneumonia due to exposure and so could not testify. But Officer Lawlis said, "In my professional opinion, the man must have been exposed to *Patty Does Providence*."

The other assault was called in at 4:30 A.M. by a hysterical college senior, Trudy Picklemeyar, who heard her roommate moaning as she returned to her dorm room after a late night at the library. She opened the door cautiously, saw a struggle going on, and ran to call the police. When Officer Lawlis arrived, he found her roommate, Kathy Klaw, in bed with another student, Dick Donaldson. An open physics book lay on the floor and among the bedclothes were a calculator, a mechanical pencil, and a job application form for NASA. Questioning Miss Klaw, the officer learned that both she and Dick had attended *Patty Does Providence*, attracted by the half-price tickets. Dick, a senior physics major, is her fiancé. They often spent the night together when

Trudy was out at the library. Apologizing for disturbing the officer, they bid him good-night.

Lionel Standard, the film reviewer for the *Dullsburg Journal*, testified that he had enjoyed the film, but he admitted that it had "no artistic value" as a story or as cinema. Bettina Crocker, a housewife and mother of three children, testified that she was "shocked" to learn that her 16-year-old son had attended the showing of *Patty Does Providence*. She heard him discussing the film over the phone with a classmate. She declared that the film taught her son "about the birds and the bees" and led him to believe that whores were nice people. She wanted the film banned. Billy Crocker, her son, testified that he did indeed see the film, gaining admittance with a false ID, which he also used to buy beer in bars. He liked the film. He said that it was "not more raunchy than other X-rated films."

Tom Terrific, a carpenter, testified that he saw the film and found it "moving." Unlike other pornographic films, this one had a message and should, he said, be shown to all girls in their mid-teens who were, like Patty, lambs ready to be led astray. Milo Shilton, English professor at Fox, testified that banning the film would violate Artco's freedom of speech. He cited John Milton, a seventeenth-century poet and philosopher, as a defender of the position that banning obscene books or other offensive material only makes these materials more attractive to potential consumers. Kathy Klaw testified that she and Dick enjoyed the film because they had never before seen an X-rated film and because it was exciting to see how a NASA engineer lived. Sam Spewak, physical education instructor at Dullsburg High, testified that Artco's sex education films were "straightforward, open, excellent."

Jurisdiction Cited During the Proceedings

Town of Kannot v. *Cinema LXIX* (1965): This ruling condemned Cinema LXIX for showing *Terri and the Trolls*, a film that, like *Patty Does Providence*, tells the story of a girl who becomes a prostitute and then repents. In this plot, however, the descent to vice is a dream in which Terri enters a fairy-world inhabited by trolls. Her sexual fantasies lead her when she wakes to vow that she will always be virtuous. The ruling banned such films "which contain patently offensive scenes" from the town on the ground that this kind of pornography offended the community at large.

Town of Wilnot v. *Kaufman* (1967): In this case the judge acquitted John Kaufman, owner and manager of the Dead End Theater in Wilnot, Wyoming, of charges of "purveying prurient material" related to his showing of *Pussy in Boots*, an Artco Film. The judge's opinion defined *obscenity* as "that which explicitly displays or describes in detail abnormal sexual behavior engaged in by humans or animals." *Pussy in Boots*, he ruled, displayed "normal sexual behavior" and so was acceptable.

Snyder v. *Tillwell College* (1972): The judge ruled that Tillwell, a private college, was entitled to offer an evening of pornographic films for its students. The student body, he argued, "was sexually aware" and so could distinguish desirable from undesirable sexual relationships. No one outside the student body was admitted to the porno festival, and no attempt was made to disguise the nature of the films when they were advertised.

Supreme Court Definitions of Obscenity: The United States Supreme Court has set up several standards by which material is to be judged obscene, and it is well settled that material must fail these tests before it can be suppressed. The tests are as follows:

1. *The "social value" test.* The core of this opinion in the leading case is found in the following language: "All ideas having even the slightest redeeming social importance—unorthodox ideas, controversial ideas, even ideas hateful to the prevailing climate of opinion—have the full protection of the guarantees, unless excludable because they encroach upon the limited area of more important interests. But implicit in the history of the First Amendment is the rejection of obscenity as utterly without redeeming social importance."

2. *The "prurient interest" test.* "However, sex and obscenity are not synonymous. Obscene material is material which deals with sex in a manner appealing to prurient interest. The portrayal of sex, e.g., in art, literature, and scientific works, is not itself sufficient reason to deny material the constitutional protection of freedom of speech and press. Sex, a great and mysterious motive force in human life, has indisputably been a subject of absorbing interest to mankind through the ages; it is one of the vital problems of human interest and public concern. A thing is obscene if, considered as a whole, its predominant appeal is to prurient interest, i.e., a shameful or morbid interest in nudity, sex, or excretion, and if it goes substantially beyond customary limits of candor in description or representations of such matters."

3. *The "patently offensive" test.* "These magazines cannot be deemed so offensive on their face as to affront current community standards of decency—a quality that we shall hereafter refer to as 'patent offensiveness' or 'indecency.'"

4. *The "hard core pornography" test.* "The inquiry for the court, therefore, is whether the publication is so entirely obscene as to amount to 'hard core pornography' (not necessarily dealing with deviant sex relations since while there is a pornography of perversion, 'pornography' is not limited to the depiction of unnatural acts)."

Opening Out

This last section, returning to and building on ideas raised earlier, takes further the work of critical thinking and critical writing in defining a subject (Smith) and introducing it (Salomon, Munson); in using figures of speech (Loewenstein) and figures of thought (West); in analyzing style (Carnicelli) and achieving verbal dexterity (Beum).

How can students best be motivated (Olson) and prepared (Tabbert) for the research paper, whether for a brief inquiry into the history of words (Geiger, Farmer), or an extended consideration of current writing about science (Goldberg)?

The volume concludes with special applications to three common college phenomena: attending lectures (McAllister), listening to popular songs (S. L. Brown), and, for teachers "across the curriculum," grading papers (West).

Definitions and Assumptions in the Teaching of Writing

Charles Kay Smith,
University of Massachusetts–Amherst

In college courses students are often asked to read fairly difficult essays and books and respond to this reading in writing. Although writing about self is important to personal development and a good way to get students started and comfortable about writing, a component of interactive reading, writing, and thinking could make any composition course more useful to students. Writing in response to reading is not simply a shift of idiom from informal writing about the self to a more formal, impersonal, academic voice. To write good responses to reading requires at least the ability to generate alternative definitions of concepts not to be found canned in dictionaries: the intellectual craft of questioning conventional assumptions and generating fresh alternatives for organizing a written response. The student's response must demonstrate intelligent understanding of the original author's position together with an awareness of the similarity to or difference from the student's own position, which may or may not be critical of the original author. In short, the student must learn to read, think, and write interactively. One efficient way to accomplish this is for teachers to conduct prereading and prewriting exercises generating alternative assumptions and definitions of concepts central to the assigned reading and writing.

Becoming Self-Generating Readers, Writers, and Thinkers

An assumption can be defined as a stated or unstated, conscious or unconscious generalization or belief that tends to govern writing and thinking. Assumptions about the meaning of concepts are called definitions. Definitions, as I am using the term, are not merely foregone conclusions that can be looked up in a dictionary but are, rather, tools that help probe the nature of concepts. It is useful to realize that definitions are rarely definitive—that is, definitions almost always need redefinition in order to fit changing cultural institutions or new intellectual or ethical contexts for which you intend to use them. Definitions and assumptions lie behind and help to determine even the simplest acts of writing. Thus reading well and writing freshly require practice in redefining and reassessing underlying assumptions.

Redefinition is a fundamental mode of intellectual inquiry that can be used to deepen and expand understanding of almost any reading and writing assignment. Here are syntactical cues for five tools of redefining and assumption-generating that, when fully employed, enable deep and diverse inquiry into the nature of words, concepts, problems, and even institutions.

Redefining Concepts: A Thinker's Basic Toolkit

Generical: "X is a kind of A, but differs from all other A's with respect to the following . . . or is X a kind of Y? . . . or perhaps it could be said to be a kind of Z? . . ."

Lexical: "At historical time T, X meant E; at time T'' X no longer means E but can mean F, G or D, etc.; and these changes in meaning may provide insight into human society and mind." (You may have to use the multivolume *Oxford English Dictionary* in the Library Reference Room.)

Assumptive: "The concept can be defined as a set of interrelated basic assumptions as follows. . . ."

Operational: "The definition of X is given by the following description of its function or by describing a way of measuring X . . . or perhaps there is another function or way of measuring X. . . ."

Biographical: "When I was 12 years old, I thought that X meant J; then when I got to be 16, I decided it meant K; but now I think X means L."

Using the Basic Tools

The five preceding tools, each illustrated by a different redefining syntax, are not difficult to use. A little practice will make these five syntaxes a set of easily accessible mental crowbars with which to pry into the nature of concepts in several different directions to discover diverse meanings. For example, the redefining tools could be practiced in the following class exercise to elicit many subliminal or unarticulated assumptions about love:

Few humans, young or old, are uninterested in love. Few subjects in literature during the last two and a half millennia have been interpreted in such rich variety. Yet without some knowledge of this variety, much of life as well as much of the best literature in our culture remains a closed book. A whole class might use redefining tools as playful methods of inquiry to pry out at least five different meanings from the concept of love. Then, with the class broken into several small writing workshops, students could practice organizing each of the alternative meanings of love "brainstormed" by the class into a paragraph by expanding the phrases and clauses of each redefining syntax into complete sentences. In this way students could organize and write five different one-paragraph definitions of *love.* Notice that the five redefining tools can serve not only as methods of inquiry but also as five forms of organization for paragraphs or essays.

"Brief History of the Idea of Love," which I wrote for my students illustrates how the basic tools of redefining might be used to inquire into the nature of love and, at the same time, quickly provides some historical background and cultural diversity that may be an aid to understanding and feeling the resonance in the literature of love:

READING

C. K. Smith

BRIEF HISTORY OF THE IDEA OF LOVE— A Symposium of Some of the World's Great Lovers

Generical definition of *love* that paraphrases Plato [428–348 B.C.]: Love is a kind of motive force that impels us toward beauty, the beauty of an earthly object to begin with, but ultimately we are impelled beyond all earthly forms to the more perfect beauty of abstract ideas—concepts like perfect Justice, perfect Truth, perfect Goodness. As Diotima explains in my masterpiece on love—the *Symposium:*

> And the true order of going, or being led by another, to the things of love, is to begin from the beauties of earth and mount upwards for the sake of that other beauty, using these steps only, and from one going on to two, and from two to all fair forms to fair practices, and from fair practices to fair notions, until from fair notions he arrives at the notion of absolute beauty, and at last knows what the essence of beauty is.

Without love, human thought and action would have no motive or expression. To love is to be human. Considering the power of desire that attracts people to one another, sexuality is a natural way for love to manifest itself, yet it would not be right to imagine that sexuality would be love's highest expression. The beauty of fleshly face or figure is that toward which love only in its first phase impels us. The love of one fair form, so long as we are guided by the best that is in us, will next concern itself with all fair acts and ideas, and finally love will move us, with a joyful passion toward the contemplation of ideals and essences like Truth, Justice, and Goodness. And then it may be said that the nature of Love, guided by our most discriminating reason, enables a human to attain ultimate unity with the divine and pure knowledge of all heavenly forms. It is in such striving to perfect our gross humanity that we make of life a work of art that becomes a part of immortality.

Lexical definition of *love* first in the spirit of an *early Christian* of the first century A.D., such as Paul, second in the spirit of typical Medieval and Renaissance *courtly romance*, and finally in the spirit of an eighteenth- to twentieth-century *modern sentimentalist:*

Early Christian. It is not Plato's definition of ambitious *eros*, or desire, that impels Divine Love but rather *agape*, or love as a kind of disinterested benevolence. Human love is but a pale counterfeit of divine agape. The original of love is the Creator's unmotivated love overflowing in His creation. The extraordinary power of love among humans is testimony to the exceeding power of Divine Love. The human creature's highest love should be a longing to be reunited with the Creator from Whose spontaneous love we spring. For only God is the source of all love, all creativity, and all good. The Son of God has redeemed fallen humanity with an excess of His Love. We can never merit such Love but only worship the Savior and the Father with all the love that is in us and hope for a divine gift of grace that will save us and make us worthy of the Love that gave us eternal life. For God is Love, and in loving Him with our whole heart and soul we become one with Him. "In a word, there are three things that last forever: Faith, Hope, and Love; but the greatest of them all is Love."

Courtly Romance. Love slakes its thirst on frustration, is nourished by the very obstacles put in its way, and grows to robust maturity on impediments and impossibilities. The more intensely social and religious forces attempt to repress romantic love, the more passion flames. Marriage is but a travesty of love. True love flourishes only in adultery. The lover is enthralled by an abject servitude in adoration of his beloved, who grants him only fleeting favors with little mercy for all the pain of denial. In order to bear this sweet agony the lover must be as much in love with love itself as with the beloved. Often Romance includes transcendent Platonic strivings after immortality and Christian religious strains such as the adoration of the Virgin Mary and dangerous religious quests like the discovery and retrieval of the Holy Grail used by Christ at the Last Supper and lost in legend.

Consider the archetype of romance—the tale of Tristan and Isolde. It is an ancient legend made mysterious by magic potions and spells. The loyal knight, Tristan, is on a mission for his king to fetch from a far land the king's betrothed, Isolde. During that long journey, Tristan and Isolde fall fiercely in love. Knightly honor and unbreakable betrothal vows frustrate and fan the fire of passion and increase both danger and desire. The strongest of social bonds, loyalty to the commands of God and king, forever bar the lovers from earthly fulfillment. No remedy for the ecstasy and agony of desire exists but the transcendent consummation of love–death, and it is only in death that Tristan and Isolde can find ultimate fulfillment. Romantic love must be self-destructive and therefore tragic. And the tragedy of love is a theme higher and more sublime than universal freedom, peace, war, morality, or religion.

Modern Sentimentalist. As Romance explained to us, flammable passion needs hard obstacles to rub it into flame. Over the last two centuries we have reconciled what were in courtly love the arch-enemies: marriage and passion. But passion pales as social and moral absolutes weaken from the eighteenth through the twentieth centuries and become less oppressive obstacles to love. The flame dampens and sputters in the sodden drizzle of a humdrum marriage. Love has been domesticated by bourgeois business as usual, tame rationality, sexual sanction in marriage, and the docile how-to-achieve-orgasm (clearly illustrated) manuals. Great passion has been miniaturized to conjugal senti-ment, cool eroticism, possessive jealousy, love of money, status, marriages of economic and social convenience, conspicuous consumption, having it all. Eric Segal sums it up in *Love Story,* "Love means never having to say you're sorry."

Assumptive definition of *love* paraphrasing Freud (1856–1939): I fear I must disagree with the idealistic assumptions of Plato and Early Christian and prick the fanciful illusions of Courtly Romance as well as the middle-class compla-cencies of Modern Sentimentalist. The strongest and most important of all human instincts is the sex drive. Love did not civilize and render us inherently peaceful. Our genetic inheritance—the id—is aggressive, lustful, savage, self-ish, and anything but social and orderly, whereas the superego is but the barely adequate outer garment that represses our naked needs and makes of human existence the tragedy that it must ever be. Love is the pale, repressed, and domesticated version of a selfish, violent, and essentially antisocial instinct of sex.

In the human infant, sex is first aimed at parents but, when this direction is inhibited, the original energy is deflected toward other more socially appro-priate objects of affection. Such is the origin and normal development of human love. This we must finally face—all love is narcissistic. Mirrored in our lover's eyes we behold, reflected, the real object of our affection. Any idealization of love, either of God or of a human lover, is illusion and mere wish fulfillment. The mature love of adult humans is, to be sure, more highly sublimated and socially benign than is the polymorphous perversity of infan-tile incest. Yet even mature love, no matter how socially we embellish it and idealistically we express it, is but aim-inhibited infantile incestuous genital lust.

Operational definition of *love* in the spirit of sociobiologist: I tend to agree with Freud more than with anyone else I have listened to so far. But even he seems to be blowing this subject out of all proportion. The way I see it, love is just another instinctive bodily function no more mysterious than hunger, thirst, or elimination. Love is a "releaser" for a more or less stereotyped courtship behavior. According to an experiment that gave adrenalin injections to one group of men and merely a placebo solution to another, neither group knowing what kind of injection they received, the adrenalin-injected group asked much more frequently for the phone numbers of strange women at a social engagement than did the nonadrenalin group. These results suggest that any fearful or exciting experience that would stimulate the secretion of ad-renalin would facilitate the "release" of courtship behavior. The more exciting the occasion, the greater the secretion of adrenalin, the more likely is love. Love and war may well go together, as may love and almost any kind of excitement, from violent storms to horror movies or revival meetings or protest marches. That adrenalin-producing experiences increase the likelihood of falling in love has been easier to understand since the investigations into sexual function and dysfunction by Masters and Johnson. These scientists have operationally defined love in terms of muscle contractions, heart rate, body temperature, tissue condition, engorgement and color, endocrine activity and blood pressure, most of which are directly related to the production of adrenalin in the body.

Biographical definition of *love* might begin with a youthful belief in courtly romance (as above), and then a sentimentalist view of love, followed by bitter disillusionment with any possibility of love, until finally the following view of love has matured that might be termed *postromantic humanist:* We who live at the end of the twentieth century are not more decadent or cynical than those who have gone before. We are attempting an idealism only the greatest lovers of the past have been ready to risk. History was satisfied with marriages that worked if only they united a fortune with a name. What courage it takes to walk clear-eyed, with intelligence and faith, into a modern marriage, knowing that it must bear the strain of striving for transcendent love, savage sexual passion, shameful failures, ever-forgiving friendship, mutual aid in the teeth of a vicious world, and if no other misery yet the certain heartbreak of sickness, death, and age. In two frail hearts all human yearnings for all time are now aflame. In short, we look to love and marriage to fulfill all desires at all times for all people. Because this is clearly impossible, the foundation of modern love is cooperative compromise built on friendship based on mutual understanding of similarities and differences in emotional, physical, and social characteristics of both partners. We are learning to understand ourselves and one another and accepting what we discover with respect and friendship. Ours is not the worst of times, though our poets are always saying they told us so.

WRITING
ASSIGNMENTS
1-4

1. How are the diverse interpretations of love in the views expressed in the "Brief History of the Idea of Love" woven together and related in modern descriptions of love to be found in films, soap operas, and advertising? Give concrete examples.

2. Generate at least two or three memorable concrete examples from your own reading or experience to illustrate a definition from "Brief History of the Idea of Love."

3. Can you think of additional assumptions about or definitions of *love?* By explaining in more detail the meaning of your ideas and then giving interesting concrete examples to illustrate them, develop your ideas into full paragraphs.

4. Let us turn from love to consider the concept of maturation. Use each of the five redefining tools to pry out as much meaning in the concept of maturing as possible. Now write each new alternative in a paragraph organized by expanding the phrases and clauses of the appropriate redefining syntax into separate, complete sentences.

> Compose a sort of symposium of different ideas about growing up, just as was done for love.

The intellectual freedom to read and write well relies on having a rich variety of assumptions and definitions from which to choose. For this reason I avoid giving students only one way of thinking about anything, even though I am sometimes passionately convinced that my assumptions are absolute and universal. I try always to generate with class help many good alternatives so that students are forced to judge among many possibilities. This process is the surest way I have found to help students care about their own ideas and understand why they hold them, while at the same time allowing them the intellectual flexibility of having alternatives with which to change their minds when they desire—in short, to become self-generating thinkers and writers. When sufficient depth and range of understanding about the possible meanings of *love* and *growing up* have been achieved for the entire class, students are ready for a task of much more scope and challenge than would have been likely without such preparation.

WRITING ASSIGNMENT 5 James Joyce's short story "Araby" concerns loving and growing up in our own century and culture, but it demands close reading. We may be too accustomed to narratives on T.V. and in movies that make their point with such brutal and obvious visual directness that little thinking need be done to "get the idea." But unless we read "Araby" actively we may be left wondering, "What was the point? What was Joyce trying to say and so what?" The following questions (to be answered in a two- to four-page essay) are intended to help students interpret the story:

1. How does Joyce define *love* in "Araby"? Do you agree with his definition? What are the probable social and psychological consequences of defining *love* in this way, or in your way?

2. How does Joyce define *maturation* or *growing up* in "Araby"? Do you agree with his definition? What are the probable social and psychological consequences of defining *maturity* in Joyce's way, or in your way?

3. How and why are *love* and *maturity* related in the very last sentence of "Araby"?

The Introduction as "Contract"

Willis A. Salomon,
Trinity University

Anyone who has written essays knows the challenge of writing even a functional introduction. For most of us, no matter how practiced we become, the introduction often takes as long to produce as the rest of the draft. The difficulties of writing effective introductions are coextensive with the fundamental challenge that essay writing presents: finding a specific, interesting *focus*. For this reason I spend significant time on writing introductions in my composition classes. Because of my students' own experience with the frustrations of focusing thoughts for an essay in an introductory paragraph or two, I have little trouble putting across the following lesson on writing "intros."

I generally begin a class on introductions with a quotation from the preface to G. E. Moore's *Principia Ethica* (Cambridge, 1903):

> It appears to me that . . . difficulties and disagreements . . . are mainly due to a very simple cause: namely to the attempt to answer questions, without first discovering precisely what question it is you desire to answer.

I present Moore's dictum for two reasons: (1) It states the necessity of knowing, if only generally, the *direction* we wish our thoughts (and thus our essay) to take; and (2) it points up what I take to be the primary function of the introductory paragraph or paragraphs of an essay—proposing a "problem." One must be careful, however, with how one defines and qualifies the word *problem*. One must be careful, that is, not to lead formula-hungry students to begin every essay with something like, "The problem I want to discuss is. . . ." I try to head off this misunderstanding by emphasizing the *function* of introductions rather than giving students a typology of *forms* (or *formulas*). I *do* eventually catalogue strategies, as I shall illustrate. But I do so in terms of their function in setting up what my favorite composition text, William J. Brandt's *The Craft of Writing* (Prentice-Hall, 1969), calls "the reader-writer" contract—the way in which "almost all writers . . . begin their writing by setting up an expectation of something about to happen" (p. 6) and by implying that what follows "will resolve the problem in some way" (p. 7). As Brandt's comments suggest, an introduction should lead into an essay rather than provide an abstract of it—which, in effect, would conclude the essay before it has begun. I have found that students easily grasp the contract metaphor. It makes student writers more aware of the responsiblity to engage and hold the reader, to give him or her something familiar yet unresolved (and thus in need of resolution), and to see the writer's work as part of a public transaction that they themselves can control.

Introductions, I tell the class, usually move, as in the proverbial "funnel," from the general to the specific, or, even better, from the given (or known) to the controversial (or unknown). An introduction must *focus* the essay on some problem or issue, and then state or imply that the author will then resolve it. To this end, I give students what I take to be three basic characteristics of an effective, well-focused introduction: (1) context, through any material that can be taken as true by most readers without explanation, whether in the form of a maxim, a definition, an opinion (testimony), or a description of a familiar thing or a plausible or familiar state of affairs; (2) focus, the problem per se that is proposed; and (3) the rationale or justification for broaching the issue (to gain the reader's assent to the importance of the problem). Here, however, I issue a warning: Be careful not to give your answer to the problem before you've looked at it and at the evidence that addresses it in the body of the paper. Students often think focus means declaring a full-blown, final word thesis, when doing so strangles, as we know, the movement through supporting material to a conclusion. Following is a list of strategies to which I call attention in class and the respective essays that illustrate them:

1. statement of a problem (Walter Percy, "The Loss of the Creature")
2. presentation of a problem in the form of a question (Edward Hallett Carr, "The Historian and His Facts")
3. statement of focus and intention (Martin Luther King, Jr., "Letter from Birmingham Jail")
4. description of a tension, opposition, or dichotomy in a subject that needs to be addressed (George Orwell, "Politics and the English Language")
5. brief, direct (though not complete) statement of a thesis (Lewis Thomas, "On Natural Death")
6. description/narration as a context to focus a conflict (George Orwell, "Shooting an Elephant")

After going over the examples with students, the *strategic* function of introductions in the reader–writer contract needs again to be emphasized, in order to close the lesson on the side of *function* rather than *formula*, function being determined by the demands of the subject and the audience addressed.

WRITING
ASSIGNMENT

Take a topic with which you are comfortable and about which you have thought enough to have a thesis (motivated by reading or by class discussion) and write two different introductions that will lead the reader into a paper that argues that thesis.

Sample Performance of the Assignment

The following two introductions, each from a student paper, focus on the topic of affirmative action quotas. The first, a two-paragraph introduction, exemplifies the first strategy, the "statement of a problem." The second, a single introductory paragraph, exemplifies the second strategy, the "presentation of a problem in the form of a question." A brief commentary follows each example.

Student Introduction 1

In the wake of obvious discriminatory practices toward women and minority groups by employers and educational institutions, the United States government enacted a series of affirmative action measures designed to counteract these practices. One result of this legislation was the creation of quotas, or prescribed ratios for the selection of women and minority group members, aimed at ensuring the equal representation of these groups in the workplace and in educational institutions. Through these quotas a designated number of positions would be guaranteed to specified groups as determined by race, ethnicity, or sex, thus minimizing the possibility of discrimination and ensuring that minority and female applicants would have equal opportunities for jobs and schooling.

Although the "quota system" would seem to be motivated by the best of intentions, a necessary consequence of it involves a situation where an employer or a selection committee must decide between two applicants: a minority member who may not fulfill all of the position's requirements, and an applicant who does not help satisfy the demands of the quota but who is better qualified for the position itself. In many cases affirmative action measures require the choice of the minority member or woman to fill the legislated quota and thereby provide an opportunity for success not otherwise available. Yet selections made on this basis often concern us, since we generally believe that true equal opportunity includes all candidates, without possible exclusions resulting from legislated quotas. Thus a conflict lies in determining which ideas of opportunity most reflect the objectives for our society regarding equality of opportunity.

Commentary

The first paragraph *contextualizes* the topic with reference to (1) recent history ("obvious discriminatory practices"), (2) environment (universities and the workplace), (3) a definition (*affirmative action* as "prescribed ratios for . . . selection"), and (4) the aim of such programs ("minimizing the possibility for any discrimination"). The second paragraph then *focuses* on a problem: in providing opportunities for those historically denied them, we will perforce take opportunities away from those who already have them. The *rationale* for raising this issue is self-evident. Equality is a common topic, and university admissions and job placement are ongoing concerns of our students. As the second paragraph closes, a "contract" is established with the reader whereby affirmative action quotas will be addressed in terms of their potential to promote social equality, a concept that will of course be defined, either formally or operationally, as the student moves into an argument. Further, it is obvious, I think, that the body of this essay will eventually argue against affirmative action quotas as a means of ensuring equal opportunity, moving then to a meritocratic defense of consistent standards. This latter stance is suggested by the order of the conflicting arguments summarized in the second paragraph. First, the justification of quotas is given, and then the "reverse discrimination" premise is brought in, potentially undercutting the argument for quotas. In this way the writer's stance is suggested, *but is not so obtrusive as to cut off a reasonably fair inquiry into the issue.* (It should also be noted here that this student introduction could easily be classed with the fourth strategy listed previously—"description of a tension." I have placed it with the first type simply because the author speaks explicitly about a problem. Because issues are by nature dichotomous, categories 1 and 4 are bound to overlap.)

Student Introduction 2

Institutions of higher learning generally have admissions standards and requirements designed to limit the number of students who enroll for a given year or semester. These requirements include high school courses and grades, "personal statements," letters of recommendation, and standardized test results. An outline is usually followed, and students who meet the institution's requirements are granted admission. Exceptions, however, are often made for students belonging to minority groups. "Objective" standards are sometimes lowered to give minorities an equal opportunity at a quality education, an opportunity that has been denied them in the past. With such admissions procedures some questions arise: How equal is this opportunity when seen through the eyes of a nonminority applicant? How flexible should an institution be when considering an application? Most importantly, do affirmative action policies such as these in college admissions provide for the achievement of equality and, hence, the elimination of prejudice, as it is sometimes claimed?

Commentary

This introduction limits itself to affirmative action in college admissions. Its *context* arises from the account in the first three sentences of the typical admissions procedure at a "selective" college or university. It then *focuses* on the fairness issues raised by concessions to minority status in the admissions process, raising them in a series of three questions. The questions refer, in order, to reverse discrimination, the desirable degree of concession to minority status, and, in the master question to which the first two lead, the potential of such admissions procedures to eliminate prejudice. In this way the student contracts with the reader to discuss the issue, but also to discuss its features in this order, thus creating a clear expectation for the structure of the essay that will follow. Like the first example, this introduction seems to be leading to an argument against concessions to minority applicants. But it also leaves the issue open enough to interest the reader in the possibility of an informed, reasonable treatment of it.

Student Introduction 3

In the past few decades, television has become a major part of American culture. Many people spend more time in front of their television sets than they spend at any other waking activity. With the increased use of the medium come the potentially adverse effects of its use. Critics accuse television programming of being too graphic, too sensational, too commercial. Television, they argue, blurs the distinction between reality and fantasy. Viewers, as a result, are not required to think, as those who control the medium are mainly concerned with advertising revenue. Television's critics, while seldom offering a viable solution to what they see as a major problem, continue to denounce the medium. However, while television never seems to meet its critics' expectations, it is not the arch-enemy of society, as it is sometimes claimed. Television is nothing more than an entertainment source, and an excellent one at that. So, while critics continue to bemoan the influence of television, they fail to realize that television will never have serious adverse effects on society because its primary aim is simply to entertain the masses.

Commentary

In this example the student declares too much of the thesis in the last three sentences, choking the movement into the body of the essay, and, in effect, concluding the essay in the introduction. What the introduction should do is to raise the issue and suggest the author's stance, stopping short of a premature peroration. Instead of saying, "This is how it is," a successful introduction says, "Let's look at this for this reason." Although there are clearly many other possible ways to improve this introduction, keeping its *focus* open rather than conclusive would improve it considerably and help the author to see the issue more clearly. After all, that television is "just" entertainment doesn't mean it can't have the adverse effects its detractors fear.

LESSON READINGS

Walker Percy, "The Loss of the Creature," in *The Message on the Bottle* (New York: Farrar Straus Giroux, 1959).

Edward Hallett Carr, "The Historian and His Facts," in *What Is History?* (New York: Knopf, 1961), Chapter 1.

Martin Luther King, Jr., "Letter from Birmingham Jail," in *Why We Can't Wait* (New York: Harper & Row, 1963).

George Orwell, "Politics and the English Language" and "Shooting an Elephant," in *Shooting an Elephant and Other Essays* (Orlando, FL: Harcourt Brace Jovanovich, 1950).

Lewis Thomas, "On Natural Death," in *The Medusa and the Snail* (New York: Viking, 1979).

FOR FURTHER READING

William J. Brandt, *The Craft of Writing* (Englewood Cliffs, NJ: Prenticc-Hall, 1969).

Beginning and Ending

Miriam Munson,
Washington University

I have found that at the beginning, writing students can learn a great deal from fairly specific instructions about what kind of thing to say in expository essays, and even from specific examples of what they might say about particular topics. Such an approach may seem at odds with the goal of teaching students to express their own ideas. But it can also be thought of as a version of the rhetorical process of *inventio,* in which the use of appropriate topics allows writers to discover ideas they did not know they had, or indeed in some cases, were capable of. In addition, the imitation of examples helps the writer to develop an authoritative voice. The method works particularly well for openings and conclusions, which tend to be a bit more formulaic than the other parts of essays. But it can also be used successfully for whole essays on a particular text or piece of art or music.

In talking about openings of essays, I always remind students of the familiar and only partly facetious description of the three parts of an essay: Say what you're going to say, say it, say what you said. This dictum confronts writers immediately with one of the most puzzling aspects of essay writing: the need to repeat material without seeming repetitious.

The opening, where you say what you're going to say, represents the first opportunity to state a thesis that will be developed in the body and reasserted in the conclusion, and this prospect often makes students nervous about divulging it any earlier than they can help. With the intention of capturing the reader's attention through suspense, students often deliberately avoid mentioning their thesis in the opening. They would prefer it to emerge gradually in the body of the essay so that the closing can seem simply to embody the reader's own conclusions. I warn students that this approach, however appealing it might sound, demands great skill to bring off. What is more likely to happen is that the baffled reader, unable to make out the direction of the writer's train of thought, will lose interest and either throw the essay aside or wish to do so.

I also point out that by withholding information from the reader, writers do not create *suspense.* If we think of the great works of suspense, from *Beowulf* to *Rear Window,* we can see that the audience has very clear expectations of what is likely to happen. The writers involved play with those expectations, and the audience pays attention because they are wait-ing to have them fulfilled. Writers of essays must create similar expecta-tions in their readers. Far from losing their interest, "saying what you're going to say" captures attention more effectively than being mysterious about it.

At least it will if it's done in a certain way. The job of the introduction is not just to say what you're going to say, but to explain why it's important and how it fits in with what other people have said. Without this kind of context, whatever claims the essay will embody exist in a vacuum; with them they have relevance and significance. I tell students as a rule of thumb that people who have never read anything on a topic should be able to pick up an essay and make sense of the opening paragraph. Later, such readers might get lost in technical details, but from the opening they should be able to see what the claim is and how it fits into some ongoing debate.

At this point, I find that I have to be more specific, and one way that works well is to look at openings of journal articles in various academic fields. From this examination we can usually derive an ideal first paragraph on which students can model the openings of their own research papers by following, more or less closely, these steps:

1. Use the first sentence to describe recent work fairly specifically related to your topic:

In recent years, much attention has been given to the problem of _____.

2. In two or three sentences, give examples of this work, that is, describe two or three of the most important recent contributions to discussion of the topic:

X, for example, has shown how _____. Similarly, Y presents evidence that _____. Z, on the other hand, has argued that _____.

3. In another sentence, describe a new approach to the problem, and say that you are going to take this approach:

So far, however, no one has approached the problem of _____ from the point of view I shall adopt in this paper, namely that _____.

4. Tell how this approach clarifies issues that others have not been able to elucidate:

From this point of view, it will become clear that _____.

Students seem to recall being told that an opening paragraph should move from the general to the specific, and this recollection often leads them to begin their essays very far away from their topics. I like to point out to students that the patterns we have outlined move from the general (the area of interest) to the specific (your claim) but that the step is not a big one. The descriptions of other people's work are at about the same level of generality as the statement of the thesis. Nevertheless, the step is big enough to provide a context for the thesis. After the opening, the body of the essay descends into particularity for each point supporting the thesis. At no point will the reader be lost in generalities whose connection with the thesis is not clear.

Students are also troubled by having to repeat their thesis in the conclusion; they find it hard to imagine how to keep the last paragraph from sounding just like the first. Examination of the conclusions of the journal articles suggests a model ending that helps with this problem. Such an ending can be sketched out along these lines:

1. Use the first sentence to say that your new approach to the problem helps solve it. Because this is now a conclusion, use a word like *thus* or *then*.

   Approaching the topic from the point of view of _____, then, sheds new light on several of its puzzling aspects.

2. Use the sentences in the body of the paragraph to summarize the evidence in each of the paragraphs or sections of the essay. You might have such a sentence for each of the paragraphs or sections, and they may contain such transitional words and phrases as *first, moreover, in addition, furthermore,* and *finally.*
3. Finish the paragraph, and the paper, with a sentence or two restating your conclusion in a manner as rhetorically exciting as possible.

   Clearly, then, _____.

From this model, students can see that although the thesis itself is repeated, its context here is completely different from that of the opening. There it appears from the perspective of other work in the field, and it is offered *as* a thesis, still to be demonstrated. In the conclusion, on the other hand, the thesis appears in the context of its supporting evidence and is offered as the conclusion of the argument summarized there. This difference of context ensures that the thesis, though repeated in the conclusion, will not sound repetitious.

Actually, of course, the conclusion occurs twice in the model closing, once as the opening sentence and once at the end. But even these two occurrences need not sound repetitious, because at the very end of the essay, the writer can present it with some real rhetorical flair. I tell students that this is the place to try for the kind of fireworks appropriate to a finale: balance, antithesis, and alliteration can all be used in the final statement of the thesis to send the reader away feeling persuaded.

Sometimes, however, this is also the point at which the writer begins to feel that the thesis and its implications are clear. Things come together for the first time in the excitement of the conclusion, and when you look back at the opening; you see that the thesis there is not at all the same as that in the conclusion. Indeed, I tell students, this happens so frequently that it's almost worth regarding first versions of introductions as tentative, as ways of getting started, and as placeholders until you have presented all your evidence and can see just where it leads. I urge students to return at this point to the opening. By rewriting it in connection with the closing, they will produce a more sharply focused introduction and one that will lead the reader willingly into the body of the essay and on to its persuasive ending.

WRITING
ASSIGNMENT
The writing assignment that follows this lesson provides a chance for students to see that this procedure works. I ask them to rewrite the opening of a recent paper in light of its conclusion and with the help of the formulas and advice brought out in our discussion. Most students see the value of an introduction that clearly directs the reader to the point of the essay; and if they rewrite unfocused introductions along the lines suggested, they will also see a great improvement in their papers.

Figuring Out

Joseph F. Loewenstein,
Washington University

Perhaps the most successful sequence of assignments in a second-semester freshman course called "Rhetoric and Oratory" came toward the end of the semester, after I had spent weeks questioning the possibility of a disinterested rhetoric. Eight or nine weeks into the semester, the students began to realize how thoroughly effective writing is drenched in purpose, how saturated in will. We devoted much time to the study of revisions by famous writers to demonstrate the significance of "mere" stylistic choices. I also spent a good deal of the second half of the term encouraging a nearly antiquarian interest in the traditional taxonomies of schemes and tropes—most easily accessible in Richard Lanham's *Handlist of Rhetorical Terms*—to prepare the students for the first of a sequence of assignments. They

WRITING
ASSIGNMENT

were challenged to produce a page or so of "figureless" prose; I suggested, but did not stipulate, that they hold themselves to a single sustained passage of description. I hinted that writing figureless prose might be an impossible task; as a gesture of sympathy I did the assignment as well.

Next, we had a vigilant and bemused session in which we hounded out as many of the residual figures as we possibly could. I rightly assumed that it would be easy enough for the students to excavate the buried metaphors, though they did feel some uneasiness about confronting the insistently connotative, suggestive dimensions of language. They discovered that what they wrote inevitably had an expressive side.

IN-CLASS
EXERCISE

For the rest of the semester this "disfigured" piece of writing became the basis for a series of exercises on ornamentation. As we continued to read the classics of modern oratory—by Sheridan, Webster, King, and Nixon—we would identify the various figures used and their local rhetorical function, and then use them to embellish the "disfigured" piece. On one day, we were to find ways to use anaphora; on the next, metonymy; on the next, personification; and so on. Obviously, the results varied. Some students found an occasion for bathos (though even the most obsessive wags soon tired of this), whereas others took the arbitrary imposition of the ornate as a challenge to their sense of restraint and understatement. No matter; they were becoming richly calculating.

286

IN-CLASS
EXERCISE

At about the same time, I used sentence-combining exercises to help extend the student's syntactic range, exercises in which students were given sentences from the prose of respected modern writers broken down into component "kernels," and from those components were to reconstruct or refashion the writer's original.[1] Here it seemed to me that the sustained exercise of a variety of syntactic skills was more important than the single-minded and scrupulous application of isolated rhetorical schemes. The two sets of exercises—sentence-combining to develop syntactic resources and "prescribed" ornament to encourage an attitude to expression at once playful and deliberate—complemented each other nicely.

All the solutions to the problems of "figuring out," even the bathetic ones, proved useful in class, for each enabled the students to observe the pressures exerted by stylistic choices both on the meaning of discourse and on its tone. But the chief advantage of the exercises is that they enabled students to examine issues of voice and decorum in a *disinterested* fashion: The "personality" of the work was determined, to a large extent, quite artificially, so they had little psychological investment in the literary *manner* of these pieces. The prose, they felt, wasn't *quite* theirs, and they were thus liberated from shame and free to tinker, to admire what they might have inadvertently let loose. Looking at prose both theirs and not theirs allowed them analytic responses that grew cooler and subtler, and their exercises consequently became more witty and more supple.

---

[1] See William L. Stull's *Combining and Creating: Sentence Combining and Generative Rhetoric* (New York: Holt, 1983).

Analogy, Metaphor, and Etymology in Thinking

Michael West,
University of Pittsburgh

Though some of my paper assignments in composition courses are short enough to be written on the board, whenever possible I like to give students substantial directions approaching the length of their own required essays. Since improving written communication is the point of the course, a teacher does well to demonstrate his or her own skills at length on occasion. Answering one set of essays with an assignment for the next set not only makes for vital written dialogue between teacher and class but reduces the amount of individualized comment-writing necessary. But it's important that the assignment resonate with the teacher's own voice. For that reason when I adapt another teacher's assignment, there's usually considerable editing involved in producing my own version to harmonize with my classroom persona, which is tantalizing, contentious, and mildly authoritarian. My particular brand of classroom humor leavens this. But good humor is idiosyncratic. Teachers adapting the following assignment may wish to spice it with their own jokes and observations while jettisoning some of my material. With that general caveat, the exercise may do others good service.

It's designed to follow a couple of earlier exercises that stressed the importance of structure and categorization for creative thought (and of organization for good student papers). I like to argue in gestalt terms that perception relies on the lenses of preconception and necessarily must do so. A purely open mind would be a purely empty mind, I tell the class, incapable of orienting itself perceptually in the blooming, buzzing welter of sensory experience. Without categories we are visually and intellectually blind (a couple of classroom experiments help flesh this out). But if significant thought has a generalizing thrust, is prejudice then inescapable? This naturally leads to the question of where our intellectual categories come from and how we can keep them from ossifying into prejudices. Such classroom discussion forms the background of my assignment on metaphor.

If you favor terse assignments, some of my exposition can be deleted and handled in classroom discussion. For this section of the course the reading material is Thoreau's "Where I lived and What I Lived for" from *Walden*. Here's my handout.

The Roots of Time

What is the role of analogy in thought? Philosophers have often distrusted arguments from analogy. If the world can be likened to a watch, does that mean there must be a Divine Watchmaker? Arguing from metaphor may seem childish in comparison with logical analysis, which revolves around the capacity to distinguish. Analysis is at bottom separating things into different categories; and categories are essential to thought, for without them no general conclusions seem possible. All men are mortal, Socrates is a man, ergo Socrates is mortal—this syllogism depends upon fitting Socrates into the right category. But how do we form the categories that enable us to make meaningful distinctions? From similarities. Nature does not create human beings with labels reading *Man*—or even *homo sapiens*. Before we can scientifically *distinguish* dogs from cats, we must first *perceive an analogy* between a dachshund and a St. Bernard, an analogy that we create perhaps as much as perceive.

Can we even think about thinking without relying on metaphors? Some philosophers have held that all theories of consciousness are grounded in some *radical* (look up the etymology of this word, please) physical analogy. Thus eighteenth-century thinkers often talked about the mind as if it were a *mirror* that reflected nature, whereas many nineteenth-century thinkers imagined the mind as a *lamp* that cast its own light out into nature. Each metaphor both expressed and shaped a distinctive view of thought. Indeed, some philosophers would argue that no theory of thought can do more than clarify the particular physical analogies in which that theory is rooted. That is, to explain thought we can only say what thought is *like*. Does the etymology of the word *idea* (look it up, please) suggest what sensory analogy underlay the Greek view of thought? Many philosophers have puzzled about how to connect the two realms of body and mind, and there is still no generally accepted account of their relation. But perhaps thinking is not quite so immaterial a process as the abstract diction of your earlier essays has sometimes suggested.

Like it or not, thinking is radically metaphorical. So are many words. Get rid of the notion that metaphor merely clothes the naked idea decorously, that figurative language is only icing on any half-baked cake of thought, spread there chiefly to render it tempting to children and English teachers. Rightly used, metaphor is not a way or prettifying thoughts after they have been conceived; rather it is one of the most powerful tools for creating thought. To look for similarities between disparate phenomena can be the first step toward wisdom. If some teacher told you that the great age of Greek *ideas* had little in common with our dreary culture of *video*, what might a smart student reply? (Again I assume that a smart student should become interested in the derivation of words. The *really* smart student might even become interested enough to look up the etymology of *etymology*.)

Time, said Einstein, is the fourth dimension. "Time," said Thoreau in a paragraph that you should study closely, is "but the stream I go a-fishing in." That definition concludes his account of where he lived and what he lived for. Our class discussions will begin to suggest how Thoreau used both figurative language and etymology to shape not only his prose style but his life's style. Neither is a style that you will probably want to re-create for yourself. But I assure you that both your prose and your life can use shaping.

WRITING ASSIGNMENT Begin now. Wherever you live, whatever you live for, what is time to you? Write a two- to three-page essay (ca. 750 words) on your own sense of time. In what physical analogies is this highly abstract concept rooted? What concrete evidence from your own life best defines time? Birthdays? Clocks? Rainy Sundays? Sexual initiation? The death of a grandparent? The deadline for this paper? When did you first become aware of time, and how? If no dictionary were handy, how would you explain the concept to a foreigner who said that his language had no one word that seemed to crop up in all the contexts that the English word *time* does? But please, no simple-minded quotation from Webster, for this exercise assumes that a dictionary's definitions are much less interesting than its derivations. (Why is that?) I will not be enlightened to learn that time is "a nonspatial continuum in which events occur in apparently irreversible succession." Would Einstein agree? Would a scientist's definition of time differ generically from a poet's definition of time, or would both be essentially poetic descriptions? Is time the stream you go a-fishing in or a polluted river that you worry about drowning in? How far is your sense of self rooted in times before you were born? Do you have an independent identity, or is it defined through relations to people *like* you?

These questions are meant to be suggestive, *not* an outline. Like Thoreau, you must shape yourself. So shape up. Your *independently organized* essay should deal with some but by no means all of these questions and with some others that you yourself generate. It should include some discussion of Thoreau's sense of time and at least one anecdote from your own experience (neither need be lengthy—less than a paragraph would suffice) illustrating some larger ideas about time. You should evolve these ideas in accordance with Thoreau's dictum, "My head is hands and feet." Elsewhere in *Walden* Thoreau dismissed people who seek to kill time by remarking contemptuously, "As if you could kill time without injuring Eternity!" Killing time with this essay is therefore inadvisable. If the process of writing it does not lead you to have at least one new thought about time, then you will have failed, no matter what grade you receive.

Meanwhile, back at the ranch. . . . If the assignment and the Thoreau chapter are handed out three meetings in advance of the essay deadline, one or two of the following meetings can begin exploring aspects of Thoreau's thought and style pertinent to this section of your course. Thoreau's poetic prose shows a mind constantly testing society's abstract categories against each other, of course, and—more important—against his own concrete experience. Students will need help appreciating this, but presumably most English teachers have been trained to give it. You might start with the first two paragraphs of the chapter and trace his inspired punning on *survey, premises, cultivated, deed,* and *live.* Or with the passage where the sleeper-ties of the railroad become human sleepers. Much of Thoreau's wordplay is etymological, of course. His prose is therefore ideal for demonstrating how physical analogy not only generated most of the categories by which we make sense of the world, but will regenerate them if we allow it to.[1]

Any discussion before the due date should leave the final paragraph unbroached and say nothing about his treatment of time. When the essays come in, you will discover that they teem with the obvious physical evidence in which our sense of time is rooted: weather, days, seasons, years, all the solar phenomena. But few if any students will have used this concrete evidence to speculate that time might not be linear, like a stream, but cyclical, like the sun. This can be the theme of your discussion when the papers are returned. With a little prodding—and after some classroom discussion drawing perhaps on Mircea Eliade's *The Sacred and the Profane*—students can entertain the idea that holidays were originally holy days, when one stepped outside linear, chronological, secular time and into what Eliade calls sacred time, a timeless fusion of past and present. Some students will then assert that when they attend Communion on Christmas Eve, the time is not "Christmas 1987" as announced by TV newscasters but what an earlier age called "Christ-tide," so that they are present at the perennial birth of Christ *in illo tempore.* Such concepts of cyclical and mythic time make for challenging, provocative class discussion. More important, they allow the teacher to make good on his claim that if students had only exploited the concrete details of their own experience analogically, they would be able to generate novel ideas far more interesting than the tired, physically deracinated clichés that are too often their intellectual stock in trade.

Obviously my exercise assumes that good writing is inseparable from good thinking. I am trying to root out the naive student's assumption that style is something you lay on with a trowel, that he already has nifty ideas and just needs a verbal technique for expressing them. Teachers who share this goal should find Thoreau a useful ally, since he so clearly fuses fresh writing with innovative living so as to discourage superficial notions of style.

LESSON READING

Henry David Thoreau, "Where I Lived and What I Lived for," from *Walden*, ed. J. Lyndon Shanley (Princeton, NJ: Princeton UP, 1971).

---

[1] If all this sounds enticing but unfamiliar, see my "Scatology and Eschatology: The Heroic Dimensions of Thoreau's Wordplay," *PMLA*, 89 (1974), 1043–64, and other authorities cited therein.

FOR FURTHER READING

Mircea Eliade, *The Sacred and the Profane: The Nature of Religion*, trans. Willard R. Trask (Orlando, FL: Harcourt Brace Jovanovich, 1959), Chapter 2.

A Balanced Style: The Double Rewrite Method

Thomas Carnicelli,
University of New Hampshire

This is a lesson on style. I assign Donald Hall's essay "An Ethic of Clarity" (from Hall's anthology *The Modern Stylists*) to be read before class. With its stress on clarity and simplicity, Hall's essay is representative of the attitude toward style that dominates composition teaching today. When the students come in, I ask them to set the essay aside, then give them a handout containing two alternative versions of Hall's opening paragraph:

A. 1. Ezra Pound, George Orwell, James Thurber, and Ernest Hemingway don't have much in common: a great poet who became a follower of Mussolini, a disillusioned left-wing satirist, a comic essayist and cartoonist, and a great novelist. 2. If anything, they show how different modern writers are. 3. Yet one thing brings them together. 4. They share a common idea of good style, an idea that good prose must be clear and simple. 5. This attitude toward style was known to earlier writers, but it has never been so widely held as it is today.

B. 1. Ezra Pound, George Orwell, James Thurber, and Ernest Hemingway have little in common: a great poet who became a follower of Mussolini, a disillusioned left-wing satirist, a comic essayist and cartoonist, and a great novelist. 2. They could easily represent the diversity of modern literature. 3. There is, however, one thing that unites them. 4. They share a common idea of good style, an idea of the virtues of clarity and simplicity. 5. Although this attitude toward style was not unknown to earlier writers, never before has it been so pervasive and so exclusive.

Before I describe what might go on in the class, let me explain the handout. Hall's original paragraph is a mixture of what might be conveniently termed "informal" and "formal" elements. What I've done in rewriting is to separate those elements to make one consistently informal version (A) and one consistently formal version (B). In A, I've used native English words, which tend to be concrete in reference and down-to-earth in tone, and a relatively colloquial syntax. In B, I've used French–Latin borrowings, which tend to be abstract in reference and elevated or intellectual in tone, and the syntax of formal written English. I've tried to use as many of Hall's own words as possible and to convey his ideas as fully as linguistic resources permit. I've also tried not to stack the deck in favor of either version.

After the students have read the handout, I ask them to characterize the style of each of the versions. I'm looking for "informal–formal," but "spoken–written" or "simple–complex" usually come up as well, and will be useful later on. Tentative agreement on "informal–formal" can usually be reached quite quickly. Then I ask the students which version they prefer and, almost invariably, the class splits right down the middle. That result will also be useful later.

After this brief general discussion, we make a line-by-line comparison of the two versions. Throughout it, I keep a steady focus on the idea of level of formality, in both diction and syntax. Here's a composite of some of the class discussions I've had.

Sentence 1. A's "don't have much in common," with its contraction and folksy understatement, is much more informal than B's rather British-sounding "have little in common." Other than that, the two versions are identical.

Sentence 2. A has an elliptical phrase, "If anything," which is common in speech. It also has the common English verb *show*, whereas B has the more intellectual French–Latin equivalent *represent*. A remains concrete and personal, with *different modern writers*, whereas B relies on long Latinate abstractions: *the diversity of modern literature.* Students strongly prefer B to A, for two reasons: In A, there is an awkward double take after *different*; A's *show* suggests conscious intention on the part of the writers— an absurd notion—whereas B's *represent* indicates that someone else is interpreting the situation.

Sentence 3. Both versions are short and fairly simple. Syntactically, A is the more informal; it starts with a conjunction and ends with a preposition (actually, an adverb)—two things that purists rail against. The key difference is, of course, in the verbs. A's native English *brings together* is much too concrete; it suggests that the writers got together to form a Political Action Committee. B's French–Latin *unites*, while retaining a slight political flavor, is sufficiently abstract to suggest that some outside interpreter is perceiving the unity. Because *unites* makes much better sense, students strongly prefer B's version of line three. Discussion of *unites* can be taken farther, though. Since it is a verb that can take a human or at least an active subject, I often ask what it is that actively unites the various writers. "The fact that they have the same view of good style" is hardly an active subject. What might be behind this fact? What might be making the writers think in the same way? Ultimately, it could be some active historical force, something like The Modern Spirit, or at least Donald Hall's interpretation of that spirit. This question is, admittedly, more concerned with the nature of history than with the nature of style, but it often proves to be the highlight of the class discussion.

Sentence 4. A is "clear and simple" throughout, in both diction and syntax. In its first half, B is identical to A, but the second half of B is another matter entirely: three Latinate abstractions—*virtues, clarity, simplicity.* Sensing a sharp contrast between content and style, students usually object to this piling up of long words: B is anything but simple in its praise of simplicity. This observation becomes more interesting later on, when students find out that B is Hall's own version, word for word.

Sentence 5. Students usually continue to be annoyed by what they regard as pomposity in B. They consider B's syntax highly artificial: Although they do not notice the opening subordinate clause and tolerate *not unknown,* they object to the inversion of *never before;* and they much prefer the syntax of A, with its simple coordination and normal word order. So, too, they prefer A's relatively simple diction, in contrast to the Latinate adjectives *pervasive* and *exclusive,* which even the best students have some difficulty understanding in this sentence.

After the class has analyzed each version in detail, there is still no clear preference for one over the other. Line 1 is much the same in each version. Version A is preferred in lines 4 and 5; version B, in lines 2 and 3. It is now time for the class to examine Hall's original paragraph.

> Ezra Pound, George Orwell, James Thurber, and Ernest Hemingway don't have much in common: a great poet who became a follower of Mussolini, a disillusioned left-wing satirist, a comic essayist and cartoonist, and a great novelist. If anything, they could represent the diversity of modern literature. Yet one thing unites them. They share a common idea of good style, an idea of the virtues of clarity and simplicity. This attitude toward style was not unknown to earlier writers, but never before has it been so pervasive and so exclusive.

As soon as they read the paragraph over, students can see that Hall's style is a mixture, a balance, of elements identified before as informal or formal. Hall's balanced style impresses them; they can see how carefully he blends the various elements within each individual sentence. I have never had a class that did not prefer Hall's version to the other two. Although some students will still object to the second parts of Hall's lines 4 and 5 they will also concede that the presence of informal elements elsewhere helps to balance the tone of the passage as a whole. If discussion continues, I will agree with the objections to the second part of line 4; I do find the extreme contrast between content and style distracting. I will, however, defend Hall's paired adjectives in line 5 by pointing out that "so pervasive and so exclusive" says more than A's "so widely held," which leaves out the idea of exclusiveness. I will also attempt to explain that this omission in A was not deliberate on my part; I simply could not come up with a "simple" equivalent of Hall's original phrasing. I will invite the students to try for themselves, and, after a few attempts, they often conclude that long words do have their uses.

I have found this lesson to be useful in two main ways. First of all, it provides students with a way of discussing prose style; it gives them specific features to look for. More important, I think, the lesson emphasizes the value of a balanced style, a style that makes intelligent use of the varied resources of the English language.

This emphasis on a balanced style is especially needed today, when the ideal of the Plain Style so dominates the field. In the writing textbooks, in the Doublespeak committees, as well as in Donald Hall's essay as a whole, there is a strong tendency to equate clarity and simplicity with moral virtue and to regard complexity as morally suspect. These concepts need to be sorted out. Clarity is indeed a virtuous end. Simplicity can be a means to that end, but not the only means and not always the best means. Complexity, too, may serve virtue. At least since the Norman Conquest, any English prose worth its intellectual salt has contained some mixture of more formal diction and syntax. Complex thoughts often require complex language as well as syntactical structures, and—as this lesson illustrates—even an argument in praise of simplicity is likely to makes use of the more formal register of English style.

The method behind this lesson can be applied in a variety of ways. By far the best is to have students do the rewriting themselves. Many of the current textbooks do use student rewriting of passages, but in a one-sided way: Students are given some grotesque piece of academic or bureaucratic jargon and asked to simplify it. Hall's own text, *Writing Well*, has some excellent exercises of this type. This is a valuable practice, but I'd suggest adding some exercises that point in the other direction. How about asking students to rewrite passages written in a successful formal style? Would *The Declaration of Independence* or *The Gettysburg Address* really sound better in Plain Style? Then again, one can ask students to rewrite passages written entirely in simple sentences, as in such sentence-combining texts as *The Writer's Options* by Diaker, Kerek, and Morenberg. This type of exercise is a proven way to expand a student's stylistic repertoire.

WRITING
ASSIGNMENT 1

WRITING
ASSIGNMENT 2

Finally, to use the double rewrite method presented in this lesson, one can take almost any example of good intellectual discourse and ask students to write formal and informal versions of it. Here, for example, are two student rewrites of the first sentence of George Orwell's "Politics and the English Language."

> Although most people who consider the issue at all would admit that the English language is deteriorating, it is generally assumed that we cannot by conscious action do anything about it.

> Most people who bother with the matter at all would admit that the English language is in a bad way, but they also believe that we can't do anything about it, no matter how hard we try.

Although this essay has been widely used by advocates of the Plain Style, students who work closely with Orwell's own prose will find the same judicious balance of formal and informal elements that I have been emphasizing. If students read what Orwell actually says, they will find that he is careful not to equate clarity and simplicity. He states that reform of the English language "is not concerned with fake simplicity and the attempt to make written English colloquial," that reform does not "imply in every case prefering the Saxon word to the Latin one, though it does imply using the fewest and shortest words that will cover one's meaning." Hence, even George Orwell, widely considered the patron saint of the Plain Style, can be used to support a more balanced view of English style, and of the teaching of English style.

LESSON READING

Donald Hall, "An Ethic of Clarity," in *The Modern Stylists* (New York: Free Press, 1968).

Freedom Through Form: A Prose Sestina

Robert Beum

Most of our students today have backgrounds where television is big, reading small, and writing barely extant. They come to us as viewers, not as readers or writers. Habituation to passive reception from a screen has denied them the active imaginative participation required by, and for, the written word—and it has denied them the word itself, limited them to the clichés, the jargon, and the rhetoric useful to advertisers, sitcom actors, and politicians. And television is only one of a host of technologies and private or group activities that, constantly overstimulating the sensibility, raise the threshold to a level from which it is difficult to come down to the quieter one of words equably building an argument or deftly modulating from one tone to another. If we are honest with ourselves, we know that, as teachers in an age where lived experience is mindless mass activities and technological hyperstimulation, we are asking almost too much. We are asking—no, requiring—the restive city boy to join us in the unwired country and not only to discern but to accept its virtues, and to do so rather precipitously.

About ten years ago I worked out a lesson—I have been using it regularly since then—that does go a ways toward bridging the gap between wordless overstimulation and thoughtful composition. The students themselves have made the claim, which is why I stick with this lesson.

I make it the first written assignment. It requires no outside readings, no library hours, no poll taking, not getting together in discussion groups. The only thing needed to orient the class is thirty minutes of explanation abundantly supported by illustrative examples on the blackboard or on handout sheets. What I explain is something that belongs to the psychology of creativity: the *heuristic principle*, the power of a pre-established form (pattern or framework) to stimulate the imagination in such a way as to facilitate composition and to lead to felicitous discoveries—to result in fresh, if not absolutely original, phrases and turns of thought.[1]

---

[1] In our *Prosody Handbook* (New York: Harper & Row, 1985, pp. 80–81 and 102–103) Karl Shapiro and I attempted a commonsense analysis of the heuristic value, for verse composition, of the restrictions imposed by meter and rhyme.

I explain that though restrictions or limitations imposed on composition might seem, on first thought, to act as hindrances, experience shows that the opposite is often, probably more often, the case. I remind my students that in most kinds of creative or constructive work, even play (consider the function of rules in any game), people usually find it helpful to have some sort of model, pattern, or guideline. Without that, one is often at a loss: How to begin? How to proceed? The pattern—which need not be followed slavishly—helps us get the job done because it focuses our activity and frees us from the bewilderment of being faced with virtually infinite choice. The pattern is at once a path and a light on that path. I remind students that all but a tiny fraction of the world's most highly regarded poetry has been written within some form of metrical or rhetorical limitation: it has meter, or it rhymes, or it counts the number of syllables per line, or it builds on the basis of syntactical parallelism. I also point out that even after adopting the discipline of a framework, one retains quite a lot of freedom to work in whatever direction one chooses, to develop one metaphor or another, to establish this tone or that—one even remains free to change metrical horses in the middle of the stream.

I explain the core of the heuristic principle as follows. When we write within a definite framework, when there is a pattern to which we "must" conform, we find that some of the words we might want to use just won't fit, won't fulfill the pattern: They're too long or too blunt or accented in the wrong place to make the right rhythm. So we throw them out and keep on searching for choices that fit really well. If we're lucky (and the bigger our vocabularies, the luckier we tend to be), we eventually come up with words that fit into place so well they make the imagination tingle: We've created vivid, fresh, or even entirely original phrases and images—and they aren't mere novelties but support the composition as a whole.

The very fact that we have to do more than just make sense—we have to make sense that fits a pattern—tends to prevent us from writing off the tops of our heads. The pattern has erected an obstacle, all right, but it's partly an obstacle that helps keep us from taking the easy way out—the stock figures, the commonplaces, the clichés that come all too easily when we have the unlimited freedom to do what comes naturally.

The necessity of the pattern becomes the mother of our invention in diction, phrase, figure, turn of thought itself.

I suggest to the students that one thing they will learn through this lesson is that when we are writing we don't always know exactly what we are going to say, or want to say, until we start putting the words together. Before we start to write we may have some point we wish to make, but the very act of writing may modify it, make it vastly richer, more precise, more piquant. Before it ever becomes finished statement or "expression," a piece of writing exists as a process of exploration leading gradually to discoveries about language, thought, and oneself.

My lesson is really a sort of game, and one short enough not to be exhausting. I ask the students to proceed in the spirit of play and exploration, and sometimes I point out that what they will be doing is a prose adaptation of *bouts rimés* (boo-reemay), or "rhymed ends," a poetry game played for centuries in Europe, especially in France, where the game was probably invented. In *bouts-rimés* someone draws up a list of words that rhyme with one another and hands the list to another person who has to build a poem that uses the rhymes in the order in which they appear on the list. If the words listed are *hoof, giraffe, roof, laugh, half, say, today*, and *riff-raff*, someone might produce the following stanza:

> Without the sound of breath or hoof
> Two awkward graces, both giraffe,
> Nibble the ivy on my roof,
> And someday, probably, I'll laugh,
> But now I don't feel well by half:
> "For twenty years, my dear," I'll say,
> "We've grown a salad, and today
> They ordered it . . . they aren't—riff-raff."

People as unlike as Alexandre Dumas, Dante Gabriel Rossetti, and Ford Madox Ford have been devotees of the game and have affirmed its benefits to imagination and verbal skill.

In verse forms like the sestina, rondeau, villanelle, and triolet, the writer's ingenuity meets its ultimate test. In these forms a set of perhaps arbitrarily selected sounds is repeated several times, each time in a predetermined order. The rules are so demanding that they are perhaps as likely to inhibit as to release creativity, but even such a formidable challenge sometimes brings wonderful things from the poet, as it does in Robert Bridges' graceful yet substantial "Triolet":

> When first we met we did not guess
> That Love would prove so hard a master;
> Of more than common friendliness
> When first we met we did not guess.
> Who could foretell this sore distress,
> This irretrievable disaster
> When first we met?—We did not guess
> That Love would prove so hard a master.

The instructor should probably point out, as I usually do, that all rhyming poetry (no matter what the rhyme scheme) in effect requires the poet to regard the rhymes somewhat in the way one regards "home" in a game like backgammon or parchesi: One keeps throwing the dice of words, and when the right combination appears, one can get "home"—to the rhyme—or at least advance in that direction.

No matter what kind of rhyming verse the instructor presents, most students usually see right away that the best preparation for any game of rhyme (or for my adaptation of the game) is a large vocabulary and a well-limbered ingenuity; many students also see that playing such games in itself actually helps initiate that limbering process and enhances one's desire for a bigger stock of words to draw on.

<table>
<tr><td>WRITING
ASSIGNMENT</td><td>Here is the lesson:</td></tr>
</table>

Using your imagination to visualize such things as a place, an object, an action, or a person—or all together—write a seven-sentence paragraph of description or narration. Each of your seven sentences must use one of the seven words listed below, and the word must come either at the beginning or at the end of the sentence in which you use it. All seven words are to be used but used only once (i.e., one word per sentence). Welcome unusual conceptions or phrases as long as they are meaningful and contribute to the effectiveness of the whole sequence of sentences.

inscription	distance	accurate	clear
soon	abundance	green	

If that set of seven words will not work for you, try this one:

isthmus	formidable	raging	done
outcroppings	vertically	accessible	

Almost any set of relatively familiar and nontechnical words will do: Sufficient application and ingenuity will always find some way to construct a meaningful passage around them.

One may vary the lesson as one likes. Several sets of words may be given, or only one. The number of words may be reduced to five or expanded to ten. One may stipulate that the words are to be used only at or very near the ends of their sentences. I have often changed the stipulations and have never noticed any distinct differences in the results.

The following three paragraphs are presented on a handout to provide my students with examples of what can be done with the assignment.

1

She picks up the comb, turns to the mirror, and has left the room: the silver becomes its own space, and she's there. Bright leaning, bending, turning, she commands it. Vulnerable space!—it just yields more light and more light and asks no release. Chemise, glass boxes, bottles, brooches break into iridescence and she combs it in. She'd gather the morning light if she could—and it would be right for the bits of sky in that oval face. She takes one step back and stands still. Seems to approve; but the glass stays ready: if she requires it, it will have to dance.

2

They misnamed it—it ought to be called a formal stiff, not a formal dance. The stiff folks I habitually go out of my way not to meet collect there. Somehow they see the point of it. For them it must be—though I don't see how—some sort of release. Anyway, that night it was a beast I had to face. I think I probably closed my eyes as I walked in. And Jane tells me I was known that evening as the one who stands—still.

3

The sun is having its morning dance. In this kitchen, though, everything, even the light, is still. Softly blotched and streaked, a honeydew melon on the counter keeps a patient face. Without blinking it takes me in. But none of this stillness is domestic: it promises to gather momentum toward some unpredictable release. It goes to the heart and does its own dance there. Show me a poem that hasn't seen it.

The arbitrary words are *there, it, release, in, face, still, dance.* The stipulation is that these must be used, in any order, as the last words of seven sentences that form a unified, meaningful, and reasonably interesting paragraph.

The models are designed to be sufficiently different to suggest the wide range of possibilities and to demonstrate how "forced" imagination may at least avoid the routine in thought and phrasing and lead us toward the experience of genuine creativity.

My follow-up is to read (at the next class session) three or four of the choicest student specimens, drawing attention to what is freshest or most vivid in them.

Exposition, not narration or description, is the focus of most composition courses, but a little variety never hurts, and many students, especially at the outset of a course, welcome the opportunity to do something brief, concrete, and imaginatively open. There is nothing to prevent the instructor from using the result merely as a diagnostic paper or as an ungraded exercise.

Giving Students a Personal Stake in Research

Carol Booth Olson,
University of California–Irvine

Bill Klein had just discovered that his mother had been diagnosed as a diabetic. He immediately conjured up an image in his mind of "a sickly, skinny person who had to inject needles containing insulin into her body everyday." But he actually had no clear understanding of what diabetes was, what the symptoms and causes were, or if there was a cure. What age group did the disease affect? How common was diabetes? Was it hereditary? He wanted to know.

Eli Espiritu had accumulated a "scanty nest egg" over the years and was just waiting for the right high-yield investment to come along. "Silver Soars" newspaper headlines during the silver boom of 1979 had caught his attention and he had been watching this fluctuating market with interest ever since. He was now ready to "concentrate [his] effort into researching the silver ore." He would base a decision about whether and how much to invest in silver on his findings.

At the age of twenty-six, Mary Gutierrez had no marital prospects in line and very little inclination to seek out a husband. But she did have a strong maternal instinct and was considering taking her "future by the reins" and guiding it "down the path of motherhood" by adopting as a single parent. "Does this idea seem too naive to women who have already raised a child?" she wondered. "Am I painting too rosy a picture of my eligibility to adopt?" She felt she had the right motives for adopting and more then enough love to give. But she had to ask herself, "Could I possibly give my child the same love and care that comes from a two-parent household?"

With these questions and others like them in mind, my Freshman Composition students embarked on a quest for knowledge that would culminate in what Ken Macrorie has called the "I Search" paper, a piece of thoughtful, investigative research into a topic that had immediate relevance to each writer. He has named it "I Search" to emphasize that "there's an *I* doing the searching and writing that affects the bend and quality of the truth in the work."[1]

What I like best about the "I Search" assignment is that it encourages students in active research out of a genuine need to know. So often, the traditional research paper is a passive enterprise in which the student merely analyzes and restates the results of someone else's intellectual inquiry, an inquiry in which he may have no personal investment. When I think of research, I think of more than a visit to the card catalogue and weekends spent in the library stacks. I think of firsthand activities like writing letters, making telephone calls, initiating face-to-face interviews, and going on field trips—supplemented by the valuable information that can be obtained from pertinent journals and books. I agree with Macrorie that the dictionary definition of research as a "patient study and investigation in some field of knowledge, undertaken to establish facts and principles" leaves out "the basic motivation for the whole effort."[2] My students are rarely patient about anything. I would rather have them get so involved in a topic that they launch their hunt for information in several different directions simultaneously than to have them bored before they begin, dragging their bodies down to the library, simply going through the motions of searching. Because the students have a stake in this paper, I find that after the initial excitement of getting started, they will sit down and take an objective look at what needs to be done and avail themselves of all the accessible secondary sources.

Based on Macrorie's guidelines, I developed a handout describing the "I Search" paper, which I distribute to students and explain in class at least three weeks before they are expected to decide on a topic they wish to pursue. (I have designated a three-part format to be written in progressive stages as opposed to Macrorie's four-part structure.)

The "I Search" Paper

WRITING
ASSIGNMENT 1

Description. This paper is designed to teach the writer and the reader something valuable about a chosen topic and about the nature of searching and discovery. As opposed to the standard research paper where the writer usually assumes a detached and objective stance, the "I Search" paper allows you to take an active role in your search, to experience some of the hunt for facts and truths firsthand, and to provide a step-by-step record of the discovery process.

Topic. The cardinal rule is to choose a topic that *genuinely* interests you and that you need to know more about. You may want to research teen-age alcoholism, a second career in interior design, the effects of divorce in the American family, the pros and cons of several popular diets, etc. The important

---

[1] Ken Macrorie, "The Reawakening of Curiosity: Research Papers as Hunting Stories" in *Practical Ideas for Teaching Writing as a Process,* ed. Carol Booth Olson (Sacramento: California State Department of Education, 1986), p. 111.

[2] Ken Macrorie, *Searching Writing* (Rochelle Park, NJ: Hayden, 1980), p. 162.

point is that you choose the topic you will investigate rather than having the instructor select a topic or even provide a number of options.

Format. The paper should be written in three sections: What I Know, Assume, or Imagine; The Search; What I Discovered.

What I Know, Assume, or Imagine. Before conducting any formal research, write a section in which you explain to the reader what you think you know, what you assume or what you imagine about your topic. For example, if you decided to investigate teen-age alcoholism, you might want to offer some ideas about the causes of teen-age alcoholism, provide an estimate of the severity of the problem, and create a portrait of a typical teen-age drinker, etc., prior to conducting your search.

The Search. Test your knowledge, assumptions, or conjectures by researching your topic thoroughly. Consult useful books, magazines, newspapers, films, tapes, etc., for information. When possible, interview people who are authorities on or are familiar with your topic. If you were pursuing a search on teen-age alcoholism, you might want to check out a book on the subject, read several pertinent articles in a variety of current magazines, make an apppointment to visit an alcohol rehabilitation center, attend a meeting of Alanon or Alcoholics Anonymous, and consult an alcoholism counselor. You might also ask a number of teen-agers from different social and/or economic backgrounds what their firsthand exposure to alcohol has been and whether they perceive any alcohol "problem" among their peers.

Write your search up in narrative form, recording the steps of the discovery process. Do not feel obligated to tell everything, but highlight the happenings and facts you uncovered that were crucial to your hunt and contributed to your understanding of the topic. Document all your sources of information, using formal footnote form when appropriate. You will be required to consult a minimum of two primary and two secondary sources.

What I Discovered. After concluding your search, compare what you thought you knew, assumed, or imagined with what you actually discovered and offer some personal commentary and/or draw some conclusions. For instance, after completing your search on teen-age alcoholism, you might learn that the problem is far more severe and often begins at an earlier age than you formerly believed. You may have assumed that parental neglect was a key factor in the incidence of teen-age alcoholism but now find that peer pressure is the prime contributing factor. Consequently, you might want to propose that an alcoholism awareness and prevention program including peer counseling sessions be instituted in the public school system as early as sixth grade.

(NOTE: The three-part format of this paper can be organized explicitly—for example, set off with subheadings—or implicitly.)

Bibliography. At the close of the report attach a formal bibliography listing the sources you consulted to write your paper.

I also provide students with a sample abstract written during the previous semester so they can get a firm grasp of what is involved in writing an "I Search." (A model abstract is provided below.)

Using the "I Search" handout and model paper for reference, students spend several weeks thinking about a topic they are genuinely interested in researching. Allowing enough lead time for students to mull over various paper options is extremely important. Otherwise, they may latch on to the first idea that comes to mind without seriously considering whether they truly need to know about that topic. To help students "discover" their topic, I ask them to keep a pocket notebook handy and to record every question that comes to mind that they genuinely need to know about. These lists of questions can then be arranged in order of urgency to help students focus on an issue of real importance to them.

WRITING ASSIGNMENT 2 After the students have selected their topic and checked to make sure research sources are available, I ask them to write up an abstract (not to exceed one page in length) in which they explain *what* their topic is, *why* they have chosen it, and *how* they intend to go about searching and writing. A sample abstract follows:

Abstract for "I Search" Paper on Procrastination

For almost as long as I can remember, I've had this nasty habit of procrastinating—postponing until tomorrow what could easily be completed today. This is especially true of the way I handle written work (like papers for this class, for instance), which have established due dates and a reader with high expectations.

I'd like to take a close look at why I procrastinate and suffer all the anxiety caused by putting things off until the last minute. Maybe I can learn something that will not only make my behavior more understandable but will enable me *to do something about it!* Then I'll hire myself out as a consultant to all my fellow procrastinators.

Speaking of fellow procrastinators, I'll start by interviewing my friends and also try to make an appointment with a counseling psychologist. Maybe talking to a time management consultant would be useful too. I've checked at the library in the *Reader's Guide to Periodicals* and it looks like *Psychology Today* is my best bet for secondary sources. I didn't see any entire books on the subject, but maybe I can also find a chapter in a couple of books.

I usually try to allot at least one hour for students to meet in peer groups to share their abstracts and exchange ideas about their perspective topics. Not only are students good at helping each other clarify and refine their ideas about what they're planning to do and why, but they serve as valuable resources in determining how to go about searching for information. Often students are able to direct their peers to firsthand resources. A student wishing to investigate whether she should train to become a nurse practitioner, for example, may find that another student knows and can arrange for an interview with someone in that profession. While the class is engaged in peer groups, I also have an opportunity to review each student's abstract and offer my responses and suggestions in individual conferences. Most often I assist the students in narrowing down their topics and broadening their research sources.

Before students begin writing their "I Search" papers it is important to clarify the criteria on which their work will be evaluated:

1. Paper is written in three sections. (Format may be explicit or implicit.)
   a. What I Know, Assume, or Imagine (prior to the search)
   b. The Search (testing knowledge, assumptions, or conjecture through documented research)
   c. What I Discovered (comparing what you thought you knew with what you learned and offering commentary and conclusions)
2. Topic lends itself to investigation and discovery.
3. Paper displays evidence of all levels of critical thinking and offers special insight into the topic discussed.
4. Main points of the essay are well supported with examples.
5. Writer uses ample transitions between ideas, paragraphs, and sections.
6. Writer varies sentence structure and length.
7. Writer uses precise, apt, or descriptive language.
8. Writer generally uses effectively the conventions of written English.
9. The Search portion of the essay is properly documented with footnotes in correct form.
   a. Paper includes references to a minimum of two primary and two secondary research sources.
   b. Paper includes a formal bibliography.
10. Writer uses research effectively as a supplement to, but not a substitute for, his or her own ideas.
11. Paper conveys a clear sense of the author's "voice" or style.
12. Author takes an active rather than a passive role in the search.
13. Paper is a genuine learning experience for the writer and the reader.

When you give students a personal stake in research and encourage them to bring everything they know about writing to their project, they produce some of their best work. In addition, they often discover something that has far more value than a grade. Bill Klein, for example, learned that his mother can still live a long and relatively normal life with the proper medical care and nutrition and that the hereditary theory of diabetes is discounted by most doctors. After completing his research on the silver market, Eli Espiritu gained enough knowledge to invest $1000 in silver bullion and commemorative coins. Mary Gutierrez decided that some children are often better off with single mothers than with two-parent families and that she had the "courage and confidence" to assume the responsibility. But she discovered, to her surprise and dismay, that infants and young children are rarely placed in single-family homes. In fact, the average age of adoptees is twelve. When faced with becoming the new mother of an adolescent almost half her age, Mary decided to wait and reconsider her options.

Perhaps the person who benefits most from this comprehensive learning experience is the teacher. I am able to play the dual role of teacher and student, and with each new paper, I gain a wealth of information. Moreover, because writing these papers is more meaningful to my students, reading them is more meaningful to me.

Summarizing and the Conventions of the Research Paper

Russell Tabbert,
University of Alaska

We expect a lot when we assign the standard academic research paper—more perhaps than we realize. Though we explain and demonstrate topic choosing, library searching, information extracting, organizing, developing, and documenting, we may not give enough attention to the stylistic conventions of summarizing and presenting secondary research material. We require that the borrowed information flow smoothly to support and develop the topics being discussed, yet we also demand to be kept regularly aware that it is coming from sources. Balancing on that thin line, I've discovered, does not come naturally or easily for many students.

WRITING ASSIGNMENT To provide explicit practice in the stylistic and mechanical conventions of summarizing secondary material, I give my students an assignment at about the point in the research project where they are finishing up note taking and just getting ready to write. Though this paper distracts them temporarily from their own work, it does, I've found, forestall many problems that would seriously weaken the research paper itself.

For the assignment I choose a relatively short, clearly structured piece of argumentation. When I pass it out I explain briefly the general nature and purpose of the exercise, and I tell them to study the essay carefully and to be prepared to discuss it. At the next class we explicate the content to make sure that everyone understands the claim and has identified the supporting arguments. Then in portions of a couple of class meetings I explain the summary assignment and identify the stylistic and mechanical skills that it is intended to develop. At this point I pass out a successful student summary from a previous semester together with the original article on which it was based.

Because I like well-packaged products, I tell my students to give their summary a one-paragraph introduction that begins at some point in the broader context and gradually funnels down to the specific issue at hand. At the end of this paragraph or at the beginning of the next, the author and title of the article should be tied in. Following this should be a sentence or two that signal briefly the main claim(s).

The body should consist of several well-developed paragraphs that correlate with the structure of the article's argument. You, the summarizer, should keep your voice out of it. Present the reasoning as objectively and fairly as possible.

When you are done, don't just drop it. Give it a concluding paragraph in which you step back and react to the piece. Help the reader of your summary evaluate the ideas, put them into perspective, gauge their significance, spot their weaknesses, and so on. Get us smoothly out.

So much for the framework of the assignment. Next I explain, illustrate, and have the students practice the stylistic devices and mechanical conventions for presenting information from secondary sources. To emphasize that this involves more than just sprinkling in footnote or page numbers, I don't have my students do any documenting for this summary assignment.

The main point to be made is that all quotations (I exaggerate a bit) and most paraphrases/summaries must be signaled by tying the source's last (usually) name or a pronoun into an attributing structure early in the sentence. There are two such devices that I especially emphasize because they can be used effectively with both quotations and summary/paraphrase:

1. In the first, the source's name (or a pronoun) is the main sentence subject, the main verb is one from a set of what might be called "attributing" verbs (such as *think, feel, claim, argue, report, state, say,* etc.), and the quoted statement or summary/paraphrase is a full clause embedded as the direct object with the *that* subordinator.

Source Name	+	*Attributing Verb*	+	*that* + Clause
"Jones		argues		that the Superfund
		states		
		etc.		

   is woefully inadequate for the cleanup that is needed."

   For variety the name/pronoun + verb can be placed parenthetically within the clause, usually between the subject and verb. The *that* is not present:

   "This misunderstanding, Jones argues, has caused problems in implementing the program."

2. Another useful device, though it can't be used as frequently, is the formula *according to* + source name followed by the full sentence quotation or summary/paraphrase:

   "According to Jones, the tax reform bill has a little of nothing for everyone."

   Here too the attribution can come within the content sentence:

"Such a revision would, according to Jones, improve the chances of success greatly."

I also use the summary assignment to review the mechanics of quotation. Because so many students are uncertain about the colon in connection with quotation, I make the following slight oversimplification· Use the colon to set off a full sentence quotation that has been introduced by a full sentence. That is, at the end of the attributing lead-in there is a full pause, usually after a noun that points forward to the quotation:

> From his studies Jones has drawn the following conclusion: "The EPA was mismanaged for purely political ends during the early years of this administration."

This is also the point to explain ellipsis, punctuation with closing quotation marks, capitals at the beginning of quoted sentences, the editorial brackets, and the handling of long quotations.

When they come to write their introductions, I urge my students not to use a quotation as the first sentence of a paragraph. At that spot we usually expect a generalization in the words of the writer, not of a secondary source. I also discuss the reasons one would choose to quote. And to prevent the frequent overreliance on quotation, we discuss the proportion of quoting to other development in a secondary source paper, making sure the quotations do not take over the paper and produce a pastiche.

Although in the research paper we encourage blending information from a variety of sources, there are usually a few sections where a stretch of writing must rely on one source or authority. The summary assignment provides an opportunity to practice smooth attributing in these situations too. I advise my students to modulate between sentences that use last name attribution, ones that simply continue presenting the information, and ones that use personal pronoun attribution. If the development from the same authority goes into a new paragraph, the first attribution should come early in the new paragraph and should be the name, not the pronoun.

One final point that I find requires comment is the question of tense in the attributing verbs. Because I usually choose a relatively contemporary essay to summarize, the assignment doesn't represent the potential complexity that can occur in actual research writing. For the summary I can simply claim that the standard convention applies: Use present tense for the attributions because we assume that the ideas presented in the source have current validity. Many whole research papers and large portions of most others will have exactly this relationship to their sources. However, two exceptions should be pointed out:

1. Use the past tense with specific activities, such as research studies, that are being referred to as events in the past:

"In his 1977 study of seventh graders, Jones found that the effect of parental income was negligible."

However, in generalizing from this we would attribute with a present tense verb if the generalization is being treated as having current relevance:

"Based on his research, Jones concludes that the effect of parental income is negligible."

2. Use the past tense with ideas, beliefs, theories, and so on, that are being treated as historical artifacts:

"Sapir and other linguists of his generation believed that the phoneme has psychological reality."

To us academics who have been reading and writing scholarly material for years, all this may seem familiar and obvious. But for many students— even those who are writing well on assignments involving personal experience, analysis, interpretation, and so on—all this is a major challenge. We are asking them to produce a stylistic register that they have had little chance to practice. Usually my students do not do especially well on their first attempt at it in this summarizing assignment. After reading, marking, but *not* grading their papers, I confer with each student and go over the problems. Then I assign a revision. By the time they have finished, they are much more ready to handle their own research material smoothly.

Understanding Words: Meanings Across Disciplines, Meanings Across Time

William Geiger and Ann Farmer,
Whittier College

CLASS 1   We have several objectives in this assignment. We want our students to realize that a relatively small number of words (and corresponding concepts and relationships) govern thinking in all academic disciplines. Next, although these words are frequently used, with the consequence that everyone thinks their meaning is "self-evident," the words differ in their meaning from utterance to utterance and from person to person. If these words are not recognized and carefully defined, the resulting discussion (whether spoken or written) may well issue in vagueness and misunderstanding. *Form* means different things to a Platonist, an Aristotelian, a businessman, a diplomat, a contractor, a swimming coach, an art historian, and an English literature professor or composition teacher. Next, an emphasis on the ambiguity of these seemingly simple words acts as a corrective to the kind of vocabulary building many of our students experienced preparing for the SAT. In addition, this exercise forces students to use standard dictionaries as guides to verbal understanding. Fifth, an awareness that these words have numerous meanings gives students further insight into the arbitrary nature of classification, in which purpose determines meaning. Sixth, if students become sensitive to the highly ambiguous nature of these key words, they will be more likely to try to determine what they and others mean and thus avoid either misunderstanding or fruitless argument. Finally, understanding these words helps turn students from problem makers into responsible problem solvers.

WRITING
ASSIGNMENT 1   In *How to Read a Page*, I. A. Richards presents a list of 103 key words, words that govern and direct all our thinking. Here is Richards's list:

Amount, Argument, Art, Be, Beautiful, Belief, Cause, Certain, Chance, Change, Clear, Common, Comparison, Condition, Connection, Copy, Decision, Degree, Desire, Development, Different, Do, Education, End, Event, Example, Existence, Experience, Fact, Fear, Feeling, Fiction, Force, Form, Free, General, Get, Give, Good, Government, Happy, Have, History, Idea, Important, Interest, Knowledge, Law, Let, Level, Living, Love, Make, Material, Measure, Mind, Motion, Name, Nation, Natural, Necessary, Normal, Number, Observation, Opposite, Order, Organization, Part, Place, Pleasure, Possible, Power, Probable, Property, Purpose, Quality, Question, Reason, Relation, Representative, Respect, Responsible, Right, Same, Say, Science, See, Seem, Sense, Sign, Simple, Society, Sort, Special, Substance, Thing, Thought, True, Use, Way, Wise, Word, Work[1]

Choose *one* of the 103 words in Richards's list and write a two- to three-page essay in which you show several of your chosen word's major meanings in at least three academic disciplines. You may use textbooks from other courses, quotations from various of your professors' lectures, and quotations from books found in your college or university as matrices for your word's various meanings.

Note: This assignment gives you experience in several areas of importance to your continuing education. First, it gives you a chance to perceive the context or situation that gives your word meaning. Second, it gives you a chance to investigate the ambiguity or multiple meanings of an important word. Next, it gives you a chance to conduct research using sources from several fields, thus allowing you to make valuable connections among the several fields you will study in college. Fourth, it gives you an opportunity to see the fundamental utility of classification as an analytic tool in your classes. Finally, it gives you a chance to see the applicability of the concepts of ambiguity and context in fields other than "English."

Our experience with this composition assignment demonstrates that it serves well as an introduction to composing a complex research paper; it functions as a manageable "mini-research paper." This assignment also allows students to see connections among the several courses they take during the freshman year. Students thus gain an increased sense of confidence in their studies and see more clearly the role of language as a tool of thought in all their courses.

CLASS 2   Once students understand that our most common words have the greatest number of meanings, we then consider how meaning in any given passage depends on the time and the place it was written, the author's interest, and his purpose for writing it.

WRITING   Each of you is to work with the word listed beside your name. Each word
ASSIGNMENT 2   is a common word that had a different meaning or meanings in the past than it has now.

---

[1] I.A. Richards, *How to Read a Page* (New York: Norton, 1942), pp. 22–23.

By using an unabridged dictionary and/or the *Oxford English Dictionary* in the reference section of the library, discover three different historical contexts for your word, one of which must use an earlier, no longer common, meaning.

The earliest meanings can be found by looking at the etymology for each word and/or at the definitions that are labeled *Obsolete* or *Archaic*. In some unabridged dictionaries the current definitions are listed in chronological order (the first known meaning first; the second, second; etc.). Spend a little time reading the dictionary front matter so that you know what information you can find in the word entries and where.

After you have found what you are looking for, conclude with a few general statements about the evolution or accretion of the word's meanings.

angel,	*enthusiasm,* n.	*paradise,* n.
arrive, v.	*fond,* adj.	*pretty,* adj.
awful, adj.	*girl,* n.	*queen,* n.
bureau, n.	*halo,* n.	*silly,* adj.
butcher, n.	*horse,* n.	*steward,* n.
car, n.	*humor,* n.	*undertaker,* n.
clown, n.	*lewd,* adj.	*valve,* n.
dear, adj.	*lust,* n.	*villain,* n.
doom, n.	*minister,* n.	*vulgar,* adj.
dope, n.	*nice,* adj.	*wench,* n.
eager, adj.	*noise,* n.	*worm,* n.

Examples:

Idiot is originally from a Greek word meaning "private person." It was later borrowed into English from French and used by English speakers to mean an uneducated or common man as Henry More used it in the Preface to his *Complete Poems* (1647): "It would be safer to ask the judgement of young lads or Countrey idiots . . . than those lubricous wits and overworn Philosophers" (*OED*, Vol. V [H–K], p. 21). It also developed the meaning of a person who is severely deficient mentally as in this quotation from *A Briefe Treatise of Testaments and Last Wills* by Henry Swinburne in 1590: "An Idiote or a naturalle foole is he, who not withstanding he bee of lawfull age, yet he is so witlesse, that hee can not number to twentie, nor can tell what age he is of . . . nor is able to answer to any such easie question" (*OED*, Vol. V [H–K], p. 22). Although it is still used as a label for people with very low IQs, Americans more often hear it used in casual conversation as a label for someone we think has done something stupid: "You idiot, why did you lock the keys in the car?"

When we are reading works written in the seventeenth century or earlier, we need to be aware that the author might very possibly only mean "a common or uneducated person" rather than someone severely mentally retarded or someone who has done something foolish. Therefore we can correctly interpret More to mean that in some circumstances an uneducated man's judgment is more accurate than an educated man's rather than that severely mentally deficient people have more brains than "wits and Philosophers" do.

Diaper entered English from Old French during the Middle English period (1100–1500 A.D.) as the name of a textile fabric, usually linen, woven in a small diamond-shaped pattern, but sometimes used as the name of a richer fabric. Henry Bradshaw refers to the richer fabric in 1513 in *The Life of St. Werburge of Chester:* "The tables were couered with clothes of Dyaper Rychely enlarged with syluer and with golde" [*OED*, Vol. III (D–E), p. 318]. By the 1800s in England, *diaper* was often used to mean the pattern itself and could refer to such a pattern in media other than fabric as in Sir G. Gilbert Scott's *Gleanings from Westminster Abbey* (1861): "The glass . . . is decorated on its face with gold diaper" [*OED*, Vol. III (D–E), p. 318]. In the earlier 1900s in the United States, *diaper* was most often used as the name for rectangles of cotton cloth used on babies. Now cloth diapers have been almost entirely replaced by synthetic disposable diapers that are neither woven nor of natural fibers nor patterned.

If we were unaware of *diaper*'s earlier meanings of patterned cloth or geometrical designs, references to diapers on Communion tables or on walls and windows of castles and cathedrals would only bewilder us.

We give the class handouts consisting of these two examples we have written ourselves, and we point out the use of transitional words *(now, also, although, therefore)* and varying sentence structures (simple to complex) to provide as seamless a sequence of sentences as possible.

LESSON READING

I. A. Richards, "How a Reader Might Improve," in *How to Read a Page* (New York: Norton, 1942), Chapter 1, pp. 17–25.

Scientific Writing and Writing About Scientific Subjects

Gail Goldberg,
Goucher College

I have found that my students often approach with some trepidation a unit devoted to writing a research paper on a natural science topic. Those unfamiliar with the conventions of scientific writing associate the discipline with ponderous terms and indecipherable graphs; those familiar with such conventions have often been trained in a particular paper format that leads to a class's worth of identical lab reports of accounts of findings. To achieve some sort of common ground and to increase understanding of, and familiarity with, various characteristics of writing associated with this discipline, we discuss the distinctions between scientific writing and writing about science.

I bring to class copies of six different accounts of a recent medical study, including the original report in the *New England Journal of Medicine*. Depending on the students' abilities as readers, one might distribute copies of these materials beforehand to the whole class. I find the immediacy of in-class reading to be productive, however, and my students respond well when given the opportunity and responsibility to convey a unique perspective. Therefore as students enter the classroom, I give a copy of each account to each student, and they spend the next few minutes reading. I ask the students to consider the following questions as they apply to the articles read:

What does it say?
For whom is it written?
How do you know?

If everyone has read the journal article, one might begin with calling attention to the abstract or eliciting a summary like the following:

While most cigarette smokers have higher activity levels of lipoprotein lipase (LPL), an enzyme which controls the storage of fat by the body's fat cells, smoking inhibits the action of this enzyme. When smokers stop smoking, their rate of weight gain is proportional to their pre-cessation level of the enzyme. This suggests that LPL plays a role in regulating body weight.

No matter which strategy is used, I expect that some class members will remain unclear about the study after a preliminary explanation. I call first on the student (fortunately a biology major) who has read the original *NEJM* report, and she gives an articulate and thorough explanation of the reported phenomena. She identifies the intended audience as scientists and medical specialists because she recognizes various conventions of form that characterize readings from her science courses; these include standard headings and subheadings to mark sections for easy reading, graphs and tables, and a preliminary abstract, which she reads to us. She also points to characteristic stylistic devices including the frequent use of the passive voice ("data were analyzed," "the enzyme was measured"), the language of hypothesis ("it seems possible," "could be," "may be"), and many technical terms *(adipocyte, triglyceride).*

I note that, unlike members of the scientific community, I tend to consider information from the perspective of someone schooled in the humanities and usually employ a style and format more appropriate to discourse in that discipline. To demonstrate, I give an informal "translation" of the study, which is welcome to several students "lost" during the earlier explanation. I explain that people who smoke are generally thinner than nonsmokers and that most smokers gain weight when they stop smoking. I pause to poll students, to illustrate these generalizations (I ask, for example, "How many of you have ever smoked?" "How many of you have tried to stop smoking?" "How many of you gained weight when you stopped smoking?"). I then draw a Pac-man figure on the chalkboard, and explain that it represents a fat cell. When smoking blocks weight gain, something happens in the fat cell (Pac-man) that makes it "hungry." The level of lipoprotein lipase (LPL), the enzyme that regulates the uptake and storage of fat, increases. More LPL means that more fat can accumulate in these cells. Some smokers already have high LPL levels, whereas others have lower LPL levels; but in each instance, smoking blocks fat accumulation. I draw a muzzle on Pac-man's open jaws, and explain that smoking, in effect, muzzles Pac-man. But when the muzzle (smoking) is removed, the starved cell starts to gobble up fat. Those smokers with high LPL levels will gain a great deal of weight and are usually the ones who go back to smoking.

Although a few of my students who have never smoked are still somewhat detached at this point, attitudes change with the next question. I ask, "How many of you have ever dieted and lost weight, only to find that you eventually stopped losing in spite of continued dieting, and ultimately put some (if not all) of the lost weight back on?" There is almost unanimous confirmation of this situation and deeper engagement now in the topic. Referring back to Pac-man, I point to the fact that the phenomenon of LPL levels when smoking is similar to that which occurs during weight reduction. At some point during dieting, LPL levels increase. Fat cells become "hungrier" and more efficient at absorbing fat. That is why when you diet, at a certain point you don't lose more weight, no matter how hard you try. Your fat cells are working so hard they defeat your intentions, and (sad to say) they usually win.

Someone jokes at this point that English teachers will forever be using analogies, even ones as far-fetched as Pac-man. This precipitates the question that is central to this lesson: What *is* an appropriate style for recording new findings on scientific subjects? Some students reject excessively stylized elements in the reports they've just read. One student criticizes as too melodramatic the *St. Louis Post-Dispatch* account, which centers on a "microscopic villain that may be the culprit behind two sad reasons people fail to lose weight"; the same student finds too colloquial certain expressions (like "go off the weed" and "when folks diet") in the same source. Instance after instance of vagueness, exaggeration, and inappropriate informality surfaces. Through this identification and discussion of excesses in writing, students distinguish a more straightforward style for relaying scientific information.

At one point, we locate statements in two articles (paragraph 4 of the *Hopkins Magazine* and paragraph 6 of the article from *Health*) that cover the same point. We compare style, to identify characteristics that are unique to each, and relate this to the intended audience and purpose for each article. While the *Hopkins Magazine* article is heavily weighted with direct quotation from one co-author, the article from *Health* projects the journalist's voice by means of such devices as the use of first person, frequent rhetorical questions, transitional markers *(now)*, and italics for emphasis. Students identify readers of the first publication as individuals seeking news of the institution and those of the second as individuals interested in self-help advice. The class decides that given the task of informing an educated audience about a new scientific development, neither stylistic strategy would be appropriate.

Suddenly, someone recognizes another example of "slanted" information; the reports in the *Hopkins Magazine* and Baltimore papers "star" the doctor now working at Johns Hopkins, whereas the St. Louis papers feature the researcher based at Washington University. The students wonder who has done most of the work. Which parts of the study should be attributed to each investigator? This gives me the opportunity to explain the significance of order of authorship. In the case of this *NEJM* article, the two researchers should be credited equally. Had there been three or more names, the first and last place would have designated those who should receive the most credit, the primary investigator and the senior member of the team.

Our focus on the lack of objectivity in some examples of scientific journalism gives way to a focus on other matters of content. Students discover errors, for example, in the number of participants reported in the *St. Louis Post-Dispatch*. A comparison of information shared by these reports reveals that most articles did identify the original source in the *NEJM*. With the exception of the *St. Louis Post-Dispatch* account, which placed misleading emphasis on an "anti-fat pill," most sources referred to the important association between elevated LPL levels in smokers and dieters, but made clear that the study promises no immediate impact for those interested in weight loss. We then turn attention to the *Globe Democrat* article, which is detailed, concise, and accurate, and as such comes closest to a report of new findings that the students will soon write. This journalist, however, has relied on direct quotations and information obtained during a press conference instead of on the original report, with a concomitant emphasis on the researcher instead of on the research performed. Students conclude that accuracy, objectivity, and thoroughness are features that ought to be evident both in scientific writing and in writing about science, and yet they recognize that their task will be somewhat unlike both the journalist's and the scientist's.

By the end of class students have suggested, discussed, and agreed on criteria they will follow for a review paper on current investigation in some field of the natural sciences. From their observations and exchanges, the conventions of style, format, and content appropriate to writing about the natural sciences have become more meaningful and more clear-cut. Among these features are the following:

1. a style that is clear, compact, and comprehensible
2. an objective and impersonal tone
3. little or no direct quotation
4. the use of specialized, technical language, with explanation of unfamiliar terms when necessary
5. content that is accurate, complete, and verifiable (can be confirmed in other sources)
6. ample detail (names, dates, statistics)
7. the systematic organization of information, with sections appropriately labeled
8. a graph or table for compact review of information if necessary

At the next class meeting, I distribute the assignment (see below), and we discuss possible topics and procedures. This assignment, a report on changing scientific perspectives toward an object, condition, or phenomenon, does not simply test students' acquaintance with the conventions we've just considered, but provides the opportunity to make decisions and exercise control over a complex body of information. Students discover that beyond shaping the form, style, and substance of their papers, the discussion of scientific writing and writing about the sciences is useful as they make informed choices about research materials, distinguishing between popular journalistic sources (or identifying with more conviction those elements that they recognize as inappropriate in those sources) and more objective, scholarly journals. They might choose case studies on AIDS victims from *Rolling Stone*, for example, but not editorial remarks from that paper, or use an abstract from the *Journal of Clinical Investigation*, but not the extremely technical accounts of methods or results from that publication. This preliminary exercise sharpens their critical ability and their sense of the appropriate in style and audience.

WRITING
ASSIGNMENT

Select a particular natural object, condition, or phenomenon about which there is current interest and on which scientific perspective has changed (let's call that topic X). Your aim is to inform an interested and educated audience about what has led to the most current thinking about X, behavior toward X, or observation of X within one scientific community. You may wish to focus instead on how X itself has changed, rather than on how scientists' perception of X has changed. For example, you might want to select an animal species and consider changing attitudes about animal behavior ("How has scientific thinking about gorilla intelligence changed?") or changing behavior toward an endangered species ("How have scientists' efforts helped to prevent the extinction of the peregrine falcon?"). You might want to examine current medical practice or thought as it relates to a particular illness or therapy. ("What progress has medical science made in the treatment of herpes?")

Your purpose is *not* to get involved in issues, although your topic *may* be controversial. Neither will you focus on competing claims about X or on the personalities who have made them. You will clearly, accurately, and objectively convey to your readers what has led up to the perspective on X today. Beyond defining what X is, you will want to show *how* the treatment of X, the understanding of X, the attitude toward X, or the behavior toward X *has changed*. The time span that you will want to consider will vary, depending on your topic.

Once you've considered several possible topics, use a library search to locate resources, and narrow your choice of topic to one that seems workable. Select a topic about which there is *current* interest and on which a number of articles have been written recently. If you can't think of where to start, pick one branch of learning involving the study of the natural world (biology, chemistry, physics, geology, astronomy, botany, zoology, etc.). Find a journal in that field and flip through a recent issue for ideas.

Be sure to evaluate sources, to select ones that treat your topic responsibly and accurately. Avoid overly stylized or clearly biased reports. As you locate and read recent material on your topic, make sure you select at least a few sources that give background information so that you can explain what changes involving X have taken place. Then organize the information into an appropriate pattern by considering the sorts of questions your readers might have about X. ("What exactly is X?" "When did it first attract our attention?" "What did we think previously about X?" "How has our thinking changed?" "What is the significance of this change?") Paraphrase the information from your original sources before you incorporate it in your paper, and document wherever necessary. In style and form, this report of changing perspectives should conform to the characteristics of writing on scientific subjects which we explored in class. Avoid colloquialism, exaggeration, irony, humor, and excessively figurative language. Use headings and subheadings as necessary, and include tables or graphs if necessary to demonstrate a change that you're reporting.

Some library resources for natural science papers:

Science
Science News
Time
Newsweek
U.S. News and World Report
Harvard Medical School Health Letter
Discover
American Health
Scientific American
Science Digest
Bioscience
Psychology Today
New York Times
Nature
Sports Medicine
New Scientist
National Geographic
Environment
Omni

READINGS

SMOKING ALTERS METABOLISM, RESEARCH AT W.U. SHOWS

Traditionally, smoking has been looked upon as a behavioral problem. Programs designed to help smokers change their evil ways dealt with smoking as a prolonged bad habit that needed to be replaced with a better behavior pattern.

But now researchers at the Washington University Medical School in St.

From *St. Louis Globe-Democrat*, Feb. 3, 1984. Reprinted by permission of Los Angeles Times Syndicate.

Louis have found that smoking alters your metabolism, and that could be what makes it hard to stop.

The researchers theorize that smoking keeps you thin by monkeying with your internal enzymes. Try to quit and your enzyme activity drops. Bango! You've gained weight. The more distorted your metabolism, the harder it may be to give up smoking, the researchers speculate.

So if the theory's true, and you want to quit smoking successfully without gaining weight, it would probably help to rev your metabolism with extra exercise.

Robert M. Carney, Ph.D., and Andrew P. Goldberg, M.D.

WEIGHT GAIN AFTER CESSATION OF CIGARETTE SMOKING
A Possible Role for Adipose-Tissue Lipoprotein Lipase

ABSTRACT   Cigarette smokers weigh less than nonsmokers and gain weight when they stop smoking. Increased activity of lipoprotein lipase in adipose tissues in some smokers may represent a compensatory response to their reduced body weight. Consequently, we hypothesized that the enzyme's activity may be related to the rate at which smokers gain weight when they stop smoking. To test this hypothesis, we measured body weight and fasting lipoprotein lipase activity in adipose tissue in 15 cigarette smokers before they stopped smoking. The changes in body weight during the first two weeks of abstinence were correlated with the base-line lipase activity in these smokers ($r = 0.82$, $P < 0.0002$). This relation remained significant in the 12 subjects who were still abstinent at three weeks ($r = 0.63$, $P < 0.03$).

These results suggest that lipoprotein lipase activity in adipose tissue has a counterregulatory role in the maintenance of body weight and adipose-tissue mass in smokers. The higher the level of lipase activity when the weight-reducing influences of cigarettes cease, the greater the rate at which weight is gained during the first three weeks of abstinence. (N Engl J Med 1984; 310:614–6.)

From the Departments of Psychiatry, Preventive Medicine, and Medicine, and the Lipid Research Center, Washington University School of Medicine, and the Jewish Hospital of St. Louis, St. Louis, Mo. Address reprint requests to Dr. Goldberg at the Gerontology Research Center, Metabolism Section, Baltimore City Hospital, 4940 Eastern Ave., Baltimore, MD 21212.

Supported by a contract (N01 HV2 2916L) and a Clinical Research Center grant (RR 00036) from the National Institutes of Health.

Schwartz and Brunzell have shown that the activity of adipose-tissue lipo-protein lipase, a key enzyme in the regulation of the uptake and storage of triglyceride fatty acid by the adipocyte,[1] is higher in obese white subjects who have lost weight than in weight-stable obese controls.[2] They found that the level of lipoprotein lipase activity in adipose tissue increased in obese white subjects after substantial weight loss but returned to lower levels when the weight was regained.[3] Noting that most of the metabolic indexes that are abnormal in obese subjects return to normal after weight loss, Schwartz and Brunzell interpreted the unexpected rise in lipase activity in obese subjects after weight loss as a "counterregulatory" response to the decrease in body weight.[2-4] Reitman et al.[5] performed similar studies in Pima Indians both before and after weight loss and found that the levels of lipase activity in adipose tissue at both times were lower in this group than in matched whites. They suggested that there may be genetic differences among various types of obesity that determine the level of lipoprotein lipase activity in adipose tissue. Perhaps the increase in such activity in certain obese subjects after weight loss represents a compensatory response by the fat cell to a reduction in its size and reflects an attempt by the body to maintain a predetermined mass of adipose tissue. Such an increase in lipase activity may improve the efficiency of triglyceride storage by the adipocyte and reduce the rate of weight loss, thereby playing a part in the maintenance of a stable body weight.

Cigarette smokers usually weigh less than nonsmokers, and most smokers experience a rapid weight gain when they stop smoking.[6] Brunzell et al. have reported higher fasting levels of lipoprotein lipase activity in adipose tissue in cigarette smokers than in a group of nonsmokers matched for age and sex.[7] Because of an alteration in their energy metabolism or a reduction in their caloric intake, cigarette smokers often maintain a stable weight that is lower than it would be if they did not smoke. Consequently, their elevated levels of lipoprotein lipase activity may be indicative of a metabolic condition that is similar to that reported in subjects who have lost weight. It is possible that the level of lipase activity in adipose tissue while one is smoking may influ-ence the amount of weight that is gained shortly after the "weight-reducing" influences of cigarette smoking cease. This study was designed to test this possibility by measuring the activity of lipoprotein lipase in adipose tissue in otherwise healthy adults before they stopped smoking cigarettes and then documenting at weekly intervals the subsequent changes in their body weight after they stopped smoking.

Methods

SUBJECTS   Eighteen cigarette smokers (13 women and 5 men) ranging in age from 28 to 67 years (mean ± S.D., 44.4 ± 10.5 years) were studied after providing informed consent. All smoked at least 20 cigarettes per day (mean, 28 ± 7 cigarettes; range, 20 to 43) for at least five years (mean, 23 ± 8 years; range, 9 to 35). Their mean relative body weight was 106.2 ± 13.6 per cent of their ideal body weight for height (Metropolitan Life Insurance Tables, 1959), and their body weights ranged from 52 to 105 kg (mean, 65.3 ± 14.5 kg). The 12 male nonsmoking controls ranged in age from 22 to 46 years (mean, 30 ± 8); their mean relative body weight was 107.5 ± 12.3 of ideal body weight, and their body weights ranged from 63 to 95 kg (mean, 77 ± 12 kg). All participants had normal levels of plasma triglyceride and cholesterol.[8] The weights of both groups of subjects had been stable for at least six months before study, and none of the subjects was taking a medication known to affect lipid or glucose metabolism. Fasting plasma glucose levels and thyroid, liver, and renal function were normal in all subjects.

Only 15 of these 18 original subjects (11 women and 4 men) refrained from smoking cigarettes after two weeks in the program. After three weeks, only 12 subjects remained abstinent. The data were analyzed after two and three weeks of smoking cessation in all 15 subjects and then at three weeks for the 12 who remained abstinent.

PROCEDURE   The heparin-releasable form of lipoprotein lipase activity was measured in adipose tissue obtained from the buttock by needle aspiration within four days before subjects stopped smoking, in the morning after a 12-hour fast. The enzyme activity was measured on a glyceryl-1-14C trioleate substrate and expressed as the amount of free fatty acid hydrolyzed per minute.[9,10] Fat-cell size was determined and lipase activity was expressed per cell as well as per gram of adipose tissue.[9] One milliunit of enzyme activity is defined as being equal to 1 neq of free fatty acid hydrolyzed per minute.[9,10] Increasing the sodium chloride concentration to 1 M inhibited lipoprotein lipase activity by 93 ± 3 per cent (n = 15). The intraassay coefficient in variation for lipase activity in tissue taken from two sites on the buttocks of these subjects was 10.5 per cent. The intraassay coefficient of variation (12.2 per cent, n = 5) was determined by measuring the activity of a known postheparin plasma pool (stored at $-70°C$) in each assay.[10]

Subjects consumed their own diets at will throughout the study. None had been acutely ill for at least one month before study, and all remained healthy during the study. The subjects were not told their lipoprotein lipase levels or the experimental hypothesis until the study was completed. All were weighed on the day of the adipose-tissue biopsy and then weekly thereafter.

STATISTICAL METHODS Data were analyzed by means of Student's t-test, univariate linear regression, and step-wise, linear multiple-regression analysis.[11] All data are expressed as means $\pm$ S.D.

Results

The activity of lipoprotein lipase ranged from 1.0 to 10.7 (3.7 ± 2.6) mU per 10^6 fat cells and from 1.2 to 12.4 (7.0 ± 3.6) mU per gram of fat in the 15 smokers. In the nonsmoking controls, levels of lipase activity ranged from 0.5 to 6.8 (2.4 ± 2.0) mU per 10^6 fat cells and 1.4 to 11.1 (4.1 ± 2.7) mU per gram of fat. The relation between the activity of lipase per cell and relative body weight (percentage of ideal body weight) was significant in the nonsmokers (r = 0.64, $P<0.03$, n = 12) but not in the smokers (r = 0.08, P not significant, n = 15). Similar correlation coefficients were found when lipoprotein lipase activity was expressed per gram of fat (r in nonsmokers = 0.58, $P<0.05$; r in smokers = 0.12, P not significant).

After 15 subjects abstained from cigarettes for two weeks, changes in body weight ranged from -1.4 to $+4.1$ kg, whereas after three weeks the range was -0.5 to $+3.2$ kg. At two weeks the correlation coefficient between lipase activity and the change in body weight was r = 0.82 ($P<0.0002$, Fig. 1) when

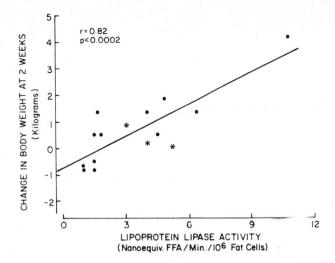

Figure 1. Relation between the Change in Body Weight during the Two Weeks Immediately after Cessation of Smoking and Fasting Levels of Lipoprotein Lipase Activity in Adipose Tissue in the 15 Subjects Who Successfully Stopped Smoking for Two Weeks. Lipoprotein lipase activity is expressed in milliunits of enzyme activity per 10^6 fat cells. One milliunit of enzyme activity is defined as being equal to 1 neq of free fatty acid (FFA) hydrolyzed per minute. The three subjects who resumed smoking by the third week are identified by asterisks rather than closed circles.

activity was expressed as milliunits per 10^6 fat cells, and r = 0.67 (P<0.006) when it was expressed as milliunits per gram of fat. At three weeks correlation coefficients for these relations were no longer significant at r = 0.49 (P not significant, n = 15) for lipase activity per 10^6 fat cells and at r = 0.34 (P not significant) for lipase activity per gram of fat. A step-wise, linear multiple regression, which included the number of cigarettes smoked per day, the number of cigarette pack-years, percentage of ideal body weight, absolute body weight, and fat-cell size as predictor variables, revealed that lipase activity per cell before the cessation of smoking was the best single predictor of weight gain at two weeks (R^2 = 0.69, P<0.0001). No other variable added significantly to the relation; that is, the increase in R^2 was not significant. When all six variables were added to the model, R^2 was increased to 0.84 (P<0.008). Similarly, lipase activity per cell was the best predictor of weight gain at three weeks (R^2 = 0.26, P<0.05), with an R^2 of 0.29 (P<0.05) for all six variables. The univariate correlation coefficients between the smokers' changes in body weight at two and three weeks and the number of cigarettes smoked per day, number of pack-years, percentage of ideal body weight, absolute body weight, and fat-cell size were not significant (Table 1).

The distribution of the data suggested that the subject who gained 4 kg and had the highest enzyme activity per cell might be a statistical outlier. Removing her data from the two-week analysis reduced the magnitude of the correlation coefficient between lipase activity and the change in body weight, but the relation remained significant per cell (r = 0.59, P<0.02, n = 14) and

Table 1. Correlation Coefficients for Possible Predictors of the Change in Body Weight after Cessation of Smoking in 15 Subjects.

POSSIBLE PREDICTOR [*]	CORRELATION COEFFICIENT	
	AT 2 WK	AT 3 WK
LPL activity/10^6 cells	0.82 [†]	0.49
LPL activity/gram of fat	0.67 [‡]	0.34
No. of cigarettes/day	0.36	0.24
No. of pack-years	0.06	0.17
Relative body weight	−0.05	0.01
Body weight (kg)	−0.20	−0.08
Fat-cell size	0.38	0.26

[*] LPL denotes lipoprotein lipase.
[†] P<0.002.
[‡] P<0.006.

per gram of fat (r = 0.56, P<0.04). Removal of the three subjects who resumed smoking cigarettes and reported decreasing their caloric intake at three weeks made the relation between the change in body weight at three weeks and the activity of lipoprotein lipase per cell significant (r = 0.63, P<0.03, n = 12). There were no significant relationships between the changes in these 12 subjects' weights at three weeks and the number of cigarettes smoked per day (r = 0.04), percentage of ideal body weight (r = 0.07), absolute body weight (r = −0.09), number of pack-years (r = −0.001), or fat-cell size (r = 0.25).

Discussion

The results of this study demonstrate that the fasting level of lipoprotein lipase activity in adipose tissue before a subject stops smoking is correlated with the change in body weight that will occur during the first two weeks of abstinence. The amount of weight gained was greatest in the smokers who had the highest baseline levels of lipoprotein lipase activity in adipose tissue. This weight gain was not significantly related to the subjects' base-line relative or absolute body weight, fat-cell size, number of cigarettes smoked per day, or number of cigarette pack-years. A step-wise, linear multiple regression showed that lipase activity per cell before cessation of smoking was the best single predictor of weight gain at two weeks, accounting for 69 per cent of the total variance. An additional 14 per cent of the variance could be accounted for when fat-cell size, relative and absolute body weight, number of pack-years, and number of cigarettes smoked per day were added to the model. The linear relation between the activity of lipoprotein lipase in adipose tissue and the change in body weight at two weeks was lost by the third week, when three of the subjects resumed smoking and altered their diets to prevent their body weight from increasing further. A reanalysis of the data with these subjects excluded revealed that at three weeks the significant relation between the change in body weight and the base-line activity of lipoprotein lipase remained.

There was no attempt to determine whether smoking cessation was associated with a decrease in basal metabolic rate, as suggested by Glauser et al.,[12] or with an increase in appetite, as implied by Burse et al.[13] Regardless of whether the observed changes in weight were mediated by a more efficient conservation of energy or an increase in caloric intake, levels of lipoprotein lipase activity before smoking cessation were significantly predictive of the short-term weight change that was associated with abstinence from cigarettes.

The activity of lipase in adipose tissue was not manipulated directly in this study, and one cannot therefore infer that a causal relation exists between the enzyme's activity and the amount of weight gained after smoking cessation. However, the ability of the adipocyte to assimilate triglyceride and increase its size is primarily regulated by lipoprotein lipase.[1] Thus, it seems quite possible that this predictive relation could be causal, provided of course that the "weight reducing" influences of smoking have ceased and that there is an adequate supply of triglyceride available for uptake by the fat cell.

The data from this study are consistent with a counterregulatory role for lipoprotein lipase in the maintenance of the mass of adipose tissue and hence the body weight of persons who have lost weight. The increase in lipoprotein lipase activity in the fat cells of smokers may be a mechanism that helps their bodies maintain their mass of adipose tissue. Circulating triglyceride would therefore be shunted preferentially to the adipocyte to maintain its size. Although we do not know the mechanism or mechanisms regulating lipoprotein lipase under these conditions, we do know that persons with elevated levels of enzyme experience a rapid increase in body weight when the weight-reducing influences of cigarette smoking are stopped. Thus, the measurement of lipoprotein lipase activity may be useful clinically in predicting a smoker's potential for weight gain upon quitting smoking.

We are indebted to John Grundhauser for statistical assistance, to Philip Cryer and his staff for the use of the Clinical Research Center, to Richard Florman and John Crain for technical assistance, to Edwin Fisher for referring the subjects, and to Phyllis Anderson for assistance in the preparation of the manuscript.

References

1. Robinson D. The function of the plasma triglyceride in fatty acid transport. In: Florkin M., Stotz EM, eds. Comprehensive biochemistry. Amsterdam: Elsevier, 1970:51-116.
2. Schwartz RS, Brunzell JD. Increased adipose-tissue lipoprotein-lipase activity in moderately obese men after weight reduction. Lancet 1978; 1:1230-1.
3. Idem. Increase of adipose tissue lipoprotein lipase activity with weight loss. J Clin Invest 1981; 67:1425-30.
4. Brunzell JD. Endocrine disorders and adipose tissue lipoprotein lipase. In: Hessel LW, Krans HMJ eds. Lipoprotein metabolism and endocrine regulation. Amsterdam: Elsevier/North-Holland, 1979:27-34.
5. Reitman JS, Kosmakos FC, Howard BV, Taskinen M-R, Kuusi T, Nikkila EA. Characterization of lipase activities in obese Pima Indians: decreases with weight reduction. J Clin Invest 1982; 70:791-7.
6. Comstock GW, Stone RW. Changes in body weight and subcutaneous fatness related to smoking habits. Arch Environ Health 1972; 24:271-6.
7. Brunzell JD, Goldberg AP, Schwartz RS. Cigarette smoking and adipose tissue lipoprotein lipase. Int J Obesity 1980: 4:101-3.
8. Manual of laboratory operations: Lipid Research Clinics Program. Vol. 1. Lipid and lipoprotein analysis. Bethesda, Md.: National Institutes of Health, 1974. (DHEW publication no. (NIH)75-628).
9. Pykälistö O, Smith PH, Brunzell JD. Human adipose tissue lipoprotein lipase: comparison of assay methods and expressions of activity. Proc Soc Exp Biol Med 1975; 148:297-300.

10. Goldberg A, Sherrard DJ, Brunzell JD. Adipose tissue lipoprotein lipase in chronic hemodialysis: role in plasma triglyceride metabolism. J Clin Endocrinol Metab 1978; 47:1173-82.
11. Snedecor GW, Cochran WG. Statistical methods. 6th ed. Ames, Iowa: Iowa State University Press, 1967.
12. Glauser SC, Glauser EM, Reidenberg MM, Rusy BF, Tallarida RJ. Metabolic changes associated with the cessation of cigarette smoking. Arch Environ Health 1970; 20:377-81.
13. Burse RL, Bynum GD, Pandolf KB, Goldman RF, Sims EAH, Danforth ER. Increased appetite and unchanged metabolism upon cessation of smoking with diet held constant. Physiologist 1975; 18:157, abstract.

Roger Signor

ENZYME THAT FOILS DIETERS RAISES HOPE FOR ANTI-FAT PILL

Dreams of developing an "anti-fat" pill have moved a step closer to reality because of basic research at Jewish Hospital.

Scientists there have put their fingers on a microscopic villain that may be the culprit behind two sad reasons people fail to lose weight:

In one situation, smokers go off the weed and promptly gain weight; in the other, nonsmokers go on rigorous diets but fail to lose their extra pounds.

The study at Jewish Hospital shows that their failures may be the result of a tiny culprit called an enzyme—not because they are "fudging" on their diets.

In a study of 27 smokers, Jewish Hospital scientists found that the enzyme—a type of protein that speeds up or slows down processes within cells—becomes hyperactive inside fatty tissue cells after a person kicks the smoking habit.

The little villain fingered by scientists here has a very long alias: "adipose-tissue lipoprotein lipase." Adipose is a nice way of saying fat.

Robert M. Carney, director of behavioral medicine at Jewish Hospital, has been on the trail of this enzyme's cruel work for several years. His latest exposé of the culprit appears in today's issue of the New England Journal of Medicine.

What Carney and his colleagues have shown in their studies of smokers who quit is that when they stop puffing, the villainous enzyme starts working against natural factors that result in "shrinking" of their fat cells.

In previous studies, Carney and others found that these fat cells get smaller when people smoke regularly. They also shrink when folks diet.

"But what we've found now is that the activity of the enzyme increases" after the smokers quit, Carney said in an interview.

This increased activity of the enzyme is what "seems to counteract" the natural reduction in size of fat cells, he said.

From *St. Louis Post-Dispatch*, March 8, 1984.

"This may explain why, under certain conditions, people fail to lose weight when they stop smoking—or fail when they try to diet," he said.

Development of an "anti-fat" pill to counteract the enzyme-villain's role may be years away, he said.

"We don't yet have the means of manipulating the enzyme," he said. "No one's yet synthesized the enzyme in the laboratory—so we can't add more of it, or take it away (in tests)," he said.

Some drugs do act to interfere with the enzyme's activity, he said. But the severe side-effects of these drugs prohibit their use, he said.

EX-SMOKER'S WEIGHT GAIN

Doctor Suspects That Enzyme Makes Body Keep Storing Fat

Why do some people gain weight after they stop smoking?

A St. Louis study suggests that the reason may be the activity of an enzyme that helped them maintain weight while smoking but which continues encouraging their bodies to store fat after they quit smoking.

Dr. Robert M. Carney and Dr. Andrew P. Goldberg tested 15 adult volunteers for the enzyme, lipoprotein lipase, just before the subjects stopped smoking cigarettes.

Those with the highest levels of the enzyme tended to gain the most weight during the three weeks after they stopped smoking, Carney said at a press conference Wednesday at Jewish Hospital.

The study was conducted at Jewish Hospital, where Carney is the director of behavioral medicine. The correlation between lipase activity and weight gain during the first two weeks after the subjects stopped smoking was .82, far above the level considered significant. A perfect correlation is 1.0.

He said the experiment "suggests" that the lipase was the cause of the weight gain, and that doctors can accurately predict which smokers are most likely to fatten up when they quit.

Unfortunately, there is no known way to regulate the amount of lipase in the body except to use drugs with serious side effects. Carney said, however, that he hopes there might be some interest in finding a safe way to reduce lipase.

In any case, smokers who are reluctant to quit because they fear that their weight will zoom could—by means of the lipase measuring procedure the two doctors used—be encouraged to give up smoking, Carney said.

The study suggests that people whose bodies do not produce the enzyme to counteract the weight reduction associated with smoking could stop smoking without worrying about a big weight gain afterward.

Some of the people in the study lost weight after giving up smoking, he said.

The results of the study were reported in the March 8 issue of the New

From *St. Louis Globe-Democrat*, March 8, 1984. Reprinted by permission of the *St. Louis Globe-Democrat*.

England Journal of Medicine. Goldberg currently is at Johns Hopkins Medical Center.

Carney said that people who smoke generally weigh less than non-smokers, perhaps because of an alteration in their energy metabolism or a reduction in their intake of calories.

STUDY SUGGESTS YOUR FAT CELLS DETERMINE YOUR WEIGHT

Cigarette smokers usually weigh less than nonsmokers, and many smokers quickly gain weight when they stop. In a *New England Journal of Medicine* article, Andrew Goldberg (and co-author Robert Carney of Washington University) reported that smokers with high levels of the enzyme lipoprotein lipase in their fat tissue were the ones who gained the most weight.

But the smokers were simply one population under a "weight-reducing influence"—smoking—that could easily be removed, says Goldberg, an associate professor at the medical school who works in the Gerontological Research Center at Key Medical Center (formerly Baltimore City Hospitals). For high levels of lipoprotein lipase also occur in people who lost weight for other reasons.

The increased enzyme activity is a sign, Goldberg thinks, that "there is not enough fat in the fat cell." It may be part of a counterregulatory response when the person is too thin.

One function of lipoprotein lipase is breaking down triglyceride, a fatty acid, so it can be absorbed by your fat cells. Therefore high lipoprotein lipase levels, Goldberg argues, suggest that your fat cells are working harder to maintain their size. He doesn't know the mechanism by which lipoprotein lipase levels are increased, but thinks the enzyme may be produced by the fat cells themselves. Or the fat cells may signal the brain which in turn signals the pancreas. In any case, in raising the enzyme level, your fat cells are reacting to a deprived state, "in terms of what your fat cells want to be." One implication: The former smoker isn't getting fat, but returning to normal; the smoker was too thin.

"The message in whole," says Goldberg, "is that here's an enzyme that appears to be related to weight gain and weight loss." If size of fat cells is controlled by a regulatory mechanism, then each individual body may have a stable setpoint for weight. That's a biological argument for why some people are bigger than others. And it's an argument that may "allow fat people to identify why they are fat"—and so abandon guilt.

His findings may also have a clinical application, as they argue against being leaner than you should be. Very lean people have a higher than normal mortality rate, Goldberg notes. Maybe that's because their bodies work too hard to compensate for the fat that's not there. Smokers and dieters may put themselves in the same boat, according to their bodies—too thin.

From *Johns Hopkins Magazine*, August 1984. Reprinted by permission.

Barbara M. Ribakove

SMOKER'S CHOICE

To Quit May Mean Putting on Pounds
Here's Why It Happens

The one side effect of smoking doctors don't talk about is this: Smoking helps keep weight down. They don't talk about it because nobody wants you to get the idea that if you want to take weight off, you should buy a carton of cigarettes. So let us say right at the outset that smoking would be a *terrible* means of weight control. Cigarettes put you at risk for coronary heart disease, lung cancer and other major diseases that hurt you a lot more than a few extra pounds—which you can take off anyway. Some smokers become severely *under*weight, which is just as bad as being severely overweight. And when a smoker finally realizes all this and quits, she may put a lot of weight on in a hurry—virtually all of it in the form of fat.

It's that last point that we want to talk about. Andrew P. Goldberg, MD, associate professor of medicine at Johns Hopkins University School of Medicine in Baltimore, and his colleague Robert M. Carney, PhD, spent a year and a half at Washington University School of Medicine in St. Louis studying what happens to the fat cells of people who quit smoking—and they think they can now predict which people will gain the most weight when they break the nicotine habit. They do this by seeing how active a particular enzyme is in people's bodies *before* they give up cigarettes.

The enzyme in question is called *lipoprotein lipase,* and its job is to get hold of fat that's floating around in your blood and store it in fat cells, or *adipocytes.* Nothing else will do the job; if you want to put fat in a fat cell, you call out the lipoprotein lipase or forget it. When fat cells get that lean and hungry feeling (and don't forget, a healthy body requires a certain proportion of fat), lipoprotein lipase goes to work to feed them.

Now, by various biochemical means we don't fully understand, smoking makes lipoprotein lipase less efficient than it ought to be. It gets out there in the blood vessels seeking fat, but it does a poor job of capturing it and storing it. The fat cells keep demanding more and the lipoprotein lipase keeps trying harder, but though its level of activity is high, its level of productivity is low. In a lean smoker, this situation may exist much of the time.

The researchers decided to see what happens to all this activity when cigarettes are taken away. They studied 18 cigarette smokers—13 women and five men—each of whom had smoked at least a pack a day for at least five years, and each of whom now wanted to quit. The subjects ranged in age from 28 to 67 years, and in weight from about 115 to about 230 pounds; all of them had normal cholesterol and triglyceride levels. Four days before they were due to quit smoking the researchers took a small sample of fat from their buttocks with a needle to measure the activity of the lipoprotein lipase in it. The investigators also took careful histories of the subjects' eating habits, but didn't ask them to make any changes. Three of the would-be nonsmokers dropped out of the study after two weeks because they started smoking again, but the other 15 were in the study long enough to produce results.

What the researchers found was that people who had the highest levels of lipoprotein lipase activity before they quit smoking were the ones who gained the most weight after they quit—even if they barely changed their calorie intake, Apparently, stopping smoking allows the enzyme to do its job with full efficiency—and since those fat cells are still begging for food, it goes right on working overtime to feed them. Obviously, these people arc going to gain weight quickly. This relationship between lipoprotein lipase activity and weight gain is so strong that it doesn't matter how much the people weighed before, how much they smoked or even whether they started eating more after they gave up tobacco; what matters is how busy that enzyme is.

Now, this information is fascinating to a scientist for what it reveals about the way our bodies work and the high priority our systems give to maintaining a certain amount of fatty tissue, but does it have practical application? It may. It's conceivable that in the not-so-distant future a person who wants to quit smoking but is scared of gaining weight could get a lipoprotein lipase test that would either reassure her that she's not likely to gain much or would be used to determine the diet and exercise regimen she needs to compensate for her high enzyme activity during the weeks and months of withdrawal. Better still, science may find ways to manipulate lipoprotein lipase safely and effectively for the benefit of people who want to control their weight whether or not they have ever smoked at all.

Spoken Words and Writing: Review of a Lecture

Marie McAllister,
Princeton University

One pattern emerges through the complaints and praise whenever I ask the students in my composition classes to describe the writing they've done in the past. Although some students mention journals or chemistry papers, most seem to believe that, as an English teacher, I am really fishing for a list of books that they were told to read and respond to in previous classes. The assignments these students go on to describe are varied and often innovative, but they all center on a reading. Not only high school survey classes and college literature courses restrict writing this way; recently, a composition instructor from a nearby prestigious university tried to explain to me why their students are not allowed to write except in response to some written text.

Nearly every instructor agrees that students should be able to read and respond to the written word, whether those words come in the form of a poem, a news story, or a job description. Still, students need composition skills besides those involved in responding to written language. Much of my time, even as an academic, is spent in responding not to what I read, but to what I hear. Whatever their future occupations, my students too are likely to spend a greater share of their lives listening than reading. Frequently they will need to respond in writing to information or instructions given orally. The analysis, logic, and argumentation that I try to link with basic writing skills must carry over into all aspects of my students' lives, whether they are writing up a proposal after a staff meeting or simply taking coherent notes in their other classes.

As one means of ensuring that my students practice responding to what they hear as well as to what they read, midway through the semester I have them write a review of a public speaker. This assignment takes little preparation on my part other than a look at the calendar of upcoming campus speakers. It works best, though, if students have already worked on analyzing an argument, detecting fallacies or misuses of language, and writing persuasively.

In preparation for our class meeting, students read several widely differing reviews of one movie. I ask them to notice audience, focus, structure, and each reviewer's strategies as they read; I want them to begin thinking about the potential of the review form. In class we work our way from a discussion of the individual reviews to a discussion of the purposes of reviewing: consumer guide, establisher of tastes, cultural artifact, literature. This part of the class may lead to heated argument: My students always agree on the practical value of having some form of review but are often indignant at negative reviews and claim that reviewers are unfairly harsh or picky in order to have more to say. A discussion of audience here helps them see that what they think of as dull detail may be of great interest to readers more knowledgeable about camera technique or cinematic history. Such discussion also alerts them to problems they will face when they write their own reviews of a speaker.

I then turn the class to a discussion of the criteria for evaluating a public speaker. Even the many students who have never attended a public talk have watched televised speeches and taken lecture classes, and they have no trouble coming up with ideas. My students' suggestions usually take off from vaguely recollected debate team principles, and from there it is easy to bring in criteria that also apply to a good essay. A few minutes with chalk and eraser result in a list that students can carry to the lecture. Criteria from my classes fall into a few large categories: delivery (eye contact, clear and audible speaking, gestures, props, "how excited it gets you"); audience (does the level of the talk match that of the listeners?); type of talk and whether the talk meets its goals (persuasive talks must persuade, humorous talks make people laugh); organization and focus and logic; and general observations.

Toward the end of the session we spend a few minutes talking about how to turn good analysis—listening, thinking, comparing, judging—into an interesting review. Students easily recognize that movie reviews have certain formal conventions, including rating the film in some way and touching on various aspects of the film-making process, sometimes with reference to movie history or a director's previous films. We have fewer models and fewer conventions for reviews of lectures, but students are quick to agree that papers about eye contact bore everyone, whereas reviews that respond to a speaker's argument catch a reader's interest. A reminder that a review must be specific and state a thesis makes students still more aware that a simple list of good and bad points is not a review, and recalls the connection between responding to writing and responding to speech.

As the class winds up, I return once more to the purpose of a review. In the course of discussion, those students who thought reviews should do nothing but describe plot and assign the movie a number usually become more flexible. Since there is no point in telling Tuesday's readers to go hear Monday's speaker, lecture reviews find an audience only when they are interesting and well written and make a critical judgment. Students also see how a review might not only warn a reader of what to expect, but also help him or her understand or enjoy an event, or consider an issue.

WRITING
ASSIGNMENT

On this note, I ask my students to choose one of several upcoming public lectures, and hand out a list of recommendations, to give them some choice of topic and time. I've found that nearly any topic can produce good reviews, although highly specialized academic talks should be avoided. The student who protests that he or she can't go to any of the choices can visit an upper-level lecture course or evaluate a sermon, although the next discussion will be better if students have been to the same talks. Students attend the lecture, decide on an angle and thesis, eliminate unnecessary material, and write a good review of the talk they heard.

Even the students who hear what turn out to be tiresome talks always come to the next class eager to share their opinions. Indeed, students who sat through bad speakers or evasive question periods often write the most exciting reviews—and no longer feel that detailed criticism is out of place in a review. All the papers have a refreshing vitality, as if listening to spoken words had inspired students to respond in their own voices. Perhaps because we all have so much practice listening to spoken words, students prove wonderfully adept at analyzing a speaker's strengths and weaknesses, and this assignment makes them realize that they can translate these skills into writing.

FOR FURTHER READING

Five reviews of the movie *Amadeus:*
Richard Corliss, "Mozart's Greatest Hit," *Time*, Sept. 10, 1984.
Robert Craft, "B-Flat Movie," *New York Review of Books*, Apr. 11, 1985.
Pauline Kael, "Mozart and Bizet," *The New Yorker*, Oct. 29, 1984.
John Simon, "Bizet's *Carmen*, Shaffer's *Amadeus*," *The National Review*,
    Oct. 19, 1984.
Michael Walsh, "Amadeus, Shamadeus," *Film Comment*, Oct. 1984.

Popular Music: The Meaning Behind That Melody

Stuart Lee Brown,
Princeton University

One of the most enjoyable and productive units I do with my composition classes covers the major areas of popular culture, with a particular emphasis on pop songs (usually two full class meetings). The lesson on popular music can easily be used as a discrete unit in itself, for it concentrates on a crucial aspect of composition courses: the student's analytical ability.

About a week before the music sessions, I bring up the subject of popular songs and define this category as including all forms of contemporary song-writing—classic rock and roll, current rock, disco, punk, new wave, "synthepop," spiritual pop, country, and so on. I tell the students that each of them will be responsible for giving an in-class presentation on one of his/her favorite songs. This idea invariably excites the class because it involves not some "distanced" literary text, but rather an object of immediate and personal interest that has been most often reserved for casual, nonacademic discussion. (Most of the following instructions for the music sessions could readily be adapted for a handout to save time during this earlier, preparatory class meeting.)

I then inform my students that they must tell me their chosen songs in the class meeting just before the music sessions so that we avoid any duplication of choices. In addition, for the actual class presentations everyone is asked to make photocopies of the lyrics and to bring in a taped (cassette) recording of the song; I volunteer to provide the tape player to be used for all of the song reports. Depending on the length of an individual song and the degree of the class's familiarity with it, either it will be played in its entirety or, more likely, some representative, precued snippet will be presented just before the student's report. I suggest that the students should keep the taped excerpts brief—no more than one or two minutes.

I tell them that over the next week they should make an intense analysis of their songs, jotting down in their notes all of their observations, no matter how unrelated they may seem. They should not only spell out for themselves what the words say on the surface, but they must also tease out of the lyrics and musical style any further meanings and implications. To clarify what they can look for, I give them the following questions to ask themselves (the instructor should feel free to modify these questions if they do not suit his/her interests):

- Can the lyrics be treated as a self-contained poem with musical accompaniment? As such, can I base my interpretation on this poem's imagery, symbolism, figurative language, tone, etc.? Does the music itself complement this analysis in any way?
- What is the psychological make-up of the song's persona, that is, if a person is implied at all? How does this affect my interpretation? (A persona here would be the personality or character behind the song who is speaking the actual lyrics, often to an implied other person.)
- How do the song's "hooks" function? (These are the recurrent catchy phrases and sounds—verbal and/or musical—that stick in your memory and onto which your recall of the song as a whole is "hooked.")
- If I've seen a music video for this song, how were its visual style and content related to the song's musical style and lyric-content? Did the video make explicit the lyrics' story, or did it add a new dimension? Did I really need the video to appreciate the song? If so, what does this imply about the current state of popular music?
- How successful is/was this song, especially on the various *Billboard* charts? For what kind of an audience was the song written? How is this reflected in its airplay and chart status (i.e., airplay on white stations versus black stations, hard rock stations versus mainstream white "pop," status on club play/black singles charts versus hot 100)?
- What is this song's place in the context of other major works by this performer/group? Is some specific style or way of thinking developed within this creative output? [Students are usually encouraged to pursue this idea only if the performer(s) wrote the material.]
- Does the song have a goal? In other words, is it trying to do something to me, the listener? What is its message or moral, if any? If there is a message, does the music itself suit it? Does the individual performance contribute effectively to the song's goal?
- How are male sexuality and female sexuality portrayed? Does the song draw on (or subvert, for that matter) any stereotypes?
- What was the historical/social/political milieu within which the song was conceived? What commentary or criticism does the song make on this context? Does the song act as a cultural artifact, revealing and defining the society that produced it?

I never expect my students to answer fully for themselves all of these questions, but for those who are not quite sure of what to think about for their analyses these ideas provide a number of provocative possible directions.

In conjunction with these questions, I assign two types of readings: a critical/analytical (i.e., "academic") work and the latest issues of two popular music magazines. I usually have my students skim through the magazines, giving the most attention to the articles that examine styles and trends; I have them study the different charts provided in each magazine and also look at the album reviews, since they often have critiques of specific songs. As for the more academic reading, I provide them with excerpts from a single, rather recently published book.[1] Although the work's primary concern is British music, the assigned selections are quite helpful in terms of American music and popular music in general. (I still consider the readings as supplementary rather than essential to this unit; it is really the individual student's own special knowledge that contributes the most to the analysis.)

At the end of our last class before the music unit, I present to the students my own pop song report (which follows the lesson). Not only does this break the ice, but it also gives them an immediate model to use for comparison when they are putting together their own presentations.

For the actual in-class oral reports, each student should focus on one aspect of his or her extensive analysis that can be presented coherently in three to five minutes. Before we begin the reports at our first music meeting, I encourage the students to write down in their notes any questions or comments that might come to mind during the presentations; after each report I allow a few minutes for discussion of these audience responses. Depending on the size of the class, the reports can be completed within two meetings at most. When the last report has been given, we engage in a more general discussion of any musical trends that we have discovered in the songs presented and in the assigned readings.

WRITING ASSIGNMENT   A written assignment is due a week after the oral reports are completed. I ask my students to take one of two approaches to the assignment: They can use the material that they just presented and the feedback from the class in a more thoroughly detailed analysis of the song; or they can take from their original notes the observations and insights that had to be omitted from the oral report and organize them into a cogent interpretative essay. The paper's length is set at two to five pages.

From my experience, these papers are unusually well polished and tightly constructed, probably because of the several stages of development they pass through (i.e., "brainstorming" analytic notes, preparation for oral report, presentation and responses, and the usual outlining for the essay). Furthermore, because of the personal nature of the project, the papers have

---

[1] Iain Chambers, *Urban Rhythms: Pop Music and Popular Culture* (London: Macmillan, 1985).

about them a special energy and enthusiasm uncharacteristic of most analytical college essays.

FOR FURTHER READING

The most current issues of *Billboard* and *Rolling Stone* magazines.

READING

Stuart Lee Brown

POP SONG REPORT

The Pointer Sisters: Neutron Dance

I don't want to take it anymore
I'll just stay here locked behind the door
Just no time to stop and get away
'Cause I work so hard to make it everyday

Whoo oooh
Whoo oooh

There's no money falling from the sky
'Cause a man took my heart and robbed me blind
Someone stole my brand new Chevrolet
And the rent is due, I got no place to stay

Whoo oooh [plaintive] Whoo oooh
Whoo oooh [plaintive] Whoo oooh

Chorus:
And it's hard to say
Just how some things never change
And it's hard to find
Any strength to draw the line
I'm just burning doin' the neutron dance
I'm just burning doin' the neutron dance

Industry don't pay a price that's fair
All the common people breathing filthy air

(Lord, have mercy!)
Roof caved in on all the simple dreams
And to get ahead your heart starts pumping schemes

Chorus:
Whoo oooh, whoo oooh
I'm on fire, yeah
Well, I'm on fire, yeah

Chorus:
I know there's a pot of gold for me
All I got to do is just believe
Oh, I'm so happy doin' the neutron dance
And I'm just burning doin' the neutron dance
[these last two lines are repeated over and over
alternating and overlapping with the next four]

It's in my hands
It's in my feet
It's all over me
I can't help myself

Yeah, yeah, oh, yeah
I'm just burning . . . etc.

Allee Willis, Danny Sembello

With "Neutron Dance," the Pointer Sisters reached the peak of their long line of pop music hits released from the *Break Out* album during 1983 and 1984—hit singles including "Jump (For My Love)," "Automatic," "I'm So Excited," and "I Need You." It achieved a wider kind of popularity than the other songs, beyond its strong "Top Ten" Billboard Chart status, because of its prominent presence in that year's smash hit movie *Beverly Hills Cop*, starring Eddie Murphy. The song plays toward the beginning of the film during a hectic chase scene that wreaks inestimable damage across an equally hectic city; certainly, its furiously paced, agitated beat proved to be a perfectly suited and memorable accompaniment to this wild fast-action sequence. In addition, "Neutron Dance"—besides being a "big" movie song and a top of the chart success—was also a major dance hit, played constantly on dance music stations ("black stations") and in all types of dance clubs. In other words, during its reign of popularity, one could hardly help but hear it no matter what popular culture context one entered—whether listening to the radio (either "white"/Top Forty or "black" stations), going to the cinema, or dancing the night away in a favorite club or discotheque. Even now, in 1986, long after it finally fell off the charts, this song has clout as a "classic" on radio stations, still getting a fair share of airplay as an "oldie."

As with so many extremely popular songs, its lyrics have gone by relatively unnoticed, or at least they have not been seriously considered by most listeners. As mentioned before, "Neutron Dance" has an unusually fast, almost manic rhythm and beat; in fact, anyone who has danced to this song knows that it whips you along at a breakneck speed and leaves you thoroughly exhausted at its conclusion. It seems fitting, then, that its lyrics actually speak not of romantic or sexual love, as do most of the Pointer Sisters' songs, but of a modern-day, urban world gone crazy with its dizzying pace of living.

The first stanza describes the singer/persona's state of mind. Harried by the wild rush of city living, she decides to stay locked inside the safety of her home; there is no opportunity to escape from it all other than this one, since working full time, just to break even, takes up all of her life. The nervous, throbbing beat underscores the sense of anxiety and complements the persona's nearly paranoid attitude.

After a catchy phrase or "hook" (the "whoo oooh" sung by the three sisters), the second set of lyrics addresses various levels of personal crisis. The woman's money is gone, stolen by her dishonest lover, her new car has likewise been taken by car thieves, and she faces eviction since she can no longer afford the rent. In just a few lines, every possibility of hope and personal happiness is "deconstructed" before our eyes: economic security, romantic love, the American Dream of working class success (the "brand new Chevrolet"), and even the safe retreat of one's own home offered in the first stanza.

The interjection of "whoo oooh" is now embellished with a doleful echo, just before the sisters begin the actual chorus (this chorus repeats twice during the song). The chorus first observes how things seem to remain inexplicably at their worst and how one is rarely strong enough to keep up the barrier ("to draw the line") between one's own sanity and the insanity of the world outside. The second part of the chorus is probably the most frequently reiterated line in the song; it is the only so-called escape available to the persona: "I'm just burning, doin' the neutron dance."

The last whole stanza moves the commentary away from the individual, common person's life to the general public. The men of "industry" are getting away with murder, leaving "all the common people breathing filthy air (Lord, have mercy!)"; brutal reality (the crumbling of "roof caved in") comes crashing down on the "simple dreams" of poor people; and finally, in order to succeed in the world of the work force, one must be dehumanized, reduced to the back-stabbing, dot-eat-dog ethic ("start pumping schemes"). After the chorus comes back twice during some transitional music, a couplet closes off the main body of lyrics ringing with a peculiar irony: "I know there's a pot of gold for me/All I got to do is just believe." Of course, believing in this illusory "pot of gold" is the source of the persona's current problems.

A frenetic coda is provided by a number of alternating and overlapping lines that, I believe, ultimately suggest the real meaning of the song's title, one that is no longer an "escape" from reality: ". . . I'm just burning, doin' the neutron dance/It's in my hands/ . . . my feet/ . . . all over me/I can't help myself." The greatest insanity of this contemporary world gone mad can be nothing less than the constant threat of a nuclear holocaust, and there is no more inhuman or absurd product of this nuclear threat than the neutron bomb—a weapon that destroys only living beings, leaving inanimate material properties intact. This darker meaning of "neutron dance" changes the effect of the song entirely, for this dance is not some healthy form of escapism (i.e., dance your cares away), but a desperate self-abandonment, a hysterical dance of death, a *danse macabre*.

Correcting Grammatical Errors Beyond the Composition Course

Michael West,
University of Pittsburgh

Any English teacher knows the hopelessness of trying to improve student writing solely in composition courses if other courses do not also demand good writing. Too often they don't. In recent years many institutions have launched so-called writing-across-the-curriculum programs to address this problem. But not enough has been done to help faculty in other disciplines share the burden of enforcing reasonable standards for writing.

Commonly, such programs are aimed at students who have passed required freshman composition, where they supposedly mastered the mechanical principles of correct writing, if not the art of good writing. But any teacher of upper-level courses will testify how fragile, evanescent, and elusive even the debased ideal of mechanical correctness proves. What is one to do? Find out what handbook the students already own and refer them to that for an explanation of their mistakes? Then one may be working with several different handbooks in one class. Require students in your class to buy yet another handbook? However pleasing to publishers, such merry pluralism confuses students. Research suggests that they all too often fail to consult the handbooks to which they are referred out of class. Moreover, handbooks are increasingly expensive. Even the shortest now take a noticeable chunk out of one's textbook budget, which the historian, psychologist, or teacher of English literature would really prefer to devote to texts in his specialty.

With the spread of tutorial centers for writing, there is a better way. In my literature courses fulfilling writing-across-the-curriculum requirements I now dispense with handbooks altogether. When I hand back papers at the end of a class, I've noticed that students scrutinize their comments and grades in the hallway with a curiosity and emotional energy that will probably have dissipated before they return to their dorms and their faithful, ineffectual handbooks. So I have composed the world's briefest handbook, which I attach to all corrected papers for immediate reference. Reproduced here, it can nevertheless fit neatly on two sides of one 8 × 11 sheet of paper when typed in elite and dittographed:

Common Grammatical Errors, and a Few Venial Solecisms[1]

The circled word is misspelled. See dictionary and don't repeat mistake; proof-read.

Subject does not *agree* with verb in number. Sentences of that kind **is** undesirable. You might even say that that kind of sentences **are** undesirable.

The harsh cry of the awk-bird fluttering through the Amazonian jungle of your prose. I'm too lazy to explain just what's *awkward,* so the problem you figure out.

You have awkwardly repeated the same word or phrase at close quarters, this *awkward repetition* making your vocabulary appear more impoverished than it is.

You've either omitted the necessary *apostrophe* or misused one. "The slave's rebellion" differs importantly from "the slaves' rebellion." We have "woman's Lib" and "women's Lib," but not "womens' Lib." Plurals and polysyllables ending in *s* form the possessive just by adding an apostrophe, thus: "States' rights," "a mistress' appeal." But monosyllables ending in *s* add *'s,* thus: "the boss's power." Don't forget mine!

Capitalize the triply underlined letter properly, or do *not Capitalize* it.

Some sort of *comma fault,* so insert needed comma at caret. Most fall in three classes:

1. Set off introductory adverbial clauses with a comma, thus:
   If you write this sentence without a comma, you will be wrong. RIGHT!
   BUT N.B.: Whoever writes this sentence without a comma is certainly right. WHY?
   ALSO N.B.: In writing this sentence without a comma you will probably be safe. WHY?

2. Punctuate compound sentences with a comma like this, and you will seldom err.
   N.B.: Compound predicates differ from compound sentences and like this may need no comma.
   WRONG: Commas alone can join two sentences, they're strong little devils.
   To join them use a semicolon or a coordinating conjunction, thus:
   RIGHT: Commas alone can't join two sentences; they aren't strong enough.
   RIGHT: Commas alone can't join two sentences, for they aren't strong enough.
   Common coordinating conjunctions are *and, but, or, nor, while, as, so, for.*
   BUT N.B.: *However, moreover, alternatively, besides, therefore, thus, ac-*

---

[1] Copyright © Michael West. Reprinted by permission.

cordingly, indeed, etc. are not conjunctions but adverbs, which need semicolons to link sentences.

p;   WRONG: Commas are useful things, they can join sentences together just like this.

RIGHT: Commas are useful things, but they can't join sentences sans conjunctions.

p;   WRONG: Commas are useful things, indeed they can stitch sentences together.

RIGHT: Commas are useful things; however, sometimes you need a semi-colon.

3. Sharply parenthetic expressions, like this one that I'm writing now, may need commas.

  BUT: Weakly parenthetic expressions like this one need no commas.

  N.B.: How does enclosing "like this one" in prior sentence with commas alter its meaning?

c   Nonrestrictive clauses, participial phrases, and words in apposition or direct address are all forms of parenthetic expression requiring commas.

no c   Don't punctuate borderline parenthetic expressions occurring within a sentence, like this particular phrase with a single comma. Use either two commas, like this, or better yet *no comma*, for the same reason that one never uses a single parenthesis.

dang!   This rustic oath is reserved for rubes with *dangling* modifiers. Reading a sentence like this one that I'm writing now, a loud guffaw often breaks from my lips. WHY?

dic   Faulty *diction.* The subscribed word may not mean what you think, whatever that is. English idiom may require that a word be used only to certain constructions. The squiggled word may be too sesquipedalian or too laid back for your context.

e.g.?   *Exempli gratia,* for the sake of example? I.e., provide one. I.e., *id est,* that is.

frag   *Sentence fragment.* The sentence being incomplete. Whereas one expects more.

gr   *Grammatical error* of some sort, perhaps involving pronouns. A reader who it displeases to see a pronoun in the wrong case may be bothered by it failing to be in the possessive case when used thus with gerunds. Or some other outright blunder.

hy/adj   *Hyphenate* compound adjectives properly. Otherwise you blur a crucial distinction between "an ill-hyphenated phrase" and an "ill hyphenated phrase." Hyphens at the end of lines must fall between syllables as marked in the dictionary.

ital   *Italicize* titles of lengthy words by underlining—and words discussed as such, like ital.

mix met   Blossoming luxuriantly, *mixed metaphors* can carry one into strange seas of thought. Leave them to Shakespeare, who knew how to handle them.

¶/no ¶   Either begin a new *paragraph* at caret, or combine your little diddly paragraphs into one.

‖ struc   *Parallel structure* demands that thoughts of the same form be expressed by words of the same form, thus—not "by speaking similarly." If two terms in

a series are nouns, the third should not be participial, nor even a participle, alas. Scorn or neglect of this principle is wrong, and even scorn for and neglect of it are not very good.

p./no p — *Punctuate* with a *period* at the caret, or remove circled period. You figure out why.

p;/no; — *Punctuate* with a *semicolon* as explained above, or remove your improper semicolon. N.B.: Semicolons are generally used only where you could also use a period, as here; the clause on each side of the semicolon must be a sentence in its own right. But . . .

p; — After an independent clause, *punctuate* with an anticipatory *colon* for three purposes: to introduce a list, an illustrative quotation, or an expansion of the previous clause.

quotes — "When are *quotation marks* necessary, students have asked, and how should we use them?" "To enclose direct quotations," I reply. "And terminal punctuation goes *inside* them!"

redun — The bracketed word [*redundantly*] duplicates another in your sentence. Cut it out!

ref? — The *reference* of the underlined word is unclear, **which** can often cause ambiguity. Avoid using relative pronouns that refer to a whole clause, not to a noun or noun phrase.

*/^* — "Use a slash thus when quoting verse, / So that the lines fare none the worse. But carets serve to mark a break / Between words linked through your mistake."

split inf — To fully understand my dislike of *split infinitives*, realize that the adverbial wedge is usually a vague intensive that would be better omitted than placed elsewhere.

struc sprawl struc — *Structure* has somehow gone awry in this sprawling pile of phrases and clauses which probably does not mean what you want quite, so try breaking it down and unless that's impossible figuring out some clearer order and more in line with the logical and grammatical relations borne by the words to each other, which is probably possible.

tense seq — I see that earlier you used another tense, so this *tense sequence* surprised me.

wdy — *Wordy.* Fewer words will do. Wordiness obscures meaning, jeopardizes you, and insults me. Whereas verbose writers waste my time, concise writers take their time to save me time. This I appreciate. Treat words like money; rewrite this passage for a telegram.

✓ — *Check.* Congratulations! You have managed to say something worth saying.

You will notice that this little style sheet is not simply a table of correction symbols referring the student elsewhere. It also gives a largely self-contained explanation of the *principles* violated by the most common student errors. It does this concisely by making the description of the principles generally exemplify the error involved, in an ironically authoritarian fashion that most of my students find amusing. They like it—if anything, too much.

That such a style sheet has limitations and dangers I am well aware. It may encourage students to equate correct writing with good writing. But let me explain how I use it in upper-level literature courses at a middling university with an average verbal SAT of 480. At the beginning of a course I lecture students fervently on the importance of writing well, not just correctly. But reasonable correctness is a precondition for good writing, I explain, necessary though not sufficient. Moreover, bad writing can be usefully divided into two categories: poor writing and incorrect writing. "The domestic feline reposed on the carpet without lying down" is an extremely awkward and redundant sentence compared with "The cat sat on the mat." But we would not say that it contains an out-and-out error, whereas "The kat sit on the Mat" contains three outright mistakes. Mistakes in the latter category I denominate *gross errors,* and I tell students that I cannot regard as satisfactory writing that averages more than three gross errors per typewritten double-spaced page—that is, I cannot grade papers that sloppy on the C level, no matter how brilliant otherwise; the ceiling grade for sloppily proofread work is D plus.

Some of my literature courses require three papers over the semester. What typically happens is this. Despite my direct warnings about proof-reading carefully 25 percent of the class receives D's on the first paper. That is returned corrected together with my style sheet. We discuss four sample duplicated papers in class—an A, a B, a C, and a D—emphasizing the intellectual differences between bad writing, adequate writing, and really good writing and stressing the largely symptomatic role of mechanical errors. Potentially hard-core cases are referred to our Writing Workshop, a noncredit tutorial center for composition like that found on many campuses nowadays, to be sure that students understand the principles behind errors that a brief style sheet may not clarify for them. (Some students, for example, do not know the meaning of grammatical terms like *clause.*) On the second paper the number of D's falls to about 10 percent. It also is returned, accompanied by the style sheet, in the folder that students must use for submitting work; thus their prior work is accessible to me when I correct later papers, and repeated errors can be suitably discouraged. By the third paper 95 percent of the class can submit mechanically tolerable prose as defined by my rigid, frigid, but objective statistical criterion. Some are also writing much better in more important ways.

Many, of course, are not. My style sheet is not a panacea. An error-oriented approach cannot of itself produce good writing; it can only discourage some of the more annoying symptoms of bad writing. By focusing attention so narrowly on the symptoms it risks neglecting the underlying etiology of the disease. For that reason, when I am teaching a course devoted entirely to composition, with weekly papers required, I avoid introducing the style sheet until midway through the semester. This allows me to establish as firmly as possible the more fundamental truth that poor writing is rooted in poor thinking, which despite popular folklore proper "grammar" by itself cannot remedy. But my sheet is flexible enough to lend itself to various pedagogical contexts and approaches—especially if the teacher adopting it edits the humor to accord with his or her classroom persona.

Though symptomatic relief is not a cure, it remains a respectable medical goal. However laudable the original impulse behind "writing-across-the-curriculum" programs, many faculty in other disciplines who are suddenly saddled with the responsibility for teaching writing will have some difficulty, I suspect, getting even symptomatic relief. If a style sheet like mine were adopted and distributed widely throughout an institution, so that teachers in any discipline could use it while correcting and attach it when returning student papers, that school would soon lodge some basic rules of punctuation, at least, more permanently in student minds. Though perhaps one sheet cannot teach the basic rules of punctuation, it can help students remember what they have already been taught but would prefer, alas, to forget.

It is pedagogically irresponsible for faculty in upper-level course not to mark mechanical errors when correcting papers, on the comforting theory that such mistakes are too minor or too elementary a feature of weak writing to deserve comment. If they will not stigmatize such errors specifically themselves, then they should abandon that plaintive, age-old academic refrain, "Why don't they teach them about such things in the English department!" But in upper-level courses it is also pedagogically irresponsible to devote much class time to re-explaining mechanical principles that the majority of the class has already absorbed. And it may prove fiscally irresponsible to have skilled faculty in other disciplines trying to tutor laggard students individually in grammar when that task can be better handled at a writing center by tutors trained and equipped for the job. In this situation a style sheet can be a very useful tool for motivating sloppy students, reminding forgetful students, and identifying the minority of ignorant students so that they can be given tutorial help. It thus allows the teacher in "writing across-the-curriculum" courses (or in upper-level English courses) to concentrate his or her classroom discussion of student writing more profitably on rhetorical concerns like invention, organization, and argument.

APPENDIX

Further Lessons in Abbreviated Form

These lessons are arranged alphabetically by author; for particular topics, consult the index.

Denis Baron *(University of Illinois)* attempts to make explicit to his students the extent to which some of our attitudes toward English are based "on the misinformation and myth that pervade our ideas about language." The question he raises—"What aspect of the English language would you change?"—can produce a wide-ranging discussion of both the language itself and questions of usage—issues like irregular spelling, euphemism and taboo, sexism, and particular individual preferences and irritants in current usage. The lesson is based on the reading of two essays, Orwell's "Politics and the English Language," and Randolph Quirk's "Natural Language and Orwellian Intervention" [in *The English Language Today*, Sidney Greenbaum, ed. (Oxford, England: Pergamon, 1985)]. The class examines Orwellian—and other—ideas of linguistic correctness and is alerted to the danger of mechanically applying any of Orwell's "rules" or other linguistic prescriptions, no matter how sound in general. The writing assignment is a paper describing a time when the writer felt pressure to change some aspect of his or her use of language.

Sally Buckner *(Peace College)* assigns two successive papers in which students rework the same material, a profile of a particular person. The first paper must show the reader what that person is like, allowing the subject to reveal himself or herself through dialogue, setting, gesture, behavior, and so on. The reader is to infer a single general impression; the writer is to avoid explicit generalization ("She is one of the kindest women I know." "He values honesty above all things.") The second paper is avowedly analytic, and the implied generalization of the first becomes the explicit thesis; the reader has little to infer. The subject is analyzed, with each paragraph concerned with one significant characteristic—appearance, temperament, motive, and so on. Students are reminded that this second paper should be no less lively and engaging than the first, although its job is to state generalizations and thoroughly support them.

Ronald R. Butters *(Duke University)* Borrowing a critical idea from Robert Scholes, Butters introduces the vital importance of point of view (and of "little words") in writing by having students change the pronouns in Hemingway's "A Very Short Story." The original is in the third person; students experiment by consistently transforming either *he* or *Luz* to *I*—thus telling the story from a new point of view—and then making whatever modifications seem necessary to make the revised story "sound right" for the speaker.

The exercise raises several fruitful questions: Why does Hemingway choose to tell the story from the point of view that he does, rather than from that of one of the characters? What are the advantages? What possibilities have been deliberately excluded? What is lost (or might be gained) by changing to a first-person view?

Ruthmary Deuel *(Department of Pediatrics and Neurology, Washington University School of Medicine)* suggests that dyslexic college students (and others struggling with the concept and execution of a proper paragraph) skip four rather than two spaces between paragraphs in typing their papers. The exaggerated spacing throws each paragraph into relief and reminds the student of his or her obligation to it as a structure.

Catherine Golden *(Skidmore College)* introduces students to the differences between speech and writing by first asking them to read as "dialogue" a page of transcript of a conversation between three speakers, and to draw inferences about each. The repetitions, pauses, fragments, and run-on sentences usually lead them to conclude that the speakers are emptyheaded, poorly educated, or suffering from speech impediments. Golden then plays the actual tape of the conversation and students are surprised at how much more sensible it seems (and how normal the speakers seem) when discourse is heard rather than read. These observations lead to a discussion of the different principles—regarding diction, sentence patterns, and so on—governing speech and writing and to a discussion of the end of Plato's *Phaedrus* (274d–279c), where Socrates claims the superiority of speech.

These discussions provide the basis for a first assignment in which students tape and transcribe a brief interview and a second in which they explicate and then agree or disagree with Socrates' argument.

William J. Gracie, Jr. *(Miami University)* teaches his class to analyze how and why magazine advertising manipulates audiences: "I begin by showing my students several magazines ads and ask them to comment on what they see: spatial arrangement, color, position of models, the importance or (sometimes) the unimportance of language in the ads, and so forth. I usually begin with two or three cigarette ads—not necessarily all of them advertising the same cigarette. I then move on to two or three cigarette ads for the *same* product as those ads appear in two or three *different* magazines: my students are invariably surprised to discover that the same product may be presented in quite different ways in different magazines, and I am usually pleased that another example of 'audience' has been presented in a painless way. Having discovered that the same product uses quite different strategies as we compare, say, a cigarette ad as it appears in *Time, Playboy,* and *Ms.,* the class is usually intrigued enough to respond imaginatively to a whole series of discussion questions: Why is there more language in one ad than in the others? What can we say of body language in the ads? Can we describe the appeal of the ads—in other words, do they appeal to our fantasies, our aspirations or fears, our needs? Which?

To avoid loosely organized papers (descriptions of one ad followed by another), it is important to stress the placement and strength of the thesis statement that will announce the position of the writer and control the structure of the paper.

Students have two options in their papers: First, they may discuss how the same product is advertised in three or four current periodicals; or, second, they may discuss how one magazine seems to affect the advertisements of three or four products within that magazine. In my experience, two thirds of the class chooses the first option, while the remaining third, intrigued to discover that one can discern an audience for the *New Yorker* or *Rolling Stone* by examining the products they advertise, writes unusually perceptive analyses. Last year one woman concentrated on how AT & T reaches out and touches in four distinctly different ways in four magazines: *Campus Voice*, *Woman's World*, *Newsweek*, and *Business World*. Another noted the prominence of mirrors, reflection pools, and doubling in a number of ads within a single magazine *(Glamour)*. She was able to say something about the audience of that magazine as well as its identity—and was also able to address the subject of the whole through its parts: Our students can see more clearly many things they have looked at previously with only half-open eyes.

Marlene Griffith *(Laney College)* places all student papers in an envelope on Library Reserve. Each student is expected to read three papers, using criteria developed in class—for example: What catches my attention? At what point did I get lost—or gain interest? What's the point? What evidence is most persuasive for me? The students write their comments, which are later clipped to the original paper together with the teacher's comments. This process creates a clearly defined audience and provides real responses. Writing is to be read. It also makes writers shift chairs, to become readers, editors, critics, and—again—writers.

Editors' suggestion: In any composition assignment that draws on the widespread practice of having students read and criticize their classmates' papers, each student can be given the problem of completely rewriting another student's paper after analyzing the problem it presents.

John P. Harrington *(Saint Peter's College)* assigns a description of a painting in a unit designed to demonstrate that writing, like painting, is the result of conscious decisions. Using any inexpensive poster reproduction taped to the blackboard, preferably of a busy painting full of variety and detail, he asks students to make a written list of absolutely everything they see in the picture. (Students are encouraged to examine the picture as closely as possible and, if they wish, to discuss it with one another.) Pooling their observations in a master list on the blackboard and discovering what they may have overlooked, students are ready to see the painting, in all its detail, as a series of conscious choices. Questions about pictorial composition ("Why did the artist take this physical point of view instead of another? What would be different if the physical point of view were moved?") lead to questions about written composition—about rhetorical perspective and ways of controlling the responses of readers. In the written assignment, a descriptive essay on the picture, students can see that their own choices in ordering their observations, arranging words in a sentence and sentences within a paragraph, are analogous to the choices made by an artist working in a different medium.

Darwin L. Hayes *(Brigham Young University)* introduces students to the problem of finding the right distance in objective reporting. Ralph E. Lapp's account of a small nuclear accident in "The Death of Louis Slotin" [in *A Treasury of Science*, Harlow Shapley, Samuel Rapport, and Helen Wright, eds. (New York: Harper & Row, 1958)] demonstrates the power of understatement through the self-effacement of the narrator, which makes us feel as well as see and judge for ourselves the extent of Slotin's heroism. Students then write an account of something they have observed going on, something obviously wrong that people knew was wrong but allowed to continue until catastrophe came. Students are to report clearly, specifically, objectively what occurred without telling the reader what to think. Their language is to be objective, charged neither negatively nor positively. And they are to keep themselves out of the account, at least enter it as little as Lapp does, reporting the world of the incident straight, without judgment and without explicit interpretation.

Editors' suggestion: Choose one paragraph from Lapp's essay and rewrite it, making the narrator as intrusive as possible. Students can then determine how a subjective treatment of the same material can undermine the dramatic effect.

Farida Hellal *(University of Algiers)*   At the beginning of an advanced course that combines composition with literary analysis, Hellal introduces students to the necessity of combining compositional and literary skills by closely considering with the class a relatively unsuccessful paper from the preceding year—on a topic they will themselves soon attempt. An initial session is spent on word and sentence-level problems: diction and connotation, vagueness, definition of key terms, usage, and the like. The second session takes up larger rhetorical problems of stance, strategy, and intent—and particularly the question of how an analytic paper can be, indeed must be, at once "objective" and yet "personal."

As all the students have recently had courses in early American literature and history, a frequent first topic is "The Moral and Religious Strain in American Colonial Literature." The most common mistake students make in addressing such a topic is to assume that a good paper can simply be conceived and organized "according to the facts": that is, by marshaling a few commonly accepted generalizations—concerning, say, Puritanism and the colonial experience—and commenting on a few representative authors, chronologically considered. In the class's discussion of a paper embodying these faults, the following points emerge:

1. One's selection of the facts necessarily reflects a personal thesis; facts become meaningful only to the extent that they reflect an idea being worked out.
2. Interpretations become richer, more interesting, and more reliable when they draw on the writer's information and experience outside the immediate scope of the paper.
3. "Facts," when not properly exploited, may be mere padding or, when not critically examined, mere clichés indulged in to evade the true issues and obscure the "subjectivity" of the argument.
4. One should avoid sweeping generalizations and demonstrate an awareness of the implicit as well as explicit issues underlying the topic. A good paper will be both "objective" and "personal" in that it will be solidly grounded not only in literary and historical fact but also in one's sympathetic grasp of the difficulties—theological, moral, practical, and rhetorical—of the writers of the time.

Katharine T. Hoff *(Rider College)*   gives the same deceptively simple in-class writing assignment in two successive lessons early in the semester: "Describe the classroom—one paragraph, ten minutes" (no other instructions). The first time, after two or three volunteers read their work, the class examines what it has heard, considering, "What is the point of the paragraph? How is this point supported and developed?"

"Some paragraphs turn out to be nonparagraphs: collections of random details; some have central topics but few precisely rendered supporting details; still others have topics and some carefully observed details but no considered order for the details. An occasional paragraph meets all the criteria of focus, development, and organization."

The second time, when students are again asked to write a one-paragraph description of their classroom, they are alerted beforehand to the choices behind a real paragraph: how choosing a point of view and an audience can enable them to choose the best details and the best words to convey an attitude toward both subject and audience. What if the writer were an interior designer trying to persuade the college to refurnish and redecorate its classrooms; or a lighting specialist analyzing the adequacy of lighting at the request of the college; or a teacher complaining about distracting noise in the classroom; or a student feeling claustrophobic and wishing for the class hour to end—or a novelist or playwright setting the scene for a particular action by creating for the reader a particular way of seeing the room?

The exercise—given twice—dramatizes the idea of what a real paragraph is and why it must be focused, organized, and developed.

Michael D. Hood *(Belmont Abbey College)* In a course devoted to teaching students how to construct a coherent argument, Hood uses the enthymeme to show students both how to analyze the arguments they read and how to invent the arguments they wish to write. In reading, students learn to determine a writer's thesis and to reconstruct its supporting argument. Crucial to this analysis is (1) identifying and proving the "Because" clause (e.g., we should all vote *because otherwise the will of the people will not be expressed)*, and (2) identifying, and then accepting or rejecting, the assumption or major premise on which the argument depends (e.g., it is good/necessary that the will of the people be expressed in elections). In writing their own arguments, students are similarly expected to identify and construct a controlling enthymeme.

Robert E. Hosmer, Jr. *(Mount Holyoke College)* prepares students to write essays on the relation between child and parent. First, to uncover basic assumptions, he asks students to write brief statements of their own in response to a series of statements, including the following: "The fundamental defect of fathers is that they want their children to be a credit to them" (Bertrand Russell); "When I was a boy of fourteen, my father was so ignorant, I could hardly stand to have the Old Man around. But when I got to be twenty-one, I was astonished at how much he had learned in seven years" (Mark Twain); "When I was a kid, a father was like the light in the refrigerator. Every house had one, but no one really knew what either of them did once the door was shut" (Erma Bombeck). In addition, the class considers possible definitions for *mother* or *father*, colored as they might be by the chronological age of the child, the period and culture in which he or she lives, the fact that the parent is alive or dead, and so on. Next, the class reads analytically and discusses Virginia Woolf's "Leslie Stephen" and Doris Lessing's "My Father," identifying differences of voice and tone, the means by which each writer establishes the dominant impression, and each writer's understanding of the term *father*. Finally, drawing on the writing, discussion, and reading up to this point, students are asked to write a 500-word essay on the father-child relationship. Some possible topics are "Three Fathers: Woolf's, Lessing's, and Mine," "Fatherhood—A Definition," or "Twentieth-Century Fathering."

Editors' note: This unit can of course be adapted to a paper on the mother-child relationship, drawing on apposite readings.

Gertrude Reif Hughes *(Wesleyan University)* In hopes of persuading students that creativity is compatible with serious thought, that one can simultaneously cultivate one's "voice" and write a carefully considered argument, Hughes asks students to write an "open letter" on a public issue addressed to someone close to them. This format permits (and requires) the personal investment in the subject of both writer and addressee. But as the letters are also "public" they must present the topic in such a way that its general interest—including perhaps something of its history, and of the moral and political conflicts it entails—is made clear.

Models are found in open letters by Frederick Douglass to his former master, Captain Thomas Auld (originally published in William Lloyd Garrison's abolitionist journal *The Liberator*) and by James Baldwin to his nephew (Part One of *The Fire Next Time*). Both are analyzed for their "private" and "public" elements, and for the complex interplay of writer, addressee, topic, and reading audience. Although sympathy and antipathy are distributed differently in the two letters (Douglass and his readers are aligned against the addressee; Baldwin and his addressee are aligned against some readers), in both the "private" element tends to establish the writer's expertise and authority, while his effort to involve a wider audience in this ostensibly private matter lends the subject urgency and importance.

The assignment is then to write a similar letter to two audiences: one, a person (real or imagined) with whom the writer has a personal relationship; the other, members of the public who may sympathize with or learn from the letter. Care must be taken to find a combination of topic and addressee that will make for a dramatic argument: Students write, for example, to their sisters about abortion, to former teachers about changes needed in the educational system, and so on. It is also necessary to have in mind a definite "public," as Douglass does in writing for abolitionists. Students are cautioned to imagine both audiences, private and public, in every paragraph; to use *you* throughout, not just at the beginning; to include details appropriate to the addressee; and to include facts and arguments needed to appeal to the wider audience.

Mary Jane Hurst *(Texas Tech University)* asks students to keep notes on what they read throughout the semester, looking for examples of good and bad writing, with particular attention to organization, method of development, and striking words, phrases, and sentences. Notes are to be taken (on 4×6 cards) for essays examined in class, articles in magazines or journals, textbooks from other classes, and leisure reading. This practice not only encourages more efficient note taking, but also helps students learn to manage their reading and studying. It also provides the basis for the final writing assignment, which is to enumerate and describe the characteristics of writing they have come to appreciate, illustrating those characteristics with examples drawn from their own reading.

Ojars Kratins *(University of California, Berkeley)* has devised a sequence that trains students to see and remember an object in its particularity. The lessons are designed to correct the tendency of inexperienced writers to fall back on general categories in describing what they see ("tree") rather than particular images ("a straight-limbed, white-trunked, thirty-three-foot-high quaking aspen at the end of September").

Taking the class outdoors, with paper and pen, he asks each student to choose a particular object and concentrate on seeing it as fully as possible for five minutes, deliberately refraining from free association. (If the students study designated objects, they can later compare different descriptions of the same object.) Then, without looking at their object again, the students are asked to write for ten minutes, with no attempt at organizing their data, on what they remember seeing.

Taking a fresh piece of paper, the students are asked to write nonstop "first, about what it was like simply trying to *see* the object while trying *not to think about it*, and second, to write about the experience of trying to *describe* what was seen."

Back in the classroom, the students compare what they have written and discuss the differences among them in perception and memory, drawing conclusions about the experience of observing and describing and the part that language and the self play in coloring what we see. Most important, the class has had an experience in disciplined and precise observation and visualizing.

Frederick K. Lang *(Brooklyn College)* Near the end of a sequence of assignments comparing various elements in two writers, Lang encourages student to leave the security of the standard comparison/contrast format by asking them to "play-act" as well as write, becoming one of the two writers under consideration and having that writer talk to or about the other. If, for example, the class has been reading Joyce and Kafka, the assignment might run as follows:

Make believe that either Joyce or Kafka is a self-absorbed magazine editor. Then make believe that the other one is an aspiring writer who has sent in a short story to the self-absorbed editor's magazine. Where are you going to get a short story on such short notice? Simple: *Dubliners* or *The Penal Colony* stories, depending on whom you have cast as whom in this scenario. Your editor is self-absorbed because he writes short stories himself, has had a book of them published (*Dubliners* or *The Penal Colony* stories, depending . . .), and has been hailed as a genius. So he will publish the story he has received only on the condition that the aspiring writer make major changes; he is very specific about these changes, and all of them are based on his own conception of what a short story should be and do. In other words, the self-absorbed editor wants to make the aspiring writer's short story as much like his own writing as he can. In fact, he is so self-absorbed that he doesn't stop at explaining to the aspiring writer what he wants done; he shows him by pointing to specific things in his own stories (*Dubliners* or *The Penal Colony* stories, depending . . .). Remember, he has suggestions for everything: plot, characterization, style, theme, imagery, and anything else he can think of. (If the self-absorbed editor is Joyce, he will probably insist on an "epiphany.") Sometimes he shows the writer what he wants by rewriting things himself (in this he is like a hard-to-please English teacher). The self-absorbed editor makes his demands in a letter to the aspiring writer. Write that letter.

Marion H. Larson *(University of Minnesota, Minneapolis)* combines analysis of sales letters and magazines to introduce students to problems of audience and persuasion. Sales letters ("junk mail") are examined for clues to their intended audience and for elements that appeal specifically to these readers. Magazines are examined for the type and presentation of ads; for the approach, content, and language of articles; and for any stated editorial policy. The effect of different audiences may be seen particularly well in articles on the same topic found in different magazines. For an assignment, students are asked to pick a single magazine and, using what they can discover about its audience, write a persuasive letter to potential subscribers.

Joseph Loewenstein *(Washington University)* uses a series of three assignments to address questions of authority and the proper use of reference works. An initial discussion exposes the range and variety of possible appeals to authority—the lawyer's precedent, the scientist's data, the poet's Muse—and the frequent inadequacy of the student's all-purpose resort to the dictionary. (How useful is Webster's definition of *justice* to a discussion of Aeschylus?) Students are then sent off to collect several definitions of such potent words as *love*, *law*, or *enthusiasm*, consulting among others the *Oxford English Dictionary* and polemical lexicographers like Samuel Johnson or Ambrose Bierce. The differences and their possible causes are discussed.

Students are then asked to prepare a short annotated bibliography for a field in which they have some expertise, the aim being to show an inexperienced researcher how to find valuable information in that field. Students are encouraged to get help from appropriate faculty members. Loewenstein checks the bibliographies while still in draft for adequacy and instructs in the conventions of footnote and bibliography. The final versions are distributed in class and the compilers explain in detail how one might use (and not use) each reference work.

The final assignment is to write a five- to seven-page critical essay on a single reference work, taking into consideration the historical context in which the work was produced, its generic conventions, its anticipated market, and the history of its use. Students are urged to cite frequently from the work and cautioned not to distort their data. This caution underlines the point of the whole sequence: that data, sources, and authorities must be handled with extreme care if one is to avoid misrepresentation.

Elaine Lux *(Laboratory Institute of Merchandising, New York City)* To stimulate imaginative and logical thinking in her students, Lux uses Eudora Welty's "A Worn Path" as an illustration of the expressive power of the metaphor of the journey in writing about an individual life. The particularity with which Welty uses the metaphor—establishing the sense of place (terrain, trees, obstacles), season, mood—stimulates possibilities for the students in themselves describing the details of their "life's journey" and thinking about its possible purpose or meaning. Students can then explore other possible analogies (a river, a game, a war, etc.) and, choosing one, work through the comparison in some detail in a written assignment. "One young man wrote about life as a long hallway with many locked rooms along it and many turns leading into the unknown. . . . He was a very quiet young man, and I had not known anything of what he was experiencing inside. His well-written and powerful essay not only helped me to be a better teacher to him, but his expressing his inner gloom seemed to free him to participate more in class."

Reta Madsen *(Webster University)* engages her students in research papers about famous trials that have left unanswered questions about the justice of their verdict. This research enables students to feel that "what they say is meaningful because they have discussed it or worked it out for themselves"—unlike papers on topics (like "Reproduction in the Fruit Fly") for which they have only to consult their course textbooks or similar sources to reproduce what is known on the topic.

The list of possibilities contains names as disparate as Socrates, Jesus, Joan of Arc, Alfred Dreyfus, Oscar Wilde, the Scottsboro Boys, Sacco and Vanzetti, Alger Hiss, Julius and Ethel Rosenberg, the Berrigan brothers, Lieutenant Calley, General Westmoreland and CBS, and Claus von Bülow. The students look into the circumstances of the trial, the particular assumptions and values of those trying and judging the accused (as well as the assumptions of the accused), and the special circumstances attendant on the person's punishment. Any conclusions students form about the justice or injustice of the trial must be supported *with evidence.* Since students, like most of us, tend to interest themselves in human subjects more readily than in nonhuman subjects, they become more involved in their cases—and more willing to ferret out the facts.

Allan A. Metcalf *(MacMurray College)* takes current issues of *The New Yorker* as the common reading matter for his second-semester research and writing class, and concentrates on introducing students to the world of civilized lucidity in the magazine's nonfiction prose—both the short pieces in "The Talk of the Town" and the longer essays.

There is resistance to be overcome, because students feel ignorant of cultural and historical allusions (Pepys, Biedermeier, Margaret Mead) and mocked by the humor. Weekly assignments of one-page research papers explaining allusions ease the first kind of resistance, and study of the magazine's plain style helps with the second.

Toward the end of the semester the students get their culminating assignment: to report in 1000 words on something they have observed or done, writing as if for "The Talk of the Town." Class discussion on the day of the assignment is of the elements of *New Yorker* style, elicited inductively from examples in recent issues. The discussion locates five distinct qualities (some, not surprisingly, echoing Strunk and White's *Elements of Style*):

1. Definite, specific, concrete detail.
2. Plain, direct words.
3. The first person—being explicit about the reporter's perspective.
4. Placing that first person in the background.
5. *The New Yorker* attitude: calm, thoughtful, interested, not angry or partisan; trying to see others as they see themselves.

The second and third characteristics are at odds with most academic writing, but all five reflect the academic spirit (at its best) as well as *The New Yorker*'s: "And if any single principle transcends all the others and informs all the others it is to try to tell the truth." Provided with a copy of this recent statement of principles ("Notes and Comment," *The New Yorker* 22 April 1985, 35–36), the students set out and return a week later with unusually successful and happy pieces of writing.

An alert student may observe that the five qualities do not include a strong thesis and logical organization. Essays to exemplify those qualities must be sought elsewhere. But five principles are quite enough for one worthwhile assignment.

Elray L. Pedersen *(Brigham Young University)* gives his class a series of exercises suggesting the analogy between appropriateness in dress and appropriateness in language. He offers a list of hypothetical situations requiring a choice of suitable dress: painting a room, applying for a job as a checker in a local discount store, playing football, working as a machinist, playing in a symphony orchestra, attending a college class, attending a funeral. He then equates language with dress and gives examples of various "styles": Tuxedo English (formal, written), Sports Clothes English (everyday, informal), and so on. A suggested writing assignment is to retell a fairy tale such as "The Three Bears" in different kinds of English.

Richard Peifer *(Butte Community College)* teaches "The Five-Person Paragraph" to have students demonstrate to themselves that ideas must be held together as they develop from a topic sentence through to the end of a paragraph.

He divides the class into groups of five and has each student write the first sentence of a topic or a story. The students exchange papers and add a sentence that carries on the idea of the previous sentence. When the papers have made the round of five, each student reads all the papers in the group. Within each group the best of the five papers is then selected and read aloud. (Note that each student will have had a part in the creation of the best paragraph.)

Even though five different minds wrote each paragraph, it will become apparent that where transitions or other connecting material was used, the ideas hung together, and in their absence the paragraphs fell apart.

This lesson can be done either before or after a formal lesson in linking sentences, but it is perhaps better to do it before: The five-person paragraphs should come as a surprise and a delight.

Jeffrey L. Porter *(College of Charleston)* To engage students in argument and encourage debate, Porter poses as a sample question one that provokes controversy as playfully—rather than abstractly—as possible: "Do you think Walter Mitty is a hero of the imagination, a victim of middle-class pettiness, or an outright nincompoop?"—rather than "through his portrayal of Walter Mitty, how does Thurber describe the role of the imagination in everyday life?" Students team up in the debate, defining their terms and defending their assertions collaboratively, forming judgments about what qualifies an action as good. Once students realize, through debate in class, that assent cannot be taken for granted, they must translate their responses into a strategy to justify their point of view. "If the original question has proven arguable during class debate, it should qualify as a paper topic."

R. Baird Shuman *(University of Illinois)* **1.** To encourage students to write for a broad audience with diverse background and interests, Shuman assigns an early short paper in which they either (1) write about something they are familiar with in such a way that newcomers to the subject can understand it or (2) write about something they are themselves just beginning to explore so that they convey a sense of discovery to the reader. These short papers (500 words maximum) should aim not to be exhaustive, but to convey the writer's enthusiasm for a subject, and to entice, interest, and inform readers. To help generate content, students may, if they wish, use another piece of writing—a magazine article, a set of directions, or whatever—and respond to it. With or without such a source, their papers should focus on their own experiences and reactions. This assignment is particularly useful in a semester in which a research paper will later be required, as it gives students practice in responding to (rather then merely citing) sources and in interpreting special knowledge to a wider audience.

2. To help recover (and increase) the fluency students have often lost over the summer, Shuman uses an enjoyable classroom exercise in timed, sequential, collaborative free-writing, which in turn serves as the basis for the students' first paper. Students are divided into small groups of three or four; each writes as much as possible, on any subject, for three minutes; papers are exchanged and read, and each student continues the paper he or she now has for four minutes; papers are again exchanged and read (each receiving a paper he or she has not yet seen) and the third contributor continues the paper for five minutes. Each student retains the paper for which he or she was the final contributor, and, at the next class, turns in (1) a clean, copy-edited version of the class exercise and (2) a radically revised version, consistent in tone and purpose, based on the material in the exercise paper. Through this exercise and assignment, students increase their fluency, get to know their classmates better, do some productive group work, and can see how serious writing may sometimes begin in play.

Carol J. Singley *(Brown University)*   **1.** In a course in argument and persuasion, Singley has students analyze and imitate letters of appeal for various political and charitable causes to help make the transition from the terse discourse of advertising to the more sustained kinds of persuasion found in such fields as politics, business, law, and religion. The letters are analyzed for format (What creates maximum readability? optimum length? What might be the response of different audiences to different formats?), for the Aristotelian appeals (logical, emotional, ethical), and for the "You Appeal," the writer's direct attempts to engage readers and make them feel important and understood.

The assignment that follows asks students to assume that they have been hired by some organization (Moral Majority, Planned Parenthood, or whatever) to write a letter soliciting the active support of residents of their home state. Two versions of the letter will be needed, one for a supportive audience of those who have contributed money within the past five years and a second for a neutral or hostile audience of those who have never identified themselves with the organization in any formal way. The goal of the letter will be to persuade people to show support for the organization in one or all of three ways: (1) make a financial contribution, (2) write to legislators urging action, (3) volunteer time and effort to advance the cause.

A follow-up assignment might ask students to work with the same topic but address their appeals and arguments to an even more general audience of newspaper readers through an editorial or letter to the editor. In any case, students are now ready to attempt longer, more fully developed pieces of persuasive writing.

2. Noting that we too often ask our students to perform complex analytical or critical writing tasks without adequately preparing them, Singley teaches a lesson in summary and synthesis to provide a bridge between descriptive or narrative writing and the expository essay. Students read three or four personal essays on a topic and then treat them step by step to arrive at a synthesis:

Step 1. Consider "what happens" in each essay, and record each significant event in a single sentence, with a minimum of interpretation or abstraction.

Step 2. Jot down words or phrases that best express the theme, topic, mood, or tone of each event recorded in Step 1.

Step 3. Referring to your responses in Steps 1 and 2, write a sentence that conveys the general meaning or message of each significant event in the essay. (At this level students combine reporting with analysis and interpretation.)

Step 4. Using all of your notes, write one or two statements that characterize the essay as a whole. (In this step students move to more comprehensive interpretations that may be called the theme or thesis of the essay. These statements provide the basis for synthesis in Step 5.)

Step 5. (Go on to this step only after you have completed Steps 1–4 for each essay you have read.)

Refer now to your topics and generalizations for each essay (Steps 2 and 4). What points of similarity or difference can you find among the essays? Write these comparisons and contrasts down in sentence form.

Step 6. What conclusions of your own did you draw from these essays? Do you have preferences for one view over another? What, in your opinion, are the most valuable and least valuable points in each essay? (This step helps students arrive at their own tentative thesis about the topic, providing a structuring principle or shape for the synthesis of the essays.)

This exercise provides a framework for complex cognitive tasks, while allowing each student maximum freedom of interpretation within it. It is readily adapted to a wide range of discourse.

Jack Sullivan *(Rider College)* assigns a movie review, 300–400 words, early in the term as a concise, unintimidating, enjoyable form of writing. "The point is to get students to convert strong images, impressions, and judgments into words as quickly as possible." The review requires preliminary note taking; it must state the film's purpose, judge its success, and produce concrete examples to support that judgment, choosing specific moments that demonstrate the film's distinctive qualities or specific elements (acting, dialogue, camera technique, pacing). This is an exercise in arguing in support of a position, documenting opinions, describing scenes (favorite or otherwise), and interpreting (relating individual parts to the whole). The paper requires no special knowledge of film technique or the vocabulary of film criticism.

At the end of the semester, the assignment is given again so that both teacher and students can measure progress in writing.

Sylvia Tomasch *(University of Wyoming)* teaches a sequence on "Language Awareness and the Origins of Common Words," introducing students to two major concepts: The first is that English has had a long history, beginning before it was English, and that its evolution is a response to human conditions. The second, a corollary to the first, is that English, spoken or written, is a tool rather than a barrier and that as such it responds to individual control.

Students are asked to find out the origins of some common words. Class discussions reveal patterns of word formations (e.g., acronyms, clipped forms), establish the two main roots of modern English (Germanic and Romance), and emphasize the responsiveness of language to changing environments (e.g., geographical, political, technological). Not incidentally, students discover dictionaries as sources for more than definition or spelling.

To pique student interest, Tomasch begins with the origins of the months and days of the week to discover that: "eternal conditions and natural forces (war, love, thunder, spring) dominate the words in both sets . . . ancient meanings, antique usage, archaic forms—these are the foundations on which modern tongues are built." An investigation of the origins of personal names (of students as well as her own) suggests the special linguistic conditions of the United States and reinforces the idea, newly conceived of in most cases, that not only has language changed in the past but it is still doing so at this very moment, and is very different from the monolithic, static stumbling block students have learned to fear. Because language is itself an essential component of the processes that created our culture, having students become explicitly aware of it means that they come to see themselves not only as the products of the world as given but as part of the process of creating the worlds that are to come. As possible subjects for future papers, students investigate some of these words in the *OED:* skirt, shirt, apron, napkin; boycott, lynch, sandwich, diesel; Frigidairc, Klccncx, Vaselinc, Xerox; scuba, radar, laser; electrocute, smog, laundromat; wig, bus, taxi, cab, van, flu; guitar, magician, umbrella, squirrel, ukelele, moccasin, cookie, loot, algebra; snob, slang, pooch, quiz.

Irwin Weiser *(Purdue University)*   In preparing students to write reviews on any subject, Weiser makes a special point of carefully identifying (1) appropriate criteria for the subject and (2) the audience's relation to the subject. Science fiction movies should not be judged by the standards of musical comedy, nor fast-food franchises by those of gourmet restaurants. Appropriate criteria for, say, a rock concert might include such things as musical ability, sound quality, showmanship (special effects, light shows, etc.), audience behavior, and the cost and quality of related merchandise. If they are potential "consumers," the review may be intended as persuasive; if, however, the subject has "come and gone," the review may be primarily informative; if a significant part of the audience has already experienced the subject, the review may be primarily evaluative.

Dexter Westrum *(Ottowa University, Kansas)*   In a noncredit remedial writing course, Westrum assigns an interview with an "expert" in a subject each student feels he or she knows a good deal about. The students prepare by making a list of questions, and when they are told that they themselves are the "experts," interview one another in order to write a profile. The experience reassures students who feel inhibited about writing and helps them gain the "habit of patience, the skill of mining material."

Angela Williams *(The Citadel)*   To instill confidence in her students and demonstrate to reluctant writers that writing can be enjoyed, Williams assigns the writing of letters. As a first assignment, students write letters to the teacher describing themselves as writers, giving a history of their efforts that will reveal how they feel about writing. Then the class discusses why it is easier to write a letter than a formal paper and how the conventions of the letter produce a ready-made beginning, middle, and end. Further assignments include a letter to a parent making the case for something the writer wants, then letters to Dear Abby, the school newspaper, school officials, and so on. The point is to use letter writing of increasing formality as a springboard for the expository essay. In the course of the unit students are referred to their handbooks for model letters, and the class reads letters by famous people—Napoleon, Shelley, Beethoven, Poe, Franklin, Johnson, Martin Luther King (chosen from *A Treasury of the World's Great Letters*) as well as novels like Alice Walker's *The Color Purple.*

Allison Wilson *(Jackson State University)*   For students alienated by critical terminology, Wilson teaches Tolstoy's *The Death of Ivan Ilyich* as a personal literary encounter, carefully avoiding the vocabulary of academic criticism and encouraging students to approach a work of fiction in terms of their own experience and reflection. The first assignment, a chapter-by-chapter plot summary that fixes the events clearly in their minds, is followed by a paper examining why in each case the secondary characters react as they do to Ivan's illness and death. In each case students not only interpret feelings, motives, and behavior in Tolstoy's story but explore why they as readers identify themselves more readily with particular characters than with others. The paper is intended to help students to discover their own feelings about the characters and events, to appreciate the validity of these feelings (as well as those of their classmates), and to produce both personal and textual evidence in support of their responses.

Thia Wolf *(Miami University)* uses role-playing exercises at the beginning of the course as a stimulus to better reading and writing. To develop her students' powers of understanding human motivation she contrives to simulate the situation in Shirley Jackson's "The Lottery" by distributing bits of folded paper from a large black box. The student drawing the marked paper pretends to be Mrs. Hutchinson, the character in the story who draws the marked paper. This student must then, sitting in the center of a circle, answer *in character* all the questions with which he or she is peppered by the class, questions that must probe the character's feelings and behavior. All the students then examine their own feelings and behavior during the role-playing exercise, which has presented them with much to be examined—their own anxiety, relief, selfishness, hypocrisy, blind obedience, and so on. The written assignment is to write about some principle of human behavior that has become clear in the course of the class session. "Armed with these insights, students can begin a series of assignments which ask them to examine puzzling kinds of behavior in individuals they know, group behavior, and finally, if they want to take this plunge, their own behavior in difficult situations."

James Thomas Zebroski *(Slippery Rock University of Pennsylvania)* assigns, as an alternative to the conventional research paper, an ethnographic report in which students closely observe an aspect of life (e.g., working patterns and attitudes toward work) in a particular community, visiting the site they choose at least four or five different times, taking detailed field notes, and finally synthesizing their findings. Students must prove one significant point about the cultural community they have been visiting, use concrete examples, description, and direct quotation, distinguishing carefully the language used at the site from their own language in writing the report. They are reminded that they are writing for one another and that their report must enlarge one another's knowledge of a particular way of life. "No one in our class has been to your site, and yet we could all fit in better there because of your report."

The reports are duplicated and collated into a book that is then discussed by the class.

EX

ABOUT THE AUTHORS

Sondra J. Stang teaches in the English Department at Washington University, where she has given composition courses at all levels during the last twenty-five years. Her published work includes three volumes on Ford Madox Ford; she is also the editor of *The Ford Madox Ford Reader* and coeditor of Ford's manuscript *A History of Our Own Times,* to be published in 1988.

Robert Wiltenburg directs the composition program and trains new teachers of writing at Washington University. He has taught at the University of Rochester, SUNY-Geneseo, St. John Fisher College, and the Eastman School of Music. His other major interest is in literature of the English Renaissance, and he has published articles on Shakespeare, Jonson, and Milton.